Favorite Recipes® *of America*

VEGETABLES

including fruits

FAVORITE RECIPES PRESS,
Louisville, Kentucky

Contents

© Favorite Recipes Press, 1968
Post Office Box 18324
Louisville, Kentucky
Library of Congress Catalog Card No. 68-25331

Introduction

Vegetables—the entire family from artichokes to zucchini—are one of the best food buys available. They rank high in vitamins and minerals but are low in cost and calories.

Vegetables and fruits are an indispensable part of any meal. They display a rainbow of color and present a treasure chest of different tastes—some subtle, others distinctive.

The color and crispness of homemade relishes, the tang and texture of marinated vegetables and the innumerable flavors of our other vegetable and fruit dishes—these luscious gifts from Mother Nature are good for you.

At last, a complete collection of recipes for vegetables and fruits which are practical, will bring out the delicate flavors of the food, and yet keep all of the vitamin-laden goodness.

These choice recipes were selected from the more than 50,000 in my files. Included are favorite recipes of Americans from all sections of the country—north, south, east and west.

Some of the recipes in the Vegetables Cookbook are old family favorites, handed down from mother to daughter for generations. Others are the latest, most up-to-date recipes you can find.

These recipes are for every meal whether it is Wednesday lunch, Sunday dinner or in-betweens. Some are ideal for dinner-on-the-grounds at church and community socials, others are suited to backyard barbecues. There are quick, easy-to-fix recipes for especially busy homemakers. And there are those that require longer, slow cooking for their indescribable flavors. Such variety means you're sure to find "the" recipe for any meal.

Each recipe was home tested by an American cook just like yourself and each one is personally endorsed by the homemaker whose name appears under the recipe. We know that you will value this unusual collection of vegetable and fruit recipes and will use it for years to come.

Treat your family to a new dish today. It will quickly become one of your family favorites, too.

Mary Anne Richards
Staff Home Economist
Favorite Recipes Press

VEGETABLES ARE DELICIOUS

Not too many years ago otherwise good cooks looked with disdain upon those ordinary foods . . . vegetables. These cooks considered vegetables good for you . . . but not very good to eat.

The fault was not with the vegetables, but with the cooks. The vegetables were carelessly selected, boiled to a pulpy, unappetizing mess and then tossed haphazardly into a bowl for serving.

Fortunately, times have changed. Now, good cooks take pride in selecting their vegetables and in preparing them in delectable ways. They serve vegetables that are tender-crisp, colorful, flavor-rich and vitamin-laden. The gentle art of undercooking these good gifts from Nature's bounty has found its place in American kitchens.

In America, we are fortunate in being able to enjoy vegetables anytime of the year—broccoli, green beans, crunchy corn, asparagus, baby green peas—and every other kind.

Almost everything that is grown the world over is carried in good supermarkets. If it isn't fresh, it's frozen. And if it isn't frozen, it's in a can. No other cooks are as fortunate as Americans in having an excellent choice of foods. Take advantage of this superb variety. Branch out instead of letting your vegetables be the stepchild of your creative cooking. Try several new vegetable dishes each week. It will be a wonderfully delicious adventure.

The Best Vegetable Buy

Your vegetable adventure begins with selecting fresh vegetables with a careful eye. Look for firm, unblemished vegetables that have a bright color.

Greens should be crisp. Some vegetables like asparagus should not have seeding. This indicates age. Potatoes, onions and carrots are old if they are sprouting. Keep fresh vegetables only a brief time after buying them.

The most convenient vegetables are canned. They don't have to be refrigerated until opened and a brief reheating is all they need before eating. Americans have made canned vegetables the most popular by eating more of them than any other types.

Vegetables come in a variety of can sizes. The most commonly available and the approximate amount of vegetable in each:

Can Size (net weight)	Contents
8 or 8½ ounces	1 cup
12 ounces	1½ or 1¾ cups
16 or 17 ounces	2 cups
1 pound, 4 ounces	2¼ or 2½ cups
1 pound, 13 ounces	3¼ or 3½ cups
6 pounds, 2 to 12 ounces	12 to 13 cups

Most like fresh vegetables in color, flavor and texture are frozen vegetables. They also usually cost more than canned vegetables. For good quality frozen vegetables, buy from a reputable dealer who stocks reliable brands of frozen food and has a rapid turnover.

Choose firm, clean packages. You can be sure the food has already lost quality if packages have softened. Frozen food is safe to eat as long as the package remains frozen, but a storage temperature of 0° F. or lower is necessary to maintain highest quality.

Buy only frozen foods that are displayed in a refrigerated cabinet made for that purpose. Avoid frozen vegetables that are stacked outside the frozen food cabinet even though they may be packed in dry ice. Look for a thermometer in the cabinet. If there is one, it should register 0° F. or lower.

When shopping, plan to pick up frozen foods last. It's a good idea to protect frozen foods in an insulated bag or double paper bag in warm weather. At home, put packages into the freezer as soon as possible.

Dried vegetables take up less storage room than the other kinds of vegetables. Mature dry legumes, including dry peas, beans and lentils in this group, are relatively inexpensive. However, they take more preparation time than vegetables in other forms. Some dried foods such as dehydrated potatoes and sweet potatoes cost slightly more than comparable fresh products, but can be prepared much faster.

Keeping Fresh Vegetables

Most fresh vegetables remain top quality for only a few days even under ideal conditions.

Vegetables such as corn, beans and peas lose sweetness in a short time as sugar converts to starch. Green, leafy vegetables quickly wilt and change flavor as water evaporates from tissues.

Most fresh vegetables will stay crisp if put in covered containers or plastic bags and stored in the refrigerator. If you wash lettuce, celery and other leafy vegetables before storing, drain thoroughly since too much moisture can hasten decay.

Sort vegetables before storing. Discard or immediately use any bruised or soft vegetables. Don't store them with firm vegetables. A storage guide for fresh vegetables:

STORING FRESH VEGETABLES

VEGETABLE	LENGTH OF STORAGE TIME IN REFRIGERATOR
Asparagus	1 or 2 days
Beans, lima	1 or 2 days shelled 3 to 5 days unshelled
Beans, snap	3 to 5 days
Beets	1 or 2 weeks—remove tops
Broccoli	1 or 2 days
Brussels sprouts	1 or 2 days
Cabbage	3 to 5 days
Carrots	3 to 5 days—remove tops
Cauliflower	3 to 5 days
Celery	3 to 5 days
Corn	1 or 2 days—store unhusked and uncovered
Cucumbers	3 to 5 days
Eggplant	1 or 2 days—store at room temperature (60° F.). If air is dry, keep eggplant in plastic bag to retain moisture.
Greens (spinach, kale, chard, collards, beet, turnip and mustard greens)	1 or 2 days
Lettuce or other salad greens	1 or 2 days
Mushrooms	1 or 2 days
Okra	3 to 5 days
Onions, green	1 or 2 days
Onions, mature	Several weeks—store at room temperature (60° F.) in loosely woven container with good air circulation. Onions sprout or decay if temperature or humidity is too high.
Parsnips	1 or 2 weeks
Peas, green	1 or 2 days—store uncovered
Peppers	3 to 5 days
Potatoes	Several weeks—store in dark, dry place with good ventilation at 45 to 50° F.
Radishes	1 week—remove tops
Rutabagas	2 weeks
Summer Squash	3 to 5 days
Winter squash, hard rind	Several weeks—store in cool, dry place at about 60° F.
Sweet potatoes	Several weeks—store at 60° F.
Tomatoes	1 to 2 weeks—keep unripe tomatoes at room temperature away from direct sunlight until ripe, then, refrigerate, uncovered. Too much sunlight prevents development of even color.

COOKING VEGETABLES CAREFULLY

To keep the highest number of vitamins, quality, color and taste in vegetables, cook them carefully.

Orange pigment is the most stable of all colors in vegetables. It stays bright even when the vegetable is withered. It doesn't change with heat, acid or method of cooking and it won't dissolve in cooking water. While it does dissolve in fat, this is usually not a problem because most of the fat used on vegetables is eaten with them.

Long overcooking may dull the bright appearance of orange vegetables, but this is due to a change in the sugars rather than in the color.

Pretty white vegetables such as turnips and cauliflower stay white if you avoid overcooking them. Strong alkaline solutions cause white vegetables to turn brown. If the water you use is hard, be sure to add a tablespoon of vinegar or lemon juice to the cooking water. This acid neutralizes the alkaline content of hard water. One teaspoon of cream of tartar also does the trick.

Chlorophyll, a very temperamental coloring agent, causes the green color of vegetables. It dislikes heat and will absolutely not tolerate acids. For best results in cooking green vegetables, use a small amount of boiling water—not more than ½ inch in the bottom of the pan. Cook uncovered for the first three minutes to allow some of the volatile acids, formed when the cells soften, to escape in the steam. Cover and cook to the tender-crisp stage. Since acid turns green vegetables to a bronze color, let family and guests add vinegar, lemon juice or tart dressing at the table.

Red foods change color according to the acid or the reaction of the cooking process. For instance, red cabbage cooked in alkaline-reacting milk will have a slightly blue cast, while that covered with an acid sauce will have a bright clear color.

Usually food with a clear red color is more appetizing than that with blue tones. Reach for the acid if your red vegetables look blue. Red cabbage cooked with a tart apple, for example, adds both a new taste and enough acid to keep the color of the cabbage bright.

Remove all vegetables from the cooking pan when they are slightly underdone. They will finish cooking while you handle them.

7

WAYS TO COOK VEGETABLES

There are several basic ways to cook vegetables:

BOIL

Cover and cook in a small amount of water. At the boiling point, bubbles continually rise and break on the surafce of the liquid.

STEAM

Cook vegetables on a rack over vigorously boiling water or in top part of a double boiler.

FRY

Cook in moderate amount of fat or oil. Vegetables, such as onion rings and eggplant, are delicious when dipped into a batter and deep-fat fried.

PANFRY

Cook in a skillet with a small amount of hot fat.

BAKE

Place whole vegetable, such as potatoes, in heated oven and cook; or grate or cut vegetable into small pieces and cook covered in the oven.

BROIL

Cook directly over or under open heat or fire until light browned. When broiling, baste vegetable with fat, flavored sauce or sugar glaze.

Cook vegetables only until they are tender. This keeps the best flavor, color, texture and food value in vegetables. For the most nutritive value, cook them whole in skins. To shorten cooking time, cut, slice, dice or coarsely shred vegetables.

Thawing before cooking is not necessary for most frozen vegetables. Leafy vegetables, however, cook more evenly if thawed just enough to separate the leaves before putting them into boiling water. Follow package directions when cooking commercially frozen vegetables.

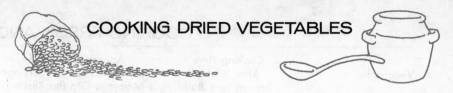

COOKING DRIED VEGETABLES

Before cooking whole peas and dry beans, soak overnight. Then cook; or boil peas and beans for 2 minutes, remove from heat and soak for 1 hour before cooking.

Cooking times for beans that take an hour or longer to cook can be shortened by adding a small amount of baking soda to water at the beginning of the soaking period. If tap water is of medium hardness, adding ⅛ teaspoon soda to the water for each cup of dry beans reduces the cooking time about one-fourth. Measure soda exactly—excessive soda affects the flavor and nutritive value of beans.

General directions for boiling dry beans, lentils and peas are:

1. Add the amount of water recommended for the vegetable in the boiling guide that follows. Boil for 2 minutes then soak for 1 hour before cooking; or, if more convenient, soak beans overnight.

2. Add 1 teaspoon of salt for each cup of vegetable and boil gently for the time specified in the guide. Stir only a few times during cooking.

3. To prevent foaming when cooking great northern, red kidney, pinto or pea beans, add 1 tablespoon of bacon drippings or other fat to the cooking water for each cup of beans.

Lentils and split peas may be boiled or baked without soaking. Use 2½ cups of water for each cup of lentils. Oven cooking is recommended for split peas unless they are to be pureed because they break up easily when cooked by other methods. For each cup of split peas, add 1½ cups of water. Boil for 2 minutes then soak for 30 minutes. Place in a baking dish; cover and bake at 350° F. for 25 minutes.

If acid ingredients such as tomatoes, catsup or vinegar are included in the recipe, add them late in the cooking period when beans are almost tender. Acids delay softening of the skins.

Boiling Guide For Dried Vegetables

VEGETABLE	AMOUNT OF WATER	BOILING TIME	YIELD
Black beans	3 cups	2 hours (about)	2 cups
Blackeye peas, cowpeas	2½ cups	30 minutes	2½ cups
Cranberry beans	3 cups	2 hours (about)	2 cups
Great Northern beans	2½ cups	1 to 1½ hours	2½ cups
Kidney beans	3 cups	2 hours (about)	2¾ cups
Lentils	2½ cups*	30 minutes	2½ cups
Lima beans, large	2½ cups	1 hour	2½ cups
Lima beans, small	2½ cups	45 minutes (about)	2 cups
Pea (navy) beans	3 cups	1½ to 2 hours	2½ cups
Peas, whole	2½ cups	1 hour	2½ cups
Pinto beans	3 cups	2 hours (about)	2½ cups

*Add this amount of water; no soaking required

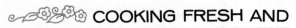

Vegetable	Cooking Time After Water Returns to a Boil		Approx. Amount As Purchased for Six Servings (About ½ Cup Per Serving)	
	MINUTES			
	FRESH	FROZEN	POUNDS FRESH	OUNCES FROZEN
ASPARAGUS				
Whole spears	10 to 20	5 to 10	2½	24
Cuts and tips	5 to 15		1¾	
BEANS, lima	20 to 25	10 to 20	2¾ in pods	16
BEANS, snap	15 to 30	15 to 25	1	16
BEETS				
Young, whole	30 to 40		2½ with tops;	
Older, whole	45 to 90		1½ without	
Sliced, diced	15 to 25		tops	
BROCCOLI				
Heavy stalks	15 to 20	8 to 15	1¾	20
Flowers only	10 to 15	5 to 10		
BRUSSELS SPROUTS	10 to 20	10 to 15	1¼	16
CABBAGE				
Shredded	3 to 10		1¼	
Wedges	10 to 15		1½	
CARROTS				
Young, whole	15 to 20		1½ without	
Older, whole	20 to 30		tops	16
Sliced or diced	10 to 20	5 to 10		
CAULIFLOWER				
Separated	8 to 15	5 to 8	2	20
Whole	15 to 20		2	20
CELERY, Cut up	15 to 18		1½	
CORN, On cob	5 to 15	3 to 5	3 in husks	32
KALE	10 to 15	8 to 12	1¼ untrimmed	24
OKRA	10 to 15		1¼	

FROZEN VEGETABLES

Vegetable	Cooking Time After Water Returns to a Boil		Approx. Amount As Purchased for Six Servings (About ½ Cup Per Serving)	
	MINUTES			
	FRESH	FROZEN	POUNDS FRESH	OUNCES FROZEN
ONIONS, Mature	15 to 30		1¾	
PARSNIPS Whole	20 to 40			
Cut	10 to 20		1½	
PEAS	8 to 20	5 to 15	3 in pods	20
POTATOES Whole, small or medium	25 to 40			
Quartered	20 to 25	10 to 12	1½	21
Diced	10 to 15			
RHUBARB, Cubed	10 to 15			
RUTABAGAS, Cut up	20 to 30			
SPINACH	3 to 10	5 to 14	2 untrimmed or 1½ pre-packaged	24
SQUASH, Summer Sliced	10 to 20	10 to 12	1½	24
SQUASH, Winter Cut Up	15 to 20		3	
SWEET POTATOES, Whole	25 to 35		1½	
TOMATOES, Cut Up	7 to 15		1¼	
TURNIP GREENS	10 to 15	15 to 20	2¾ untrimmed	28
TURNIPS Whole	20 to 30		1¾ without tops	
Cut up	10 to 20			

SEASONING VEGETABLES

Vegetable	Ways to Prepare	Season With
ARTICHOKES	Simmered in water until tender	Basil, chive, curry, dill, thyme, almonds, b a c o n , cheese, crumbs, croutons, red wine, butter.
ASPARAGUS	Boiled, steamed, baked	Basil, caraway, celery seed, marjoram, nutmeg, oregano, tarragon, anchovies, bacon, cheese, lemon, mushrooms, sausage, scallions.
BEANS	Boiled	Cheese, crumbs, croutons, horseradish, basil, caraway, dill, sage, chives, thyme, bacon, onion.
BEETS	Boiled, baked	Allspice, basil, caraway, mint, poppy seed, sage, tarragon, c h e e s e , sausage, honey, mustard, onion.
BROCCOLI	Boiled, baked, raw flowerettes	Basil, curry, garlic, oregano, almonds, anchovies, bacon, cheese, crumbs, sausage, ham, lemon.
BRUSSELS SPROUTS	Boiled, baked, stuffed	Basil, celery seed, oregano, tarragon, thyme, bacon, nuts, cream, crumbs, sausage, lemon, mustard.
CABBAGE	Pan stirred, baked, steamed, braised, raw	Anise, basil, bay leaf, caraway, celery seed, oregano, rosemary, s a g e , savory, thyme, bacon, cheese, croutons, sausage.
CARROTS	Steamed, boiled, braised, raw	Cinnamon, chives, cloves, ginger, mint, mustard, rosemary, almonds, croutons, honey, lemon and orange, scallions, sugar, marshmallows.

Vegetable	Ways to Prepare	Season With
CAULIFLOWER	Steamed, boiled, raw in salads	Caraway, chives, curry, dill, ginger, n u t m e g , savory, thyme, cheese, c r e a m , crumbs, sausage, lemon, vinegar and sugar.
CELERY	Raw, sauteed, boiled, baked	Chives, curry, dill, fennel, ginger, majoram, tarragon, almonds, bacon, cheese, sausage, o l i v e s , onions, white wine.
CORN	Boiled, baked, steamed	Celery seed, chervil, coriander, marjoram, nutmeg, rosemary, sage, savory, tarragon, bacon, cheese, croutons, mustard, onion, relish, bell pepper, scallions, Worcestershire.
CUCUMBER	Raw	Allspice, basil, chives, dill, mustard, tarragon, thyme, anchovies, bacon, cheese, lemon, mushrooms, onion, soya.
EGGPLANT	Baked, boiled, fried, mashed	Allspice, basil, celery seed, coriander, curry, garlic, ginger, nutmeg, thyme, anchovies, b a c o n , sugar, onions, soya.
GREENS	Boiled	Basil, celery seed, curry, garlic, marjoram, nutmeg, oregano, rosemary, sage, t a r r a g o n , bacon, nuts, cheese, animal fat, mushrooms, onion, sausage, ham, butter.
MUSHROOMS	Buttered and simmered	Anise, basil, bay leaf, celery seed, garlic, ginger, nutmeg, oregano, rosemary, bacon, nuts, cheese, cream, croutons, crumbs, scallions, red wine, brandy.
OKRA	Steamed with butter, fried, boiled	Chili powder, garlic, mustard, oregano, bacon, croutons, sausage, ham, onion, pimento.
ONIONS	Boiled, fried, braised, broiled	Allspice, bay leaf, cinnamon, chili powder, clove, marjoram, mustard, oregano, thyme, bacon, nuts, cheese, cream, croutons, sausage, ham, vinegar and sugar, brandy.

Vegetable	Ways to Prepare	Season With
PARSNIPS	Boiled	Celery seed, cinnamon, clove, ginger, mustard, nutmeg, tarragon, bacon, cream, honey, oil or butter, sherry, brandy.
PEAS	Simmered in water until tender, steamed with butter, boiled	Anise, basil, celery seed, chives, mint, nutmeg, oregano, rosemary, nuts, bacon, cheese, coconut, cream, sausage, ham, onion, scallions.
PEPPERS	Sautéed, broiled	Bay leaf, chili powder, curry, dill, garlic, ginger, mustard, thyme, anchovies, bacon, cheese, crumbs, sausage, mushrooms, lemon.
POTATOES	Boiled, baked fried, braised, steamed	Celery seed, chives, curry, dill, garlic, ginger, sage, marjoram, bacon, nuts, cheese, onion, mushrooms, olives, scallions, horseradish.
SQUASH, SUMMER	Boiled, baked, steamed	Basil, celery seed, curry, ginger, marjoram, garlic mint, oregano, rosemary, bacon, cheese, crumbs, croutons, mushrooms, onion, soya.
SQUASH, WINTER	Baked	Cinnamon, clove, curry, ginger, nutmeg, nuts, marshmallows, cream, orange, honey, lemon, brandy, rum.
SWEET POTATOES	Baked	Cinnamon, clove, curry, ginger, nutmeg, nuts, marshmallows, cream, orange, honey, lemon, brandy, rum.
TOMATOES	Broiled, sautéed, baked, stewed, boiled	Basil, bay leaf, chili powder, chives, curry, garlic, ginger, rosemary, sage, thyme, anchovies, bacon, cheese, cream, croutons, crumbs, mushrooms, olives, onion, oil or butter, vinegar and sugar.
TURNIPS AND RUTABAGAS	Boiled	Celery seed, cinnamon, clove, ginger, mustard, nutmeg, tarragon, bacon, cream, honey, oil or butter, sherry, brandy.

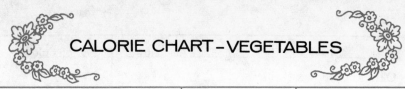

CALORIE CHART – VEGETABLES

Food	Amount	No. of Calories
VEGETABLES		
Asparagus		
Cooked	1 c.	35
Canned, white or green		
med. spears	6 spears	20
Beans		
Canned, baked, pork and		
molasses	½ c.	154
Lima, immature, cooked	1 c.	150
Red kidney, canned	½ c.	108
Snap, green, cooked	1 c.	25
Canned	1 c.	45
Waxed, canned	½ c.	20
Beets		
Fresh, cooked, diced	1 c.	70
Canned	½ c.	38
Broccoli, cooked	1 c.	45
Brussels sprouts, cooked	1 c.	60
Cabbage		
Cooked	1 c.	40
Raw, coleslaw	1 c.	100
Carrots		
Canned	1 oz.	5
Cooked, diced	1 c.	45
Raw, 5½ x 1-inch	1 carrot	20
Cauliflower, cooked,		
flowerbuds	1 c.	30
Celery, raw	Large stalk	5
Collards, cooked	1 c.	75
Corn		
Canned, cream-style,		
white	½ c.	91
Canned, cream-style,		
yellow	½ c.	92
Canned, whole kernel,		
white	½ c.	70
Canned, whole kernel,		
yellow	½ c.	75
Cooked, 1 ear 5 inches		
long	1 ear	65
Cowpeas, cooked, immature	1 c.	150
Cucumbers, raw, pared	6 ⅛-in. slices	5
Dandelion greens, cooked	1 c.	80
Endive, curly	2 oz.	10
Kale, cooked	1 c.	45
Lettuce, 4¾-in. diameter		
head	1 head	70
Mushrooms, canned	1 c.	30
Mustard greens, cooked	1 c.	30

Food	Amount	No. of Calories
Okra, cooked, 3 x ⅝-in. pod	8 pods	30
Onions, mature		
Cooked	1 c.	80
Raw, 2½-in. diameter	1 onion	50
Parsnips, cooked	1 c.	95
Peas, green	1 c.	
Canned, solids and liquids	1 c.	170
Cooked	1 c.	110
Peppers, sweet		
Green, raw	1 medium	15
Red, raw	1 medium	20
Pimento, canned	1 medium	10
Potatoes, medium		
Baked, peeled after baking	1 potato	90
Boiled, peeled before boiling	1 potato	90
French-fried, 2 x ½ x ½-in. pieces		
Cooked in deep fat	10 pieces	155
Frozen, heated for serving	10 pieces	95
Mashed, milk added	1 c.	145
Mashed, milk and butter added	1 c.	230
Pumpkin, canned	1 c.	75
Radishes, raw	4 small	10
Sauerkraut, canned	1 c.	30
Spinach, fresh cooked or canned	1 c.	45
Squash, cooked		
Summer, diced	1 c.	35
Winter, baked, mashed	1 c.	95
Sweet potatoes		
Cooked, medium, 5 x 2 in.		
Baked, peeled after baking	1 potato	155
Boiled, peeled after boiling	1 potato	170
Candied, 3½ x 2¼-in.	1 potato	295
Canned	1 c.	235
Tomatoes		
Canned or cooked	1 c.	45
Raw, about 3 per lb.	1 tomato	30
Tomato juice, canned	1 c.	50
Turnips, cooked, diced	1 c.	40
Turnip greens, cooked	1 c.	45
Vegetable juice cocktail, canned	1 c.	40

Compiled from USDA Yearbook of Agriculture.

Artichokes and Asparagus

Artichokes

> ¼ c. salad or olive oil
> 2 tbsp. lemon juice
> 2 sm. bay leaves
> 1 clove of garlic, split
> 1 tsp. salt
> Dash of pepper
> 4 lge. artichokes

Boil 6 quarts water with oil, lemon juice, bay leaves, garlic, salt and pepper. Trim stalks from base of artichokes; cut a 1-inch slice from top of each. Remove tough bottom row and discolored leaves; snip off spiky tips of leaves (about ¼-inch). Wash artichokes in cold water; drain. Tie each with string to hold leaves in place. Place in boiling water; reduce heat. Simmer, covered, for 30 minutes or until base if soft. Drain well; remove string. Serve with sauce, lemon butter or mayonnaise. Yield: 4 servings.
Personal Comment: An artichoke is eaten by pulling off 1 leaf at a time with the fingers, dipping it in sauce and pulling it through the teeth in order to scrape off the tender inner side of the stalk end; the leaf is then discarded. The pale young leaves in the center, when pulled up, reveal the fuzzy choke; this is lifted out and discarded, leaving the heart, which is eaten with a fork.

Marjorie Francis, Montgomery, Ala.

 ## Artichoke Casserole Supreme

> 12 artichokes
> 1 tsp. salt
> 1 c. boiling water
> 1 clove of garlic, crushed
> 1 tbsp. salad oil
> ¼ c. lemon juice
> Chopped cooked seafood, chicken or turkey
> Medium white sauce

Break off stems from artichokes to about ½ inch; remove outer leaves and thorny leaf tips. Tie with string to keep leaves in place. Cook, covered, in 1-inch boiling salted water seasoned with garlic, salad oil and lemon juice for 30 minutes. Remove carefully; trim stem. Alternate layers of artichoke hearts, seafood and sauce in baking dish. Bake at 350 degrees for 20 minutes. Yield: 6 servings.

Mrs. Kelley Storey, Home Economics Teacher, Paris, Tex.

Artichoke Hearts Elegante

    1 pkg. frozen artichokes
    1 tbsp. dried minced onion, dehydrated
    1 clove of garlic, crushed
    1 tbsp. chopped parsley or ½ tbsp. dried parsley
    ½ c. dry bread crumbs
    1 tsp. salt
    Freshly ground pepper
    ¼ c. olive oil
    2 tbsp. water
    4 tbsp. grated Parmesan or Romano cheese

Cook artichokes in boiling salted water for 5 minutes; drain well. Place in buttered baking dish. Mix all remaining ingredients; sprinkle over artichokes. Bake at 400 degrees for 20 minutes or until soft. Yield: 4 servings.

Mrs. Robert Still, Tacoma, Wash., Favorite Recipes Food Fair

 ## Artichoke Hearts In Parmesan Custard

    2 9-oz. pkg. frozen artichoke hearts
    ½ c. canned tomatoes, drained and chopped
    1 tsp. salt
    ¼ tsp. pepper
    ¼ tsp. garlic salt
    2 tsp. chopped parsley
    ½ c. grated Parmesan cheese
    ¾ c. water
    ¼ c. olive oil
    6 eggs, beaten

Place unthawed artichoke hearts in bottom of greased 2-quart casserole. Sprinkle with tomatoes, salt, pepper, garlic salt, parsley and Parmesan cheese. Pour in water and olive oil. Bake, covered, at 350 degrees for 1 hour. Pour eggs over cooked artichokes; bake, uncovered, for 15 to 20 minutes or until eggs are set. Yield: 8 servings.

Mrs. Marvel Swenson, Home Economics Teacher, Sauk Rapids, Minn.

 ## Artichoke Hearts In Lemon Butter

    ½ c. minced onion
    ½ clove of garlic, crushed
    2 tbsp. butter
    ¾ c. chicken broth

(Continued on next page)

2 15-oz. cans artichoke hearts
3 tbsp. lemon juice
1 ½ tsp. salt
1 tsp. oregano
¼ tsp. grated lemon rind

Saute onion and garlic in butter until transparent; add broth and artichoke hearts. Season with lemon juice, salt, oregano and lemon rind. Simmer gently for 10 minutes or until artichokes are heated through. Yield: 6-8 servings.

Florence B. Fisackerly, Home Economics Teacher, Inverness, Miss.

 ## Artichoke Hearts And Pecans

2 No. 2 cans artichoke hearts, drained
1 c. sweet cream
2 tbsp. butter
2 tbsp. flour
Salt and pepper to taste
Tabasco sauce to taste
½ c. broken pecans
¼ c. bread crumbs
2 tbsp. Parmesan cheese

Stand artichoke hearts in small casserole. Blend cream, butter and flour; cook until thickened, stirring constantly. Season with salt, pepper and Tabasco sauce. Pour sauce into casserole; add pecans. Sprinkle with bread crumbs and cheese. Bake at 300 degrees until bubbly. Yield: 6 servings.

Selma Sailors, Diller, Nebr.

 ## Artichoke-Lobster Newburg

3 pkg. frozen artichoke hearts
1 bay leaf (opt.)
2 cans cream of mushroom soup
5 tsp. chopped onion
6 tbsp. sherry
1 tsp. salt
¼ tsp. garlic salt
¼ tsp. pepper
4 c. cooked lobster, cut into bite-sized pieces
1 c. grated cheddar cheese

(Continued on next page)

Cook artichoke hearts according to package directions; add bay leaf during cooking. Drain. Combine soup, onion, sherry and seasonings; mix well. Arrange artichoke hearts and lobster in casserole. Add soup mixture; top with cheese. Bake at 400 degrees for 15 minutes. Serve with wild rice if desired. Yield: 8 servings.

Mrs. Hugh G. Fly, Jr., Wheeler AFB, Hawaii

 ## Artichokes A La Maria

  1 tbsp. minced onion
  1/3 c. olive oil
  1 tbsp. flour
  1 c. boiling water
  2 carrots, sliced
  1 bunch fresh green onions, chopped
  1 tsp. peppercorns
  1 tsp. salt
  1 tsp. dill weed
  2 pkg. frozen artichokes
  Juice of 1/2 lemon

Saute minced onion in oil. Add flour, water, carrots and green onions. Cook for 10 to 15 minutes. Add spices, artichokes and lemon juice. Cook for 45 minutes or until vegetables are tender but not watery. Yield: 6 servings.

Ruth Bender, West Lafayette, Ind.

 ## Artichokes With Parsley Sauce

  2 10-oz. pkg. frozen artichokes or 4 c. cooked artichokes
  3 tbsp. butter
  3 tbsp. flour
  2 c. milk
  1/2 tsp. salt
  1/8 tsp. pepper
  2 tbsp. minced parsley or parsley flakes

Cook frozen artichokes according to package directions. Drain; dice. Melt butter; stir in flour. Add milk gradually; cook until thickened, stirring constantly. Add salt and pepper; fold in minced parsley. Combine with artichokes; heat thoroughly. Sprinkle with paprika. Yield: 8 servings.

Lois Sandell, Home Economics Teacher, Nevada, Iowa

Artichokes Santa Cruz

6 artichokes
Salt
¼ lb. fresh mushrooms, chopped
¼ c. chopped green onions
½ c. chopped cucumbers
2 tbsp. salad oil
1 6-oz. pkg. frozen king crab meat, thawed and chopped
½ lb. cooked cleaned shrimp, chopped
2 hard-cooked eggs, chopped
½ c. mayonnaise
½ c. sour cream
2 tbsp. chopped fresh dill or 1 tsp. dill weed
⅛ tsp. white pepper
2 tbsp. lemon juice

Wash artichokes; cut off stems at base and remove small bottom leaves. Trim tips of leaves and cut off about 1 inch from top of artichokes. Stand artichokes upright in deep saucepan large enough to hold snugly. Add ¼ teaspoon salt for each artichoke and 2 to 3 inches boiling water. Cover and boil gently for 35 to 45 minutes or until base can be pierced easily with fork; add more boiling water if needed. Turn artichokes upside down to drain. Gently spread leaves and remove choke or thistle portion from center of artichoke with metal spoon. Saute mushrooms and onions in oil until tender, but not browned. In large bowl, combine mushrooms with cucumbers, crab meat, shrimp, eggs, mayonnaise, sour cream, dill, 1 teaspoon salt, pepper and lemon juice. Chill; fill prepared artichokes with salad. Serve garnished with lemon wedges and parsley as desired. Yield: 6 servings.

Lucy Steel, Rahway, N. J.

 ## Chicken-Artichoke Casserole

1 2-lb. fryer chicken, cut up
1 ½ tsp. salt
¼ tsp. pepper
½ tsp. paprika
1 pkg. frozen artichoke hearts, thawed
1 6-oz. can sliced mushrooms
2 tbsp. flour
3 tbsp. cooking sherry
⅔ c. chicken consomme
½ c. melted butter

Sprinkle chicken pieces with salt, pepper and paprika; arrange in casserole. Place artichoke hearts and mushrooms in and around chicken. Blend flour with sherry and consomme in blender on high or 10 seconds. Pour sauce

(Continued on next page)

over chicken. Add melted butter. Bake in preheated 350-degree oven for 1 hour and 15 minutes.

Mrs. Barbara I. Barker, Home Economics Teacher, Arlington Heights, Ill.

 ## Filbert-Stuffed Artichokes

> *4 med. artichokes*
> *½ c. chopped toasted filberts*
> *½ c. seasoned dry bread crumbs*
> *¼ c. chopped pimento-stuffed olives*
> *1 clove garlic, pressed*
> *2 tbsp. melted butter or margarine*
> *Boiling water*
> *1 tsp. salt*

Wash artichokes. Cut off stems at base and remove small bottom leaves. Trim tips of leaves and cut off about 1 inch from top of artichokes. Combine filberts, crumbs, olives, garlic and butter; stir with a tossing motion to coat mixture with the butter. Spoon between leaves of artichokes. Stand them upright in a deep saucepan large enough to hold snugly. Add 1-inch boiling water and salt. (Pour water around, not over artichokes.) Cover and boil gently 35 to 45 minutes, or until base of artichokes can be pierced easily with a fork. Add more boiling water, if needed. Serve with additional melted butter, if desired.

Photograph for this recipe below.

Chilled Artichokes With Garlic Mayonnaise

6 lge. artichokes
Lemon juice
Boiling salted water
1 c. mayonnaise
1 clove of garlic, mashed
Paprika

Wash artichokes thoroughly in cold water; drain. Turn each on its side; slice off thorny top 1/3 of the way down. Cut off stem to make a flat base; remove small leaves around base. Cut thorns from tips of outer leaves with scissors; rub cut edges with lemon juice. Turn on cut end; press firmly to separate leaves slightly. Carefully scoop out fibrous center leaves and fuzzy core with small spoon. Stand artichokes in 1 inch of boiling salted water. Simmer, covered, for 30 minutes or until tender. Drain; chill, covered, for 1 hour or longer. Blend mayonnaise and garlic. Spoon into artichokes; sprinkle with paprika. Yield: 6 servings.

Mrs. Elizabeth Hayton, Kelso, Wash.

 ## Mildred's Artichokes

6 lge. artichokes
Juice of 1 lemon
6 lge. onions, thinly sliced
½ c. olive oil
½ c. water
Salt to taste
¾ tsp. monosodium glutamate

Remove stems from artichokes; peel off tough outer leaves. Lay each one on its side; cut off an inch or more of the tops so that only the very tender portion of leaves remain. Halve lengthwise; remove choke portion. As each artichoke is prepared drop it into cold water to which half the lemon juice has been added. Saute onions in oil; place artichoke halves cut-side down on onions. Add water and remaining lemon juice; sprinkle with salt and monsodium glutamate. Simmer, covered, for about 45 minutes, or until tender. Serve cold as an accompaniment or appetizer. Yield: 6 servings.

Mrs. Mildred Callahan, Home Economics Teacher, Miami, Fla.

 ## Shrimp And Artichoke Casserole

1 10-oz. pkg. frozen artichoke hearts
¾ lb. cooked shrimp
¼ lb. fresh mushrooms, sliced
2 tbsp. butter

(Continued on next page)

1 tbsp. Worcestershire sauce
¼ c. dry sherry
1 can cream of mushroom soup
¼ c. grated Parmesan cheese
½ tsp. salt
¼ tsp. pepper
 Paprika
 Parsley

Arrange artichoke hearts in buttered baking dish. Arrange shrimp over artichokes. Saute mushrooms in butter for 6 minutes; add to shrimp and artichokes. Mix Worcestershire sauce and sherry with soup; pour over ingredients in baking dish. Sprinkle with cheese, salt, pepper and paprika. Bake at 375 degrees for 30 to 40 minutes. Garnish with parsley. Yield: 4-6 servings.

Mrs. Forbes S. Hascall, Bloomfield Hills, Mich.

 ## Stuffed Artichokes

4 med. artichokes
⅔ c. fine dry bread crumbs
1 tsp. grated cheese
1 tbsp. plus 1 tsp. chopped parsley
1 tsp. salt
¾ tsp. pepper
2 c. water
2 tbsp. olive oil

Remove outside lower leaves from artichokes; cut off stems. Cover with cold salted water; let stand for 20 to 30 minutes. Blend bread crumbs, cheese, 1 teaspoon parsley, salt and pepper. Wash artichokes; spread open leaves. Place mixture between leaves. Stand artichokes in skillet; add water, remaining parsley and olive oil. Cook, covered, for 30 minutes or until tender. To eat, pull out leaves one by one. Yield: 4 servings.

Sister M. Joanna, Home Economics Teacher, Newfield, N. J.

 ## Asparagus

Fresh asparagus
Salt
Butter

Break stems at farthest point from tips where they snap easily. Wash thoroughly and tie with white string in bunches (enough in each bunch for 1 serving); stand bunches upright with stems in boiling water in deep saucepan. Cook covered until tender, about 15 to 30 minutes. Season with salt and butter to taste; remove string to serve.

Barbara Hallman, Montgomery, Ala.

April Asparagus

2 pkg. frozen asparagus
2 green onions, chopped
6 stuffed olives, chopped
1 tbsp. capers
1 tsp. salt
½ tsp. thyme
⅓ c. red wine
¼ c. wine vinegar
¾ c. olive oil
½ tsp. pepper

Cook asparagus according to package directions; drain. Combine remaining ingredients; pour over warm asparagus, making sure dressing coats all asparagus. Let stand for several hours. Yield: 6-8 servings.

Denise L. Hodnette, Pensacola, Fla.

 ## Asparagus-Almond Casserole

1 recipe cream sauce
¼ lb. grated American cheese
4 cans green asparagus pieces, drained
½ c. blanched almonds
Bread crumbs
Paprika

Make thick cream sauce; add cheese. Stir until dissolved. In casserole, layer asparagus, cheese sauce and almonds; sprinkle top with bread crumbs and paprika. Bake in 350-degree oven until bubbly.

Mrs. J. Hart Caughey, Hon. V. Pres., Allied Officers' Wives' Club, Naples, Italy

 ## Asparagus Almondine

¼ c. slivered blanched almonds
¼ c. butter
¼ tsp. salt
2 tsp. lemon juice
2 c. cooked asparagus, drained

Saute almonds in butter until golden, stirring occasionally; remove from heat. Add salt and lemon juice; pour over hot asparagus. Let stand for a few minutes before serving. Yield: 4 servings.

Katherine W. Rebbe, Home Economics Teacher, Wakefield, Neb.

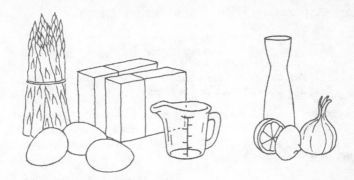

 Asparagus Bearnaise

　2　pkg. frozen asparagus
　1　½ tsp. monosodium glutamate
　3　egg yolks
　2　tbsp. lemon juice
　¼　tsp. minced onion
　¼　tsp. minced parsley
　½　tsp. dried tarragon
　　　Dash of cayenne
　½　c. butter

Prepare asparagus according to package directions; season with monosodium glutamate. Blend egg yolks, juice, onion, parsley, tarragon and cayenne. Melt butter; blend into egg mixture, stirring or beating constantly. Serve immediately over hot asparagus. Yield: 8 servings.

Mrs. Ruth B. Marsh, Home Economics Teacher, Millersville, Pa.

 Asparagus Casserole

　3　tbsp. butter
　4　tbsp. flour
　1　½ c. milk
　　　Salt and pepper to taste
　1　tsp. grated onion
　1　can or 2 c. asparagus, cooked and cut
　6　hard-boiled eggs
　　　Bread crumbs

Make white sauce of all ingredients except asparagus and eggs. Alternate in casserole layers of asparagus, sliced eggs, and white sauce. Top with sauce. Sprinkle with bread crumbs and bake at 400 degrees until browned.

Mrs. Hulett C. Smith, Wife of Governor of West Virginia, Charleston

Asparagus With Fried Onion Rings

2 sm. cans asparagus tips
1 ½ c. grated American cheese
1 can mushroom soup
1 sm. can evaporated milk
1 3½-oz. can fried onion rings

Drain asparagus tips and place in well-greased casserole. Cover with grated cheese. Mix soup and milk well; pour over asparagus and cheese. Cook for 30 minutes at 350 degrees; sprinkle onion rings over top and brown 10 minutes longer. Yield: 8-10 servings.

Mrs. S. L. Norrell, Cleburne, Tex.

 ## Asparagus-Macaroni Loaf

⅓ c. instant nonfat dry milk powder
2 tbsp. flour
1 tsp. salt
⅛ tsp. pepper
1 c. water
2 eggs, slightly beaten
3 oz. Gruyere cheese, shredded
1 10-oz. pkg. frozen asparagus, thawed
Pimento
4 c. cooked elbow macaroni

Sprinkle combined dry milk powder, flour and seasonings on surface of water in double boiler. Beat with rotary beater just until blended. Add eggs and cheese. Cook over hot water, stirring constantly, until cheese is melted and sauce has thickened. Arrange asparagus spears and pimento in bottom of buttered 1½-quart loaf pan. Cut remaining asparagus into small pieces and stir into sauce. Add macaroni to sauce and mix lightly. Pour into loaf pan. Bake in 325-degree oven for 50 to 60 minutes or until set. Remove from oven. Turn out loaf onto a warm platter. If desired, garnish with thin slices of cucumber and lemon.

STELLAR SAUCE:

3 tbsp. instant nonfat dry milk
1 10½-oz. can cream of celery soup
½ c. water
3 oz. Gruyere cheese, shredded
Few grains of pepper

Sprinkle dry milk powder onto surface of soup in top of double boiler; stir until blended. Stir in water and cheese. Cook over hot water, stirring constantly, until cheese is melted and the sauce is piping hot. Add pepper. Serve with Asparagus-Macaroni Loaf.

Mrs. Walter Apple, Madison, Wis.

Asparagus And Mushroom Casserole

3 c. medium cheese sauce
2 14½-oz. cans asparagus, chopped
2 sm. cans sliced mushrooms, drained
1 tsp. finely chopped chives or green onion
1 tbsp. sliced pimento
2 hard-cooked eggs, sliced
Bread crumbs
2 tbsp. butter, melted

Combine cheese sauce, asparagus, mushrooms, chives, pimento and eggs. Spoon into greased casserole. Combine crumbs and butter; sprinkle over mixture. Bake at 350 degrees for 15 minutes. Yield: 6-8 servings.

Amie B. Benton, Eugene, Ore.

 ## Asparagus Parmigiano

1 ½ lb. fresh asparagus, cooked or 2 pkg. frozen asparagus, cooked
1 onion, chopped
1 garlic clove, minced
3 tbsp. oil
1 tsp. salt
¼ tsp. Tabasco
1 1-lb. can tomatoes
¼ tsp. thyme
1 8-oz. can tomato sauce
4 oz. mozzarella cheese, thinly sliced
2 tbsp. grated Parmesan cheese

Drain asparagus and arrange in shallow baking dish. Saute onion and garlic in oil until golden. Add salt, Tabasco and tomatoes. Simmer, uncovered, for 10 minutes. Add thyme and tomato sauce; simmer 20 minutes longer. Pour sauce over asparagus. Place slices of mozzarella cheese over top. Sprinkle with Parmesan cheese. Bake at 350 degrees for 30 minutes. Yield: 6-8 servings.

Photograph for this recipe on page 17.

 ## Asparagus Polonaise

3 tbsp. butter
3 tbsp. flour
1 tsp. salt
2 tsp. dry mustard
1 c. milk
1 egg, beaten

(Continued on next page)

2 c. diced cooked chicken
1 tbsp. dry sherry
2 c. asparagus, cooked
½ c. bread crumbs
½ c. grated cheese

Blend butter, flour, salt and mustard in double boiler; gradually add milk, stirring until smooth and thick. Combine egg and small amount of sauce; stir into remaining sauce. Add chicken and sherry. Place asparagus in 1½-quart casserole; cover with sauce. Sprinkle with mixture of crumbs and cheese. Bake at 400 degrees for 20 minutes. Yield: 4-6 servings.

Mrs. Robert W. Hughes, Asheboro, N. C., Favorite Recipes Food Fair

 ## Asparagus Au Printemps

1 lb. fresh asparagus
2 tbsp. butter
1 tsp. chicken seasoned stock base
1 tsp. Mei Yen seasoning
¼ tsp. grated lemon rind
¼ tsp. sweet basil
1 tsp. cornstarch
½ c. water
2 lge. ripe tomatoes, coarsely chopped

Cut tough ends from asparagus. Steam asparagus for 15 minutes or until just tender. Melt butter in small skillet; blend in stock base, seasoning, lemon rind and sweet basil. Blend cornstarch with water; add to butter mixture. Cook, stirring constantly, until mixture boils and thickens. Add tomatoes to sauce. Cook for 2 to 3 minutes longer. Turn asparagus out onto heated serving dish; spoon sauce over asparagus. Yield: 4 servings.

Mrs. Elvira Schmidt, Home Economics Teacher, Frederic, Wis.

 ## Asparagus Ring

2 tbsp. butter
2 tbsp. flour
1 c. milk
1 c. grated cheese
Dash of cayenne pepper
¼ tsp. salt
3 eggs, separated
1 med. can asparagus, drained and cut
Cracker crumbs

(Continued on next page)

Melt butter; add flour. Cook until bubbly; stir in milk gradually. Cook until thickened, stirring constantly. Add half the cheese and seasonings; stir until melted. Stir in well-beaten egg yolks and asparagus; let cool. Fold in remaining cheese and stiffly beaten egg whites. Thickly butter ring mold; sprinkle with crumbs. Pour asparagus into mold; set in pan of hot water. Bake at 350 degrees for 30 to 40 minutes or until set. Unmold at once. May be filled with hot seasoned peas and water chestnuts. Yield: 8 servings.

Myrtle Little, Home Economics Teacher, Hattiesburg, Miss.

 Asparagus Souffle

> 1 pt. or 1 10½- oz. can asparagus
> 4 tbsp. butter
> 7 tbsp. flour
> ½ c. milk
> 2 ¼ tsp. salt
> Dash of pepper
> 4 eggs, separated

Cut fresh asparagus into ¼-inch pieces; simmer in boiling water until tender. Drain, reserving ½ cup liquid. Melt butter; stir in flour. Gradually add milk and reserved asparagus liquid; cook, stirring constantly, until thickened. Add seasonings. Beat egg yolks until thickened; add to sauce. Cook slowly, stirring constantly. Mix sauce with asparagus. Beat egg whites until stiffened; fold into asparagus mixture. Place in buttered casserole; place in shallow pan of water. Bake at 350 degrees for 1 hour or until fork inserted in center comes out clean.

CHEESE SAUCE:
> 2 tbsp. butter
> ¼ c. flour
> 1 ½ c. milk
> ¼ tsp. salt
> Dash of pepper
> 4 tbsp. grated sharp cheddar cheese

Melt butter; add flour. Gradually add heated milk; cook until smooth. Remove from heat. Add salt, pepper and cheese; stir until blended. Pour over souffle before serving. Yield: 6 servings.

Mrs. Howard L. Ramer, Vestal, N. Y.

 Asparagus With Sour Cream

> 2 lb. fresh asparagus
> ⅓ c. sour cream
> 3 tbsp. melted butter

(Continued on next page)

Creamed Asparagus

½ c. soft bread crumbs
½ tsp. crumbled basil leaves
½ tsp. salt
½ tsp. paprika

Cook asparagus in small amount of salted water. Place in single layer in 12 x 8 x 2-inch pan. Spread with sour cream. Combine butter, bread crumbs, basil, salt and paprika; sprinkle over asparagus. Bake at 375 degrees for 8 to 10 minutes or until bread crumbs are browned. Yield: 6 servings.

Kathryn G. Roller, Hammonton, N. J.

Asparagus On Toast

1 lb. fresh asparagus
4 slices bread
1 c. milk
2 tbsp. (heaping) flour
Salt to taste
Butter
Grated cheese
Paprika
Parsley

Wash fresh asparagus and cut off white ends. Cook in slightly salted water. Toast bread on both sides; dip crusted edges in water in which asparagus was cooked. Heat milk in double boiler. Combine flour, salt and small piece of butter; add to milk. Cook, stirring often to keep mixture smooth. Place bread on platter. Dot with small amount of butter. Spread cooked asparagus over toast. Cover with hot milk sauce. Sprinkle with grated cheese and paprika. Garnish with parsley. Yield: 4 servings.

Rena A. Decatur, Peabody, Mass.

Creamed Asparagus

Green whole asparagus, canned
Cracker crumbs
Butter
White sauce
Grated cheese

Line bottom of pan with asparagus. Cover with fine cracker crumbs, butter dots, and a layer of medium white sauce. Repeat until amount to be served is reached. Top with cheese and bake, covered, about 30 minutes.

Mrs. John J. McKeithen, Wife of Governor of Louisiana, Baton Rouge

Chilled Asparagus Lemonette

    1 *med. onion, finely chopped*
    2 *tbsp. lemon juice*
    ¼ *c. water*
    ½ *c. Sauterne*
    ⅛ *tsp. garlic salt*
    ½ *tsp. dried salad herbs*
    2 *tbsp. salad oil*
    ¾ *tsp. salt*
    2 *lb. fresh asparagus, cooked*

Blend well all ingredients except asparagus. Pour over asparagus. Cover; refrigerate for several hours. Drain; serve on crisp salad greens. May be garnished with pimento strips.

Mrs. Marlys Garman, Lake Geneva, Wis.

 ### Crusty Asparagus Casserole

    1 *No. 2 can asparagus, chopped*
    1 ⅛ *c. cheese cracker crumbs*
    1 *c. grated American cheese*
    2 *pimentos, chopped*
    3 *eggs, beaten*
    2 *c. milk*
    1 *tsp. salt*
    Dash of pepper
    ¾ *stick butter, melted*

Combine asparagus, crumbs, cheese and pimentos; pour into 9 x 13-inch baking dish. Mix remaining ingredients; pour over asparagus mixture. Bake at 350 degrees for 35 to 40 minutes. Yield: 12 servings.

Mrs. F. Horton Highfill, Huron, S. D.

 ### French-Fried Asparagus With Sauce

    1 *can asparagus spears, drained*
    ½ *c. flour*
    2 *eggs, lightly beaten*
    2 *tbsp. milk*
    1 *c. cracker crumbs*

Roll asparagus spears in flour; dip into eggs beaten with milk. Roll in cracker crumbs. Fry in deep fat until golden brown.

(Continued on next page)

MOCK HOLLANDAISE SAUCE:
>1 4-oz. pkg. cream cheese
>1 tbsp. lemon juice
>1 egg yolk

Blend cream cheese, lemon juice and egg yolk. Serve cold over hot asparagus.
Yield: 4 servings.

Louise Cole, Arlington, Va.

 Elegant Asparagus Casserole

>1 lge. can asparagus spears or tips, drained
>1 can cream of mushroom soup
>1 c. toast cubes, buttered
>2 tsp. dried parsley flakes
>Dash of black pepper
>Dash of paprika
>1 can cheese soup

Place asparagus in a 1½-quart casserole. Some may be reserved to decorate top, if desired. Add mushroom soup that has been thinned with a little asparagus liquid. Cover with toast cubes. Mix seasonings with cheese soup which has also been thinned with asparagus liquid. Spread over top of casserole. Bake at 350 degrees until bubbly or about 30 minutes.

Mrs. Paul D. Spradlin, Russellville, Ala.

 Parmesan Asparagus

>2 green onions, chopped
>¼ c. butter or margarine
>1 tbsp. flour
>½ tsp. salt
>Dash of pepper
>½ c. asparagus liquid
>2 14-oz. cans or jars asparagus spears, drained
>½ c. light cream
>2 tbsp. diced pimento
>½ c. grated Parmesan cheese

Cook onions in butter until tender; stir in flour and seasonings. Add liquid from asparagus and cream. Cook until thickened, stirring. Add pimento. Arrange asparagus in shallow baking dish. Pour sauce over asparagus; sprinkle with Parmesan cheese. Bake at 400 degrees for 20 minutes or until asparagus is heated and cheese is lightly browned. Yield: 6-8 servings.

Mrs. Eleanor V. Puckett, Home Economics Teacher, Huntersville, N. C.

Goldenrod Asparagus

    1 No. 1 can asparagus and juice
    3 hard-cooked eggs
  12 stuffed olives
    2 c. medium white sauce
    Buttered toast

Heat asparagus in juice. Chop egg whites and olives; add to sauce. Arrange hot asparagus on toast; cover with sauce. Garnish with sieved egg yolks. Yield: 6 servings.

Mrs. Ethel G. Burns, Chinook, Mont.

 ## Ham And Asparagus Rolls

    2 cans asparagus spears, drained
    6 thin slices ham
    6 slices toast
    4 tbsp. butter
    4 tbsp. flour
    Pepper
  ¼ tsp. salt
    2 c. milk
  ½ lb. grated cheese

Place several spears of asparagus on each ham slice. Roll; secure. Broil until hot; place on toast. Melt butter; blend in flour, seasoning and milk. Cook until thickened, stirring constantly; add cheese. Pour over rolls on toast. Yield: 6 servings.

Annie Maude Brown, Home Economics Teacher, Baldwyn, Miss.

 ## Salmon And Asparagus Chantilly

    1 1-lb. can salmon
    Milk
    4 tbsp. butter
    4 tbsp. flour
    2 tsp. grated onion
    1 tsp. dry mustard
    2 tsp. salt
    Dash of pepper
    2 tbsp. mayonnaise
    2 tsp. parsley flakes
    3 hard-cooked eggs, sliced or quartered
    1 pkg. frozen asparagus spears, cooked and drained

(Continued on next page)

Drain salmon, reserving liquid. Remove skin and bone. Add enough milk to salmon juice to make 2 cups liquid. Melt butter; blend in flour. Add milk and salmon juice; cook until smooth and thick. Add onion, mustard, salt, pepper, mayonnaise and parsley flakes. Combine sauce, salmon, eggs and asparagus spears. Place in shallow 11 x 7-inch baking dish. Bake at 350 degrees for 30 minutes. Yield: 4 servings.

Gertrude Pautsch, Wessington, S. D.

 ## Souffle With Asparagus

 2 tbsp. butter
 2 tbsp. flour
 ¾ c. hot milk
 ½ tsp. salt
 Dash of cayenne
 ½ lb. yellow cheese, sliced
 4 eggs, separated
 1 can asparagus tips

Combine butter, flour, milk, salt and cayenne; cook over low heat until thickened and smooth. Add cheese; stir until melted. Add beaten egg yolks; cool. Fold in stiffly beaten egg whites. Arrange asparagus in casserole; add cheese mixture. Bake in 350-degree oven for 30 minutes. Yield: 8 servings.

Mrs. A. R. Mason, Officers' Wives' Club, Williams AFB, Ariz.

 ## Spicy Asparagus

 ⅔ c. white vinegar
 ½ tsp. salt
 ½ c. sugar
 3 sticks cinnamon
 1 tsp. whole cloves
 1 tsp. celery seed
 ½ c. water
 2 lge. cans green asparagus

Boil vinegar, salt, sugar, spices and water. Pour over asparagus. Cover; chill for 24 hours. Drain; serve. Yield: 6 servings.

Mrs. Mary J. Higgins, Home Economics Teacher, Marietta, Ga.

Beans

Baked Beans Supreme

1 lge. can pork and beans
1 c. catsup
1 tsp. mustard
1 tsp. Worcestershire sauce
2 tbsp. brown sugar
6 slices salt bacon
1 lge. onion, sliced

Mix beans, ½ cup catsup, mustard and Worcestershire sauce; pour into buttered baking dish. Sprinkle brown sugar on top; arrange bacon slices and onion alternately over top. Pour remaining catsup over bacon and onion slices. Bake at 300 degrees for 2 to 3 hours. Yield: 8-10 servings.

Mrs. Beulah K. Sanders, Home Economics Teacher, Goldonna, La.

 ### Bean Chowder Casserole

1 ½ lb. ground beef
2 med. onions, chopped
1 lb. brown beans, cooked
2 8-oz. cans tomato sauce
2 6-oz. cans tomato paste
2 tbsp. chili powder
2 tbsp. sugar
¼ tsp. garlic powder
⅛ tsp. salt

Place ground beef and onions in skillet on medium heat; brown slightly. Add all other ingredients and mix thoroughly. Place in casserole; cover and bake at 350 degrees for 30 minutes. Yield: 6 servings.

Mrs. Margaret Kemp, Mountain View, Ark.

 ### Bean Rarebit

1 ½ c. dried beans
3 c. grated cheese
1 ½ tbsp. butter
1 ½ c. ginger ale or beer
2 eggs, beaten

Cook beans; drain. Melt cheese and butter; add ½ cup ginger ale or beer. Blend remaining ginger ale or beer with eggs; stir into cheese mixture. Cook until thickened, stirring constantly. Pour over beans; serve. Yield: 8-10 servings.

Emily Rickman, Danville, Va.

Brunch Beans

> 3 cans pork and beans
> 2 unpeeled apples, chopped
> 3 onions, chopped
> Juice of 2 lemons
> Butter, the size of a walnut
> 2 tbsp. shredded coconut
> 1 tsp. curry powder
> ⅛ tsp. pepper

Place 1 can pork and beans in ungreased casserole; top with layer of apples and onions. Repeat twice. Sprinkle lemon juice over top. Slice butter in small pieces over top of beans. Bake in 350-degree oven till heated through. Remove from oven. Sprinkle with shredded coconut, curry powder and pepper. Bake 20 minutes longer. Yield: 6 servings.

Mrs. D. C. Leonard, Olustee, Okla.

 ### Deviled Baked Beans

> 2 1-lb. cans baked beans
> 1 c. pickle relish
> ½ c. catsup
> 1 tbsp. prepared horseradish
> 1 tsp. dry mustard
> ½ tsp. chili powder
> 1 tsp. Worcestershire sauce
> ¼ c. brown sugar
> 1 tbsp. butter or margarine, melted
> 2 sm. corn muffins, crumbled

Place 1 can of beans in greased 1½-quart casserole; cover with relish. Combine catsup, horseradish, mustard, chili powder, Worcestershire sauce and brown sugar; spoon one-third of the mixture over the relish. Add remaining beans and remaining seasonings. Blend butter and crumbs; sprinkle over casserole. Bake at 375 degrees for 30 minutes or until brown and crusty. Yield: 8 servings.

Mrs. William S. Smith, Officers' Wives' Club, Lemoore, Cal.

 ### Fiesta Beans

> ⅓ c. brown sugar, packed
> ½ c. strong coffee
> 1 tbsp. vinegar
> 1 tsp. dry mustard
> ½ tsp. salt

(Continued on next page)

2 lge. cans oven-baked beans
1 onion, thinly sliced
¼ c. brandy (opt.)
4 slices bacon, chopped or whole strips

Mix together in saucepan brown sugar, coffee, vinegar, mustard and salt; simmer for 5 minutes. Alternate layers of beans, hot sugar syrup, and onion rings in a 2-quart casserole. Cover and bake at 350 degrees for 45 minutes. Stir in brandy; top with bacon squares. Continue baking, uncovered, until bacon is cooked, about 30 minutes. Yield: 8 servings.

Mrs. Georgia M. Wilson, Home Economics Teacher, Prescott, Ariz.

 ## Old-Fashioned Bean Bake

¼ c. unsulphured molasses
1 tbsp. prepared mustard
1 tbsp. vinegar
3 1-lb. cans baked beans in tomato sauce
2 med. onions, sliced
2 tomatoes, sliced

Combine molasses and mustard; add vinegar. Mix well. Turn beans into casserole or baking pan; stir in molasses mixture. Arrange onion and tomato slices on top of beans, or layer with beans. Bake at 375 degrees for 35 minutes. Yield: 8 servings.

Photograph for this recipe below.

Home-Baked Great Northern Beans

   1 lb. Great Northern beans
   1 bay leaf
   1 tsp. salt
   ½ tsp. dried thyme or savory
   1 onion, sliced
   1 tbsp. dry mustard
   ½ c. dark brown sugar
   1 12-oz. bottle catsup
   Ham slices or split frankfurters (opt.)

Wash beans; place in large kettle. Cover with water; heat to boiling. Remove from heat; let stand for 1 hour. Add bay leaf, salt and thyme; simmer until beans are tender but not mushy. Add onion, mustard, brown sugar and catsup; mix well. Pour into large pan or bean pot. Cover; bake for 4 to 6 hours at 250 degrees. Stir beans occasionally; add water as needed. Thirty minutes before serving, add slices of ham or frankfurters. Yield: 10-12 servings.

Wilma Bryant, Sebree, Ky.

 ### Baked Green Beans And Mushrooms

   14 slices fresh white bread, cubed without crusts
   ½ c. melted margarine
   2 cans cut green beans, drained
   2 cans sliced or chopped mushrooms, drained
   Salt and pepper
   1 sm. onion, diced
   1 can cream of mushroom soup, undiluted
   ⅓ soup can milk
   1 3¼-oz. pkg. toasted slivered almonds (opt.)

Preheat oven to 400 degrees. Toss bread cubes with margarine; spread half of mixture evenly into bottom of greased 2-quart casserole. Cover with beans; top with mushrooms. Sprinkle evenly with salt, pepper and onion. In medium bowl, combine soup and milk, mixing well; pour over beans. Top with remainder of bread cubes and almonds. Bake for 30 minutes. Yield: 8 servings.

Mrs. F. T. Murphy, Sarasota, Fla.

 ### Cheesey Green Beans

   1 No. 303 can cut green beans
   2 tbsp. flour
   2 tbsp. butter

(Continued on next page)

1 c. milk
¼ tsp. salt
1 3-oz. jar Old English cheese spread
1 3-oz. jar chopped pimentos
1 can mushroom soup
1 c. crushed Ritz crackers

Heat green beans in a saucepan. Make a white sauce with flour, butter and milk. Add salt, cheese spread, pimentos and soup to white sauce. Pour beans into 1½-quart casserole dish; pour soup mixture on top. Mix lightly; top with cracker crumbs. Brown in a 350-degree oven for 20 minutes. Yield: 6 servings.

Janis Callaway, Atlanta, Ga.

Curry Beans

½ c. chopped onion
½ tsp. curry powder
2 tbsp. corn oil
1 pkg. frozen French-style green beans, separated
1 tomato, chopped
1 tsp. salt
¼ tsp. ground coriander (opt.)

Saute onion with curry powder in oil. Add remaining ingredients; stir and cook for several minutes. Reduce heat and simmer for 10 minutes. Yield: 4 servings.

Sundri Watumull, Honolulu, Hawaii, Favorite Recipes Food Fair

Dill Seasoned Green Beans

2 No. 2 cans cut green beans
2 tsp. dillseed
1 tbsp. bacon drippings
Bean stock
Milk
4 tbsp. melted butter
4 tbsp. flour
Salt and pepper
Few drops of Tabasco sauce
Soup croutons

Cook beans, dillseed and bacon drippings for 30 to 40 minutes; drain. Blend bean stock with enough milk to make 2 cups; combine with remaining ingredients. Cook until thickened, stirring constantly. Layer with beans and croutons in 1½ to 2-quart casserole. Bake at 350 degrees for 15 to 20 minutes. Yield: 8-10 servings.

Mrs. Bernice Bagwell, Home Economics Teacher, Waco, Tex.

Fresh Green Beans

1 lb. fresh green beans
Seasoning to taste

Snip off ends of beans; sliver French beans on diagonal or leave whole. Drop beans in boiling water or part boiling water and part boiling stock. Reduce heat immediately; season to taste. Simmer, covered, for 30 minutes to 1 hour. Correct seasonings. Cooking time depends on tenderness and stage of development of beans; young, slightly underdeveloped beans are most desirable and require less cooking time. Bacon, salt pork, ham hock or butter may be substituted for stock.

Mrs. W. H. Golson, Jr., Atlanta, Ga.

 ## Garlic Beans

1 to 2 cans French-cut or whole green beans
1 med. onion, sliced
5 cloves of garlic (opt.)
½ c. sugar
1 c. vinegar
1 c. salad oil
½ tsp. salt

Drain beans; place in casserole with onion and garlic. Sprinkle with sugar; let stand for 2 to 3 hours. Blend remaining ingredients; pour over beans. Cover; refrigerate for 24 hours. Drain before serving. Yield: 10-12 servings.

Thrath C. Curry, Home Economics Teacher, Carrollton, Ala.

 ## Goldenrod Beans

1 ½ tbsp. fat
2 tbsp. flour
½ tsp. salt
⅛ tsp. pepper
Bean stock
3 hard-cooked eggs, separated
½ can evaporated milk
1 ½ lb. whole beans, cooked
2 tbsp. mayonnaise

Melt fat; blend in flour, seasonings and ½ cup bean stock. Cook until thickened, stirring constantly. Cook for 2 minutes longer. Chop egg whites; add with milk to beans. Heat to serving temperature. Force yolks through sieve. Add mayonnaise to sauce; pour over beans. Sprinkle with yolk. Serve hot.

Mrs. L. E. Crawford, Home Economics Teacher, Adel, Ga.

German-Style Green Beans

    1 No. 303 can green beans
    6 slices bacon
    2 tbsp. flour
    2/3 c. sour cream
    1/4 tsp. salt
    1 tsp. cider vinegar

Drain 1/3 cup stock from beans; heat beans in remaining liquid. Fry bacon until crisp; blend flour in drippings. Add bean stock, sour cream, salt and vinegar. Cook until thickened, stirring constantly. Drain beans; arrange in serving dish. Top with sour cream mixture; sprinkle with crumbled bacon. Yield: 4 servings.

Pauline Brown, Lone Wolf, Okla.

 ## Governor's Favorite Green Beans

    2 lb. tender Kentucky Wonder green beans
    1 stick of butter
    2 tsp. salt
    White pepper
    2 tbsp. chopped pimentos

Wash beans well; cut off each end and split lengthwise. Let stand in ice water for about 1 hour. Tie in small bunches with white string. Parboil until tender; do not overcook. Drain well; place in serving dish. Melt butter; add pimentos. Pour over beans; sprinkle with white pepper and serve.

Mrs. Winthrop Rockefeller, Wife of Governor of Arkansas, Little Rock

 ## Green Bean Puff

    4 c. cooked green beans, drained
    1/4 c. finely diced celery
    3/4 c. mayonnaise
    1 tsp. mustard
    1/4 tsp. salt
    1 tsp. vinegar
    1/4 c. milk
    1 egg white, stiffly beaten
    1/4 tsp. paprika

Combine hot beans and celery in 5-cup casserole. Blend mayonnaise, mustard, salt, vinegar and milk. Fold egg white into the mixture; pile lightly on top of beans. Sprinkle with paprika. Bake at 400 degrees for 15 minutes or until sauce puffs and browns and beans are thoroughly heated. Yield: 4 servings.

Sister Rose Marie, Home Economics Teacher, Grand Forks, Minn.

Green Bean Croquettes

2 tbsp. margarine
2 ½ tbsp. flour
⅔ c. milk
½ tsp. salt
2 tsp. minced onion
¼ tsp. Worcestershire sauce
1 No. 2 can cut green beans, drained
2 c. coarse whole wheat bread crumbs
¾ c. fine whole wheat bread crumbs
1 egg, slightly beaten with 2 tbsp. cold water

Melt margarine in small saucepan; blend in flour. Add milk slowly; cook, stirring constantly, until very thick. Add salt, onion and Worcestershire sauce. Chop or mash beans; add coarse bread crumbs and hot white sauce. Mix well. Chill. Shape mixture into croquettes, using 1 tablespoon for each. Roll in fine bread crumbs; dip into egg mixture. Roll again in fine crumbs. Fry in small amount of hot fat in skillet until browned. Serve with chili sauce. Yield: 5 servings.

Mrs. Glenn Waldrop, Robert Lee, Tex.

 ## Green Beans Almondine

2 tbsp. butter
2 tbsp. flour
½ tsp .salt
1 c. milk
1 can whole string beans, drained
¼ c. slivered almonds

Melt butter; add flour, salt and milk. Cook until thickened, stirring constantly. Place beans in buttered casserole; cover with white sauce. Sprinkle with almonds. Bake at 350 degrees for 20 minutes. Yield: 4-6 servings.

Mrs. Rhea DaLee Thomas, Home Economics Teacher, Norton, Tex.

 ## Green Beans Bearnaise

6 pkg. frozen French-style green beans
¾ c. melted butter or margarine
3 6-oz. cans evaporated milk
3 tbsp. vinegar
1 ½ tsp. salt
½ tsp. thyme
½ tsp. tarragon
1 ½ tsp. chopped parsley

(Continued on next page)

1 tbsp. grated onion
9 egg yolks, slightly beaten
1 ½ beef bouillon cubes

Cook green beans according to package directions; drain. Set butter over hot water; stir in milk, vinegar, salt, thyme, tarragon, parsley and onion. Stir constantly until smooth; if mixture should start to curdle, add 1 tablespoon boiling water and beat with rotary beater. Pour half the hot sauce into egg yolks, stirring constantly; return to remaining mixture in double boiler. Add bouillon cubes; cook until very thick, stirring frequently. Serve over hot beans. Yield: 24 servings.

Mrs. Naomi Blatt, Lancaster, Ohio

 ### Green Beans Bechamel

2 lb. green beans, cooked and drained
½ c. butter
4 tbsp. flour
1 c. rich chicken stock
1 c. light cream
Salt to taste
Grated nutmeg to taste
½ c. slivered almonds
½ c. freshly grated Parmesan cheese
½ c. cracker crumbs

Place beans in buttered casserole. Simmer ¼ cup butter with flour for 2 to 3 minutes; stir in chicken stock and cream. Cook until thickened, stirring constantly. Season; pour over beans. Sprinkle with almonds, blended cheese, crumbs and remaining butter. Boil until brown. Yield: 8 servings.

Robbie Hanks, Sutherlin, Ore., Favorite Recipes Food Fair

 ### Green Beans With Cream Cheese Sauce

1 can whole string beans
1 4-oz. can mushrooms, drained
1 tbsp. butter
1 3-oz. pkg. cream cheese
1 tbsp. light cream (opt.)
¾ tsp. celery seed
¼ tsp. salt

Cook beans in juice until half of juice remains; drain. Saute mushrooms in butter. Soften cream cheese; blend in cream, celery seed and salt. Spoon cheese sauce over hot beans; garnish with mushrooms. Yield: 4 servings.

Mrs. Janice King, Commerce, Tex.

Green Beans With Mixed Herb Butter

  1 lb. green beans
  ¼ c. butter or margarine
  ¾ c. minced onions
  1 clove of garlic, minced
  ¼ c. minced celery
  2 tbsp. sesame seed
  ¼ tsp. rosemary
  ¼ tsp. dried basil
  ¾ tsp. salt
  ¼ c. snipped parsley

Wash and trim beans; cut crosswise into thin slanted slices. Cook beans, covered, in ½ inch boiling salted water for 15 minutes or until tender; drain. Melt butter in saucepan; add onions, garlic, celery and sesame seed. Saute for 5 minutes. Add remaining ingredients. Simmer, covered, for 10 minutes. Toss well with beans. Yield: 4 servings.

Jo Anna Littrel, Columbus Junction, Iowa

 ### Green Beans Napoli

  1 1-lb. can green beans
  4 tbsp. salad oil
  ¼ tsp. garlic salt

Heat beans; drain. Add oil and garlic salt. Toss lightly.

TOPPING:

  1 tbsp. butter, melted
  ¼ c. cornflake crumbs
  ½ tsp. paprika
  4 tbsp. grated Parmesan cheese

Combine butter and crumbs; stir over moderate heat until crumbs are golden. Blend in paprika; remove from heat. Add cheese; toss lightly. Serve over beans. Yield: 4-6 servings.

Mrs. Raymond Schmelze, LeRoy, N. Y.

 ### Green Beans In Wine Sauce

  3 slices bacon, diced
  1 med. onion, sliced
  3 tbsp. sugar
  2 tsp. cornstarch
  3 tbsp. tarragon vinegar
  ½ c. sherry wine
  4 c. cooked green beans

(Continued on next page)

Saute bacon and onion. Add sugar, cornstarch, vinegar and wine. Cook until thickened, stirring constantly. Pour over hot beans; serve. Yield: 8 servings.

Marjorie Ann Inman, Home Economics Teacher, Valparaiso, Ind.

 ## Green Beans-Swiss Cheese Casserole

Butter
2 tbsp. flour
1 tsp. salt
¼ tsp. each Accent and white pepper
1 c. sour cream
1 tsp. prepared mustard
1 No. 1 can French-cut green beans
½ c. grated Swiss cheese
2 tbsp. instant onions

Grease a 1-quart baking dish. Preheat baking dish. Preheat oven to 350 degrees. Heat 2 tablespoons butter in pan; add flour, salt, pepper and Accent. Heat until it bubbles. Remove from heat; gradually add sour cream and mustard, stirring constantly. Heat, but do not boil. Drain beans; add beans, cheese and onions to sour cream mixture. Toss gently. Pour in baking dish; top with bread crumbs which have been browned in 1 tablespoon butter. Heat 15 to 20 minutes or until hot. Yield: 6 servings.

Mrs. Harold G. Young, Sterling, Colo.

 ## Oriental Green Beans

2 10-oz. pkg. frozen green beans
2 1-lb. cans bean sprouts, drained
2 5-oz. cans water chestnuts, drained and sliced
¾ tsp. salt
1 10½-oz. can condensed cream of mushroom soup
½ c. unblanched sliced almonds, toasted

Cook beans according to directions on package, about 8 minutes; drain. Add sprouts, salt, chestnuts and soup; mix and heat thoroughly. Add half of almonds and mix. Serve immediately, sprinkling with remaining almonds. If desired, serve sprinkled with soy sauce. Yield: 8-9 servings.

Mrs. Lurleen B. Wallace, Governor of Alabama, Montgomery

Parmesan Green Beans With Croutons

    ¾ c. small bread cubes
    3 tbsp. salad oil
    1 tbsp. vinegar
    1 tsp. minced onion
    ¼ tsp. salt
    1 No. 2 can cut green beans, drained
    2 to 3 tbsp. Parmesan cheese

Saute bread cubes in 2 tablespoons oil until brown. Blend remaining oil with vinegar, onion and salt. Add beans to bread cubes; cover with vinegar mixture. Heat; stir frequently. Sprinkle with cheese; serve. Yield: 4-6 servings.

Mrs. Jo Ann Gray, Home Economics Teacher, Waxahachie, Tex.

 Sour Cream-Bean Casserole

    2 pkg. frozen French-style beans
    2 tbsp. flour
    1 tsp. salt
    ¼ tsp. pepper
    2 tbsp. butter
    1 carton sour cream
    ½ c. grated sharp cheese

Cook beans as directed on package; drain. Add flour, salt, pepper and butter; mix well. Mix cream with bean mixture; pour into shallow baking dish. Top with grated cheese. Bake in 350-degree oven for 15 minutes.

Mrs. Charles D. Cope, Atlanta, Ga.

 Sweet-Sour Green Beans

    1 No. 303 can green beans, drained
    8 slices bacon
    1 tbsp. brown sugar
    ½ tsp. salt
    Dash of pepper
    ¼ tsp. paprika
    ¼ tsp. dry mustard
    3 tbsp. vinegar
    1 tbsp. water

Combine bean stock and bacon; cook until stock is nearly evaporated. Remove bacon; add beans. Cook, covered, for 15 minutes. Blend dry ingredients with vinegar and water; add bacon. Heat to boiling; serve over beans. Yield: 4 servings.

Mrs. Dorothy Sue Hill, Home Economics Teacher, Oberlin, La.

Southern-Style Fresh Pole Beans

¼ lb. salt pork
1 lb. pole beans
¾ tsp. salt or to taste
Raw onion rings

Wash salt pork and score; make a crosswise cut through the center down to the rind and then three or four crosswise slashes. Place in a kettle with ½ inch boiling water. Cover and cook for 35 minutes or until meat is tender. Remove tips from pole beans; cut into 1-inch pieces. Wash and add to pork with salt. Cover and cook for 20 minutes or until beans are tender-crisp. Garnish with onion rings. Yield: 6 servings.

Mrs. Sue Miller, Huntsville, Ala.

 ## Surprise Green Bean Casserole

3 or 4 slices bacon
1 can French-cut green beans
1 can stewed tomatoes
½ c. chopped onion
Salt and pepper to taste

Cut bacon into bite-sized pieces. Cook until crisp. Drain green beans and tomatoes. Mix all ingredients in casserole dish. Bake 15 to 20 minutes at 350 degrees. Yield: 3-4 servings.

Mrs. William W. Lewis, Officers' Wives' Club, Las Vegas, Nev.

 ## Kidney Bean Casserole

1 med. onion, chopped
1 green pepper, chopped
1 c. water
1 can kidney beans
1 can mushrooms, drained
Salt and pepper
Butter

Cover onion and green pepper with water; cook until tender. Drain. Combine beans, mushrooms, green pepper, onion, salt and pepper; dot with butter. Bake at 350 degrees for 30 minutes.

Mrs. Richard Ridenour, Fairmont, W. Va.

Baked Kidney Beans

2 No. 303 cans kidney beans, drained
2 lge. onions, chopped
1 lge. green pepper, chopped
1 ¼ c. sugar
1 c. catsup
3 slices bacon, diced

Combine all ingredients in a casserole. Bake at 350 degrees for 2 hours. Yield: 8 servings.

Mrs. Bill Joe Culver, Pawhuska, Okla.

 ### Kidney Bean And Bacon Casserole

1 lb. bacon
1 lge. onion, sliced
1 7-oz. pkg. macaroni, cooked and drained
1 can kidney beans and juice
2 cans vegetable soup

Brown bacon and onion, draining off excess fat; break into bits. Combine with remaining ingredients in a 9-inch casserole. Bake at 250 degrees for 1 hour. Yield: 6 servings.

Mrs. Luella Nelson, Superior, Wis.

 ### Kidney Beans In Red Wine

2 c. dried red kidney beans
4 slices bacon, cut up
1 tsp. salt
1 tbsp. grated onion
2 tbsp. butter
2 tbsp. flour
Freshly ground black pepper
1 c. dry red wine

Cover beans with water; soak overnight. Simmer in soaking water with bacon and salt for 2 hours. Drain; keep hot. Saute onion in butter for 5 minutes. Add flour, pepper and wine; cook until thickened, stirring constantly. Blend with beans. Canned kidney beans or black beans may be substituted for dried kidney beans. Yield: 6 servings.

Mrs. Ella S. Ballard, Clayton, N. M.

MKB Casserole

¼ lb. salt pork
1 lb. dried kidney beans
Salt and pepper to taste
1 lge. onion, chopped
1 med. green pepper, chopped
1 c. grated cheddar cheese
1 6-oz. can tomato paste
2 slices bacon

Fry salt pork and pour off excess fat. Add beans and water to cover; cook until tender. Add salt, pepper, onion, green pepper, cheese and tomato paste; mix well. Pour into a large casserole; top with bacon strips. Bake at 300 degrees until bacon is cooked. Yield: 8 servings.

Mildred R. Piper, Honolulu, Hawaii

 ### Pasta Fagoola

1 onion, chopped
1 green pepper, chopped
1 clove garlic, chopped
Olive oil
1 c. elbow macaroni
1 can kidney beans
Parmesan cheese

Saute first 3 ingredients in ¼ cup olive oil. Cook macaroni as package directs and drain. Add kidney beans and top with plenty of cheese. Place in casserole; bake at 350 degrees until nicely browned. Yield: 6-8 servings.

Mrs. P. T. Dix Arnold, Gainesville, Fla.

 ### Lentil Casserole

1 lb. lentils
2 tbsp. chopped onion
2 tbsp. chopped green pepper
2 to 3 stalks celery, chopped
⅛ lb. butter or margarine
4 tbsp. flour
3 c. lentil stock and top milk
1 tsp. seasoned salt
½ tsp. salt
1 sm. can tomato sauce

(Continued on next page)

Soak lentils for several hours or overnight; cook until tender. Saute onion, pepper and celery in butter until tender. Add flour and lentil stock with milk; cook until thickened, stirring constantly. Add seasonings and tomato sauce; pour over lentils. Pour into 8½ x 1½-inch casserole. Bake at 300 degrees for 1 hour and 30 minutes to 2 hours, stirring occasionally. Add liquid as needed to maintain desired consistency. Yield: 8 servings.

Margaret Tisdale, Home Economics Teacher, Memphis, Tenn.

 Baked Lima Beans

> 2 c. dried lima beans
> 6 c. water
> ½ tsp. soda
> 1 c. sour cream
> ½ c. brown sugar
> ½ c. catsup
> ½ tsp. dry mustard
> 1 tsp. salt

Soak beans in water and soda overnight. Cook for 45 minutes in same water; add remaining ingredients. Place in casserole. Bake at 275 degrees for 2 hours. Yield: 10 servings.

Clotele Pease, Home Economics Teacher, Minneapolis, Minn.

 Baked Lima Beans With Tomato Sauce

> 1 ½ c. dried lima beans
> 5 c. cold water
> 4 slices bacon, cut into 1-in. pieces
> ⅓ c. minced celery
> ½ c. minced onion
> ¼ c. diced green pepper
> 1 clove of garlic, minced
> 2 tbsp. flour
> 1 ½ c. canned tomatoes
> 2 tsp. salt
> ⅛ tsp. pepper
> 2 tbsp. sugar

Soak washed beans overnight in 3 cups cold water; add remaining water. Cover; bring to boil. Simmer for 30 minutes or until tender; drain. Place in 1½-quart casserole. Brown bacon; add celery, onion, green pepper and garlic. Cook until vegetables are tender. Stir in flour, tomatoes, salt, pepper and sugar. Cook until thickened, stirring constantly. Pour sauce over beans. Bake, covered, at 300 degrees for 1 hour. Yield: 4 servings.

Mrs. Elizabeth Lehew, Home Economics Teacher, Coloma, Mich.

Butter Beans A La Karen

4 egg yolks
2 sticks butter or margarine
2 tbsp. grated onions
2 tbsp. tarragon vinegar
½ tsp. salt
½ tsp. pepper
½ c. water
½ tsp. beef flavoring
Butter beans or lima beans

Beat yolks carefully; place in double boiler. Add 1 stick margarine and all remaining ingredients except beans. Stir gently but steadily over low heat for 15 minutes or until sauce is of custard consistency. Serve over fresh butter beans or frozen baby lima beans, which have been cooked in salted water with remaining margarine. Yield: 6 servings.

Mrs. James T. Cook, Jr., Marianna, Fla., Favorite Recipes Food Fair

Fresh Lima Beans

1 qt. freshly shelled lima beans
Seasoning to taste

Wash beans thoroughly, filtering through hands to remove grit and waste completely. Place beans in saucepan; cover with boiling water. Season to taste. Simmer for 30 minutes to 1 hour. Correct seasoning. Young tender beans require less cooking time than the larger, more fully developed ones. Stock, bacon, ham hock or butter may be added for extra flavor while cooking.

Martha Williamson, San Diego, Cal.

Lima Bean Casserole

2 c. frozen lima beans, cooked according to package directions
½ c. chopped pimento
1 c. grated cheese
1 c. white sauce
2 tbsp. tomato catsup
½ c. bread crumbs
2 tbsp. butter (softened)

Combine beans, pimento, cheese, white sauce and catsup in casserole. Cover with bread crumbs which have been buttered. Bake at 350 degrees for 30 minutes. Yield: 6-8 servings.

Mrs. Thomas Byrd, Nashville, Tenn.

Chili Lima Beans

3 pkg. frozen green lima beans
3 tbsp. butter
1 ½ tsp. salt
¼ tsp. pepper
1 can undiluted mushroom soup
1 8-oz. pkg. cheddar cheese
2 cans or 1 4-oz. pkg. frozen chopped green chili

Cook frozen beans as directed on package, adding butter, salt and pepper. When tender, drain; place beans in buttered casserole. Heat soup, cheese and chili until cheese is melted; pour over lima beans. Bake at 350 degrees for about 20 minutes. Yield: 6-8 servings.

Mrs. Ernestine Sanford, Socorro, N. M.

 ### Copenhagen Limas

1 10-oz. pkg. frozen limas
¼ c. milk
¼ c. crumbled bleu cheese
¼ c. fine dry bread crumbs
1 tbsp. melted butter

Cook limas in unsalted water according to package directions. Heat milk with cheese, stirring until cheese melts; add beans. Combine bread crumbs and butter; stir over medium heat until golden brown. Pour beans into serving bowl; sprinkle with crumbs. Yield: 4 servings.

Mrs. Ralph E. Smith, Garrett, Ind.

 ### Dried Lima Beans

1 lb. dried lima beans
1 ham bone
1 onion, diced
1 tbsp. salt
2 tbsp. bacon drippings
4 tbsp. flour

Place lima beans, ham bone, onion and salt in enough water to cover. Cook until beans are tender. Remove ham bone. Melt drippings; add flour and brown slightly. Add to beans and bring to a boil. Yield: 2 quarts.

Mrs. William Novak, Jr., Maywood, Cal.

Lima Bean-Olive Casserole

1 c. chopped onions
1 c. chopped green peppers
4 tbsp. olive oil or bacon drippings
1 c. chopped ripe olives
1 tbsp. chili powder
1 clove of garlic, grated
1 tsp. salt
1 tbsp. cornstarch
1 ¼ c. bean liquid
3 cans baby green lima beans
1 c. grated cheddar cheese

Saute onions and green peppers in oil. Combine olives, chili powder, garlic, salt, cornstarch and bean liquid. Heat until slightly thick. Add onions, green peppers, beans and half the cheese. Cook in a buttered casserole in a preheated 375-degree oven for 30 minutes. Sprinkle with remaining cheese; heat until cheese melts. This recipe is better if prepared at least 1 day before serving. It is excellent for freezing. Yield: 18-20 servings.

Mrs. Ivanell S. Harris, Florence, Miss.

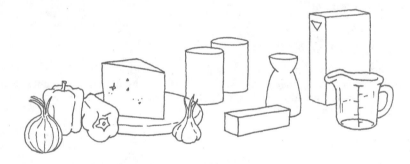

 ### Lima Beans In Sour Cream

2 10-oz. pkg. frozen lima beans
1 ½ tsp. salt
½ c. boiling water
2 tbsp. chopped onion
2 tbsp. chopped pimento
2 tbsp. butter
½ c. sour cream
⅛ tsp. white pepper

Cook beans in salted boiling water, covered, until tender; drain. Saute onion and pimento in butter; add sour cream and pepper. Combine with beans; heat thoroughly. Serve. Yield: 6-8 servings.

Ruby C. Irvine, Home Economics Teacher, Coalton, W. Va.

Lima Beans Paprika

2 pkg. frozen lima beans
1 med. onion, minced
5 stalks celery, cut in ½-in. pieces
¼ c. butter or margarine
1 3-oz. can mushrooms
2 tbsp. flour
½ tsp. salt
⅛ tsp. pepper
½ tsp. nutmeg
1 c. cream
Paprika

Cook lima beans in salted water; set aside. Saute onion and celery in butter until golden. Add mushrooms and simmer for 2 minutes. Mix flour, salt, pepper and nutmeg; add to cream. Mix well. Add to onion, mushroom and celery. Add beans. Put into casserole. Sprinkle with paprika. Bake at 350 degrees for 20 minutes or until heated through. Yield: 6-8 servings.

Mrs. Amy Hale, Knoxville, Tenn.

 ### Milano Casserole

2 c. lima beans
1 sm. can tomato sauce
½ c. grated Parmesan cheese
1 sm. green pepper, chopped
¾ c. chopped black olives
Dash of salt and pepper

Combine all ingredients, reserving a small amount of cheese for topping. Pour into buttered 2-quart casserole. Sprinkle with Parmesan cheese. Bake at 350 degrees for 30 to 40 minutes. Yield: 4 servings.

Mrs. Jon Ed Simbeck, Mancos, Colo.

 ### Quick Baby Limas

¼ lb. cured ham, thinly sliced
1 c. water
1 pt. freshly shelled or frozen baby limas
Salt to taste

Cook ham for 5 minutes in pressure cooker with water. Let pressure return to normal; add beans. Cook for 5 minutes longer in pressure cooker. Add salt. Yield: 4 servings.

Jo Anne M. Starling, Home Economics Teacher, Stedman, N. C.

Limas In Piquant Sauce

    4 c. frozen or fresh lima beans
    2 c. water
    2 tsp. salt
    ¼ c. butter
    ¼ c. flour
    ¼ tsp. pepper
    4 tsp. prepared mustard
    1 c. milk
    4 tsp. lemon juice
    ¼ c. diced pimento

Combine beans, water and 1 teaspoon salt; cook until tender. Drain; reserve liquid. Measure; add water to make 1 cup. Melt butter; blend in flour, remaining salt, pepper, mustard, bean liquid and milk. Cook until thickened, stirring constantly. Add lemon juice and pimento; pour over beans. Heat; serve. Yield: 8 servings.

Mrs. Gene Taresh, East Nicolaus, Cal.

 ## Louisiana Lima Beans

    ½ lb. small pork sausage
    2 c. cooked dried lima beans
    1 tsp. salt
    ¼ tsp. poultry seasoning
    Pepper to taste
    2 tbsp. chopped onion
    2 tbsp. shredded green pepper
    2 tbsp. butter
    1 c. milk

Parboil sausage for 5 minutes; combine with beans and seasonings in buttered casserole. Sprinkle with onion and green pepper; dot with butter. Cover with milk. Bake at 350 degrees for 25 minutes. Yield: 4 servings.

Mrs. Jo Frances Weimar, Home Economics Teacher, Alto, Tex.

 ## Savory Lima Bean Scallop

    1 ½ c. dried lima beans
    1 sm. onion, sliced
    ½ tsp. salt
    1 c. diced celery
    2 tbsp. chopped green pepper
    1 c. condensed tomato soup
    ½ c. water

(Continued on next page)

2 tbsp. melted margarine or fat
⅛ tsp. pepper
¼ c. buttered crumbs
Bacon sliced (opt.)

Soak beans in cold water for 6 to 8 hours. Drain; cover with boiling water. Add sliced onion; cook slowly until tender. Drain; add salt, celery, green pepper, tomato soup, water, margarine, pepper and additional salt to taste. Put into greased casserole; sprinkle with crumbs. Arrange bacon strips on top. Bake in 400-degree oven for 30 minutes. Yield: 6-8 servings.

Katherine B. DeKay, South Pasadena, Cal.

Western Lima Bake

1 lb. dried lima beans
2 ½ tsp. salt
½ lb. ground beef
1 med. onion, finely chopped
3 tbsp. vegetable oil
2 8-oz. cans tomato sauce
½ c. bean stock
Dash of poultry seasoning

Wash beans; soak overnight in 2 quarts water. Simmer, covered, in same water for 1 hour to 1 hour and 30 minutes or until tender. Season; drain. Place in casserole. Saute meat and onion in oil; add remaining ingredients. Pour hot over beans. Bake at 350 degrees for 1 hour or until bubbly. Yield: 5-6 servings.

Mrs. Janette Cook, Port Edwards, Wis., Favorite Recipes Food Fair

Yum-Yummy Butter Beans

2 c. dried butter or lima beans
Salt and pepper to taste
1 tbsp. olive oil
¼ c. chopped pimento
¼ c. minced onion
¼ c. chopped green pepper
¼ c. chopped bacon, fried crisp
1 can deviled ham
½ c. grated cheese

Soak beans overnight. Partially cook with salt, pepper and olive oil. Add pimento, onion and green pepper; cook until done. Stir in bacon, ham and cheese; add water to reach desired consistency. Yield: 6-8 servings.

Mrs. Ann Derrick, Home Economics Teacher, Amarillo, Tex.

Baked Beans

    2 c. dried navy beans
    1 ½ qt. cold water
    1 ½ tsp. salt
    1 sm. onion, sliced
    4 tbsp. butter or margarine
    ¼ c. catsup
    ¼ c. molasses
    1 tsp. dry mustard

Rinse beans; add to cold water. Bring to boiling point; simmer for 2 minutes. Remove from heat; cover. Let stand for 1 hour. Add 1 teaspoon salt; simmer, covered for 1 hour or until beans are tender. Drain; reserve stock. Place onion in 2-quart bean pot or casserole; add beans. Combine 2¼ cups of bean stock with butter, catsup, molasses, dry mustard and remaining salt; pour over beans. Bake, covered, at 325 degrees for 4 hours. Add liquids as needed. Uncover; bake for 30 minutes longer or until brown. Yield: 6 servings.

Mrs. Dorothy H. Lee, Allen, Okla.

 ### Navy Beans And Apple Casserole

    2 c. dried navy beans
    6 c. cold water
    1 tsp. salt
    3 lge. tart apples, peeled and sliced
    ⅓ c. (firmly packed) brown sugar
    ¼ lb. salt pork, sliced

Wash beans; place in 3-quart pan. Add water and salt; heat to boiling. Simmer, covered, for 2 hours. Drain; reserve stock. Layer beans and apple slices in greased casserole; sprinkle sugar over each layer. Add 2 cups bean stock; top with salt pork. Bake, covered, at 250 degrees for 2 hours and 30 minutes. Yield: 4-6 servings.

Winifred Hobart, Home Economics Teacher, Fairgrove, Mich.

 ### Pressure Cooked Beans

    2 c. dried navy beans
    ⅓ lb. salt pork, diced
    3 tbsp. brown sugar
    3 tbsp. molasses
    2 tsp. salt
    ½ tsp. mustard
    1 med. onion, diced
    2 tbsp. catsup
    Water

(Continued on next page)

Soak beans overnight; drain. Sear pork in 4-quart pressure cooker; add beans, sugar, molasses, salt, mustard, onion, catsup and enough water to cover beans. Cook at 15 pounds pressure for 40 minutes. Yield: 6 servings.

Mrs. Louis N. Neumeyer, Karnack, Tex.

 ### Special Baked Beans

> 2 c. dried navy beans
> ½ lb. salt pork, scalded and rind removed
> 6 sprigs parsley
> 1 lge. onion
> 1 clove garlic
> 1 green pepper
> 2 sweet red peppers
> 2 tbsp. maple syrup
> 6 tbsp. catsup

Soak beans overnight in cold water. Drain, reserving bean liquor. Put pork, parsley, onion, garlic and pepper through medium knife of food grinder; mix with beans, syrup and catsup. Cover with fresh water; simmer for 2 hours. Pour into 2-quart bean pot; add just enough bean liquid to cover beans. Cover pot. Bake at 300 degrees for 1 hour and 30 minutes longer. Yield: 6 servings.

Mrs. Orpha I. Friday, Lorimor, Iowa

 ### Pea Beans, Boston-Style

> 2 c. California or New York pea beans
> ¼ lb. fat salt pork
> 1 onion (opt.)
> 1 tsp. salt
> ½ c. light molasses
> ½ tsp. dry mustard
> 1 tbsp. sugar

Wash and sort beans; cover with cold water. Soak overnight. Drain; cover with fresh water. Simmer until skins burst. Drain; reserve stock. Scald pork; cut a ¼-inch slice off and place in 2-quart bean pot with onion. Cut 1-inch deep into rind of remaining pork at ½-inch intervals. Place beans in pot; bury pork in beans, leaving rind exposed. Bring reserved stock to boiling point; add 1 cup to salt, molasses, mustard and sugar. Pour mixture over beans; add enough stock to cover beans. Bake, covered, at 300 degrees for 6 to 7 hours. Add water as needed. Uncover; bake for 1 hour longer or until rind is crisp.

Azalee S. Bowlin, Home Economics Teacher, Greenville, S. C.

Baked Pinto Beans

    3 ½ c. cooked pinto beans or 1 No. 2½ can pork and beans
    1 lge. onion, chopped
    ½ c. chopped green pepper
    ½ c. brown sugar
    ½ tsp. salt
    ¾ c. catsup
    1 tsp. prepared mustard
    6 strips (about) bacon, diced

Combine all ingredients; place in bean pot. Lay additional strips of bacon across top. Bake at 375 degrees for 1 hour and 30 minutes. Yield: 8-10 servings.

Juline Levins, New Carlisle, Ind.

 ### Bean Pie

    1 qt. pinto beans
    Salt to taste
    1 sm. onion, chopped
    Sugar
    Vinegar
    Bacon strips

Cook beans with salt and onion until tender; mash to a paste. Put in greased pan about 1-inch thick. Sprinkle on sugar moistened with vinegar. Lay strips of bacon on top. Bake at 400 degrees until bacon is done. Syrup from sweet pickles may be substituted for sugar and vinegar.

Ruby Bendixen, Halfway, Ore.

 ### Bean Pot Pintos

    2 c. dried pinto beans
    5 c. water
    1 sm. piece salt pork
    1 sm. onion, chopped
    1 regular Coca-Cola
    ½ tsp. salt
    5 dried chili peppers

Cook beans overnight in bean pot with water, salt pork and onion. Add Coca-Cola, salt and chili peppers; cook for several hours longer. Yield: 8 servings.

Mrs. Eleanor Weatherman, Home Economics Teacher, Wink, Tex.

Idaho Buckaroo Beans

6 c. water
2 c. dried pinto or red beans, washed
1 lge. or 2 med. onions, coarsely chopped
2 lge. cloves of garlic, finely sliced
1 sm. bay leaf
Salt to taste
½ lb. smoked ham, slab bacon or salt pork
2 c. canned tomatoes
½ c. chopped sweet pepper (opt.)
2 tsp. chili powder
2 tbsp. brown sugar
½ tsp. dry mustard
¼ tsp. crushed oregano leaves or ground cumin seed

Pour water over beans; cover and soak for 12 to 15 hours. Or, if desired, bring water to a full boil. Gradually add beans so water does not stop boiling. Boil beans 2 minutes. Remove from heat; cover and set aside for 1 hour. Add onion, garlic, bay leaf and salt. Cover and bring to simmer. Cut ham into 2-inch cubes. If slab bacon or salt pork is used, wash salt off or parboil and slice through twice, not quite to rind. Add meat to beans. Bring to a rapid boil; reduce heat to a slow simmer. Cover tightly and cook for 1 hour and 30 minutes. Stir in remaining ingredients. Bring to a rapid boil; reduce heat to a slow simmer. Add more salt if needed. Cover; simmer for 2 hours or longer. Yield: 6 servings.

Photograph for this recipe on page 37.

 ### Soybean Casserole

¼ c. diced salt pork
2 c. diced or chopped celery
2 tbsp. chopped onions
2 tbsp. chopped green pepper
6 tbsp. sifted flour
2 c. milk
1 tbsp. salt
2 c. soybeans, cooked and chopped
1 c. buttered bread crumbs
½ tsp. paprika

Cook salt pork in frying pan; add celery, onions and green pepper. Stir and cook 5 minutes. Blend together flour, milk and salt. Cook, stirring, until mixture boils. Combine beans with celery mixture. Pour in casserole. Cover with crumbs; sprinkle with paprika. Bake 30 minutes at 350 degrees.

Dicy Fox, Dandridge, Tenn.

Soybean Loaf

  1 c. soybeans
  1 sm. onion
  1 c. ground walnuts
  1 c. toasted bread crumbs
 ½ *c. cream*
  2 eggs, slightly beaten
  1 tbsp. butter or vegetable oil
  Salt to taste

Soak beans overnight or longer. Pour off water; place beans in cold water. Cook for 2 hours or until tender. When nearly cooked, add onion. When well done, make a puree of beans. Add remaining ingredients; mix well. Press mixture into baking dish. Bake at 350 to 400 degrees for 45 minutes. Serve with cranberry or other tart jelly. Yield: 8 servings.

Mrs. Diane Caviezel, Enumclaw, Wash.

 ### Wax Beans Delight

  Butter
  2 No. 303 cans yellow wax beans
 ¼ *tsp. salt*
 ¼ *tsp. pepper*
 ½ *tsp. sweet basil*
 ¼ *tsp. celery salt*
 ½ *tsp. parsley flakes*
  1 sm. can mushrooms, drained
  1 can mushroom soup
 ½ *c. milk*
  1 can French-fried onion rings

Slightly grease 2-quart casserole with butter; add beans and seasonings. Add mushrooms; stir several times. Pour in soup and milk, stirring slightly. Bake 30 minutes at 350 degrees. Sprinkle on onion rings. Bake 5 minutes longer. Yield: 8 servings.

Mrs. J. E. Paganelli, Officers' Wives' Club, Norfolk, Va.

 ### Maine Yellow Eye Bean Bake

  4 c. dried yellow eye beans
  1 lge. onion
 ⅔ *c. molasses*
  3 tbsp. catsup
  2 tsp. dry mustard

(Continued on next page)

2 tsp. salt
½ tsp. pepper
½ lb. salt pork

Soak beans overnight in cold water. Drain; sort beans. Place onion in bottom of bean pot; add beans. Add remaining ingredients separately, scoring salt pork and placing on top of beans. Fill pot with hot water to cover beans well. Bake at 350 degrees for 6 to 7 hours, adding more hot water if needed. Do not add water during last hour of baking.

Mrs. Joseph F. L. Payeur, Niagara Falls, N. Y.

 ### Bean Casserole

1 8-oz. can French green beans, drained
1 8-oz. can wax beans, drained
1 8-oz. can lima beans, drained
1 can cream of celery soup
¼ to ½ c. milk
1 can onion rings

Combine beans, soup and milk in casserole; cover with onion rings. Bake at 350 degrees for 25 to 30 minutes. Yield: 6-8 servings.

Mrs. Marilyn Volin, Home Economics Teacher, Mead, Neb.

 ### Beans In Sour Cream

1 pkg. frozen green beans, cooked
1 pkg. frozen wax beans, cooked
1 pkg. frozen baby lima beans, cooked
1 pt. sour cream
½ tsp. salt
¼ tsp. pepper
2 tbsp. bread crumbs
¼ tsp. garlic salt
1 tbsp. melted butter

Drain beans; blend with sour cream, salt and pepper. Place in 1½ or 2-quart casserole. Brown crumbs, garlic salt and butter; sprinkle over beans. Bake at 350 degrees for 30 minutes. Yield: 6-8 servings.

Mrs. Betty G. Lueders, Harper Woods, Mich

Company Vegetable Casserole

 2 pkg. green beans, cooked
 1 can drained bean sprouts
 1 can water chestnuts
 1 sm. onion, chopped
 1 can cheese sauce
 1 can mushroom pieces
 1 can onion rings

Mix all ingredients except rings together; put in 10-inch greased casserole with onion rings on top. Bake at 350 degrees for 10 minutes. Yield: 6 servings.

   Mrs. Russell Kruchten, Officers' Wives' Club, Taiwan, China

 ## Creole Beans

 3 1-lb. cans pork and beans
 2 slices bacon, chopped
 1 lge. green pepper, chopped
 ¾ c. catsup
 ½ bean can water
 2 med. onions, chopped
 ⅔ tbsp. Worcestershire sauce
 ½ tbsp. salt
 ¼ c. sugar

Combine all ingredients in bean pot. Bake at 350 degrees for 2 hours and 30 minutes. Yield: 6-8 servings.

   Mrs. Mary Davis Faison, Home Economics Teacher, Weldon, N. C.

 ## Vegetable Casserole

 1 10-oz. pkg. frozen green beans
 1 10-oz. pkg. frozen lima beans
 1 6-oz. can mushrooms, sliced
 3 tbsp. flour
 2 tsp. chicken fat
 1 onion
 1 c. chicken broth
 1 c. sweet milk
 1 c. sharp cheese, grated
 1 c. bread crumbs

Cook beans and mushrooms; drain well. Make a white sauce of next 5 ingredients. Pour sauce over vegetables placed in a casserole. Top with cheese and bread crumbs; bake at 350 degrees for 20 minutes. Yield: 8 servings.

   Mrs. H. C. Evans, Morristown, Tenn., Favorite Recipes Food Fair

Broccoli and Brussels Sprouts

Baked Beets

7 tbsp. butter
4 tbsp. flour
1 c. water
¼ tsp. salt
4 tbsp. brown sugar
3 tbsp. prepared horseradish
4 c. chopped cooked beets
⅓ c. dried bread crumbs

Melt 4 tablespoons butter in saucepan; add flour and mix well. Add water slowly; cook until thickened, stirring constantly. Add salt, sugar, horseradish and beets. Mix well. Pour into greased baking dish. Cover with crumbs; dot with remaining butter. Bake at 350 degrees for 20 minutes or until crumbs are browned. Yield: 5-6 servings.

Mrs. Harry Stapleton, Massena, Iowa

 ### Beets En Casserole

3 c. sliced beets, cooked
1 tbsp. flour
2 tbsp. dark brown sugar
⅓ tsp. salt
¼ tsp. paprika
Dash of nutmeg
Dash of ground cloves
¼ tsp. cinnamon
2 tbsp. butter
2 tbsp. vinegar
¼ c. boiling water

Thoroughly blend beets with flour, sugar, salt and spices. Add remaining ingredients; pour into baking dish. Cover. Bake at 350 degrees for 25 minutes or until thoroughly heated and slightly thickened. Yield: 6-8 servings.

Mrs. J. Y. Morgan, Chester, N. J.

 ### Beets In Orange Sauce

2 tbsp. cornstarch or flour
2 tbsp. beet juice (opt.)
1 c. fresh orange juice
4 tbsp. lemon juice
2 tbsp. vinegar
2 tbsp. white or light brown sugar
½ tsp. salt

(Continued on next page)

2 *No. 2 cans baby beets, drained or 1 No. 2½ can julienne
beets*
4 *tbsp. butter*
2 *tbsp. grated orange rind*

Mix cornstarch with beet juice; add to mixture of orange juice, lemon juice
and vinegar. Cook until clear. Add sugar, salt and beets. Heat thoroughly; add
butter and rind. NOTE: Keeps well in refrigerator or freezer. Yield: 8 servings.

Mrs. Janet Long, Home Economics Teacher, Channelview, Tex.

 ## Beets With Pineapple

1 *13½-oz. can pineapple chunks*
½ *c. water*
⅓ *c. cider vinegar*
1 *tbsp. cornstarch*
½ *tsp. salt*
4 *tbsp. brown sugar*
⅛ *tsp. ginger*
2 *1-lb. cans sliced beets, drained*

Drain pineapple; reserve syrup. Blend pineapple syrup, water, vinegar, cornstarch, salt, sugar and ginger. Cook until thickened, stirring constantly. Add
beets; heat to boiling. Fold in pineapple chunks just before serving; heat. Yield:
8-10 servings.

Joan McCready, Home Economics Teacher, Missouri Valley, Iowa

 ## Boiled Beets And Greens

*Beets with leaves
Salt
Butter*

Scrub beets well; cook in boiling water until tender, about 30 to 60 minutes.
Old beets may be pared and sliced before cooking, or cooked whole and
plunged into cold water after which the loosened skins rub or slip off easily.
Season with salt and butter to taste. Cut stems and large veins from leaves,
removing damaged leaves. Steam in top of double boiler in own juices or drop
into small amount of boiling water; reduce heat and simmer 8 to 15 minutes
or until tender. Season with salt and butter.

Marjorie Gentry, Knoxville, Tenn., Favorite Recipes Food Fair

Chrysanthemum Beets

3 to 4 raw beets
1 tbsp. butter
Salt to taste

Peel and shred beets on coarse shredder or grater. Place butter, beets and salt in heavy saucepan; cover and cook over high heat until steaming. Reduce heat to low; cook for 8 to 10 minutes. Carrots may be cooked in same manner. Yield: 4 servings.

Mrs. Dorothy Soderlund, Home Economics Teacher, Milaca, Minn.

 ## Gala Beets

2 tbsp. butter
2 to 2½ c. diced or sliced beets, drained
1 to 2 tbsp. beet liquid
1 c. thinly sliced onions
¼ c. chopped celery (opt.)
Salt and pepper to taste
1 tbsp. chopped parsley (opt.)

Melt butter in saucepan; add beets, beet liquid, onions and celery. Cover and simmer for 12 minutes or until tender. Season with salt and pepper. Sprinkle with parsley before serving. Yield: 4 servings.

Mrs. Evelyn Johnson, Home Economics Teacher, Bottineau, N. D.

 ## Harvard Beets

⅓ c. sugar
⅓ tsp. salt or to taste
2 tbsp. cornstarch
½ c. mild vinegar
2 c. sliced beets or 10 to 12 sm. beets, cooked, peeled and
sliced
1 to 2 tbsp. butter

Mix sugar, salt and cornstarch; add vinegar. Boil for 5 minutes. Pour over hot beets; cover. Cook over low heat for 30 minutes. Add butter just before serving. One-fourth cup vinegar and ¼ cup water or beet liquid may be substituted for ½ cup vinegar. Yield: 6 servings.

Mrs. Anona Moore, Home Economics Teacher, Alvin, Tex.

Harvard Beets With Greens

1 tbsp. sugar
2 tsp. cornstarch
¼ c. vinegar
¼ c. water or beet juice
1 tbsp. butter
Dash of salt
1 c. cooked diced beets
2 c. wilted spinach or other greens

Combine sugar and cornstarch; add remaining ingredients except beets and greens. Cook over low heat until thickened, stirring constantly. Add beets; heat. Serve over hot wilted greens. Yield: 4 servings.

Isabelle Staley, Huron, S. D.

 ## Harvard Beet Surprise

1 tbsp. cornstarch
4 tsp. sugar
¾ tsp. salt
1 tsp. orange rind
Beet liquid
¼ c. vinegar
2 c. cubed or sliced beets, cooked
½ c. cooked raisins

Mix cornstarch with sugar, salt and orange rind; combine enough water with beet liquid to measure 2/3 cup. Blend in beet liquid and vinegar. Bring to a boil for 1 minute. Add beets and raisins. Heat to serving temperature. Yield: 5 servings.

Jean Carolyn Leis, Home Economics Teacher, Buhler, Kan.

Creamed Beets With Horseradish

2 tbsp. butter or margarine
2 tbsp. flour
½ tsp. salt
1 c. milk
3 tbsp. horseradish
3 c. cooked diced beets

Melt butter; stir in flour and salt. Add milk gradually. Cook until thickened, stirring constantly; stir in horseradish. Pour over hot beets; serve immediately. Yield: 4-6 servings.

Josephine Brighenti, Ironwood, Mich.

 ## Spiced Harvard Beets

½ tsp. salt
Dash of pepper
⅛ tsp. cinnamon
⅛ tsp. cloves
⅛ tsp. allspice
¾ c. vinegar
½ c. sugar
1 c. beet stock
2 c. sliced or cubed beets
2 tbsp. cornstarch
¼ c. cold water

Boil seasonings and spices with vinegar, sugar and beet stock; pour over beets. Let stand for 3 or 4 hours; drain. Heat liquid to boiling; stir in cornstarch dissolved in water. Cook until thickened, stirring constantly. Pour over hot beets; serve. Yield: 6-8 servings.

Mrs. Ellaine B. Scott, Dekalb, Miss.

 ## Hungarian Beets

1 1-lb. can sliced beets
1 c. sour cream
¼ c. salad dressing
1 tbsp. chopped chives
1 tbsp. lemon juice
½ tsp. brown sugar
¼ tsp. dry mustard

Heat beets; drain. Combine remaining ingredients; add to beets. Heat slowly; do not boil. Yield: 4 servings.

Linda Conner, Home Economics Teacher, Fort Benton, Mont.

Sweet-Sour Beets With Orange Marmalade

½ c. sugar
1 tbsp. cornstarch
½ tsp. salt
2 whole cloves
½ c. vinegar
3 c. cooked sliced beets
2 tbsp. margarine
3 tbsp. orange marmalade

Blend sugar, cornstarch, salt, cloves and vinegar; cook in top of double boiler until thickened, stirring constantly. Add beets; cook over hot water for 30 minutes. Just before serving, stir in margarine and marmalade. Yield: 6 servings.

Mrs. Dorothy M. Hardin, Lebanon, Ill.

 ### Zippy Beets

½ c. heavy cream
3 ½ tsp. horseradish
1 ½ tsp. salt
10 sm. beets

Heat cream, horseradish and salt. Add beets; heat thoroughly. Yield: 4 servings.

Mrs. Walter H. Mann, Jr., Bainbridge, Md.

 ### Broccoli Casserole

2 pkg. frozen broccoli
3 tbsp. butter
3 tbsp. flour
2 c. milk
Salt and red pepper
1 c. grated cheese
¼ c. almonds
6 slices bacon
½ c. buttered bread crumbs

Cook broccoli. Drain and place in greased 8 x 12-inch casserole dish. Make cream sauce of butter, flour and milk. Season to taste with salt and red pepper. Add cheese. Spread almonds and crumbled bacon over broccoli. Top with cheese sauce; sprinkle with crumbs. Bake at 350 degrees for 20 minutes. Yield: 6-8 servings.

Mrs. Stanley Greene, Ames, Iowa

Baked Broccoli A La Parmesan

　　2 pkg. frozen broccoli
　¼ c. shortening
　　1 clove garlic, cut up
　½ lb. mushrooms, sliced
　　1 can tomato paste
　　2 paste cans broccoli liquid
　¼ c. sifted flour
　　1 tsp. salt
　¼ tsp. nutmeg
　　Dash of pepper
　¼ c. grated Parmesan cheese

Cook broccoli; reserve liquid. Slice thin; arrange in buttered 6 x 10 x 1½-inch baking dish. Melt shortening; add garlic. Cook for several minutes. Add sliced mushrooms; let cook 5 minutes. Add tomato paste and broccoli liquid, combined with flour. Season with salt, nutmeg and pepper; add cheese. Cook all together in covered saucepan for 15 minutes. Pour sauce over broccoli in baking dish; sprinkle with more Parmesan cheese. Bake at 350 degrees for about 30 minutes. Yield: 8 servings.

Mrs. Robert J. Hill, Hon. Pres. Officers' Wives' Club, F. E. Warren AFB, Wyo.

 ### Broccoli-Cheese Bake

　　2 10-oz. pkg. frozen chopped broccoli
　　1 can mushroom soup
　　2 c. cheese, grated
　　Onions
　　1 clove garlic, minced
　　Salt and pepper
　　2 c. bread crumbs
　　2 tbsp. green sage or 1 tbsp. dried
　⅛ lb. butter
　　Water
　　1 c. grated cheese
　　Paprika

Cook broccoli; drain thoroughly. Add mushroom soup, 1 cup cheese, 1 medium chopped onion, garlic, salt and pepper to taste. Chopped parsley may be added and a small can of sliced mushrooms adds flavor. Turn into 12 x 7½ x 2-inch baking dish. Mix bread crumbs, sage, small grated onion and butter. Add hot water to moisten to desired consistency. Spread over casserole. Top with cheese; sprinkle with paprika. Bake 30 minutes at 325 degrees or until cheese is bubbly and lightly browned on top. This casserole may be frozen. Add approximately 30 minutes to the cooking time if using directly from the freezer. Yield: 6-8 servings.

Mrs. George Croft, Charleston, S. C.

Broccoli With Fried Onion Rings

2 pkg. frozen broccoli
1 can cream of mushroom soup
1 can French-fried onion rings

Cook broccoli according to package directions; place in 2-quart casserole. Cover with soup; top with onion rings. Bake, covered, at 350 degrees for 20 minutes. Yield: 4-6 servings.

Edna L. House, Home Economics Teacher, Edwardsport, Ind.

 ## Broccoli With Grapefruit Sections

2 lb. fresh broccoli or 1 pkg. frozen broccoli
Salt and pepper
2 tbsp. butter
1 grapefruit, sectioned

Wash broccoli. Split lengthwise all stalks thicker than 1 inch. Cook in 1 inch boiling salted water, using ½ teaspoon salt per 1 cup water, covered, for 10 to 12 minutes. If frozen broccoli is used, cook according to directions on package. Drain; season to taste. Melt butter in skillet. Add grapefruit sections; heat to serving temperature, turning once carefully. To serve, turn broccoli into serving dish, arrange grapefruit sections over top. Yield: 4 servings.

Photograph for this recipe below.

Broccoli In Cheese Sauce

> 2 10-oz. pkg. frozen broccoli or cauliflower, cooked and drained
> 1 can cheddar cheese soup
> ¼ c. milk
> ¼ c. buttered bread crumbs

Place broccoli in shallow 10 x 6 x 2-inch baking dish. Blend soup and milk; pour over broccoli. Top with crumbs. Bake at 350 degrees for about 30 minutes or until hot and bubbling. Yield: 6-8 servings.

Mrs. John L. Hansbrough, Magee, Miss.

 ## Broccoli With Mustard Sauce

> 2 tbsp. butter
> 1 tsp. salt
> ⅛ tsp. pepper
> 1 tbsp. flour
> 1 tbsp. prepared mustard
> 1 egg yolk
> ¾ c. milk
> 2 tsp. lemon juice
> 1 pkg. frozen broccoli, cooked

Melt butter; stir in salt, pepper and flour. Combine mustard, egg yolk and milk; add to flour mixture. Cook for 5 minutes or until thickened, stirring constantly. Stir in lemon juice; pour over hot drained broccoli. Serve. Yield: 3-4 servings.

Sandra Brown, Home Economics Teacher, Stowe, Vt.

 ## Broccoli With Onions

> 1 pkg. frozen broccoli
> 1 can boiled onions
> 1 can mushroom soup
> 1 can mushrooms
> 1 c. grated cheese
> ½ c. bread crumbs
> Juice of ½ lime or lemon

Cook broccoli until almost tender; combine with other ingredients in buttered casserole dish. Bake at 350 degrees for 30 minutes. Yield: 6 servings.

Mrs. Charles Meyers, Bismarck, N. D.

Broccoli Ring

2 pt. cooked chopped broccoli
1 pt. thick white sauce
1 pt. mayonnaise
Onion juice
Cayenne pepper
Salt
Accent
12 eggs

Mix broccoli, white sauce and mayonnaise; season highly with onion juice, cayenne pepper, salt and Accent. Beat eggs; add to broccoli mixture. Pour into buttered 2-quart ring mold; set in pan of water. Bake in 350-degree oven about 1 hour or until firm. Remove from mold; serve. For easy removal of mold, heat and butter ring mold before using. Yield: 8 servings.

Mrs. Henry Viccellio, Hon. Pres. Officers' Wives' Club, Robins AFB, Ga.

 ### Broccoli With Shrimp Sauce

3 pkg. frozen broccoli
¼ c. chive cream cheese
¼ c. milk
1 can frozen cream of shrimp soup
2 tbsp. lemon juice
2 tbsp. toasted almonds

Cook broccoli according to package directions. Blend cream cheese and milk. Add soup; heat and stir until hot. Add lemon juice; pour over hot drained broccoli. Sprinkle with toasted almonds. Bake 20 to 30 minutes in 350-degree oven. Yield: 6-10 servings.

Mrs. Daniel Morrow, Boise, Idaho, Favorite Recipes Food Fair

 ### Broccoli With Sour Cream

1 c. sour cream
2 tbsp. brown sugar
2 tbsp. cider vinegar
¼ tsp salt
½ tsp. mustard
1 lb. broccoli, cooked

Heat sour cream with brown sugar, vinegar, salt and mustard. Pour over hot broccoli; serve. Yield: 4 servings.

Mrs. Kathleen Garrett, Home Economics Teacher, Albertville, Ala.

Broccoli Supreme

    1 tbsp. salad oil
    1 med. onion
    1 pkg. frozen chopped broccoli, completely thawed
    1 can cream of chicken soup
    Garlic salt, celery salt and Accent to taste
    2 c. hot cooked rice
    ½ c. diced Swiss cheese

Heat oil in skillet; add onion and broccoli. Toss and stir about 5 minutes. Add soup and seasonings. Heat to boiling point, stirring constantly. Butter a 1-quart casserole; line with hot rice. Pour broccoli mix over; top with cheese. Place in 325-degree oven until bubbly and cheese is melted, about five minutes. Yield: 4 servings.

Mrs. J. A. Alger, Jr., Hon. Pres. Coast Guard Officers' Wives' Club,
Governors Island, N. Y.

 ## Egg And Broccoli Bake

    1 10-oz. pkg. frozen broccoli, cooked and drained
    6 hard-cooked eggs, halved lengthwise
    2 10¾-oz. cans condensed cheddar cheese soup
    1 c. milk
    ¼ c. butter or margarine, melted
    ¼ c. water
    2 c. herb-seasoned stuffing mix

Arrange broccoli and eggs in shallow 12 x 8 x 2-inch baking dish. Stir soup until smooth; gradually blend in milk. Pour liquid over broccoli and water; stir in stuffing mix. Sprinkle over casserole. Bake at 400 degrees for 30 minutes. Yield: 4 servings.

Mrs. Lloyd E. Clark, Meridian, Miss.

 ## Fresh Broccoli With Sour Cream Dip

    1 ½ lb. fresh broccoli
    1 wedge lemon
    1 c. French dressing
    ½ pt. sour cream
    1 tbsp. chopped chives

Cover broccoli with cold salted water; soak for 30 minutes. Drain; cut off tough part of stalk and coarse outer leaves. Steam for 15 to 20 minutes or until tender; add lemon wedge to water to prevent odor. Remove from steamer; marinate in French dressing for 3 to 4 hours. Blend sour cream and chives. Serve broccoli cold with sour cream dip. Yield: 4-6 servings.

Kay Ormiston, Home Economics Teacher, Jackson, Wyo.

Noodle-Broccoli Casserole

> 2 pkg. tiny noodles
> 1 stick butter
> 2 bunches green onions or 1 lge. white onion, chopped fine
> 2 pkg. chopped frozen broccoli, cooked
> 1 can cheese soup, undiluted
> ½ tsp. rosemary
> 1 tsp. Worcestershire sauce
> Dash of Tabasco sauce
> 1 c. grated cheese

Cook noodles; add ½ stick butter after draining. Saute onions in ½ stick butter. Mix together with broccoli, cheese soup, rosemary, Worcestershire sauce and Tabasco sauce. Cover top with grated cheese. Bake for 50 minutes at 350 degrees. Yield: 20 servings.

Mrs. Jerry M. Totten, Omaha, Neb.

 ### Rice And Broccoli Casserole

> 1 c. cooked rice
> ¼ to ½ c. chopped onion
> ½ c. chopped celery
> Butter
> 1 or 2 pkg. chopped broccoli, cooked
> 1 can cream of chicken soup
> 1 can cream of mushroom soup
> 1 sm. jar Cheez Whiz
> Grated Parmesan cheese or paprika

Form rice into crust in large greased casserole. Saute onion and celery in butter; combine with broccoli, soups and Cheez Whiz. Pour over rice; sprinkle with cheese. Bake at 350 to 375 degrees for 10 to 20 minutes or until bubbly and lightly browned.

Mrs. Angela Gish, Home Economics Teacher, Bazine, Kan.

 ### Brussels Sprouts Bake

> 2 pkg. frozen Brussels sprouts
> 1 can cream of celery soup
> 2 tbsp. butter
> ⅛ tsp. nutmeg
> ¼ c. coarsely chopped salted peanuts

Combine all ingredients except peanuts; pour into casserole. Bake at 375 degrees for 45 minutes or until tender. Sprinkle with nuts before serving.

Mrs. Doris Matsumoto, Kekaha, Kauai, Hawaii

Brussels Sprouts Casserole

> 1 pkg. frozen Brussels sprouts
> 1 c. medium white sauce
> ⅓ c. grated cheese
> ½ c. toasted bread crumbs

Cook Brussels sprouts according to package directions. Place in casserole; add white sauce. Sprinkle with cheese; top with bread crumbs. Bake at 325 degrees until cheese is melted and sauce bubbles. Yield: 4 servings.

Mrs. Mary Menking, Home Economics Teacher, Gonzales, Tex.

 ## Brussels Sprouts In Celery Sauce

> 2 qt. Brussels sprouts
> 1 ⅛ tsp. salt
> 2 ¼ c. boiling water
> 1 ½ c. diced celery
> 6 tbsp. butter
> 6 tbsp. flour
> Milk
> Dash of pepper

Remove wilted Brussels sprouts leaves; wash. Cook sprouts until tender; drain. Add salt to water. Cook celery in boiling water for 15 minutes; drain, reserving celery water. Melt butter; blend in flour. Combine celery water with enough milk to measure 3 cups. Cook until smooth and thick, stirring constantly. Add celery and pepper; pour over Brussels sprouts. Yield: 8 servings.

Mrs. Margaret Cepelka, Home Economics Teacher, Berryville, Va.

 ## Brussels Sprouts With Dilled Sour Cream Sauce

> 2 lb. Brussels sprouts or 4 10-oz. pkg. frozen Brussels sprouts
> 3 c. beef bouillon
> 1 pt. dairy sour cream
> 1 tbsp. chopped fresh dill
> White pepper, salt and onion juice to taste

Cover and cook Brussels sprouts in bouillon for 10 to 15 minutes or until tender. Cover and chill in liquid. Blend remaining ingredients for sauce and chill. Drain Brussels sprouts and serve with sauce. Yield: 8 servings.

Photograph for this recipe on page 67.

Brussels Sprouts With Chestnuts

> 2 tbsp. butter
> 2 tsp. flour
> ¾ c. chicken broth
> ¼ tsp. salt
> Pinch of white pepper
> ¼ tsp. basil
> 3 lb. fresh Brussels sprouts
> 1 ½ c. peeled, sliced cooked or canned chestnuts

Make a cream sauce with butter, flour and chicken broth. Season with salt, pepper and basil. Cook mixture until slightly thickened. Keep warm over simmering water. Cook Brussels sprouts in boiling salted water until crisp but tender. Drain thoroughly. Place sprouts in serving dish. Add chestnuts to sauce; pour sauce over sprouts. NOTE: If desired, 3 packages frozen Brussels sprouts may be substituted. Cook according to package directions. Yield: 8 servings.

Meroe E. Stanley, Home Economics Teacher, Northville, Mich.

 ## Brussels Sprouts Parmesan

> 1 pkg. frozen Brussels sprouts, cooked
> 2 slices bread, cut into ½-in. cubes and toasted
> 2 tbsp. butter
> 2 sprigs parsley, chopped
> ½ tsp. salt
> Grated Parmesan cheese

Toss Brussels sprouts with buttered bread cubes, parsley and salt; turn into hot bowl. Sprinkle generously with Parmesan cheese. Serve hot. Yield: 4 servings.

Mrs. Gladys Truitt, Home Economics Teacher, Bowling Green, Ky.

 ## Brussels Sprouts In Tomato Sauce

> 1 qt. cooked Brussels sprouts
> 1 can tomato soup
> 1 soup can water
> ¼ c. grated American cheese

Place cooked Brussels sprouts in a 1½ or 2-quart casserole. Dilute soup with water and pour over sprouts. Sprinkle cheese over top. Bake at 350 degrees for 15 minutes. Yield: 6 servings.

Mrs. Madeleine Beckman, Bath, Ill., Favorite Recipes Food Fair

Brussels Sprouts With Grapes

  2 pkg. frozen Brussels sprouts
  ¾ c. sour cream
  ½ c. slivered almonds
  ⅔ c. drained mushrooms
  1 c. seedless white grapes
  ¼ c. chopped pimento
  1 tsp. sugar
  ½ tsp. pepper
  2 tsp. salt
  ¾ c. grated American cheese
  Paprika

Cook Brussels sprouts according to package directions; drain. Add sour cream, almonds, mushrooms, grapes, pimento and seasonings. Heat in double boiler for 7 minutes. Place in serving dish; sprinkle with cheese and paprika. Yield: 8-10 servings.

Novella Mae Melton, Home Economics Teacher, Roswell, N. M.

 ## Brussels Sprouts Supreme

  2 tbsp. butter or margarine
  2 tbsp. flour
  1 c. milk
  ½ tsp. salt
  ¼ tsp. thyme
  1 5-oz. can water chestnuts, drained and sliced
  Buttered bread crumbs (opt.)
  2 10-oz. pkg. frozen Brussels sprouts, cooked

Melt butter in saucepan; blend in flour. Gradually add milk, stirring constantly, until smooth. Cook and stir until sauce boils for 1 minute and thickens. Mix in salt and thyme; fold in water chestnuts. Pour sauce over Brussels sprouts; top with buttered bread crumbs. Yield: 6-8 servings.

Irene M. Runkle, Home Economics Teacher, Nampa, Idaho

 ## Brussels Sprouts With Walnuts

  2 10-oz. pkg. frozen Brussels sprouts
  1 c. boiling water
  1 tsp. salt
  ½ c. grated process sharp cheese
  ¼ c. butter or margarine
  ¼ c. packaged spiced dry bread crumbs
  ⅓ c. chopped walnuts

(Continued on next page)

Simmer Brussels sprouts in boiling, salted water in 1½-quart saucepan for 4 to 5 minutes. Drain; turn into greased 1½-quart casserole. Dot with cheese. Melt butter in small fry pan; add bread crumbs and walnuts. Cook, stirring, until lightly browned. Sprinkle over Brussels sprouts. Bake in preheated 400-degree oven for 10 minutes. Yield: 6 servings.

Mrs. Bernadette Schoen, Home Economics Teacher, East Troy, Wis.

 ## Brussels Sprouts With Yam Frill

    ½ c. brown sugar
    5 tbsp. butter, melted
    ¾ c. orange juice
    3 tbsp. grated orange peel
    ½ tsp. nutmeg
    ½ tsp. allspice
    8 cooked yams, peeled and mashed
    2 10-oz. pkg. frozen Brussels sprouts
    ¼ tsp. white pepper

Blend sugar, 2 tablespoons butter, ¼ cup orange juice, 2 tablespoons orange peel, ¼ teaspoon nutmeg and ⅛ teaspoon allspice into yams; whip until light and fluffy. Heat to serving temperature; keep hot. Cook Brussels sprouts according to package directions; drain. Toss gently with remaining butter, orange juice, peel, nutmeg, allspice and white pepper. Cook over low heat. Yield: 6-8 servings.

Mrs. Olive Curtis, Deming, Wash.

 ## Fresh Brussels Sprouts With Pecan Butter

    2 pt. Brussels sprouts
    Chicken stock
    2 tbsp. chopped onion
    ½ tsp. salt
    ½ c. coarsely chopped pecans
    ¼ c. butter
    Pimento strips
    Parsley

Wash and trim Brussels sprouts. Soak in salted water for 20 minutes, using 1 teaspoon salt to 1 quart water. Drain and rinse with cold water. Place sprouts in pan containing 1 inch of boiling stock, onion and salt. Bring to boil and cook for 5 minutes. Cover and cook for 10 minutes or until tender, but still crisp. Drain and keep hot. Saute pecans in butter. Pour over Brussels sprouts; toss lightly. Garnish with pimento strips and parsley. NOTE: Bouillon cubes may be substituted for chicken stock, using 1 cube for each 1 cup of water. Yield: 6 servings.

Mrs. Carol Maata, Flint, Mich.

Nutmeg Fresh Brussels Sprouts

1 qt. fresh Brussels sprouts
1 ¼ tsp. salt
3 tbsp. butter or margarine
1 tsp. ground nutmeg
⅛ tsp. pepper

Wash and trim Brussels sprouts. Rinse and place in saucepan containing 1 inch boiling water and salt. Bring to a boil again; cook 5 minutes. Cover and continue cooking for 15 minutes or until Brussels sprouts are crisp but tender. Drain. Add butter, nutmeg and pepper; toss lightly. Place in serving dish or pile in center of glazed squash rings. Yield: 6 servings.

Mrs. Loretta Fowler Bennett, Home Economics Teacher, Alexandria, Va.

 ### Saucy Brussels Sprouts

1 qt. Brussels sprouts
2 tbsp. melted butter
3 tbsp. flour
1 tsp. salt
½ c. hot tomato juice
1 c. milk
¼ c. grated American cheese

Cook sprouts in boiling salted water for 15 minutes or until tender. Drain. Blend butter, flour and salt; add tomato juice. Pour mixture slowly into milk. Cook in double boiler, stirring, until thickened. Place sprouts in greased custard cups in 1-quart casserole. Cover with sauce; sprinkle with cheese. Bake in 350-degree oven for 15 minutes or until browned. Yield: 6-8 servings.

Elaine L. Smith, Union City, Ind.

 ### Sweet And Sour Brussels Sprouts

1 lb. fresh or 3 10-oz. pkg. frozen Brussels sprouts
1 tbsp. butter or margarine
¼ c. brown sugar
¼ c. white vinegar
1 tsp. cornstarch
1 tsp. grated onion
Dash of dry mustard

Cook Brussels sprouts until just tender; drain well. Melt butter; blend in remaining ingredients. Cook and stir until thickened; pour over Brussels sprouts. Yield: 5 servings.

Freda F. Bennett, Home Economics Teacher, Elgin, Neb.

Cabbage and Carrots

Baked Cabbage With Grated Cheese

1 cabbage
1 tbsp. butter
1 tbsp. flour
1 pt. cabbage stock
Salt and pepper
4 tbsp. grated cheese
Cracker crumbs

Boil cabbage for 15 minutes in salted water; drain. Add more water; boil until cabbage is tender. Drain; cool. Chop cabbage; put cabbage in buttered baking dish. Melt butter; stir in flour. Add cabbage stock; stir until smooth. Season with salt and pepper; mix in grated cheese. Pour sauce over cabbage; sprinkle with cracker crumbs. Dot with butter. Bake at 450 degrees for 10 minutes. Yield: 6-8 servings.

Mrs. Jane D. Modrall, Home Economics Teacher, Tullahoma, Tenn.

 ## Beerach

1 lb. ground meat
1 onion, thinly sliced
1 2-lb. cabbage, shredded
½ tsp. pepper
½ tsp. salt
1 recipe yeast dough

Combine all ingredients except dough; cook at medium temperature until meat is done. Drain. Roll yeast dough, which has risen once, into five or six squares or circles ½-inch thick and 6 to 7 inches wide. Place a portion of meat mixture on each; fold up edges. Seal; place in greased pan. Let rise until double in bulk. Bake at 300 degrees for 45 to 50 minutes. Serve hot or cold. Yield: 5-6 servings.

Anita Darnell, Greenville, Tex., Favorite Recipes Food Fair

 ## Cabbage Au Gratin

1 spring cabbage
Salt and pepper
6 tbsp. butter
3 tbsp. flour
1 ½ c. milk
2 slices bread, cubed and French-fried

Cut cabbage into quarters or eighths; soak in cold water until crisp. Drain well. Place in pressure cooker: add salt, pepper and 3 tablespoons butter. Steam at

(Continued on next page)

10 pounds pressure for 3 minutes. Melt remaining butter in top of double boiler over boiling water; add flour, ¾ teaspoon salt and a dash of pepper, stirring until smooth. Gradually add milk; cook until smooth and thickened, stirring constantly. Pour white sauce over cabbage in casserole; top with bread cubes. Yield: 8 servings.

Beryl Wolf, Home Economics Teacher, Gustine, Tex.

 ## Cabbage Deluxe

3 tbsp. butter
2 tbsp. flour
1 tsp. salt
Few grains pepper
1 tsp. prepared mustard
1 ⅓ c. milk
1 egg yolk, beaten
2 c. shredded cabbage
1 c. thinly sliced onions
1 c. grated cheese
1 c. toasted buttered bread crumbs

Melt butter in saucepan; blend in flour and seasonings. Cook until bubbly, stirring constantly. Add milk; cook and stir until thickened. Add egg yolk, stirring constantly; cook for 1 minute. Alternate layers of cabbage, onions, cheese and sauce in baking dish; repeat layers. Top with crumbs. Cover and bake at 375 degrees for 30 minutes; uncover and bake for 5 minutes longer. Yield: 4-6 servings.

Mrs. Eunice S. Tate, Home Economics Teacher, Malvern, Ark.

 ## Cabbage For The King

2 c. coarsely chopped cabbage
1 tsp. salt
¼ c. boiling water
1 tbsp. flour
2 tbsp. butter, melted
2 c. milk
1 tsp. salt
¼ tsp. pepper
1 c. grated cheddar cheese
¼ c. buttered cracker crumbs

Cook cabbage with salt in boiling water for 3 minutes; drain. Blend flour with melted butter; gradually add milk, salt and pepper. Cook until thickened, stirring

(Continued on next page)

constantly. Arrange cabbage and white sauce in layers in buttered casserole. Top with cheese and crumbs. Bake at 275 degrees for 1 hour. Yield: 4-6 servings.

Mrs. Maxine Muck, Adrian, Mich.

 ## Cabbage Wedges With Nippy Sauce

    1 med. head cabbage
    3 tbsp. butter, melted
    2 tbsp. flour
  ½ tsp. onion salt
    1 c. milk
    1 egg yolk
    1 tbsp. prepared yellow mustard
    2 tsp. lemon juice

Cut cabbage into 6 wedges. Cook, covered, in a small amount of boiling water until crispy tender. Meanwhile, prepare Nippy Sauce by combining butter, flour and onion salt; blend in milk and egg yolk. Cook over moderate heat until thickened, stirring constantly; add mustard and lemon juice. Spoon sauce over thoroughly drained cabbage wedges. Yield: 6 servings.

Photograph for this recipe below.

Cabbage With Sour Cream Sauce

1 med. cabbage, cut into six wedges
1 c. sour cream
¼ tsp. salt
½ c. liquid from cabbage
1 tbsp. chopped chives

Remove core from cabbage; place in saucepan with 1 inch boiling, salted water. Cook for 5 minutes. Cover and cook for 8 to 10 minutes longer. Place wedges on warm serving platter. Heat sour cream and salt in liquid from cabbage; do not boil. Remove from heat; stir in chives. Pour over cabbage. Garnish with additional chives. Yield: 6 servings.

Mary K. Porter, Home Economics Teacher, Collinsville, Ala.

 ## Company Cabbage

5 c. finely shredded cabbage
1 c. finely shredded carrots
½ c. chopped green onions and tops
½ tsp. salt
⅛ tsp. pepper
1 beef bouillon cube
¼ c. hot water
¼ c. butter
1 tsp. prepared mustard
⅓ c. chopped pecans
¼ tsp. paprika

Combine cabbage, carrots, green onions, salt and pepper in large heavy saucepan. Dissolve bouillon cube in hot water; add to vegetables in saucepan. Toss with fork to blend thoroughly. Cover tightly and cook over low heat for 5 minutes, stirring and turning once during cooking. Drain; turn into warm dish. Melt butter in small saucepan over low heat; stir in mustard and pecans. Heat thoroughly and pour over vegetables. Sprinkle with paprika. Yield: 6 servings.

Mrs. Jean C. Vandergrift, Roanoke, Va.

 ## Country-Style Cabbage

1 med. cabbage, shredded
½ c. butter
½ c. light cream
½ tsp. salt

Cover and cook cabbage in butter for 5 to 6 minutes; add cream and salt. Heat for 1 to 2 minutes. Yield: 6 servings.

Mildred D. Crow, Home Economics Teacher, Alvarado, Tex.

Cream Cheese Cabbage

5 c. cabbage, cut into ¼ to ½-in. wide shreds
1 3-oz. pkg. cream cheese
1 tbsp. cream
2 tbsp. butter
Few grains of pepper
¼ tsp. celery seed
¾ tsp. salt

Soak cabbage for 12 to 15 minutes in ice water; drain. Cook cabbage in salted, boiling water for 4 to 5 minutes; drain. Mix cream cheese and cream; add to cabbage. Add butter, pepper, celery seed and salt; mix lightly. Serve immediately. Yield: 4 servings.

Mrs. Dean Maggard, Bowling Green, Ky., Favorite Recipes Food Fair

 ## Crunchy Boiled Cabbage

1 med. fresh cabbage
2 tsp. cooking salt
8 c. boiling water
4 tbsp. butter, melted
½ tsp. pepper

Remove outside leaves of cabbage; cut into quarters. Remove core; cut into ¼-inch shreds. Place in rapidly boiling salted water; cover. Allow to boil rapidly for 3 minutes; turn off heat. Let stand for 3 minutes on burner. Cabbage should be crisp and crunchy. Uncover; drain. Add butter and pepper; serve immediately. Yield: 8-10 servings.

Sister Mary Isabels, South Orange, N.J.

 ## Elegant Cabbage With Ham

1 med. cabbage, shredded
2 c. diced ham
1 can cream of mushroom or potato soup
½ c. milk
⅓ c. buttered bread crumbs

Steam cabbage in covered saucepan with small amount of water until slightly tender; drain. Arrange cabbage and ham in alternate layers in 2-quart greased casserole. Blend soup with milk; pour over cabbage. Top with crumbs. Bake at 350 degrees for 30 minutes. Yield: 8 servings.

Mrs. Betty Holdorf, Home Economics Teacher, Grand Blanc, Mich.

Fresh Cabbage With Caraway-Cheese Sauce

1 2-lb. cabbage
Beef stock or water
1 tsp. salt
2 tbsp. butter or margarine
1 tbsp. caraway seed
2 tbsp. flour
1 ½ c. milk
⅛ tsp. ground black pepper
1 c. shredded sharp American cheese

Remove outer leaves from cabbage; save for use in salads or soup. Cut head into six wedges. Place in a saucepan with 1 inch boiling beef stock or water and ½ teaspoon salt. Bring to boiling point; boil, uncovered, for 5 minutes. Cover and cook for 5 to 10 minutes or until cabbage is tender. Remove cabbage from water to a serving dish. Place butter or margarine and caraway seed in a saucepan. Heat until butter is melted; blend in flour. Add milk, mixing well. Stir and cook until of medium thickness. Stir in remaining salt, ground black pepper and cheese. Heat only to melt cheese; spoon over cabbage wedges. Yield: 6 servings.

Mrs. Brenda Hall, Miami, Fla.

 ## Fried Cabbage

¼ lb. salt pork, cut into strips
1 med. cabbage, chopped
Salt and pepper to taste
¼ c. water

Fry salt pork until crisp; remove from pan. Combine cabbage, salt, pepper and water in drippings. Simmer, covered, for 10 minutes or until cabbage is tender and begins to brown slightly. Stir occasionally. Yield: 6 servings.

Mrs. Carla B. Davis, Home Economics Teacher, Brunswick, Me.

 ## Panned Cabbage

¼ c. butter
½ cabbage, shredded
½ tsp. salt

Melt butter in heavy frying pan or medium heat. Sprinkle cabbage with salt; place in pan with butter. Cover tightly and cook for 5 to 7 minutes, stirring occasionally. For variation add ½ cup sweet or sour cream just before serving or add 2 tablespoons vinegar and 2 tablespoons brown sugar. Yield: 4 servings.

Vera E. Ballard, Corvallis, Ore.

Fresh Cabbage-Cracker Pie

 20 soda crackers
  1 qt. cabbage, finely shredded
  1 ½ c. milk
 ½ tsp. salt
 ¼ tsp. celery seed
 ¼ tsp. pepper
 ¼ c. butter or margarine

Coarsely crumble crackers and sprinkle half over bottom of a well-greased pie plate. Fill with cabbage. Top with remaining crumbs. Pour milk with seasonings over cabbage. Dot with butter. Bake at 350 degrees for 40 to 50 minutes. Yield: 6 servings.

Mrs. Edward T. Breathitt, Wife of Governor of Kentucky, Frankfort

 ### Lynn's Cabbage

  1 cabbage, cut into 1-in. chunks
  8 slices bacon, diced
  1 green pepper, diced
  1 sm. onion, diced
 Salt and pepper
  1 ½ c. diced cheese
  2 c. medium white sauce
 Buttered crumbs

Cook cabbage in salted water until tender. Fry bacon until crisp; add green pepper and onion. Place a layer of cabbage in greased casserole; sprinkle with salt, pepper, one-third of bacon and cheese. Repeat twice. Cover with white sauce; sprinkle with crumbs. Bake at 350 degrees for 45 minutes.

Mrs. Malcolm Walter, Jupiter, Fla.

 ### Baked Red Cabbage

  2 c. coarsely chopped red cabbage
  1 c. grated cheese
  1 c. rich milk
 Salt and pepper to taste
 ½ c. cracker crumbs
  2 tbsp. butter

Place cabbage in buttered casserole; stir in cheese and milk. Season to taste; sprinkle with crumbs. Dot with butter. Bake at 350 degrees for 40 minutes. Yield: 4 servings.

Lulu Smith, Home Economics Teacher, Sand Springs, Okla.

Red Cabbage With Caraway

1 lge. red cabbage, shredded
3 tbsp. butter
2 tbsp. chopped onion
2 sour apples
1 tsp. salt
¼ c. boiling water
4 tbsp. red wine
4 tbsp. brown sugar
1 tbsp. caraway seed

Soak cabbage in cold water. Melt butter in saucepan; add onion. Simmer for 3 minutes. Add cabbage. Cover pan and simmer for 10 minutes longer. Core apples; cut into thin slices. Add to cabbage with salt and boiling water. Cover pan and simmer for 1 hour. Add more water if necessary. When cabbage is tender and water absorbed, add red wine, brown sugar and caraway seed. Simmer for 10 minutes longer. Serve hot. Yield: 6 servings.

Mrs. Lyle C. Franz, Maysville, Ky.

 ### Raisin Cabbage Rolls

¾ c. seedless raisins
½ lb. ground lean beef
1 c. cooked rice
1 tbsp. chopped onion
1 tsp. seasoned salt
¼ tsp. dill weed
2 tbsp. water
8 lge. outside cabbage leaves
1 10½-oz. can beef broth
¼ c. catsup
2 tsp. cider vinegar
2 tsp. cornstarch

Combine ½ cup raisins with beef, rice, onion, salt, dill and water. Pour boiling water over cabbage; let stand 5 minutes. Drain and cut out thick portion at base of leaf. Spoon filling on center of leaves. Fold sides in, then roll up to enclose filling. Secure rolls with toothpicks, if necessary. Place in skillet with broth. Cover; simmer until tender, 30 to 40 minutes. Remove rolls and keep warm. If less than ¾ cup pan liquid, add water to make this amount. Add catsup, vinegar blended with cornstarch and remaining ¼ cup raisins. Cook, stirring, until clear. Add rolls and heat 5 minutes. Yield: 4 servings.

Photograph for this recipe on page 85.

Saucy Cabbage Wedges

    1 2-lb. cabbage
    ⅓ c. mayonnaise
    ¼ c. milk
    4 tsp. vinegar
    1 tsp. sugar
    ½ tsp. prepared mustard
    Paprika

Cut cabbage into eight wedges; cook in boiling, salted water for 8 to 10 minutes. Combine mayonnaise and milk in small saucepan; stir until smooth. Add vinegar, sugar and mustard; mix well. Stir over low heat until hot. Pour over well-drained cabbage; sprinkle with paprika. Yield: 8 servings.

Mrs. Billie Jean McCarroll, Home Economics Teacher, Slidell, Tex.

 ## Scalloped Cabbage With Tomatoes

    1 ½ c. bread crumbs
    ¼ c. melted butter or margarine
    2 lb. cabbage, shredded
    1 No. 2 can tomatoes, drained
    1 green pepper, pimento or onion, chopped
    Juice from tomatoes
    Salt and pepper to taste

Saute bread crumbs in butter. Dip cabbage in hot water to remove rawness; drain. Layer cabbage, crumbs, tomatoes and green pepper in loaf pan. Top with crumbs; cover with tomato juice. Season. Bake at 350 degrees for 45 minutes or until cabbage is tender. Yield: 6 servings.

Berniece M. Cobb, Westminster, Colo.

 ## Skillet Cabbage

    1 tbsp. bacon drippings
    1 med. onion, finely chopped
    1 green pepper, finely chopped
    3 stalks celery, finely chopped
    1 to 2 lge. green tomatoes, finely chopped
    ½ med. cabbage, finely chopped
    1 tsp. salt
    ¼ tsp. pepper

Melt bacon drippings in skillet; add vegetables. Season with salt and pepper; mix well. Cover and cook over medium heat for 5 to 8 minutes or until cabbage is tender but crisp, stirring occasionally. Yield: 4 servings.

Hilda H. Sharp, Home Economics Teacher, Nashville, Tenn.

Stuffed Cabbage Leaves

1 ½ lb. ground beef
4 tbsp. grated onion
½ c. butter
1 ½ c. cooked rice
1 tsp. salt
1 tsp. thyme
12 lge. cabbage leaves
3 c. canned tomato sauce

Combine meat with onion; saute in butter until lightly browned. Add rice, salt and thyme; mix well. Cook cabbage leaves in boiling water for 1 minute; drain and pat dry. Spoon meat mixture on center of leaves; fold over and secure with toothpicks. Place in greased shallow baking dish; cover with tomato sauce. Cover and bake at 325 degrees for 45 minutes. Yield: 6 servings.

Mrs. Hazel Janson, Pensacola, Fla.

 ### Stuffed Whole Cabbage

1 2-lb. cabbage
2 ¼ tsp. salt
1 c. finely chopped luncheon meat
1 c. shredded American cheese
¼ c. finely chopped onion
½ c. soft bread cubes
1 tbsp. milk
¼ tsp. pepper
1 ½ c. diced fresh tomatoes
¾ c. boiling water
¾ c. bread crumbs
1 ½ tbsp. melted butter or margarine

Place whole cabbage in kettle with 1 teaspoon salt and enough boiling water to cover. Boil, uncovered, for 30 minutes or until almost tender. Remove from water; drain well. Cut off top; carefully scoop out inside leaving a 1½-inch shell. Place cabbage shell in casserole. Finely shred enough of the cabbage center to make 1 cup. Combine with luncheon meat, cheese, onion, ½ cup bread crumbs, milk, ½ teaspoon salt and pepper. Mix well; spoon into cabbage shell. Combine tomatoes, water and all remaining salt. Pour into casserole around cabbage. Cover with aluminum foil or casserole lid. Bake at 350 degrees for 1 hour. Remove from oven; sprinkle with bread cubes mixed with melted butter. Bake for 15 minutes longer or until cubes are browned. Serve with tomato sauce spooned over each portion. Yield: 6 servings.

Bess E. Alexander, Cambridge, Idaho, Favorite Recipes Food Fair

Wilted Cabbage With Cheese

7 c. shredded cabbage
2 c. boiling water
1 c. grated cheddar cheese
1 can cream of celery soup
Crushed potato chips

Cook cabbage in boiling water until wilted. Drain; place in buttered casserole in alternate layers with cheese and soup. Garnish top with crushed potato chips. Cover and bake at 350 degrees for 20 to 30 minutes. Yield: 8-10 servings.

Mrs. Verna Graves, Home Economics Teacher, Albert Lea, Minn.

 ## Baked Apple And Carrot Casserole

5 apples, thinly sliced
2 c. cooked carrots, sliced lengthwise
6 tbsp. sugar
2 tbsp. flour
Salt to taste
¾ c. orange juice

Place layer of apple slices in baking dish; cover with layer of carrots. Sprinkle with mixture of sugar, flour and salt. Repeat until ingredients are used. Pour juice over all. Bake at 350 degrees for 20 to 30 minutes. Yield: 5 servings.

Mrs. Junnie M. Goldston, Leaksville, N. C.

 ## Baked Shredded Carrots

4 med. carrots
Salt and pepper to taste
2 tbsp. butter

Grate carrots with medium grater. Place carrots in well-buttered casserole. Season and dot with butter. Bake, covered, at 325 degrees for about 25 minutes. Yield: 6 servings.

Myrtle Sellis, Home Economics Teacher, Austin, Minn.

A family-pleasing main dish, Braised Chicken and Fresh Vegetables is economical as well. Garden-fresh green vegetables add color accented by strips of bright pimento. Get ready for compliments in abundance and requests for seconds.

BRAISED CHICKEN AND FRESH VEGETABLES

1 3- to 4-lb. ready-to-cook chicken
2 tbsp. shortening
2 c. boiling water
3 tsp. salt
12 sm. whole white onions
4 ribs celery
$\frac{1}{2}$ med. green pepper
1 c. fresh snap beans, cut into 1-in. pieces
1 c. shelled fresh green peas
$\frac{1}{2}$ tsp. ground black pepper
2 tbsp. flour
3 tbsp. cold water
$\frac{1}{4}$ c. pimento strips

Wash chicken and cut into serving pieces. Brown on all sides in hot shortening in a Dutch oven or saucepan. Add boiling water and salt. Cover and cook 10 minutes. Peel onions; cut celery into 1-inch pieces and green pepper into ½-inch strips. Cover and cook 40 minutes or until vegetables are tender. Add beans, peas and black pepper 15 minutes before cooking times is up. Blend flour with cold water to a smooth paste. Add and cook 1 to 2 minutes. Add pimento. Serve hot as the main dish.

See photograph on reverse side.

California Carrot Casserole

18 to 20 med. carrots, peeled
Salt and pepper to taste
2 tsp. candied ginger, finely chopped
4 tbsp. butter or margarine
2 tbsp. evaporated milk
½ c. chopped walnuts

Simmer carrots, covered, in small amount of boiling salted water until tender. Drain and mash well; season with salt, pepper, ginger and 2 tablespoons butter. Beat well, adding milk. Pile in buttered 1-quart casserole. Sprinkle with nuts; dot with remaining butter. Bake at 375 degrees for 30 minutes. Yield: 6 servings.

Mrs. Teresa Holley, Meridian, Miss.

 ## Candied Carrots

½ c. butter or margarine
6 tbsp. brown sugar
6 carrots, cut into halves, lengthwise
1 c. water

Blend butter and sugar; add carrots and water. Cook over low heat until carrots are tender. For variety, 2 tablespoons fresh mint may be added.

Alice N. Pohl, Portland, Ore., Favorite Recipes Food Fair

 ## Carrots In Orange Sauce With Almonds

½ c. slivered almonds
1 tbsp. butter
1 ½ tbsp. brown sugar
2 tsp. cornstarch
¼ tsp. salt
⅛ tsp. cinnamon
⅛ tsp. nutmeg
1 c. orange juice
1 tsp. grated orange rind
10 to 12 carrots, cooked and cut into strips

Saute almonds in butter for 5 minutes; remove from pan. Combine sugar, cornstarch, salt, cinnamon and nutmeg; add orange juice and rind. Cook, stirring constantly, until slightly thickened and clear. Add almonds. Serve over hot shoestring carrots. Yield: 6 servings.

Mrs. Marie L. Trainor, Home Economics Teacher, Springfield, Ill.

Carrot Souffle

¼ c. butter or margarine
¼ c. diced celery
1 tbsp. finely chopped onion
½ tsp. pepper
½ tsp. salt
¼ c. sifted flour
3 eggs, separated
2 c. grated raw or cooked, mashed carrots

Melt butter; add celery, onion and seasonings. Cook until onion is lightly browned. Blend in flour. Remove from heat; add egg yolks, blending thoroughly. Blend in carrots. Fold in stiffly-beaten egg whites. Place mixture in well greased 1-quart casserole; place casserole in pan of hot water. Bake at 350 degrees for about 45 minutes or until firm in center. Yield: 6 servings.

Lois E. Clarchick, Pittsburgh, Pa.

 ## Creamed Carrots And Celery

2 c. sliced carrots
1 c. diced celery
¼ c. water
¾ c. white sauce or cream of celery soup
2 tbsp. margarine
¼ c. grated cheese
Dash of salt and pepper

Cook carrots and celery in water for 5 minutes; drain. Add carrots and celery to white sauce; add margarine, cheese and seasonings. Pour into oiled baking dish. Bake at 350 degrees for 20 minutes. Yield: 5 servings.

Leila Mae Vickrey, Tallahassee, Fla.

 ## Easy Carrot Casserole

4 c. carrots, cut into lengthwise slices
2 c. medium white sauce
2 c. potato chips

In a greased baking dish, place a layer of carrots, white sauce and crushed potato chips, ending with potato chips. Bake at 375 degrees for 45 minutes. Yield: 6-8 servings.

Zelma M. Waldron, Plymouth, Neb.

Cheese Scalloped Carrots

12 carrots, sliced
 3 onions, chopped
 ¼ c. butter
 ¼ to ½ tsp. celery salt
 ¼ tsp. dry mustard
 ⅛ tsp. pepper
 ¼ c. flour
 2 c. milk
 ½ lb. sliced cheese
    Bread crumbs

Cook carrots, covered, in 1 inch of salted boiling water until barely tender.
Simmer onion in butter; add seasonings, flour and milk to make white sauce.
Cook until smooth. In 2-quart casserole, arrange layers of carrots and cheese.
Cover with white sauce; top with bread crumbs. May refrigerate until needed.
Bake 45 minutes in 325-degree oven. Yield: 10 servings.

Mrs. M. J. Stack, Officers' Wives' Club, Jacksonville, Fla.

 ## Golden Crumb Carrots

 2 c. cooked carrots
 3 tbsp. butter or margarine
 1 c. fine bread crumbs
 ¾ c. grated American cheese

Mix all ingredients lightly in saucepan; stir over very low heat until cheese
melts. Serve hot. If desired, this optional method may be used. Put a layer of
cooked carrots in a casserole; dot with butter. Cover with a layer of bread
crumbs, then a layer of cheese. Repeat layers. Bake at 350 degrees for 20 to
30 minutes. Yield: 5-6 servings.

Eunice Zachary, McCall, Idaho

 ## Honey-Glazed Carrots

 3 tbsp. honey
 2 tbsp. butter
 ¼ tsp. grated orange rind
 1 tbsp. poppy seed
 ⅛ tsp. salt
10 to 12 sm. carrots, cooked

Combine all ingredients except carrots in a skillet; bring to a boil. Add carrots;
simmer for 10 to 12 minutes, turning frequently. Yield: 6 servings.

Mrs. Bertha Wilkins, Cresbard, S. D.

Glazed Carrots And Raisins

1 1-lb. pkg. carrots, thinly sliced
1 c. golden raisins
1 c. water
1 tsp. salt
½ c. (firmly packed) brown sugar
4 tbsp. margarine or butter
2 tbsp. lemon juice

Combine carrots with raisins, water and salt in heavy saucepan. Heat to boiling. Simmer, covered, for 30 minutes or until carrots are tender; drain. Sprinkle with brown sugar, butter or margarine and lemon juice; heat slowly until butter or margarine melts. Cook for 10 minutes or until carrots are richly glazed, stirring frequently. Yield: 6 servings.

Mrs. Kay Schneider, Home Economics Teacher, Norwalk, Conn.

 ## Julienne Carrots En Casserole

8 med. carrots, julienne
½ c. mayonnaise
2 tbsp. grated onion
2 tbsp. prepared horseradish
1 tsp. salt
¼ tsp. pepper
⅓ c. buttered bread crumbs
Dash of paprika

Cook carrots in small amount of water about 10 minutes. Place carrots and 2 tablespoons water in which they were cooked in greased shallow baking dish. Mix together mayonnaise, grated onion, horseradish, salt and pepper. Spoon sauce over carrots and stir lightly. Sprinkle with bread crumbs and paprika. Bake in 350-degree oven for 15 minutes. Yield: 6 servings.

Mrs. R. C. Giffen, Jr., Naval Officers' Wives' Club, Philadelphia, Pa.

 ## Minted Glazed Carrots

12 young fresh carrots
¼ c. butter
½ c. sugar
2 tbsp. fresh chopped mint or dried mint leaves

Wash and scrape carrots. Cook in boiling salted water until tender. Drain. Melt butter; stir in sugar. Carefully place hot carrots in skillet or shallow heavy pan. Pour sugar-butter mixture over carrots. Cook slowly until carrots are

(Continued on next page)

glazed but not brown. Just before serving, sprinkle with chopped mint. Canned baby carrots may be used. Yield: 6 servings.

Sister Mary Jude, Chicago Heights, Ill.

Herbed Carrots With Green Grapes

1 ½ lb. carrots
½ tsp. salt
1 tsp. basil
½ c. butter or margarine
1 sm. clove of garlic, crushed
½ tsp. thyme
¼ tsp. celery salt
1 c. seedless grapes (opt.)
1 tbsp. lemon juice
⅛ tsp. salt
Few grains of pepper

Wash and pare carrots; cut into 3 x ¼-inch strips. Put carrots into saucepan; add salt, basil and enough boiling water to steam. Cook, covered, for 12 to 15 minutes or until carrots are crisp-tender. Melt butter or margarine; add garlic, thyme and celery salt. Set aside. Remove carrots from heat; add grapes. Let stand, covered, for 1 to 2 minutes; drain off liquid. Stir lemon juice into seasoned butter; pour over carrots. Season with salt and pepper; toss mixture gently. Serve immediately. Yield: 6-8 servings.

Mrs. Robert A. Riffenburg, Fortuna, Cal., Favorite Recipes Food Fair

Carrot And Almond Ring

2 tbsp. butter
2 tbsp. flour
½ c. warm milk
2 c. mashed cooked carrots
½ c. grated almonds
½ tsp. salt
4 eggs, separated

Melt butter in saucepan. Add flour; blend until smooth. Gradually add warm milk. Bring sauce to a boil, stirring constantly; simmer for 5 minutes. Add carrots, almonds and salt. Lower heat; carefully blend in lightly beaten egg yolks. Simmer slowly for 4 to 5 minutes longer. Remove from heat; cool. Beat egg whites until stiff; fold gently into carrot mixture. Pour into a buttered 9-inch ring mold; place mold in a pan of hot water. Bake at 350 degrees for 50 to 60 minutes or until firm. Let stand for a few minutes before turning out onto a platter. Fill center with green peas. Yield: 8 servings.

Mrs. Francyne Trackman, Joliet, Ill.

Individual Carrot Custards

1 ¼ c. milk, scalded
2 eggs, beaten
2 ½ c. grated carrots
1 tsp. salt
⅛ tsp. pepper
1 ½ tbsp. minced onion
1 tbsp. lemon juice
4 tbsp. melted butter
Parsley

Slowly stir milk into the eggs; add all remaining ingredients, except parsley. Pour into greased custard cups; set in shallow pan of hot water. Bake at 350 degrees for 30 minutes or until knife inserted comes out clean. Unmold; garnish with parsley. If individual custard cups are not available, use a 10-inch ring mold. Yield: 8 servings.

I. Eugenia Spangler, Home Economics Teacher, Newville, Pa.

 ## Peanut-Carrot Loaf

2 tbsp. butter or fat
4 tbsp. flour
1 No. 303 can stewed tomatoes
2 c. roasted peanuts, chopped
2 c. carrots, diced
1 ¼ c. dry bread crumbs
¼ c. chopped parsley
1 ½ tsp. salt
⅛ tsp. pepper
1 onion, diced

Melt butter; add flour and stewed tomatoes. Cook, stirring constantly, until thickened. Add remaining ingredients; mix thoroughly. Mold into loaf or pack in well-greased casserole dish. Bake 1 hour at 400 degrees. Yield: 6 servings.

Mrs. D. W. Houghton, Officers' Wives' Club, Staten Island, N. Y.

 ## Pineapple Carrots

3 to 4 pkg. carrots, cut in 1-in. pieces
1 1-lb. can pineapple chunks, drained
2 to 4 tbsp. cornstarch

Cook carrots partially. Measure pineapple juice; add 2 tablespoons cornstarch to each cup juice. Cook until thickened, stirring constantly. Layer carrots and pineapple in 3-quart casserole. Cover with pineapple juice. Bake at 350 degrees until bubbly. Yield: 8-10 servings.

Ellen Scheidt, Home Economics Teacher, Karval, Colo.

Carrot Loaf With Parsley Sauce

2 c. cooked carrots
4 tbsp. butter
1 egg
5 tbsp. fine bread crumbs
1 tbsp. finely chopped onion
2 tbsp. finely chopped parsley
Seasoning to taste
1 bunch parsley
1 tbsp. flour
2 tbsp. heavy cream
Juice of ½ lemon

Combine carrots, 2 tablespoons butter, egg, crumbs, onion, chopped parsley and seasoning in greased loaf pan. Bake at 375 degrees for 25 minutes. Boil parsley in salted water for 10 minutes. Cut leaves from stalks; finely chop. Blend 2 tablespoons butter, flour and cream; cook until thickened, stirring constantly. Fold in parsley and lemon juice. Pour over carrot loaf.

Mrs. Wilda Carr, Home Economics Teacher, Holdredge, Neb.

 ## Scalloped Carrots With Cheese

12 med. carrots
1 med. onion, minced
¼ c. butter
¼ c. flour
1 tsp. salt
¼ tsp. dry mustard
2 c. milk
⅛ tsp. pepper
¼ tsp. celery salt
½ lb. Velveeta cheese, melted
3 c. bread cubes
⅓ c. melted butter

Cook carrots in water until barely tender; drain. Cook onion gently in ¼ cup butter until lightly browned. Stir in flour, salt and mustard. Stir in milk until smooth. Add pepper, celery salt and cheese; stir until cheese is melted. Place carrots in shallow casserole. Pour cheese sauce over carrots. Top with bread cubes which have been mixed with remaining butter. Bake at 350 degrees for 35 to 40 minutes. Yield: 6-8 servings.

Mrs. Virginia F. Jacka, Calumet, Mich.

 ## Scalloped Carrots With Peanut Butter

2 c. sliced carrots, cooked
1 c. white sauce
1 tsp. peanut butter

(Continued on next page)

¼ c. melted butter
½ c. bread crumbs

Drain carrots; arrange in buttered 1-quart casserole. Blend white sauce with peanut butter; pour over carrots. Sprinkle with buttered bread cumbs. Bake at 375 degrees for 20 minutes. Yield: 6 servings.

Charlotte H. Thompson, Home Economics Teacher, Claremont, N. H.

 ## Spiced Carrots

1 lb. small carrots, scraped
⅓ c. thawed orange juice concentrate
⅓ c. hot water
1 thin slice lemon
1 tsp. grated onion
2 tsp. brown sugar
½ tsp. salt
Dash of white pepper
1 1-in. piece of stick cinnamon
2 whole cloves
2 whole allspice
Several blades of whole mace
2 tbsp. butter or margarine

Place carrots into large, heavy skillet or saucepan. Mix remaining ingredients; pour over carrots. Cover tightly and bring to a boil. Simmer for 20 minutes or until carrots are tender. Remove spices before serving. Yield: 6 servings.

Sister M. Roseann, Altoona, Pa., Favorite Recipes Food Fair

 ## Zesty Carrots

6 to 8 carrots, cut lengthwise
¼ c. water
2 tbsp. grated onion
2 tbsp. horseradish
½ c. mayonnaise
½ tsp. salt
¼ tsp. pepper
¼ c. cracker crumbs
1 tbsp. butter
Dash of paprika

Cook carrots until tender. Place in shallow baking dish. Combine water, onion, horseradish, mayonnaise, salt and pepper; pour over carrots. Top with mixture of cracker crumbs, butter and paprika. Bake at 375 degrees for 15 to 20 minutes. Yield: 6 servings.

Naomi Austin, Gainesville, Tex.

Cauliflower and Celery

Cauliflower With Almond Butter

    1 sm. cauliflower
    1/4 c. slivered blanched almonds
    3 tbsp. butter

Trim outer leaves from cauliflower. Wash and cook in boiling salted water for 10 minutes or until tender. Drain; cook almonds in butter until lightly browned. Place cauliflower in serving dish; pour butter and almonds over top. Yield: 4 servings.

Helen Janis Hale, Somerset, Ky., Favorite Recipes Food Fair

Cauliflower Casserole

    1 cauliflower
    1/2 lb. fresh or 1 7-oz. can mushrooms
    1/4 c. diced green pepper
    1/3 c. margarine
    1/4 c. flour
    2 c. milk
    1 tsp. salt
    6 slices pimento cheese
    Dash of paprika

Wash and cut cauliflower into flowerets; cook in salted water 15 minutes. Drain. Saute mushrooms and green pepper in margarine. Remove mushrooms. Add flour, milk and salt to margarine in pan; cook a few minutes until flour taste is gone. Add sauteed mushrooms and green pepper to white sauce. Put half of cauliflower in a 1½-quart casserole. Cover cauliflower with 3 slices of cheese; add half of white sauce. Repeat layers, ending with white sauce. Sprinkle with paprika. Bake 15 to 20 minutes at 350 degrees. Yield: 8 servings.

Elsa M. Lindsay, Downey, Cal.

Cauliflower With Chipped Beef

    2 pkg. frozen cauliflower
    2 10½-oz. cans cream of mushroom soup
    1 ½ c. sour cream
    1 tbsp. lemon juice
    4 oz. chipped beef, shredded

Prepare cauliflower according to package directions. Place in casserole. Heat soup; add sour cream, lemon juice and chipped beef. Simmer for 2 minutes, stirring constantly. Pour over cauliflower. Yield: 6 servings.

Mrs. Doris Hunter, New York, N. Y.

Cauliflower Custard

    1 med. cauliflower
    2 eggs
    ¼ tsp. salt
    ⅛ tsp. pepper
    3 tbsp. butter
    1 c. cream or rich milk

Wash cauliflower and cook in slightly salted water for 15 minutes. Drain and chop fine. Beat egg; add salt, pepper and butter. Stir in cream. Pour into well-greased 1¾-quart casserole. Set casserole in pan of warm water. Bake at 325 degrees for 50 minutes. Yield: 6 servings.

Mrs. Hazel J. Hunter, Cave Junction, Ore.

 ### Cauliflower And Ham Casserole

    1 lge. head cauliflower
    1 c. ham, cut in small cubes
    1 10-oz. can cream of mushroom soup
    ½ c. buttered bread crumbs
    ½ c. grated cheddar cheese

Cook the whole cauliflower in boiling water for about 20 minutes. Drain and break into pieces. Place cauliflower and ham in layers in casserole. Cover with soup. Sprinkle with bread crumbs and cheese. Bake in a 375-degree oven for 25 minutes or until slightly browned. Yield: 4-6 servings.

Mrs. William Segal, Jacksonville, Fla.

 ### Cauliflower Harlequin

    1 sm. cauliflower, separated
    4 tbsp. butter, melted
    ¼ lb. boiled ham, diced
    2 hard-cooked eggs, diced
    2 tbsp. fine bread crumbs
    2 tbsp. grated Parmesan cheese

Cook cauliflowerets in boiling salted water for 15 minutes. Drain; place in well buttered casserole. Add 2 tablespoons butter; sprinkle with ham, eggs and bread crumbs. Pour remaining melted butter over bread crumbs. Sprinkle with cheese. Bake at 375 degrees for 20 minutes. Yield: 4 servings.

Mrs. C. E. Lohr, Princeton, W. Va.

Cauliflower Mold

    2 eggs
    1 can cream of celery soup
    1 lge. head cauliflower, coarsely chopped
    ½ c. grated cheese
    ½ c. soft bread crumbs
    2 pimentos, chopped
    2 tbsp. chopped onion
    1 tsp. salt
    ⅛ tsp. pepper

Beat eggs slightly; stir in remaining ingredients. Pour into buttered casserole. Set in pan of hot water. Bake at 375 degrees for 50 minutes or until firm. Serve hot. Yield: 4-6 servings.

Voncile Owens, Home Economics Teacher, Sonora, Cal.

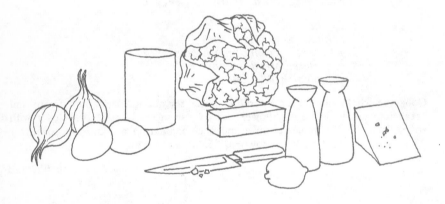

 ## Cauliflower Polonaise

    2 pkg. frozen cauliflower
    ½ c. fresh coarse bread crumbs
    6 tbsp. butter, melted
    4 tsp. lemon juice
    2 tbsp. finely chopped parsley
    2 hard-cooked eggs, finely chopped

Cook cauliflower until tender; drain. Saute bread crumbs in butter until golden brown; remove from heat and add lemon juice. Place cauliflower in serving dish; add bread crumbs and mix lightly. Sprinkle with chopped parsley and eggs. Yield: 6 servings.

Loraine Ranney, Plattsmouth, Neb.

Cauliflower With Shrimp Sauce

1 med. cauliflower, broken in flowerets
1 can frozen cream of shrimp soup
½ c. sour cream
Salt to taste
¼ c. slivered blanched almonds, toasted

Cook cauliflower, covered in salted water for 10 to 15 minutes or until tender; drain. Heat soup over low heat, stirring frequently. Add sour cream; cook and stir just until heated. Season to taste; add almonds. Pour over hot cauliflower. Garnish with parsley. Yield: 4-6 servings.

Mrs. Helen J. Mueller, Home Economics Teacher, Taylor Ridge, Ill.

 ## Cauliflower Souffle

1 lge. cauliflower
⅓ c. butter
2 tbsp. flour
1 c. milk
3 eggs, separated
3 tbsp. grated Parmesan cheese
Seasonings to taste

Boil cauliflower until tender in salted water. Separate into flowerets; remove most of stem. Place cauliflower in baking dish. Melt butter; blend in flour and milk. Cook and stir until thickened. Remove from heat; add egg yolks. Cool. Fold in stiffly beaten egg whites and cheese; season to taste. Pour over cauliflower. Bake at 350 degrees for 30 to 45 minutes. Yield: 4-6 servings.

Mrs. Dorothy Smith, Palacios, Tex.

 ## Cauliflower And Tomatoes

1 10-oz. pkg. frozen cauliflower
1 ½ c. boiling salted water
1 sm. clove of garlic, chopped
3 tbsp. olive oil
½ tsp. salt
½ c. canned tomatoes
1 tsp. chopped parsley
2 tbsp. Parmesan cheese

Place cauliflower in boiling water for 3 to 4 minutes or long enough to separate flowerets; drain. Saute garlic in olive oil until browned; remove garlic. Add flowerets to olive oil. Saute lightly; add salt and tomatoes. Cover; simmer for 5 minutes. Arrange in serving dish; sprinkle with parsley and cheese. Yield: 4 servings.

Mrs. William V. Hadden, Home Economics Teacher, Auburn, Ky.

Creamed Cauliflower

    1 med. head of cauliflower
½ c. butter
⅔ c. vinegar
½ c. chopped onion
½ c. chopped green pepper

Break cauliflower apart and cook 15 minutes in as little water as possible. Melt butter; add vinegar, onion and green pepper. Heat and serve over cauliflower. Yield: 4 servings.

          Faraba M. Millican, Junction City, Kan.

 ## Deep Fat-Fried Cauliflower

    1 egg, slightly beaten
1 tbsp oil or melted fat
1 c. milk
1 c. sifted flour
¼ tsp. salt
1 cauliflower or 2 pkg. frozen cauliflower, thawed

Combine egg, oil and milk; gradually add to mixture of flour and salt. Beat with rotary beater until smooth. Divide cauliflower into flowerets; cook in boiling water to cover until tender. Dip flowerets in batter; fry in 375 degree deep fat until delicately browned. Yield: 4-6 servings.

          Mrs. Edgar Barber, Wall, S. D.

 ## Dilly Cauliflower Au Gratin

    1 med. cauliflower
¼ c. flour
¼ c. butter or margarine
2 c. milk
½ lb. sharp cheddar cheese, shredded
½ tsp. dill seed
½ tsp. salt
⅛ tsp. pepper
4 slices dry bread, crumbled and toasted

Remove leaves from cauliflower; cut off tough part of stem. Break into flowerets; simmer for 8 to 15 minutes in small amount of salted water. Blend flour with melted butter; gradually add milk, cheese and seasonings. Cook until thickened, stirring constantly. Layer cauliflower and cheese sauce in 2-quart casserole; top with crumbs. Bake at 350 degrees for 20 minutes. Yield: 6 servings.

          Mrs. Jennette F. Buhler, Home Economics Teacher, Byron, Wyo.

Fresh Cauliflower With Cheese Sauce

1 lge. head cauliflower
2 tsp. salt
3 tbsp. butter or margarine
3 tbsp. flour
1 ½ c. milk or milk and vegetable stock
⅛ tsp. ground black pepper
½ tsp. dry mustard
1 c. shredded sharp cheddar cheese
2 tbsp. capers

Wash cauliflower and remove outer leaves, leaving tender inner leaves attached. Place whole cauliflower head in saucepan with 1 teaspoon salt and boiling water to cover. Bring to boiling point and cook, uncovered, 5 minutes. Cover and cook 20 minutes longer or until cauliflower is crisp-tender, turning head once to cook uniformly. Melt butter in saucepan. Blend in flour. Stir and cook until bubbly. Remove from heat and add milk, remaining salt, pepper and mustard. Stir and cook until sauce is medium thick. Remove from heat; add cheese and capers. Place cauliflower head in a serving dish. Pour a portion of the sauce over top of cauliflower. Serve remaining sauce in a separate bowl. Yield: 6 servings.

Mrs. Ann Volrich, Memphis, Tenn.

 ## South African Rock Lobster Over Cauliflower

6 4-oz. rock lobster tails
1 med. head cauliflower
2 tsp. salt
3 tbsp. butter
3 tbsp. flour
¼ tsp. salt
½ tsp. paprika
1 c. milk
1 c. rock lobster liquid

Drop frozen rock lobster tails into boiling salted water and cook for 5 minutes. Drain immediately, reserving 1 cup of water in which they are boiled. Drench with cold water. Remove meat from shells and cut into bite-sized pieces. Wash cauliflower in cold water to completely immerse head. Add salt and cook not longer than 15 minutes after water boils. Drain. Meanwhile, prepare white sauce of butter, flour, seasonings, milk and rock lobster liquid. Add rock lobster meat and heat thoroughly. Pour sauce over cauliflower in serving bowl and serve immediately. Yield: 6 servings.

Photograph for this recipe on page 105.

Fresh Cauliflower And Fish Luncheon Dish

1 ½ c. cold poached fish fillets or steaks (salmon, haddock or
    halibut)
1 med. head cold, cooked cauliflower
½ c. French dressing
½ head lettuce
1 tsp. salt
Dash of ground white pepper
2 tsp. fresh lemon juice
Fresh parsley for garnish
¾ c. mayonnaise
1 ½ tbsp. pickle relish

To poach fish, tie in a cheesecloth bag and place in boiling water. Cook 5 to 8 minutes or until flaky. Remove from bag and chill. Separate cauliflower into pieces and marinate in French dressing for 1 hour. Just before serving arrange lettuce on a serving platter. Flake fish and mix with salt, ground white pepper and fresh lemon juice. Pile in the center of platter. Arrange cauliflower around fish. Garnish with fresh parsley. Serve with mayonnaise mixed with pickle relish. Yield: 5-6 servings.

Photograph for this recipe below.

Low Calorie Curried Cauliflower

1 sm. pkg. frozen cauliflower
½ tsp. salt
¼ tsp. curry powder

Cook cauliflower in boiling salted water; drain. Sprinkle with curry powder. Yield: 4 servings.

Mrs. Mary L. Weaver, Schwenksville, Pa.

 ## Chinese Cauliflower

1 head cauliflower
Salt
⅓ c. hot water
2 tbsp. butter
2 tbsp. cream
Paprika, snipped chives or parsley

Wash and remove lower stalks from cauliflower; shred entire head or slice thinly. Place in skillet; sprinkle lightly with salt. Add hot water. Cook, covered, 5 to 7 minutes or until tender, but slightly crisp; do not drain. Add butter and heavy cream; heat, tossing with fork for 1 to 2 minutes. Serve at once, sprinkled with paprika. Yield: 3-4 servings.

Mrs. James L. Puryear, San Antonio, Tex., Favorite Recipes Food Fair

 ## Baked Celery

3 slices lean bacon, chopped
1 onion, thinly sliced
2 tbsp. finely chopped parsley
1 sm. clove of garlic, crushed
8 med. stalks celery
1 c. beef consomme
¼ c. soft fine bread crumbs
3 tbsp. melted butter

Place bacon, onion, parsley and garlic in well greased shallow baking dish; arrange celery stalks on top. Add consomme; cover and bake at 325 degrees for about 1 hour or until celery is tender. Saute bread crumbs in butter; sprinkle over celery during last 10 minutes of baking. Yield: 4 servings.

Rhuie Hollens, Lake Orion, Mich.

Basic Celery Dish

1 c. celery, chopped
Celery, dill or sunflower seeds

Drop celery slowly into enough boiling water to cover bottom of pan. Simmer, covered, for about 8 minutes or until tender. Season. Curry Powder or freshly grated nutmeg may be used as seasoning variations. Serve with cream sauce made with part cream and part remaining celery stock or brown celery in seasoned butter.

Mrs. R. S. Barnes, Otis, Ore.

 ## Braised Celery

1 bunch celery, cut into 1-in. pieces
1 med. onion, chopped
2 tbsp. butter
1 tsp. salt
1/8 tsp. pepper
1 c. chicken broth
Minced parsley

Combine ingredients; simmer for 15 minutes or until celery is tender.

Margaret Green, Monte Vista, Colo.

 ## Celery Almondine

4 c. finely sliced celery
1/2 c. butter
1 tbsp. chopped chives
1 tbsp. grated onion
Salt and pepper to taste
1 1/2 tbsp. flour
1 c. light cream
1/2 c. double strength chicken bouillon
1 c. sliced almonds

Simmer celery, butter, chives, onion, salt and pepper in covered saucepan slowly until tender. Remove from heat; sprinkle with flour. Stir well. Slowly add cream and bouillon; cook slowly, stirring constantly, until thickened. Boil for 1 minute. Add almonds and additional seasonings if desired.

Mrs. Rex Todd Withers, Lansing, Mich.

114

Celery With Almonds

    1 qt. cooked celery, cut into ¼-in. pieces
    1 pt. medium cream sauce
    1 can cream of chicken soup
    ½ c. grated Parmesan cheese
    1 c. blanched slivered almonds

Combine drained celery with remaining ingredients; pour into buttered casserole. Bake at 400 degrees until golden brown. Yield: 6 servings.

Mrs. M. A. Guhin, Home Economics Teacher, Aberdeen, S. D.

 ### Celery Casserole

    4 c. sliced celery
    ½ c. boiling water
    1 10½-oz. can condensed cream of celery soup
       or cream of mushroom soup
    ½ c. sweet milk
    ½ c. chopped pecans
    ⅓ c. cracker crumbs
    3 tbsp. butter

Cook celery in boiling water until tender; drain. Combine with soup, milk and pecans; mix well. Turn into greased 1½-quart casserole; sprinkle with cracker crumbs. Dot with butter. Bake at 350 degrees for 30 minutes. Yield: 6-7 servings.

Mrs. C. E. Barnette, Johnson City, Tenn.

 ### Celery Au Gratin

    2 tbsp. butter
    2 tbsp. flour
    1 c. chicken stock
    ¼ c. light cream
    2 c. cut up celery, parboiled
    ¼ c. almonds
    1 tsp. salt
    ½ tsp. pepper
    1 c. grated American cheese
    1 c. buttered bread crumbs

Melt butter in saucepan; blend in flour. Gradually add stock and cream. Cook and stir until thickened. Combine all ingredients except cheese and buttered crumbs in 8 x 8-inch pan. Top with cheese and buttered crumbs. Bake at 350 degrees for 15 to 20 minutes. Yield: 4-6 servings.

Julie Smith, Arlington, Neb.

Celery-Cheese Casserole

    4 c. coarsely sliced celery
    ¼ c. finely chopped onion
    ¼ c. chopped green pepper
    1 tbsp. butter
    3 tbsp. cream cheese
    3 tbsp. crumbled Bleu cheese
    ½ c. heavy cream
    ½ tsp. salt
    ⅛ tsp. pepper

Cook celery until tender in water to cover. Drain, reserving ¾ cup of broth. Saute onion and green pepper in butter until tender; mix in celery broth, cream cheese, Bleu cheese and cream. Stir until thoroughly blended; season with salt and pepper. Place celery in buttered 1½-quart casserole; pour cheese mixture over celery. Bake at 375 degrees for 20 minutes or until surface is lightly browned. Yield: 6 servings.

Mrs. Helen Green, St. Charles, Ill.

 ### Celery And Water Chestnuts

    4 c. celery, cut into 1-in. slices
    1 5-oz. can water chestnuts
    1 can cream of chicken soup
    ¼ c. diced pimento
    ¼ c. soft bread crumbs
    ¼ c. toasted slivered almonds
    2 tbsp. butter

Cook celery in small amount of water for 8 minutes or until tender-crisp; drain. Mix celery with sliced water chestnuts, soup and pimento. Pour into buttered casserole. Toss together crumbs, almonds and butter; sprinkle over casserole. Bake at 350 degrees for 35 minutes or until lightly browned and hot. Yield: 6 servings.

Freda H. Montgomery, Fresno, Cal.

 ### Cheese-Celery Casserole

    1 med. bunch celery, cut into 1-in. pieces
    ½ lb. Cheddar cheese
    3 hard-cooked eggs, sliced
    1 tsp. salt
    Dash of hot pepper sauce
    ½ c. slivered almonds
    2 c. cream sauce
    1 c. bread crumbs
    Butter

(Continued on next page)

Boil celery until tender. Place alternate layers of celery, cheese and eggs in buttered casserole. Add salt and a dash of pepper sauce. Add almonds; cover with cream sauce and bread crumbs. Dot with butter. Bake at 350 degrees for 30 minutes or until browned and bubbly. Yield: 4-6 servings.

Mrs. Harvyl Boaz, Paducah, Ky.

 ## Creamed Almond-Celery Parmesan

4 tbsp. butter
1 c. slivered almonds
3 c. diced celery
2 tbsp. flour
½ c. light cream
⅛ tsp. pepper
1 c. boiling chicken broth
3 tbsp. grated Parmesan cheese

In large skillet, melt 2 tablespoons butter until frothy; add almonds and celery. Saute, covered, for 15 to 20 minutes, stirring occasionally. Add remaining butter; melt. Blend in flour. Cook; stir for 1 minute. Add cream, pepper and boiling broth all at once, stirring to blend. Increase heat to moderately high. Cook; stir until sauce comes to a boil and thickens. Spoon into 1-quart casserole; sprinkle with Parmesan cheese. Place under broiler until cheese browns. Yield: 4 servings.

Mrs. C. B. Snider, Officers' Wives' Club, Leighton Barracks, Germany

 ## Creole Baked Celery

¼ c. chopped onion
3 tbsp. butter
2 c. cooked or canned tomatoes
½ clove of garlic, chopped
Salt to taste
1 c. pitted ripe olives, chopped
½ tsp. chili powder
4 tbsp. cornstarch
½ c. grated American cheese
3 c. sliced celery, cooked
½ c. buttered bread crumbs

Saute onion in butter until light brown; add tomatoes, garlic, salt and olives. Bring to boil and simmer for 5 minutes. Mix chili powder and cornstarch with small amount of cold water; add to hot olive mixture. Cook and stir until thick. Blend in cheese. Place celery in baking dish; add olive mixture. Sprinkle crumbs over top. Bake at 375 degrees for 30 minutes or until brown. Yield: 6 servings.

Mrs. Jane Wisdom, Home Economics Teacher, Hillsboro, Ill.

French-Fried Celery

2 stalks celery, washed and quartered
1 egg, slightly beaten
Fine bread crumbs
Salt

Cook celery in small amount of water for 10 minutes; drain well. Add 2 table-spoons water to egg. Dip celery into egg; roll in fine bread crumbs. Fry in deep fat at 375 degrees for 3 to 6 minutes or until golden brown. Drain on absorbent paper; sprinkle with salt. Serve hot. Yield: 8 servings.

Mrs. Jerry Mooney, Dallas, Tex.

 ### Fresh Celery Parmesan

3 doz. 2-in. ribs of celery
Meat or poultry stock or water
Salt to taste
2 tbsp. butter, margarine or olive oil
⅛ tsp. ground white pepper
⅓ c. grated Parmesan cheese

Wash celery in cold water before cutting; drain well. Place in a saucepan with 1 inch of boiling stock or water and salt. Cover; bring to boiling point and cook for 10 minutes or only until crisp-tender. Drain well and place in a shallow pan. Dot with butter, margarine or olive oil. Sprinkle with pepper and cheese. Broil until flecked with brown. Yield: 6 servings.

Mrs. Mary Williams, Mobile, Ala.

 ### Chard Or Swiss Chard

1 lb. chard
1 tbsp. butter
2 tbsp. olive oil
1 clove of garlic, minced (opt.)
Seasonings

Wash leaves thoroughly, removing coarse ribs. Shake off as much water as possible. Heat butter and olive oil in skillet; add garlic. Add chard. Cover immediately and cook over high heat until steam appears. Reduce heat; simmer until leaves are tender, 5 to 6 minutes in all. Season to taste. If ribs are to be cooked, skin stalks, increasing depth of cut into stalk when approaching base to remove any bitter flavor. Place in pan with boiling water. Cook, closely covered, for 12 minutes or until tender. Drain ribs well, reserving liquor. Serve with cream sauce made with half cream and half reserved liquor.

Cindra J. Hellman, Lincoln City, Ore.

Collards and Corn

Collards

Salt pork or bacon, sliced or scored
1 bunch collards
Salt

Wash pork; place in boiling water to cover. Reduce heat; simmer until tender. Wash greens thoroughly; remove stems, large veins and imperfect areas. Add to meat and water; salt to taste. Cook until tender, about 45 minutes to 1 hour and 30 minutes, depending on quality of leaves.

Marjorie Elliott, Columbia, S. C., Favorite Recipes Food Fair

Collards And Cornmeal Dumplings

⅓ lb. salt meat, washed and scored to rind
1 bunch collards
1 recipe Cornmeal Dumplings

Cook meat, covered, in iron pot with about 1 inch water until tender. Add collards; cook until tender. Chop well. Add Cornmeal Dumplings; cook 20 to 30 minutes.

CORNMEAL DUMPLINGS:
1 c. flour
2 tsp. baking powder
1 tsp. salt
1 c. cornmeal
2 eggs, slightly beaten
½ c. milk
2 tbsp. butter or oleo, melted

Sift flour, baking powder and salt together in bowl. Stir in cornmeal. Add eggs, milk and butter to dry ingredients. Stir until batter is mixed well. Drop by heaping spoonfuls onto waxed paper. Sprinkle with additional cornmeal. Drop dumplings into simmering collards. Cover tightly. Cook gently for 20 minutes. Do not lift cover while dumplings cook. Other greens may be substituted for collards.

Mrs. Margaret Betsworth, Pensacola, Fla.

Southern Collards And Patties

1 lge. bunch fresh collards
1 tbsp. plus 1 tsp. salt
1 tsp. sugar
¼ c. bacon fat
1 sm. ham hock or bacon

(Continued on next page)

Water
1 c. cornmeal
Hot collard broth

Wash and trim collard greens; cut up. Add 1 tablespoon salt, sugar, bacon fat, ham hock and water. Cook until tender, using plenty of liquid. Combine meal and remaining salt; add enough hot broth for consistency to shape patties. Shape mixture into patties; drop into boiling collard mixture, using enough liquid to cover patties. Cook until done. Yield: 4 servings.

Sandra Methvin, Home Economics Teacher, Elmer, La.

 ### Boston-Style Baked Corn

1 tsp. dry mustard
½ tsp. salt
2 tbsp. brown sugar
1 c. catsup
1 sm. onion, diced
2 12-oz. cans whole kernel corn, drained
2 to 3 slices bacon, diced

Combine mustard, salt, sugar and catsup in medium bowl; add onion and corn. Mix thoroughly. Pour mixture into greased 1½-quart casserole. Top with bacon slices. Bake in preheated 350-degree oven for 40 minutes or until bacon is cooked and corn is heated. Yield: 6-8 servings.

Cathie Miller, Home Economics Teacher, Jackson, Miss.

 ### Casserole Of Corn

6 slices lean bacon
1 c. milk
2 c. finely crumbled bread crumbs
2 17-oz. cans cream-style corn
¾ tsp. salt
½ tsp. chili powder
1 c. grated cheddar cheese
1 4-oz. can sliced mushrooms, drained

Fry bacon until lightly crisp; break into bits. Mix bacon with milk and bread crumbs; stir into corn with salt, chili powder, cheese and mushrooms. Mix well. Pour into a 2-quart casserole. Bake at 350 degrees for 50 minutes or until puffy and creamy soft. Garnish with additional crumbled bacon. Yield: 8 servings.

Mrs. Raymond Munnell, Indiana, Pa.

Caballero Casserole

    2 15-oz. cans tamales
    2 12-oz. cans whole-kernel corn with sweet peppers
    1 14½-oz. can pizza sauce

Set oven at 400 degrees. Cut each tamale into 6 slices and place half in bottom of 13 x 9-inch pan. Spread with 1 can corn; top with remaining tamale slices and corn. Pour pizza sauce over all.

CHEESE OLIVE TOPPING:
    ½ c. flour
    ¾ c. cornmeal
    1 envelope cheese sauce mix
    1 ½ tsp. baking powder
    1 tsp. salt
    1 egg, slightly beaten
    ⅔ c. milk
    ¼ c. vegetable oil
    2 tbsp. chopped ripe olives

Combine flour, cornmeal, cheese sauce mix, baking powder and salt in large mixing bowl; add remaining ingredients. Stir until dough forms; spoon over casserole. Bake at 400 degrees for 30 to 35 minutes. Yield: 6 servings.

Mrs. Nancy Foster, Riverside, Cal.

 ## Cheese-Corn Pudding

    1 sm. onion, chopped
    3 tbsp. butter
    3 tbsp. flour
    2 c. milk
    1 c. coarsely grated domestic cheese
    Salt and pepper
    1 chopped pimento
    1 tsp. sugar
    Pinch of marjoram
    2 to 2½ c. niblet corn
    2 eggs, slightly beaten
    Bread crumbs

Saute onion in butter; blend in flour. Gradually add milk and cheese; add salt and pepper to taste; add pimento, sugar and marjoram. Stir in corn and eggs. Pour into a shallow buttered casserole. Sprinkle bread crumbs over top and dot with additional butter. Bake at 350 degrees for 35 minutes. Yield: 4 servings.

Mrs. George M. Rooney, Officers' Wives' Club, Colts Neck, N. J.

Corn Bread Pudding

2 c. bread cubes
1 ½ c. milk
2 eggs, beaten
1 No. 303 can cream-style corn
Salt and pepper to taste
1 tsp. sugar

Combine all ingredients; let stand for awhile. Pour into buttered casserole. Bake at 325 degrees for 1 hour or until firm. Trim crust from bread before cutting into cubes. Yield: 4-6 servings.

Mrs. Donna J. Glass, Home Economics Teacher, Moorpark, Cal.

 ## Corn Caneloni

CORN MIXTURE:
2 med. onions, chopped
2 tbsp. butter
2 cans cream-style corn or 9 ears fresh corn, grated
Pinch of nutmeg
Sugar
Salt and pepper
2 or 3 tomatoes, peeled and chopped
Milk
1 or 2 egg yolks

Fry onions in butter; stir in corn. Add nutmeg, sugar, salt, pepper and tomatoes. Add enough milk to make mixture the consistency of cooked cereal. Add egg yolks just before removing from heat; stir well. Set aside.

FRENCH PANCAKES:
Pinch of salt
6 eggs
4 tbsp. flour
2 tbsp. water
Medium white sauce
Parmesan cheese

Combine all ingredients except sauce and cheese; beat until foamy. Fry quickly in lightly buttered pan. When pancake is cooked, place a spoonful of corn mixture in center and roll. Place in greased casserole. Cover with white sauce; sprinkle with Parmesan cheese. Bake at 350 degrees for 20 to 25 minutes. Yield: 8 servings.

Anne Dodenhoff Nelson, Falls Church, Va.

Corn Fritters

½ c. milk
1 c. corn
1 ½ c. flour
1 tsp. salt
2 tsp. baking powder
1 tbsp. shortening, melted
2 eggs, beaten

Blend milk and corn. Sift dry ingredients; add to corn. Add shortening and eggs; beat well. Fry at 375 degrees in deep fat until golden brown and crisp. Yield: 4-6 servings.

Mrs. Fred Kaufmann, Ucross, Wyo.

 ### Party Fritters

1 c. flour
1 tbsp. sugar
½ tsp. salt
1 tsp. baking powder
2 tbsp. shortening
½ c. milk
2 eggs, separated
2 c. whole kernel corn, drained
Confectioners' sugar

Sift dry ingredients; cut in shortening until mixture looks like cornmeal. Add milk and egg yolks. Fold in corn; fold in stiffly beaten egg whites. Fry until golden brown on both sides. Sprinkle with confectioners' sugar after draining.

Mildred L. Bailey, Home Economics Teacher, Middleport, Ohio

 ### Corn And Mushrooms

1 can buttered corn
1 8-oz. can mushrooms
Salt and pepper
Butter

Heat corn and mushrooms in kettle; drain. Add salt and pepper to taste; top with square of butter. Yield: 6 servings.

Mrs. James D. Holmes, Officers' Wives' Assn., St. Paul, Minn.

Corn-Noodle Casserole

2 med. onions, minced
2 lge. green peppers, minced
1 scant c. oil
1 No. 2 can cream-style corn
3 sm. cans mushrooms
1 c. sliced ripe olives
1 tsp. sugar
2 8-oz. pkg. noodles, cooked
Salt, pepper and Accent to taste
Cornflakes

Saute onions and peppers in oil; add next 8 ingredients. Mix gently; place in large casserole. Top with cornflakes. Bake in pan of hot water in 375-degree oven for 45 minutes. Yield: 12 servings.

Mrs. W. C. Meyer, Coronado, Cal.

 ## Corn Patties

2 eggs, separated
1 ½ c. whole kernel corn
2 tsp. flour
2 tsp. cream
1 tsp. soft margarine
½ tsp. salt
Dash of pepper

Combine beaten egg yolks with corn, flour, cream, margarine, salt and pepper. Fold in stiffly beaten egg whites. Drop by tablespoonfuls onto hot griddle greased with additional butter; cook until brown on each side. Yield: 6 servings.

Barbara A. McCrea, Home Economics Teacher, Superior, Mont.

 ## Corn-Pepper Saute With Peanuts

2 tbsp. margarine
2 tbsp. minced onion
1 12-oz. can whole kernel corn, drained
1 tbsp. chopped hot peppers
¼ tsp. salt
½ c. cocktail peanuts

Melt margarine in a small saucepan. Saute onion until tender. Add corn, hot peppers and salt; heat thoroughly. Toss in cocktail peanuts. Serve immediately. Yield: 4-5 servings.

Photograph for this recipe on page 119.

Corn Pancakes

2 c. canned corn
1 tsp. baking powder
Salt to taste
Flour
Bacon or ham fat
Milk (opt.)

Mix corn, baking powder and salt. Add enough flour to make batter; add milk if more liquid is needed. Bake on griddle or in skillet in bacon fat. Serve hot with butter and honey or jelly. Yield: 4 servings.

Mrs. Curt Taylor, Boone, Iowa, Favorite Recipes Food Fair

 ## Corn Pie

1 ¼ c. fine cracker crumbs
½ c. butter or margarine, melted
¼ c. finely chopped green pepper
1 tbsp. finely chopped onion
2 tbsp. butter or margarine
2 tbsp. flour
1 c. milk
1 can whole kernel corn
½ tsp. salt
1 tsp. sugar
2 eggs, slightly beaten

Blend cracker crumbs and melted butter; press evenly on bottom and sides of baking dish, reserving ¼ cup crumbs for top. Cook pepper and onion in butter until onion is transparent. Blend in flour and cook until bubbly; add milk and cook, stirring constantly, until thickened. Add corn, salt, sugar and eggs; mix well and pour into crust. Top with remaining crumbs and bake at 400 degrees until firm, about 25 minutes. Yield: 6 servings.

Mrs. Robert E. McNair, Wife of Governor of South Carolina, Columbia

Corn Souffle

¼ c. butter
¼ c. flour
⅔ c. milk
1 c. cooked corn, sieved
3 eggs, separated
½ tsp. salt
¼ c. grated cheese
1 tbsp. chopped green pepper

Melt butter; add flour and mix to a smooth paste. Add milk and corn; cook until thick, stirring occasionally. Remove from heat; add beaten egg yolks, salt, cheese and green pepper. Fold in stiffly-beaten egg whites; pour into greased baking dish. Bake at 350 degrees for 30 minutes. Serve hot. Yield: 6 servings.

Dicia Blevins, Calhoun, Tenn.

 ## Corn In Sour Cream

3 strips bacon
1 can whole kernel corn
½ tsp. salt
1 c. sour cream

Fry bacon crisp; pour off all except 2 tablespoons fat. Add corn, salt and sour cream; crumble bacon on top. Heat; serve. Yield: 4 servings.

Ann C. Farmer, Home Economics Teacher, Owensboro, Ky.

 ## Corn-Tamale Pie

2 lge. tamales, cut
1 garlic clove, minced
1 med. onion, finely chopped
¼ green pepper, finely chopped
¼ lb. sharp cheddar cheese, cubed
1 5-oz. jar stuffed green or black olives
1 15½-oz. can cream-style corn
1 tsp. tamale spice (opt.)
1 can tomato sauce

Combine tamales, garlic, onion, green pepper and cheese. Add some liquid from stuffed olives or ½ teaspoonful salt if black olives are used. Combine with other ingredients; place in a 9 x 13-inch baking dish. Bake at 300 to 325 degrees for 1 hour. Diced leftover roast or ½ pound cooked ground meat may be added. Yield: 6 servings.

Mrs. Clyde A. Beard, Officers' Wives' Club, Army Depot, Sacramento, Cal.

Corn And Sweet Green Peppers

  2 lge. or 3 sm. green peppers, finely chopped
¼ lb. butter or margarine
  2 12-oz. cans whole kernel corn
¼ tsp. salt or to taste
  Dash of pepper

Saute green peppers in butter for about 15 minutes; add corn and seasonings. Cover and simmer for 20 minutes or until tender. Three cups fresh corn may be substituted for canned corn. Yield: 8-10 servings.

Sister Mary Coletta, C.S.C., Home Economics Teacher, Riverside, N. J.

 ## Cream-Style Corn

1 doz. ears corn
1 stick oleo
2 tsp. salt
4 tbsp. sugar
1 c. milk

Barely clip tips off corn. Scrape milk completely out. Melt oleo in cast iron cooker. Pour corn into cooker with an equal amount of water. Add salt and sugar. Cook very slowly for 30 minutes, stirring often. Add milk and cook until thick.

Mrs. John J. McKeithen, Wife of Governor of Louisiana, Baton Rouge

 ## Crispy Corn Pie

  1 No. 303 can whole kernel corn
  1 12-oz. can beef or pork luncheon meat, cubed
  4 eggs, beaten
  2 tsp. prepared mustard
  2 tbsp. flour
¾ c. milk
  1 c. grated sharp cheddar cheese
  1 tsp. Worcestershire sauce
24 crackers, crushed
  6 tbsp. melted butter
  1 tsp. parsley flakes
½ tsp. thyme
  6 strips pimento

Add corn and luncheon meat to eggs beaten with mustard, flour and milk. Stir in cheese and Worcestershire sauce. Pour into deep 8-inch round baking dish.

(Continued on next page)

Combine crackers with butter and herbs, blending well. Sprinkle over corn mixture. Bake at 325 degrees for 50 to 60 minutes or until knife inserted in center comes out clean. Garnish with pimento. Yield: 6-8 servings.

Mrs. Eleanor Hatch, Home Economics Teacher, Joseph, Ore.

 ## Barbecued Corn

    8 ears corn
    ¼ c. barbecue sauce
    1 stick butter

Remove husks from corn. Blend barbecue sauce and butter; spread mixture generously over each ear. Wrap each ear of corn securely in heavy-duty aluminum foil. Bake over hot coals for 15 to 20 minutes, turning several times. Yield: 8 servings.

Mrs. Jo-Ann T. Charping, Greenville, S. C.

 ## Corn On The Cob

    Fresh ears of young corn

Remove husks and silk from ears of corn; drop into boiling water. Cook for 3 to 12 minutes, depending on variety and freshness of corn until tender. Serve with salt, pepper and butter.

Barbara Hallman, Montgomery, Ala.

 ## Herbed Roasting Ears

    ½ c. soft butter or margarine
    1 tsp. dried rosemary
    ½ tsp. dried marjoram
    6 ears sweet corn, husked and silked
    1 head romaine

Blend butter with herbs; spread on corn. Wrap each ear of corn in 2 to 3 leaves of romaine. Place in shallow baking dish; cover tightly with foil. Bake at 450 degrees for 20 to 25 minutes. Yield: 6 servings.

Betty Phillips, Dayton, Ohio

Peanut Butter-Grilled Corn

Corn on the cob
Peanut butter
Bacon slices

Husk and clean corn. Spread ears lightly with peanut butter; wrap in slice of bacon. Fasten with toothpick. Cook over hot coals for 10 minutes or until done, turning.

Ruth Schmitz, Home Economics Teacher, Luxemburg, Wis.

 ## Tabasco-Butter Sauce For Corn On The Cob

Corn on the cob
⅛ tsp. Tabasco sauce
½ c. melted butter

Remove husks and silks from corn. Drop into boiling salted water. Cover; boil for 5 to 6 minutes. Add Tabasco sauce to melted butter; use to brush on hot corn. Sauce may be varied with any one of the following: 1 teaspoon fresh snipped chives, ⅛ teaspoon curry powder, ⅛ teaspoon thyme or ⅛ teaspoon garlic salt.

Photograph for this recipe below.

Texas Corn

Corn on the cob
¼ c. margarine, melted
1 tbsp. chili powder
1 tsp. paprika
Salt and pepper

Wash and silk corn. Combine margarine, chili powder and paprika. Brush each ear of corn with mixture; sprinkle with salt and pepper. Wrap each ear in foil and seal. Place on cookie sheet. Bake at 350 degrees for 1 hour. Corn may be cooked on grill. Yield: 4-6 servings.

Mrs. Bill Garrison, Lancaster, Tex.

 ## Roasted Corn, California Style

Unhusked corn
Sweet butter
Salt
Pepper

Cover unhusked corn in cold water; soak for 1 hour or longer. Roast over hot coals for 40 minutes, turning as necessary. Inside husk will be moist and hot when outside is brown and dry. Remove husks; season with butter, salt and pepper.

Mrs. Bea Marsh, Sunnydale, Cal.

 ## Fiesta Casserole

2 c. canned cream-style corn
2 c. canned whole-kernel corn
¼ c. chopped ripe olives
¼ c. chopped canned pimento
¼ c. chopped onion
¼ c. chopped green pepper
2 beaten eggs
1 tsp. salt
Dash of pepper
Dash of Tabasco sauce
1 c. cracker crumbs

Combine corn, olives, pimento, onion and green pepper with eggs and seasonings; add cracker crumbs. Mix thoroughly. Pour into 2-quart baking dish. Bake in 350-degree oven for 30 to 35 minutes. Yield: 6-8 servings.

Mrs. W. H. McLean, Jr., Officers' Wives' Club, Fort Holabird, Md.

Fresh Corn In Cream

4 tbsp. butter or margarine
4 c. fresh corn, cut off cob
1 ½ tsp. salt
½ tsp. sugar
⅓ c. heavy cream
¼ tsp. pepper
Pimento
Fresh parsley

Melt butter in skillet or saucepan. Add corn, salt and sugar. Cover and cook for 10 minutes. Add cream and cook for 5 minutes longer. Stir in pepper. Cut small stars from pimento, using cookie cutter; arrange over top as desired. Sprinkle with parsley. Yield: 6-8 servings.

Mrs. Louise T. Card, Soddy, Tenn.

 ## Grandma's Corn Bake

2 cans cream-style corn
2 eggs
¼ c. cornmeal
1 clove of garlic, chopped
6 tbsp. Wesson oil
2 c. grated cheese
1 c. green chilies, chopped

Combine corn, eggs, cornmeal, garlic and oil; place layer of mixture in casserole. Sprinkle cheese and chilies over entire surface. Cover with remaining corn mixture. Bake at 350 degrees for 35 minutes or until set and lightly browned.

Retha R. Wengert, Bluewater, N. M.

 ## Hominy Casserole

1 can cream of mushroom soup
¼ tsp. red pepper
½ tsp. pepper
1 tsp. celery seed
1 tsp. Worcestershire sauce
1 tsp. salt
2 No. 3 cans hominy, drained
1 c. buttered bread crumbs or packaged croutons
½ c. slivered almonds

Combine soup and seasonings; heat thoroughly. Pour over hominy in casserole. Cover with bread crumbs and almonds. Bake at 300 degrees for 15 minutes. Yield: 12 servings.

Mrs. Leon Potts, Home Economics Teacher, Kossuth, Miss.

Hominy Luncheon Dish

¾ lb. ground meat
¼ c. minced onion
½ tsp. paprika
1 tsp. chili powder
½ tsp. sugar
1 tsp. salt
1 tbsp. yellow cornmeal
2 c. canned tomatoes
1 No. 2½ can hominy, well drained
1 c. grated cheddar cheese

Brown meat and onion; add seasonings and cornmeal. Add tomatoes; simmer for a few minutes. Pour mixture over hominy in casserole; top with grated cheese. Bake at 350 degrees until cheese is melted and slightly browned. Yield: 6-8 servings.

Mrs. Kathryn Coughlin, Bell, Cal.

 ### Kentucky-Fried Corn

6 strips bacon, cut into 1-in. cubes
4 ears medium white corn, scraped
2 sm. cucumbers, thinly sliced
1 med. onion, minced or in rings
1 lge. egg
Salt and pepper
Sugar to taste

Lightly fry bacon. Mix corn, cucumbers, onion, egg, salt, pepper and sugar thoroughly. Pour into bacon grease; fry slowly for 30 to 45 minutes. Pimento strips or green pepper slices may be used, if desired. Yield: 4-6 servings.

Mrs. Mildred Roselle, Pleasure Ridge Park, Ky., Favorite Recipes Food Fair

 ### Quick Scalloped Corn

Saltine crackers, broken in sm. pieces
2 1-lb. cans cream-style corn
Butter
1 c. milk

Butter 2½-quart casserole; place layer of crackers in bottom. Add layer of corn and a few dots of butter. Repeat layers until corn is used. Top with crumbled crackers and butter; add milk, enough to moisten. Bake in 375-degree oven for 30 minutes or until golden brown on top. Yield: 8-10 servings.

Mrs. Robert J. Coulter, Officers' Wives' Club, Minneapolis, Minn.

Scalloped Corn With Chipped Beef

½ sm. onion, chopped
3 tbsp. chopped green pepper
2 tbsp. butter
2 ½ c. cooked corn
½ c. milk
½ c. dry bread crumbs
1 sm. jar chipped beef, cut into sm. pieces

Brown onion and green pepper in butter. Combine corn, milk and crumbs; add to onion and pepper. Mix well. Stir in beef; pour into casserole. Bake at 350 degrees until lightly browned. Yield: 6 servings.

Margaret H. Peden, Home Economics Teacher, Raeford, N. C.

 ## Scalloped Corn With Oatmeal

1 can cream-style corn
¼ c. cream or milk
¼ c. quick cooking oats

Blend corn, cream and oats in casserole. Bake at 350 degrees for 30 to 45 minutes. Yield: 6 servings.

Mrs. Hugh Songer, Three Oaks, Mich.

 ## Scalloped Corn And Oysters

1 can cream-style corn
1 can oysters, drained
2 tbsp. butter
6 crackers, crushed
Salt to taste
Oyster liquor

Alternate layers of corn, oysters, butter and crackers in buttered casserole, using 1/3 of each; sprinkle with salt. Repeat layers twice. Pour half of oyster liquor over casserole.

TOPPING:

½ c. butter, melted
¾ c. cracker crumbs

Combine ingredients; spread over casserole. Bake at 350 degrees for 30 minutes or until browned. Yield: 6 servings.

Mrs. Dorothy Miller, Gering, Neb.

Cucumbers and
Eggplant

Baked Cucumbers

    ¼ c. chopped onion
    ¼ c. chopped parsley
    ½ c. margarine
    1 ½ c. bread crumbs
    2 c. tomato pulp
    1 tsp. salt
    ⅛ tsp. pepper
    4 lge. cucumbers, pared and sliced

Saute onion and parsley in margarine; add remaining ingredients except cucumbers. Cook for 5 minutes longer. Layer sliced cucumber and part of onion mixture in greased casserole; add small amount hot water. Top with remaining onion mixture. Bake at 350 degrees for 1 hour or until cucumbers are tender and top has browned. Yield 4-6 servings.

Mrs. Dorothy W. Hayes, Home Economics Teacher, Roanoke, Va.

 ## Braised Cucumbers

    ¼ c. cold water
    1 cube chicken bouillon
    1 tbsp. butter
    2 lge. cucumbers, peeled

Boil water, bouillon cube and butter until cube is completely dissolved. Cut cucumbers into 1-inch slices; add to bouillon. Simmer, covered, for 10 minutes or until cucumbers are tender. Drain; serve immediately. Yield: 2-3 servings.

Dorothy Brevoort, Former Supervisor, Home Economics Education,
Beach Haven, N. J.

 ## Creamed Cucumbers

    2 lge. cucumbers
    3 tbsp. butter
    3 tbsp. flour
    1 ½ c. milk
    ¼ c. chopped parsley
    Paprika

Split cucumbers lengthwise; remove seeds. Dice cucumbers; boil in small amount of salted water for 15 minutes. Melt butter; stir in flour. Add milk gradually; cook, stirring constantly, until thick. Combine drained cucumbers and sauce. Add parsley. Sprinkle paprika over top. Yield: 4 servings.

Mrs. D. Claude Roberts, Cambria, Wis.

Breaded Cucumbers

2 lge. cucumbers
1 egg, beaten
2 tbsp. cream
1 tsp. thyme
Cracker meal
Dash of salt
Dash of pepper
Butter or margarine

Cut cucumbers into 8 pieces each, dip into mixture of egg, cream and thyme. Roll in cracker meal; season. Fry in butter or dot with butter and broil. Yield: 4-6 servings.

Mary Ida Farmer, Home Economics Teacher, Midvale, Ohio

 ## Cucumbers In Casserole

2 lge. cucumbers, peeled
½ c. flour
1 tsp. salt
¼ tsp. pepper
¼ c. melted butter
1 ½ tsp. Worcestershire sauce
½ c. sour cream
½ c. crushed potato chips

Peel and cut cucumbers into halves lengthwise, then crosswise. Roll each piece of cucumber in combined flour, salt and pepper. Place in baking dish and pour melted butter over top. Add Worcestershire sauce, a drop at a time, over each piece of cucumber. Spread sour cream over all. Sprinkle with crushed potato chips. Bake at 350 degrees for 25 minutes until golden or fork tender. Yield: 4 servings.

Lucille Swartz, Dillon, Mont.

 ## Fresh Green Cucumbers

2 to 3 med. cucumbers, sliced ¼-in. thick
1 sm. onion, sliced
Salt and pepper to taste
½ to 1 c. vinegar

Place cucumbers and onion in bowl; sprinkle with salt and pepper. Pour vinegar over cucumber and onion slices. Serve immediately. Yield: 5-6 servings.

Mrs. Sam Whitley, Home Economics Teacher, Laneville, Tex.

Cucumber Dumplings

½ c. butter, melted
1 tbsp. flour
2 c. water
Salt and pepper to taste
Prepared biscuit mix
1 ½ c. sliced cucumber
1 c. cream
½ c. vinegar

Blend butter with flour; bring to a boil. Add water, salt and pepper; boil to make broth. Make dumplings according to directions on biscuit mix package; drop into broth. Cook until tender. Add cucumber slices, scattering over dumplings. Add cream; stir gently. Stir in vinegar. Bring to a boil; serve immediately. Yield: 6 servings.

Mrs. A. J. Althoff, Vincennes, Ind., Favorite Recipes Food Fair

 ## Cucumbers Au Gratin

3 tbsp. flour
3 tbsp. butter
1 ¼ c. milk
1 beef bouillon cube
Dash of pepper
¼ tsp. onion juice
1 c. grated sharp cheese
⅓ c. fine dry crumbs
1 ½ tbsp. melted butter
2 med. cucumbers, pared and sliced ⅛-in. thick

Blend flour with butter. Add milk gradually and stir constantly over direct heat until sauce thickens. Stir in bouillon cube, pepper and onion juice; remove from heat. Add cheese; stir until melted. Stir bread crumbs in melted butter to coat well. Layer cucumbers and hot sauce alternately in a 6-cup buttered casserole. Top with buttered crumbs; cover and bake at 325 degrees about 30 minutes. Remove cover and continue baking 10 minutes longer or until cucumbers are just tender and surface is browned. Serve piping hot. Yield: 5 servings.

Mrs. M. J. Dutschke, Louisville, Ky.

Batter-Fried Cucumbers

½ c. flour
Salt
1 egg, beaten
8 tbsp. chicken stock
12 sm. young cucumbers
Hot fat

Mix flour with a pinch of salt, egg and chicken stock to make a batter. Cut off tips of cucumbers and scrub thoroughly. Dip into batter and drop a few at a time in a kettle of 360-degree fat; fry until crisp and golden. Serve hot with sour cream and a sprinkle of fresh dill or parsley. Yield: 4 servings.

Sara Thomas, Dayton Ohio

 ## Fried Cucumbers

Cucumbers
Flour
Salt and pepper

Select firm green cucumbers. Peel and slice cucumbers ¼-inch thick. Flour well; season with salt and pepper. Fry until golden brown on each side.

Freda Holley, Orange, N. J.

 ## Scalloped Cucumbers

4 med. cucumbers, peeled and diced
1 ½ c. milk
1 tsp. salt
½ tsp. pepper
1 c. dry bread crumbs
4 tbsp. butter

Combine cucumbers, milk, salt and pepper thoroughly; fold in bread crumbs. Pour into greased 1-quart casserole; dot with butter. Bake at 350 degrees for 30 minutes. Yield: 4-6 servings.

Mrs. Stenson Terry, Home Economics Teacher, San Perlita, Tex.

Stuffed Baked Cucumbers

Cucumbers
Chopped tomato
Salt and pepper
Chopped celery
Chopped onion
Buttered bread crumbs

Cut cucumbers into halves lengthwise; scoop out centers. Chop centers and mix with all remaining ingredients except crumbs. Fill cucumber shells; cover with buttered crumbs. Bake at 375 degrees for 45 minutes to 1 hour.

Mrs. James Roberts, Raleigh, N. C., Favorite Recipes Food Fair

Dandelions Sauteed With Garlic

2 lb. fresh dandelion greens
4 tbsp. olive oil
2 cloves chopped garlic
Salt and pepper to taste

Clean and wash dandelion greens thoroughly; cut in half. Heat oil and garlic in saucepan. Add dandelions, salt and pepper. Cook about 12 minutes or until tender. Add water if too dry. Serve very hot. Yield: 4 servings.

Mary DeLorme, Home Economics Teacher, St. Johnsville, N. Y.

Scalloped Dandelions

2 tbsp. bacon drippings
2 tbsp. flour
¾ c. water
2 c. milk
¾ tsp. salt
1 tbsp. vinegar
2 tsp. sugar
1 c. dandelions, firmly packed
¼ c. minced onion
2 hard-boiled eggs, sliced

Combine drippings and flour in skillet; stir until slightly brown. Add water, milk, salt, vinegar and sugar. Cut up young tender dandelions; mix with onion. Add to sauce; do not cook after adding. Add eggs last. Do not use dandelions with flowers. Yield: 6 servings.

Sovilla Anna Yoder, Galena, Md.

Dandelion Blossoms

¼ c. milk
2 tbsp. powdered milk
1 tbsp. baking powder
1 egg
½ c. flour
Pinch of salt
16 lge. fresh dandelion blossoms
Fat

Mix all ingredients except dandelion blossoms and fat. Wash blossoms lightly; drain. Do not allow to wilt. Dip blossoms into batter; fry in deep fat until golden. Yield: 4 servings.

Elizabeth Skaggs, Cerro Gordo, Ill.

 ### Eggplant Dressing

⅓ lb. ground meat
¼ c. chopped onion
1 stalk celery, chopped
Salt and pepper to taste
1 med. eggplant, cooked and mashed
⅓ c. cooked rice
Toasted bread crumbs

Brown meat, onion and celery in skillet, stirring frequently. Salt and pepper to taste; combine with eggplant and rice in greased baking dish. Top with crumbs. Bake at 350 degrees for 15 minutes. Yield: 2-4 servings.

Mrs. Edna C. Hathorn, Home Economics Teacher, Crowley, La.

 ### Eggplant Casserole Deluxe

1 eggplant
1 onion, diced
½ stick butter
4 slices bread
3 tbsp. vinegar
1 can mushroom soup

Peel, cube and boil eggplant in salted water a few minutes until tender. Saute chopped onion in butter. Dice bread in ½-inch squares. Add bread to eggplant. Add vinegar and mushroom soup to skillet with butter and onion. Simmer to blend 1 to 2 minutes. Put all ingredients into casserole. Bake at 350 to 375 degrees 15 to 20 minutes or until bubbling. Yield: 6 servings.

Mrs. Ralph Frame, Virginia Beach, Va.

Eggplant-Bacon Casserole

1 lge. eggplant
1 lge. onion, chopped
½ c. grated sharp cheddar cheese
½ tsp. Worcestershire sauce
½ tsp. garlic salt
10 crushed soda crackers
½ c. finely chopped green pepper
½ c. light cream
Salt and pepper to taste
4 to 6 slices bacon
1 tbsp. butter

Peel and cut eggplant into 1-inch cubes. Add onion; cook in a small amount of boiling salted water until tender. Drain. Add cheese, Worcestershire sauce, garlic salt, cracker crumbs, green pepper and cream. Season with salt and pepper. Saute chopped bacon slices in a small skillet. Spoon eggplant mixture into a greased casserole; top with bacon and butter. Bake at 350 degrees for 15 to 20 minutes. Yield: 4-6 servings.

Mrs. Mel H. Patton, Officers' Wives' Club, Westover AFB, Mass.

 ### Eggplant Christina

1 lge. eggplant
⅓ c. olive oil
4 tomatoes
¾ c. bread crumbs
½ c. chopped onions
Salt and pepper
Parmesan cheese

Cook eggplant whole and unpeeled in boiling salted water. When cool, cut into cubes; pour olive oil over them. Cut tomatoes into cubes, reserving the juice. Combine crumbs, onions, salt and pepper. Arrange eggplant and tomatoes in casserole. Cover with a layer of crumb mixture, then cheese. Continue these layers ending with cheese. Pour oil and tomato liquid over casserole. Bake at 350 degrees for 30 to 45 minutes. Yield: 6 servings.

Mrs. F. R. Roberts, Hon. Pres., Naval Officers' Wives' Club, Philippine Islands

 ### Eggplant-Lamb Dish

3 ½ c. cubed lamb
½ c. olive oil
1 c. minced onions
½ c. minced green pepper

(Continued on next page)

1 3-lb. eggplant, pared and diced
1 c. raw rice, cooked
1 No. 2 can tomatoes
1 c. dry red wine
1 c. grated Parmesan cheese
⅛ tsp. cinnamon
2 tsp. salt
½ tsp. garlic salt

Brown lamb in oil. Add onions and green pepper; saute until tender. Cover; simmer until done. Cook eggplant, covered, in 1 cup salted water for 5 minutes; drain. Combine all ingredients in baking dish, reserving ½ cup cheese. Refrigerate for 6 to 8 hours. Top with remaining cheese. Bake at 350 degrees for 1 hour. Yield: 8 servings.

Mrs. F. W. Beekman, Merced, Cal., Favorite Recipes Food Fair

 ### Eggplant Clambake

2 med. eggplants
2 7½-oz cans clams, minced
2 c. cracker crumbs
2 tbsp. melted butter
3 eggs, beaten
1 tsp. salt
¼ tsp. pepper
Milk

Peel eggplants; cut in 1-inch slices. Let stand in cold water for 20 minutes; cook for 15 minutes or until soft. Drain; mash. Add clams and liquid, 1½ cups cracker crumbs, butter, eggs, salt and pepper. Add milk to desired consistency. Place in 2-quart casserole; cover with remaining crumbs. Dot with butter. Bake at 325 degrees for 40 minutes or until brown. Yield: 8-10 servings.

Marian Chisholm, Home Economics Teacher, Marblehead, Mass.

 ### Eggplant With Sour Cream

Eggplant
French dressing
1 clove of garlic
Sour cream with minced chives

Cut eggplant into ¾-inch slices; marinate in French dressing with garlic for 1 hour. Drain. Bake at 450 degrees for 20 minutes. Remove from oven and spread with sour cream. Return to oven and with door open, heat for 5 minutes. Serve warm.

Mrs. Dorothy A. Foster, Home Economics Teacher, Mathews, Va.

Eggplant Parmigiana

> 1 14½-oz. can tomatoes, Italian style
> ½ can tomato paste
> ½ tsp. oregano
> ½ tsp. basil
> 1 tsp. sugar
> ¼ tsp. salt
> 3 cloves garlic
> 2 tbsp. olive oil
> Dash of red pepper, if desired
> 2 med. eggplants
> 3 beaten eggs
> Olive oil
> 1 c. diced shredded mozzarella cheese
> 3 to 4 tbsp. grated Parmesan cheese

Combine first 9 ingredients in saucepan; cook for 20 to 30 minutes over medium heat. Slice eggplant lengthwise ¼-inch thick. Sprinkle with salt; place in colander with heavy plate on top for 15 to 20 minutes and let drain. Wipe off excess salt. Dip eggplant in eggs; brown slices on both sides in hot olive oil. Drain on absorbent paper. Alternate layers of eggplant, tomato sauce, mozzarella and Parmesan cheese in casserole. Bake in 375-degree oven for 20 minutes or until bubbling hot. This dish also makes a delicious sandwich on French bread. Yield: 6 servings.

Mrs. Renatos Prati, Officers' Wives' Club, Corpus Christi, Tex.

 ## Elegant Eggplant

> 1 lge. eggplant, peeled and cubed
> 2 tbsp. butter
> ½ c. hot water
> 2 tbsp. beef stock base
> 1 ½ tsp. Italian seasoning
> 1 c. sour cream
> 1 tbsp. instant toasted onions
> ½ tsp. salt
> ¼ tsp. pepper
> ¼ c. bread crumbs
> 2 tbsp. grated Parmesan cheese

Saute eggplant in butter for 5 minutes or until slightly tender. Combine water, beef stock base and Italian seasoning; pour over eggplant. Simmer, covered, until eggplant is tender and liquid has evaporated. Spoon into flat baking dish. Combine sour cream, onions, salt and pepper; pour over eggplant. Sprinkle with crumbs and cheese. Bake at 350 degrees for 20 to 25 minutes or until hot and brown. Yield: 6 servings.

Mrs. Helen Lipscomb, Home Economics Teacher, St. Petersburg, Fla.

Oven-Crisp Eggplant

½ c. fine cracker crumbs
½ tsp. paprika
¼ tsp. rubbed oregano
½ tsp. salt
1 egg
1 tbsp. water
2 1-lb. eggplants
¼ c. butter or margarine, melted

Mix cracker crumbs with paprika, oregano and salt; set aside. Beat egg with water. Peel eggplants and cut each lengthwise into 6 segments. Dip eggplant pieces into beaten egg and then into crumb mixture. Let stand for at least 30 minutes. Place, peeled-side down, in shallow baking pan. Drizzle with melted butter. Bake at 400 degrees for 20 minutes or until crisp.

Mrs. Charles Yeargin, Ellerton, Ga., Favorite Recipes Food Fair

Breaded Eggplant

1 sm. eggplant
American cheese
½ tsp. salt
¼ tsp. pepper
2 eggs, beaten
½ c. milk
2 c. crushed cracker crumbs

Peel eggplant; cut into ⅛-inch slices. Place 1 slice cheese between 2 slices eggplant. Combine salt, pepper, eggs and milk; beat. Dip eggplant and cheese into crumbs, egg mixture and again in crumbs. Brown in oil. May be served with mushroom or tomato sauce.

Cetha G. Kuske, Home Economics Teacher, Britton, S. D.

French-Fried Eggplant

1 med. eggplant, sliced 1 in. thick
Salt
2 eggs, beaten
½ to ¾ c. flour

Salt eggplant slices well; let stand for 5 or 10 minutes. Blend eggs and flour into a heavy batter; add 1 teaspoon salt. Cut eggplant into 1-inch strips; coat thoroughly with batter. Brown in deep fat; drain. May be frozen and reheated in oven. Yield: 6 servings.

Mrs. Virginia B. Firth, Home Economics Teacher, Smyrna, Del.

Fried Eggplant In Casserole

1 egg, beaten
½ c. milk
½ c. prepared biscuit mix
1 tsp. salt
½ tsp. pepper
1 ½ lb. eggplant, peeled and thinly sliced
Oil
3 hard-cooked eggs, sliced
½ lb. Cheddar Cheese
1 can tomato soup
6 stuffed or ripe olives

Blend egg and milk with biscuit mix, salt and pepper. Dip eggplant into batter; brown in oil heated to 350 degrees. Layer in greased casserole with eggs and cheese; cover with soup. Bake at 350 degrees until cheese is bubbly. Garnish with olives; serve hot. Yield: 6 servings.

Mrs. Edna Mae Martz, Home Economics Teacher, Upland, Cal.

 ## Eggplant Fritters

1 eggplant
1 c. cracker crumbs
2 eggs
Salt
Pepper

Peel eggplant. Slice and soak in salt water ½ hour; drain. Boil in fresh water until tender; drain and mash. Add crumbs, eggs, salt and pepper to taste. Drop by teaspoonfuls into hot fat and fry until brown. Yield: 6 servings.

Mrs. Edward T. Breathitt, Wife of Governor of Kentucky, Frankfort

 ## Texas Fritters

2 eggs
1 c. buttermilk
1 tsp. salt
½ tsp. soda
2 tsp. baking powder
1 ½ c. flour
4 tbsp. corn meal
1 med. eggplant, peeled and cubed

(Continued on next page)

Blend all ingredients except eggplant to form batter. Fold eggplant into batter; drop into frying pan in pancake sized portions. Turn once; drain on paper toweling. Serve hot. Yield: 8-10 servings.

Mrs. Mallie Venn Steger, Home Economics Teacher, Montgomery, Tex.

 ## Stuffed Eggplant

>   2 medium-sized eggplants
>   ¼ c. oil
>   1 ½ lb. ground beef
>   ¼ c. chopped onion
>   ¼ c. chopped green pepper (opt.)
>   ¼ clove garlic, chopped
>   1 ¼ tsp. Tabasco
>   1 tsp. salt
>   1 ½ c. cooked rice
>   1 tsp. lemon juice

Slice eggplants in half; scoop out and chop some of the pulp. Heat oil in skillet. Add eggplant pieces, beef, onion, pepper, garlic, Tabasco and salt; saute until eggplant is lightly browned. Toss with rice to blend all ingredients. Stuff eggplant halves with filling. Place stuffed halves, skin down, in greased baking dish. Bake in 375 degree oven for 30 minutes. Remove from oven, sprinkle with lemon juice and serve. Yield: 4 servings.

Photograph for this recipe below.

Simple Stuffed Eggplant

> *1 eggplant*
> *Salt and pepper*
> *2 tbsp. butter*
> *½ c. water*
> *2 c. crumbs*

Halve eggplant lengthwise; scoop out center pulp, leaving ½-inch rind. Cover shells with cold water. Finely chop pulp; season with salt, pepper and butter. Saute for 10 minutes, stirring constantly; add water and 1 cup crumbs. Drain shells; sprinkle inside with salt and pepper. Fill with mixture; top with remaining crumbs. Place halves in baking dish 1/3 full of hot water. Bake at 350 to 375 degrees for 30 minutes. Serve hot.

> *Marjorie Joan Mattie, Home Economics Teacher, Boscobel, Wis.*

 ### Scalloped Eggplant

> *1 eggplant, cubed*
> *2 med. onions, sliced*
> *Salt and pepper to taste*
> *1 egg, beaten*
> *1 ½ c. grated sharp cheese*
> *1 c. cornflakes or crumbs*

Cook eggplant and onions with seasonings in small amount of water until tender; drain. Mash. Combine with remaining ingredients in casserole. Bake at 350 degrees for about 1 hour. Yield: 6 servings.

> *Mrs. Don Jackson, Home Economics Teacher, Bad Axe, Mich.*

 ### Stewed Eggplant

> *1 lge. eggplant, peeled*
> *⅓ c. water*
> *1 sm. onion, chopped*
> *2 tbsp. chopped sweet pepper*
> *2 tbsp. cooking oil*
> *½ c. chopped ham*
> *1 c. cleaned shrimp*
> *Salt and pepper to taste*

Cut eggplant into 1½-inch chunks; place in saucepan with water. Cover and cook over medium heat. Saute onion and sweet pepper in oil; add to eggplant. Cook for 15 minutes or until eggplant chunks begin to soften. Add ham, shrimp, salt and pepper. Cook for 15 minutes or until shrimp is done. Yield: 3 servings.

> *Mrs. William J. van Santen, Metairie, La.*

Baked Eggplant Palermo

2 lge. firm eggplants
2 4½-oz. cans artichoke hearts, drained
2 4-oz. cans mushrooms
½ tsp. garlic powder
½ c. butter
1 ½ tsp. oregano
1 tsp. sweet basil
2 tbsp. minced onion
1 tsp. salt
2 sm. green peppers, chopped
2 sm. fresh tomatoes, chopped
1 c. Parmesan cheese

Cut eggplants in half lengthwise; cut ½-inch in from edges all around each half. Scoop out centers of eggplant to form shells. Dice center portion of eggplant; reserve. Parboil eggplant shells in boiling salted water until tender but shape retained. Drain and place in baking dish cut-side up. Cut artichoke hearts into halves. Saute mushrooms and garlic in butter; add eggplant and saute until golden. Stir in oregano, basil, onion, salt, peppers, tomatoes and artichokes; simmer for 3 to 4 minutes until heated through. Stir in ¾ cup Parmesan cheese. Spoon into eggplant shells; top with remaining cheese. Bake at 350 degrees for 20 minutes or until cheese is brown. Yield: 4 servings.

Sandra Hartman, Home Economics Teacher, Riverside, Cal.

 Mexicano Stuffed Eggplant

1 2-lb. eggplant
6 tbsp. butter or margarine
¼ tsp. finely minced garlic
½ c. diced celery
½ c. coarsely shredded carrots
¼ c. chopped onion
½ tsp. salt
¾ tsp. chili powder
½ tsp. oregano leaves
⅓ c. sliced stuffed olives
1 c. toasted croutons
½ c. chopped tomatoes

Cut a lengthwise slice from one side of eggplant. Parboil eggplant 25 minutes. Cool. Using a grapefruit knife, scoop out pulp to within ¼-inch of the skin and cut into cubes. Melt butter or margarine in a medium skillet. Add garlic, celery, carrots and onion; cook until onion is transparent. Blend in seasonings and remaining ingredients. Spoon mixture into eggplant shell. Place in a buttered baking dish and bake at 400 degrees for 20 minutes. Yield: 6 servings.

Photograph for this recipe on page 135.

Tomato And Eggplant Casserole

    1 1½-lb. eggplant
  ½ tsp. salt
  2 tbsp. butter or margarine
  2 eggs, beaten
  ¼ tsp. ground black pepper
  1 tsp. finely chopped onion
  ½ tsp. oregano leaves
  ½ c. crumbled saltines
  6 med. tomato slices
  ½ c. grated American cheese

Peel eggplant; cut into ¼-inch thick slices. Place in a saucepan with ½-inch boiling water and salt. Cover and bring to a boil; cook 10 minutes or until tender. Drain and mash. Blend in butter, egg, pepper, onion, oregano and saltines. Turn into a buttered 1-quart casserole; cover surface with tomato slices. Sprinkle with additional salt, pepper and grated cheese. Bake in preheated 375-degree oven for 25 minutes or until lightly browned on top. Yield: 6 servings.

Mrs. Dorothy G. Brown, Hackensack, N. J., Favorite Recipes Food Fair

Braised Endive (Escarole)

  1 head escarole
  3 tbsp. olive oil
  Salt and pepper

Separate leaves, discarding tough outer ones; wash thoroughly. Heat oil, add escarole and cook over low heat until tender, 10 to 20 minutes. Season and serve immediately. A garlic clove may be cooked 1 to 2 minutes in the hot oil and discarded before escarole is added, if desired.

Frances Watts, Montgomery, Ala.

Fiddlehead Tidbits

  1 can fiddleheads (fern sprouts)
  Bread
  Soft sweet butter
  Salt
  Chopped onion
  Mayonnaise

Drain fiddleheads well. Cut bread into small rounds; spread with butter. Place one fiddlehead on each round; add a dash of salt and small amount of chopped onion. Top with a small cone of mayonnaise. Yield: 4-6 servings.

Mrs. Robert W. Higbie, Jr., Manchester, Vt.

Lettuce and Okra

Kale

1 2-lb. piece bacon or cottage ham
2 to 3 lb. kale greens

Simmer meat in water to cover for 2 hours. Wash greens thoroughly, re-moving all grit and waste. Cut out bruised areas and tough stems. Add greens to simmering meat and continue cooking for 35 minutes or until barely tender. Very young greens may be washed carefully and added to a skillet in which 1 tablespoon butter and 2 tablespoons olive oil have been heated. Cover im-mediately, cooking over high heat until steam appears. Reduce heat and simmer until greens are tender, 5 to 6 minutes in all.

Mrs. E. H. Walker, Portland, Ore.

 ## Kale Loaf

¼ c. celery leaves
3 tbsp. butter
1 tbsp. flour
¼ c. vegetable stock
1 ½ c. cooked chopped kale
1 egg, beaten
¼ c. cooked diced carrots
1 ½ c. cooked rice
1 tbsp. salt
2 slices bacon

Saute celery leaves in butter; add flour, vegetable stock, kale, egg, carrots, rice and salt. Shape into loaf; lay bacon across top. Bake at 400 degrees for 30 minutes. Yield: 8 servings.

Mrs. Ava Bush, Home Economics Teacher, Grapeland, Tex.

 ## Modified Southern-Style Kale

2 c. cooked kale
1 tsp. butter or margarine
Salt and pepper to taste
3 slices bacon
3 hard-boiled eggs
Paprika

Season cooked kale with butter, salt and pepper. Fry bacon until crisp; pour off fat. Crumble bacon over kale in a serving bowl. Garnish with eggs cut in halves or quarters. Sprinkle with paprika. Serve with corn bread. Yield: 4 servings.

Mrs. R. C. Hagee, Hiwasse, Ark., Favorite Recipes Food Fair

Braised Lettuce

    3 tbsp. butter
    1 lge. solid head lettuce
    ½ tsp. salt

Melt butter in a 10-inch heavy skillet. Trim lettuce without removing core; cut into five neat wedges. Cook with cut surfaces down in butter until delicately browned, turning gently so as not to spoil shape of wedges. Sprinkle lettuce with salt; cover pan and turn heat to very low. Simmer for 15 minutes or until tender. Remove carefully to a hot serving platter, using a pancake turner or broad spatula. Serve immediately with juices. Yield: 5 servings.

Mrs. Lena Bayer, Oblong, Ill.

 ## Dutch Lettuce

    1 head lettuce
    2 hard-cooked eggs, chopped
    2 sm. onions, chopped
    ½ c. diced bacon, cooked
    ⅓ c. vinegar
    1 tbsp. sugar
    1 tsp. salt
    Bacon drippings
    4 potatoes, boiled

Let lettuce leaves stand in cold water for 1 hour or more; drain well. Alternate layers of lettuce, bacon, eggs, onions and mashed potatoes in dish. Add vinegar, sugar and salt to bacon fat; heat to boiling point. Pour over layers; serve hot. Yield: 8 servings.

Mrs. Elizabeth Stek, Pella, Iowa

 ## Leaf Lettuce

    ¼ c. vinegar
    ¼ c. water
    1 tsp. salt
    ¼ tsp. pepper
    2 tbsp. sugar
    ¼ c. chopped green onions
    1 qt. garden lettuce
    3 hard-boiled eggs

Mix vinegar, water, salt, pepper and sugar. Pour over well-mixed onion and lettuce; toss lightly. Place on oblong dish. Slice eggs lengthwise; arrange petal-fashion at each end of dish.

Carrie Courson, Hickory Flat, Miss.

Lettuce Scramble

    1 *med. hard head of lettuce*
    1 *tbsp. onion juice*
    ¼ *c. water*
    2 *tbsp. cooking oil*
    4 *lge. or 6 sm. eggs*
    ½ *tsp. salt*

Discard bruised outside leaves of lettuce. Cut remainder in bite-sized chunks. Place in large skillet with onion juice, water and oil. Cover; cook about 10 minutes. Uncover; add eggs and salt. When egg whites begin to set, scramble. Place on platter; garnish with crisp bacon or crisp garlic croutons.

Mrs. Barry Jones, Sebring, Fla.

 ## Sauteed Lettuce

    2 *tbsp. drippings*
    Chopped onion
    ¼ *c. vinegar*
    1 *qt. leaf lettuce or other greens, washed and cut*
    Salt to taste
    Pepper to taste

Melt drippings in heavy pan; add onion. Cook until soft and yellow. Stir in vinegar; add greens. Cover; heat until greens are wilted. Season with salt and pepper. Serve hot. Yield: 4 servings.

Joyce A. Hearn, Atlanta, Ga.

 ## Stuffed Mirlitons

    4 *lge. mirlitons*
    ½ *c. diced onion*
    ¼ *c. chopped celery*
    3 *tbsp. cooking oil*
    1 *c. cooked chopped shrimp*
    ½ *c. Italian bread crumbs*
    1 ½ *tsp. seasoned salt*
    ⅛ *tsp. cayenne pepper*
    ½ *c. plain bread crumbs*

Halve mirlitons lengthwise; remove seed in center. Boil until tender; scoop out meat, reserving shell for stuffing. Mash. Saute onion and celery in oil in 9 or 10-inch skillet until tender; add mashed mirlitons, shrimp, Italian bread crumbs, seasoned salt and cayenne pepper. Fill shells; cover with plain crumbs. Bake at 350 degrees for 30 minutes or until brown. Yield: 8 servings.

Mrs. Margaret A. McBride, Home Economics Teacher, Livingston, La.

Favorite Stuffed Mirlitons (Vegetable Pears)

> 3 vegetable pears
> 1 lb. ground beef
> 2 med. onions, chopped
> 2 cloves garlic, finely chopped
> 2 tbsp. cooking oil
> 2 c. water
> 3 to 4 slices toast
> 2 eggs, beaten

Boil pears whole until tender. Cut in half lengthwise and remove flat seed. Scoop out center, leaving shell. Fry meat, onions and garlic in oil on low heat until light brown. Stir often. Add water; cook about 10 minutes. Remove from heat. Soften toast in small amount of water; break into pieces. Add vegetable pear pulp and toast to meat mixture; stir in eggs. Fill pear shells. Cover with additional toast crumbs. Place in flat pan with small amount of water covering bottom. Bake in 350-degree oven until lightly browned, 15 to 20 minutes. Serve hot or cold. Yield: 6 servings.

Mrs. Dorothy Greenlow Marquart, Franklinton, La.

 Baked Mushrooms With Bleu Cheese

> 2 lb. lge. fresh mushrooms, cleaned
> ½ c. crumbled bleu cheese
> 1 c. dry bread crumbs
> ⅛ tsp. minced chives
> 2 tbsp. butter
> ¼ c. sherry
> ½ c. heavy cream

Remove stems from mushrooms; place a piece of cheese in each cavity. Saute crumbs and chives in butter until coated; add remaining cheese. Place a layer of crumbs in buttered casserole; add mushrooms, cavity-side up. Sprinkle with sherry and remaining crumbs; cover with cream. Bake, covered, at 375 degrees for 25 minutes. Yield: 6 servings.

Vivian I. Reagan, Pittsburgh, Pa.

 Creamed Mushrooms

> 1 lb. fresh mushrooms
> 2 tbsp. butter
> ½ tsp. salt
> Pepper to taste
> 1 tbsp. flour
> 1 c. milk

(Continued on next page)

Marinated Mushrooms

Wash mushrooms under cold running water; drain. Do not soak. Slice; do not peel. Place in butter in heavy saucepan with seasonings. Cover; place over medium low heat. Do not add water. After steam forms and butter melts, turn heat to medium; cook for 5 minutes. Blend flour and milk; add to mushrooms. Cook until thickened, stirring constantly. Serve at once. Yield: 4 servings.

Mrs. Nannie C. Edwards, Home Economics Teacher, Oxford, Pa.

 ## Athenian Mushrooms

½ *lb. sm. mushrooms*
½ *c. lemon juice*
⅔ *c. olive oil*
½ *tsp. Tabasco*
1 *tsp. salt*
1 *tsp. crushed tarragon leaves*

Wipe mushrooms with a damp cloth; trim off bottom of stem and cut in half lengthwise. Combine remaining ingredients and pour over mushrooms. Marinate in refrigerator overnight. Drain before serving. Yield: 2 cups.

Photograph for this recipe below.

Club Mushroom Casserole

 1 lb. fresh mushrooms, sliced
 ½ c. butter
 ⅓ c. flour
 3 c. milk
 2 tsp. Worcestershire sauce
 1 ½ tsp. salt
 ¼ tsp. pepper
 4 hard-cooked eggs, sliced
 ½ c. diced green pepper
 1 4-oz. can pimento, diced
 2 c. shredded process cheese

Saute mushrooms in butter; push aside. Blend in flour; add milk gradually. Cook until thickened, stirring constantly. Fold in remaining ingredients except cheese; place in greased casserole. Bake at 350 degrees for 30 minutes or until brown. Top with cheese. May be served with hot rice or toast. Yield: 6-8 servings.

Jean Capling, Warren, Mich., Favorite Recipes Food Fair

 ### Hot And Tangy Mushrooms

 3 lb. mushrooms
 8 cloves garlic, diced
 ¼ c. olive oil
 1 tbsp. oregano
 1 tsp. crushed red hot pepper
 3 oz. cooking wine

Boil mushrooms for 5 minutes; strain. Brown garlic in oil with oregano. Add mushrooms, hot pepper and wine. Simmer for 1 hour or until mushrooms are completely cooked. Yield: 6-8 servings.

Rose Lazzaro, Clifton, N. J.

 ### Mushroom Casserole Deluxe

 ⅓ c. butter
 1 tbsp. chopped parsley
 1 tbsp. chopped green onion
 1 tbsp. prepared mustard
 1 tsp. salt
 ⅛ tsp. each cayenne, nutmeg
 1 ½ tbsp. flour
 1 lb. fresh mushrooms, sliced
 1 c. heavy cream

(Continued on next page)

Combine first eight ingredients and blend. Place layer of mushrooms in 1½-quart greased casserole. Dot with half of butter mixture; top with remaining mushrooms and butter mixture. Pour cream over mixture. Bake, uncovered, 55 minutes at 375 degrees. Yield: 4 servings.

Mrs. Jerry Gunn, Little Rock, Ark.

 ## Italian Baked Mushrooms

1 ½ lb. mushrooms
3 tbsp. chopped parsley
1 sliver garlic, chopped
1 tsp. oregano
¾ c. coarse bread crumbs
¼ c. grated Parmesan cheese
1 tsp. salt
½ tsp. pepper
¼ c. olive oil
¼ c. bouillon or hot water

Wash mushrooms; peel caps. Slice into oiled baking dish. Sprinkle with parsley, garlic, oregano, one-half of crumbs and one-half of cheese. Season with one-half of salt and pepper. Pour oil over all. Add remaining crumbs, cheese and seasonings. Bake at 350 degrees for 25 minutes or until mushrooms are tender and tops are browned. If mixture seems dry after 15 minutes of baking, add small amount of bouillon or hot water. Serve hot.

Mrs. Ann Leak, Knob Noster, Mo.

 ## Mushroom Paprikash

1 lb. fresh mushrooms
2 tbsp. butter or margarine
1 tsp. fresh lemon juice
2 tbsp. instant minced onion
1 tsp. flour
½ tsp. salt
1 tsp. paprika
Dash of ground red pepper
¼ c. sour cream

Wash and slice mushroom caps and stems. Saute in butter or margarine and lemon juice for 5 to 6 minutes or until mushrooms are tender. Combine instant minced onion, flour, salt, paprika and red pepper; add to mushrooms. Stir and cook for 1 minute. Add sour cream; heat but do not boil. Yield: 6 servings.

Photograph for this recipe on page 151.

Mushroom-Cheese Pie

    1 ½ lb. mushrooms, cleaned and sliced
    1 c. thinly sliced onions
    4 tbsp. butter or margarine
    ⅓ c. flour
    1 8-oz. carton sm. curd, cream-style cottage cheese
    ¼ c. chopped parsley
    ¼ c. dry sherry
    2 tsp. salt
    ⅛ tsp. pepper
    2 c. sifted flour
    ⅔ c. shortening
    4 to 5 tbsp. ice water

Saute mushrooms and onions in butter until tender. Add flour; mix well. Add cottage cheese, parsley, sherry, 1 teaspoon salt and pepper; mix thoroughly. Set aside. Preheat oven to 425 degrees. Sift flour and remaining salt together. Cut into shortening. Add ice water gradually, stirring with fork. Roll out half of dough to form 12-inch circle. Line 9-inch pie plate. Roll out remaining dough for strips. Pour filling into pastry-lined pie plate. Arrange lattice strips on top. Flute edge. Bake on bottom rack of oven 40 to 45 minutes until browned. Cool 5 minutes. Yield: 6-8 servings.

Mrs. Harold Yates, Birmingham, Ala.

 ## Mushrooms Baked In Cream

    1 lb. mushrooms with 1 to 2-inch caps
    2 tsp. minced onion
    ⅓ c. butter or margarine
    ¼ tsp. pepper
    ¼ tsp. monosodium glutamate
    ¼ tsp. salt
    ¼ tsp. paprika
    ⅓ c. toasted bread crumbs
    3 slices bacon, crumbled
    ½ tsp. Worcestershire sauce
    1 c. cream

Wash mushrooms; remove stems from caps. Reserve caps. Finely chop stems. Cook stems and onion in butter over low heat until tender. Blend pepper, monosodium glutamate, salt, paprika and bread crumbs with onion and mushroom stems. Arrange mushroom caps in a shallow greased casserole. Fill with bread crumb mixture; top with bacon. Mix Worcestershire sauce and cream; pour around mushrooms. Bake at 375 degrees for 15 minutes.

Mrs. Nancy Carter, Fayetteville, Ark.

Mushroom Patties

2 c. cooked mushrooms
1 egg, beaten
½ tsp. salt
Pinch of pepper
1 sm. onion, grated or onion salt
Cracker meal
Shortening

Put mushrooms through grinder; add egg, seasonings and onion. Mix well; shape into patties. Dip patties into cracker meal; fry in shortening until golden brown. Yield: 4 servings.

Mrs. Bernice Bartosz, Stevens Point, Wis.

 ## Mushrooms A La King

3 stalks celery, finely chopped
1 lb. mushrooms
3 tbsp. butter
2 tbsp. flour
2 c. milk
Salt and pepper to taste
Paprika
3 hard-cooked eggs, thinly sliced
¼ c. sliced ripe olives
2 tbsp. sherry
Dry toast

Cook celery until tender in small amount of water; drain. Slice mushrooms; saute in butter. Stir in flour and milk; cook until thickened, stirring constantly. Season with salt, pepper and paprika; add celery, eggs and olives. Heat thoroughly; add sherry just before serving over toast. Yield: 4 servings.

Mrs. Eugenia Holderith, Home Economics Teacher, Franklin, N. J.

 ## Mushrooms Magnifique

12 lge. mushrooms, cleaned
Salt
2 tbsp. softened butter
½ c. finely chopped pecans
1 ½ tbsp. chopped parsley
½ clove garlic, minced
⅛ tsp. thyme
½ c. heavy cream

(Continued on next page)

Remove stems from mushrooms; finely chop enough stems to measure ¼ cup. Salt caps lightly. Blend butter with stems, pecans, parsley, garlic, ¼ teaspoon salt and thyme; stuff mushroom caps. Place caps in shallow baking pan; cover with cream. Bake at 350 degrees for 20 minutes, basting occasionally with cream. Yield: 6 servings.

Grace W. Beaulieu, Dracut, Mass.

 ## Mushrooms With Sour Cream And Bacon

> 2 lb. fresh mushrooms
> ½ stick butter
> 1 med. or 3 green onions
> 1 tbsp. flour
> 1 c. sour cream
> 1 tsp. salt
> ½ tsp. pepper
> 1 tbsp. minced parsley
> 3 strips bacon, cooked and crumbled

Wash mushrooms; break off stems. Slice caps into quarters if large. Saute in butter for a few minutes; add onions. Simmer, covered, for 15 minutes. Sprinkle flour over mushrooms, stirring lightly. Add sour cream, salt and pepper; heat. Do not boil. Sprinkle with parsley and crumbled bacon; serve at once. Yield: 6 servings.

Mrs. Elizabeth L. Jeffries, Home Economics Teacher, Johnson City, Tenn.

 ## Pilau Rice With Mushrooms

> 1 lb. mushrooms
> 1 med. onion, chopped
> 1 green pepper, chopped
> Few sprigs of parsley, chopped
> 1 c. canned tomatoes
> 1 tbsp. tomato paste
> ¼ c. salad oil
> 1 tbsp. butter or margarine
> Salt and pepper to taste
> 1 c. uncooked rice
> 1 c. water

Slice mushrooms into skillet; add onion, green pepper, parsley, tomatoes, tomato paste, oil, butter, salt and pepper. Cook over low heat for 10 minutes; add rice and water. Continue cooking for 10 minutes or until rice is tender; add hot water as needed. Watch carefully to keep from burning. Rice cooks more quickly if covered for part of cooking period. Yield: 4 servings.

Mrs. Fannie M. Plunkett, Jasper, Ark., Favorite Recipes Food Fair

Stuffed Mushrooms Deardon

> *Lge. fresh mushrooms*
> *Shelled and uncooked fresh or frozen shrimp*
> *Salt and pepper to taste*
> *Lemon juice*
> *Butter*

Place mushrooms, cap-side down, in glass baking dish. Stuff each mushroom with a whole shrimp. Sprinkle with seasonings, several drops of lemon juice and a dot of butter. Bake, uncovered, at 350 degrees for 20 minutes. Serve at once.

Mrs. Russell W. Deardon, New York, N. Y.

 ## Mustard Greens, Southern-Style

> *Bacon*
> *Washed mustard greens*
> *Salt and pepper to taste*

In heavy saucepan, fry several slices of bacon; fry greens in bacon fat until clear green. Add water; season to taste. Cook until tender.

Gail Epperson, Home Economics Teacher, Slidell, La.

 ## Boiled Okra

> *1 qt. tender okra with ½-inch stems*
> *Cold water*
> *1 tbsp. cider vinegar*
> *1 tbsp. bacon drippings or butter*
> *Salt*

Place okra in pan with cold water to just cover. Before water is hot, add vinegar. Do not stir okra while cooking. Boil until fork tender. Add drippings and salt to taste. Lift okra from pan carefully to serve.

Mrs. Pearl Burbank, El Dorado, Ark.

Fried Okra

6 to 8 sm. pods of okra
½ to 1 c. cornmeal or cracker crumbs
¼ c. bacon fat

Wash okra; cut off ends and slice to desired thickness. Toss okra with meal until coated. Fry in fat over medium heat for 25 minutes or until brown and crisp. Yield: 4 servings.

Mrs. Ruth Ragsdale, Home Economics Teacher, Richmond, Va.

 ### Okra Croquettes

½ c. shortening
1 egg
1 tbsp. flour
3 tbsp. cornmeal
½ tsp. salt
¼ tsp. pepper
2 c. finely chopped okra
¼ c. finely chopped onion
Fat

Heat shortening in 10-inch skillet. Beat egg; add flour, cornmeal, salt and pepper. Mix well. Stir in okra and onion. Drop from tablespoon into hot fat. Cook for 3 minutes or until golden brown, turning once and flattening with spatula. Yield: 4 servings.

Vera Faye Elledge, Home Economics Teacher, Mabank, Tex.

 ### Okra Patties

1 ½ c. okra
2 tbsp. buttermilk
3 tbsp. flour
2 tbsp. cornmeal
1 tsp. salt
⅛ tsp. pepper
1 egg, beaten
Cooking oil

Parboil okra. Drain; mash. Add buttermilk, flour, cornmeal, salt, pepper and egg. Drop by tablespoonfuls into heated oil; fry until brown. Yield: 8 servings.

Jane Johnston, Decatur, Ga.

Fritter-Fried Okra

1 c. flour
3 tsp. baking powder
½ tsp. salt
2 eggs, well beaten
⅓ c. milk
5 c. thinly sliced okra

Sift flour with baking powder and salt; add mixture of eggs and milk. Stir until smooth. Add okra and stir. Spoon into deep fat and fry. Yield: 6-8 servings.

Mrs. Patsy Cooper, Goree, Tex.

 ## Glamorized Okra

4 c. young tender okra, small pods preferred
2 tbsp. fat
1 tsp. (or more) salt
2 c. whole or skim milk

Remove stem ends from okra; wash and drain. Heat large skillet and melt fat. Spread okra evenly over bottom of skillet. Sprinkle with salt. Pour in milk. Simmer, uncovered, without stirring, over low heat until liquids have evaporated, leaving only the curd. Allow akra to brown slightly; turn carefully with spatula and brown on other side. Serve immediately with curd.

Mrs. Jewel Walker, Laurel, Miss.

 ## Okra Casserole

3 scallions or 2 leeks
2 tbsp. oil
1 clove garlic
1 lb. fresh or frozen okra
½ c. vinegar
2 c. water
2 c. stewed tomatoes
½ lb. sharp cheese, cut into ½-in. cubes

Cut scallions into small pieces; brown in oil with garlic until transluscent. Remove from heat and place in casserole. Add okra which has been soaked for 30 minutes in vinegar and water. Add stewed tomatoes. Mix; add cheese, submerging it. Bake at 350 degrees until thickened. Yield: 4 servings.

Chris Masaitis, Home Economics Teacher, Philadelphia, N. Y.

Okra Etouffe

   3 c. sliced okra
   ¼ c. cooking oil
   1 c. canned tomatoes
   1 med. onion, chopped
   1 med. green pepper, chopped
   Salt and pepper to taste
   Red pepper to taste
   ¼ c. cracker or potato chip crumbs (opt.)

Spread okra in greased casserole; cover with oil, tomatoes, onion, green pepper and seasonings. Cover loosely with foil. Bake at 400 degrees for 1 hour or until tender, stirring occasionally. Uncover; top with crumbs. Lightly brown. Yield: 3-4 servings.

Mrs. Guy Mitchell, Chataignier, La.

 Okra Pilau

   3 to 4 bacon slices, chopped
   2 c. okra, cut in rings
   1 ½ c. water
   1 c. long grain rice
   Salt and pepper to taste

Fry bacon till almost crisp in saucepan. Add okra; fry until tender. Add water, rice, salt and pepper. Cover; turn heat very low. Cook, stirring several times, for 1 hour to 1 hour and 30 minutes or until rice is dry. Yield: 4-6 servings.

Mrs. N. G. Sires, Jr., Isle of Palms, S. C.

 Scalloped Okra

   1 sm. onion, chopped
   ¼ tsp. salt
   ½ tsp. pepper
   2 tbsp. butter
   2 c. cooked or canned okra
   ½ c. grated cheese
   1 egg, beaten
   ¾ c. bread crumbs
   Buttered crumbs

(Continued on next page)

Combine chopped onion, salt, pepper and butter with okra. Layer with cheese, egg and bread crumbs in casserole. Top with buttered crumbs. Bake at 350 degrees for 30 minutes. Yield: 4 servings.

Mrs. Louise E. Keller, Home Economics Teacher, Clayton, Ga.

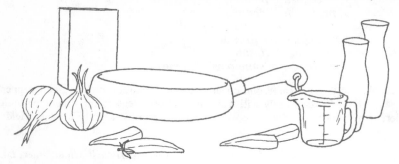

 ### Skillet Okra

> 1 c. sliced okra
> Fat
> 1 lb. ground beef
> Salt and pepper to taste
> 1 sm. onion, chopped or ½ tsp. onion powder
> 1 c. water
> 1 c. uncooked rice

Cook okra in a small amount of fat until done. Cook ground beef until slightly brown. Add okra, seasonings, onion and water; simmer until 30 minutes before serving. Add rice and enough water to steam rice. Cook until rice is tender. Yield: 4-6 servings.

Mrs. Lenis Landry, Jennings, La., Favorite Recipes Food Fair

Spanish Okra

> ¼ lb. tender okra, cut ¼-in. thick
> 2 lge. fresh tomatoes, diced
> 3 tbsp. onion, chopped
> 4 tbsp. butter
> 1 tsp. salt
> 2 tbsp. chili powder
> 3 drops Tabasco sauce
> 1 c. water

Mix okra, tomatoes, onion and salt. Saute in butter for 5 minutes. Add chili powder, Tabasco sauce and water; mix well. Cover and simmer over low heat until vegetables are tender and mixture has thickened. Yield: 6-8 servings.

Mrs. Georgia Short, Home Economics Teacher, Dell City, Tex.

Onions and Parsnips

Creamed Onions

12 onions
Butter
Salt and pepper to taste
White sauce

Boil onions in salted water. Add lump of butter, salt and pepper to liquid used to boil onions; add enough white sauce to thicken and cover onions. Serve hot. Yield: 8 servings.

Mrs. Hilda Miller, Clarks Hill, Ind., Favorite Recipes Food Fair

Creamed Onions With Dried Beef

2 lb. small onions
4 tbsp. butter
2 tbsp. flour
½ tsp. salt
2 c. milk
¼ lb. sliced dried beef, cut into pieces
1 c. bread crumbs

Cook onions in boiling, salted water for 10 minutes or until tender. Drain and place in 1½-quart baking dish. Melt 2 tablespoons butter in saucepan; stir in flour and salt. Add milk gradually. Cook and stir until sauce thickens. Cover beef with boiling water; drain immediately. Add dried beef to sauce; pour over onions. Melt remaining butter; toss with bread crumbs. Sprinkle over top. Bake at 425 degrees for 12 to 15 minutes or until brown. Yield: 6 servings.

Clara Deiter, Home Economics Teacher, Dodge City, Kan.

Creamed Onions With Mushrooms

1 c. milk
2 tbsp. butter
2 tbsp. flour
¼ tsp. salt
⅛ tsp. paprika
2 tbsp. chopped parsley
10 med. onions, cooked
½ c. mushrooms
½ tsp. grated lemon rind and juice

Blend milk, butter and flour; cook until thickened, stirring constantly. Add seasonings. Combine with onions, mushrooms, lemon juice and rind; serve hot. Yield: 6 servings.

Mrs. Anna Benda Whitescarver, Flemington, W. Va.

Creamed Onions And Peanuts

    1 tbsp. butter
    1 ½ tbsp. flour
    ½ tsp. salt
    Pepper to taste
    1 ½ c. milk
    2 c. cooked sliced onions
    ½ c. chopped salted peanuts
    ¼ c. dry bread crumbs
    1 tbsp. melted butter

Melt butter; blend in flour and seasonings. Add milk; cook over low heat, stirring constantly, until thickened. Alternate layers of onions, peanuts and sauce in baking dish. Combine bread crumbs and melted butter; sprinkle over layers. Bake at 400 degrees for 20 minutes. Yield: 4 servings.

Mrs. Josephine Kelm, Morgan, Minn.

 ## Creamed Onions With Pecans And Cheese

    18 to 20 sm. onions
    ½ c. water
    1 ½ tsp. salt
    4 tbsp. butter or margarine, melted
    4 tbsp. flour
    1 ½ c. milk
    1 c. shredded cheese
    ½ c. chopped pecans

Place onions, water and 1 teaspoon salt in 1½-quart saucepan. Cover and bring to a boil over high heat; simmer for 15 minutes or until tender. Drain. Blend butter and flour in saucepan; stir in milk and remaining salt. Cook over medium heat until thick. Add cheese and stir until melted. Add onions and heat through. Place in serving dish; sprinkle with pecans. Yield: 4-6 servings.

Mrs. Juanita Patton, Home Economics Teacher, Inola, Okla.

 ## Batter-Fried Onion Rings

    2 to 3 lge. onions
    1 c. sifted flour
    ½ tsp. baking powder
    ½ tsp. salt
    1 tsp. sugar
    ¾ c. milk
    1 egg
    2 tbsp. melted fat

(Continued on next page)

Peel onions and slice into ¼-inch slices; separate into rings. Sift flour with baking powder, salt and sugar. Combine milk, egg and fat; add to dry ingredients all at once and beat until smooth. Dip onion rings in batter and fry until golden brown in deep fat at 375 degrees. Drain on absorbent paper; sprinkle with salt. Yield: 4 servings.

Mrs. Ouida Capps, Arlington, Tex.

 ## Beefy Onion Rings

> 1 beef bouillon cube
> ½ c. boiling water
> 1 c. pancake mix
> 1 egg
> Cooking oil
> 1 onion, cut into rings

Dissolve bouillon in boiling water; cool. Beat pancake mix with egg, 1 tablespoon cooking oil and bouillon. Dip onion rings in batter; drain for a moment. Fry in 1 inch of oil heated to 350 degrees for 3 minutes, turning once.

Mrs. Wanda Winters, New York, N. Y.

 ## French-Fried Onions

> 6 med. Bermuda onions, thinly sliced
> Milk
> 2 eggs whites, stiffly beaten or 2 whole eggs, beaten
> Salt and pepper to taste
> Flour
> Fat

Separate onion slices into rings. Cover rings with milk; let stand for 30 minutes. Drain thoroughly. Dip into egg whites and seasoned flour. Fry in preheated 375-degree fat until light brown. Yield: 8 servings.

Bert Hearn, Columbia, La.

 ## Glazed Green Onions

> 12 to 15 lge. green onions, peeled
> 5 tbsp. butter
> 2 tbsp. brown sugar

Cook onions in enough water to cover until tender; drain off most of liquid. Add butter and sugar. Cook over low heat for 15 minutes or until golden brown, stirring occasionally. Yield: 6 servings.

Mrs. Martha Boyle, Home Economics Teacher, Owensboro, Ky.

Helen's Glazed Onions

    2 lb. onions
    ½ c. melted butter
    6 tbsp. sugar

Boil onions, uncovered, in large amount of boiling salted water for 20 to 40 minutes or until tender. Heat butter; add onions. Sprinkle with sugar. Simmer for 10 minutes or until onions are glazed, turning and basting frequently; sprinkle with paprika. Yield: 6 servings.

Mrs. Helen Redmon, Greensboro, N. C.

 ### Piquant Glazed Onions

    8 sm. white onions, peeled
    2 tbsp. butter
    1 tbsp. brown sugar
    1 tsp. lemon juice
    ¼ tsp. salt
    ⅛ tsp. ground ginger

Parboil onions in boiling, salted water in small saucepan for 15 minutes; drain. Melt butter in small frying pan; stir in brown sugar, lemon juice, salt and ginger. Add onions; cook over low heat, turning often, for 15 minutes or until lightly glazed. Yield: 4 servings.

Mrs. Mildred Miller, Home Economics Teacher, Chico, Cal.

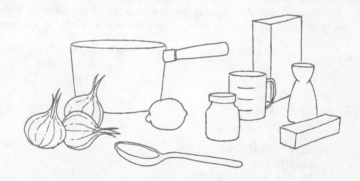

 ### Herbed Creamed Onions And Peas

    1 lb. small white onions
    1 tsp. salt
    1 lb. fresh peas, shelled
    Herbed cream sauce

(Continued on next page)

Pour boiling water over onions; let stand for 5 minutes and then peel. Place in saucepan with salt and 1 inch boiling water. Bring to boiling point, uncovered; boil for 5 minutes. Cover and cook for 15 minutes or until tender. Add peas 5 minutes before cooking time is up. Drain; mix lightly with herbed cream sauce. Serve at once.

HERBED CREAM SAUCE:

> 2 tbsp. butter or margarine
> 2 tbsp. flour
> 1 c. milk
> ½ tsp. salt
> ¼ tsp. ground basil
> ⅛ tsp. ground pepper

Melt butter or margarine; blend in flour. Remove from heat and stir in milk. Cook over medium heat until thickened, stirring constantly. Stir in seasonings; pour over vegetables. Yield: 4 servings.

Mrs. Betty Carnathan, Huntsville, Ala.

 ## Leeks Au Gratin

> 2 bunches leeks
> Boiling water
> 1 tsp. salt
> Pepper
> ½ c. grated cheese

Wash and trim leeks. Cook in boiling, salted water to cover for 15 minutes or until tender; drain. Arrange in buttered baking dish; sprinkle with pepper and cheese. Heat under broiler until cheese is melted. Yield: 8 servings.

Verlys M. Malme, Erskine, Minn.

 ## Leek Pie

CRUST:

> 2 c. sifted flour
> ½ tsp. salt
> ⅛ tsp. white pepper
> ½ c. bite-sized shredded wheat biscuits, crushed to ¼ cup
> ⅔ c. shortening
> 3 to 4 tbsp. cold water

Preheat oven to 450 degrees. Sift together flour, salt and white pepper; mix in cereal crumbs. Blend shortening into dry ingredients until particles resemble coarse cornmeal. Add a small amount of water at a time. Toss lightly until mixture begins to form pieces about size of a quarter. Place on waxed paper;

(Continued on next page)

knead dough into smooth ball. Be certain cracked edges are pressed together. Allow dough to rest 10 minutes. Roll out on floured board 1 inch larger than 9-inch pie plate; form pie shell. Bake for 20 to 25 minutes or until light brown.

FILLING:

 3 to 4 young leeks
 3 tbsp. plus 1 tsp. butter or margarine
 2 c. cottage cheese
 2 tbsp. cornstarch
 ½ tsp. salt
 ⅛ tsp. white pepper
 2 eggs
 ½ c. bite-sized shredded wheat biscuits, crushed to ¼ cup

Trim leeks within 2 inches of white portion; wash. Cut into ¼-inch pieces for about 3 cups. Saute leeks in 3 tablespoons butter until tender. Mix cottage cheese, cornstarch, salt and pepper; heat and stir until smooth. Beat eggs until thick and lemon colored. Add a small portion of cheese to eggs; mix well. Add eggs to cheese; cook until thickened, stirring constantly. Mix leeks with sauce; pour into pie shell. Toss crumbs with remaining margarine; sprinkle over pie. Return to 450 degree oven for 10 minutes to crisp crumbs. Three or four bunches green onions may be substituted for leeks. Yield: One 9-inch pie.

Mrs. Roberta Robins, Baltimore, Md.

 Mediterranean Onions

 1 lb. sm. white onions
 ¼ c. olive oil or salad oil
 1 ½ tbsp. wine vinegar
 1 ½ tsp. salt
 1 ½ tsp. salad herbs
 ¼ c. raisins

Stick toothpick crosswise through center of each onion. Cover onions with boiling water; add olive oil, vinegar, salt, herbs and raisins. Bring to a boil; simmer for 20 to 25 minutes or until tender but firm. Yield: 4-6 servings.

Mrs. Jacob Cozad, Home Economics Teacher, Indianola, Iowa

 Mountain Ramp

 2 pecks fresh ramps
 ½ gal. water
 2 tbsp. salt
 1 c. vegetable oil
 ½ lb. bacon
 1 doz. eggs

(Continued on next page)

Peel ramps; parboil in salted water until tender. Drain; place in skillet with hot oil and bacon. Turn often until completely fried. Beat eggs for 1 minute; add to ramps. Cook for a few minutes until done; add salt to taste. Serve topped with bacon. Yield: 10 servings.

Mrs. Pearl W. Criss, Webester Springs, W. Va.

 ## Onion Rings Au Gratin

2 lb. white onions, sliced
8 slices buttered toast
¼ lb. American cheese, grated
2 eggs
2 c. milk
½ tsp. salt
⅛ tsp. pepper
1 tbsp. butter
Paprika (opt.)

Cook onions in boiling, salted water until tender. Place half of toast in baking dish; arrange layer of onions and layer of cheese over toast. Repeat layers. Beat eggs slightly; add milk, salt and pepper. Pour over layers. Dot with butter; sprinkle with paprika if desired. Bake at 350 degrees for 40 minutes or until done. Yield: 8 servings.

Mrs. Ron Havenstein, Iowa City, Iowa

 ## Onion Shortcake

1 c. flour, sifted
2 tsp. baking powder
¼ tsp. salt
5 tbsp. margarine
1 ½ c. milk
6 to 8 med. onions, sliced
1 c. grated American cheese
1 egg, beaten
½ tsp. mustard

Sift flour with baking powder and salt; cut in 3 tablespoons margarine. Add ½ cup milk and stir 15 times with fork. Spread dough in greased 2-quart casserole. Saute onions in remaining margarine until lightly browned; place in casserole. Add cheese. Combine egg, remaining milk and mustard; pour over cheese. Bake at 450 degrees for 30 minutes; do not overbake. Yield: 6 servings.

Mrs. Sarah M. Gleason, East Walpole, Mass., Favorite Recipes Food Fair

Onions In Bacon

6 med. white onions
6 cubes butter or margarine
6 slices bacon
1 c. brown sugar

Skin onions and score tops; place cube of butter on top of each. Wrap each onion in slice of bacon; fasten with wooden toothpick. Arrange onions in center of double 14-inch square of aluminum foil. Top with brown sugar; close foil. Cook on grill on low heat setting for 30 minutes or until onions are tender. Yield: 6 servings.

Mrs. June Nesbitt, Home Economics Teacher, Springfield, Ill.

 Onions With Bleu Cheese

4 c. small pearl onions
4 tbsp. butter
4 tbsp. flour
2 c. milk
½ c. crumbled bleu cheese
1 tsp. salt
⅛ tsp. pepper

Lightly brown onions in butter; sprinkle flour over onions and blend. Stir in milk, cheese, salt and pepper. Cook and stir for 3 to 5 minutes. Place in serving dish and sprinkle with parsley. Yield: 6 servings.

Barbara Gaylor, Lansing, Mich.

 Onions Viennese

2 ½ lb. med. Bermuda onions, quartered
2 tbsp. sherry wine
½ c. chopped celery
¼ c. chopped pimento
1 c. mushrooms
½ tsp. marjoram
Pinch of thyme
1 tbsp. Alamo Zestful Seasoning

Cover onions with cold water and bring to a boil. Boil for 15 minutes; drain well. Add remaining ingredients.

CREAM SAUCE:
⅛ lb. butter
2 tbsp. (heaping) flour

(Continued on next page)

175

½ c. cream
1 c. milk
Cracker crumbs
Cubed cheddar cheese
Paprika

Melt butter in saucepan. Slowly blend in flour. Add cream and milk slowly. Cook over medium heat until mixture thickens. Combine cream sauce with onion mixture. Place a layer of mixture in casserole. Sprinkle cracker crumbs over top and dot liberally with cheese. Repeat. Sprinkle top with paprika. Bake at 325 degrees for 1 hour. Yield: 10 servings.

Helen Killmer, Perry, Iowa

 ## Peanut Butter Onions

3 to 4 c. chopped onions
Cream sauce
1 to 2 tbsp. peanut butter

Cook onions until tender. Combine cream sauce and peanut butter; stir into onions. If small onions are used, leave them whole. Yield: 6 servings.

Sister Mary Clarelle, Home Economics Teacher, Delphos, Ohio

 ## Onion-Cheese Pie

1 ½ c. finely chopped soda crackers
½ c. melted butter
2 ½ c. sliced onions
1 ½ c. milk
3 eggs, slightly beaten
1 tsp. salt
¼ tsp. pepper
½ lb. cheese, finely grated

Combine crackers and butter; press into 9-inch pie pan. Fry onions in additional butter until light brown and tender; place in pie crust in layers. Scald milk; add to eggs, stirring constantly. Add salt, pepper and cheese; pour over onions. Bake at 350 degrees for 40 to 45 minutes. Garnish with parsley in center. Yield: 6-8 servings.

Mrs. Ann Edwards, Home Economics Teacher, Corsicana, Tex.

Bacon And Onion Pie

    4 lge. onions, finely chopped
    Bacon fat
    3 eggs plus 1 egg yolk, beaten
    1 c. sour cream
    6 strips bacon, fried and crumbled
    Dash of salt and pepper
    ½ tsp. caraway seed
    1 9-in. pastry shell, unbaked

Fry onions in bacon fat until transparent. Combine eggs and sour cream; stir well. Combine all ingredients except pastry shell; pour into pastry shell. Bake at 375 degrees for 30 to 45 minutes. Serve warm; cut into wedges. Yield: 6 servings.

Mrs. Jack Roberts, Augusta, Ga.

 ### Onion Pie

    3 med. onions, thinly sliced
    2 tbsp. butter
    2 eggs
    1 tsp. sugar
    ¼ tsp. salt
    1 ¼ c. milk
    1 pie shell, unbaked

Simmer onions in butter until tender but not brown, adding a little water if necessary. Combine eggs, sugar and salt; gradually stir in milk. Cook and stir over low heat until thickened. Place onions in pie shell; cover with mixture. Bake in preheated 425 degree oven for 15 minutes. Reduce heat to 375 degrees; bake for 45 to 60 minutes or until well set. Yield: 6 servings.

Ruth Adams, Claymont, Del.

 ### Scalloped Onions

    6 med. onions
    ¼ c. margarine
    ¼ c. flour
    2 c. milk
    ½ tsp. salt
    2 c. grated American cheese

Slice onions and separate into rings; place in 1½-quart casserole. Melt margarine; blend in flour. Slowly stir in milk; cook until thickened. Stir in salt and grated cheese; pour over onions. Bake, uncovered, at 375 degrees for 1 hour. Yield: 6 servings.

Nita Atley, Holly, Mich.

Scalloped Apples And Onions

9 med. onions
6 med. apples
16 slices bacon, cooked and crumbled
¾ tsp. salt
1 c. water
½ c. soft bread crumbs
2 tbsp. bacon fat

Thinly slice pared onions and apples; layer with bacon in greased casserole. Sprinkle each layer with salt; add water. Saute crumbs in bacon fat; sprinkle over casserole. Bake, covered, at 375 degrees for 30 minutes. Uncover; bake for 15 minutes longer. Yield: 6 servings.

Mrs. Charlotte H. Payne, Montrose, Pa.

 ### Slivered Almond Onions

16 to 20 small onions
½ c. butter or margarine
1 c. silvered almonds

Parboil onions to loosen outer skin; remove outer skin, stem and root end. Arrange onions in shallow casserole in a single layer. Dot top of each onion with butter; sprinkle almonds over top. Cover and bake at 350 degrees for 45 minutes or until tender. Yield: 8-10 servings.

Mrs. Richard W. Hurd, Montgomery, Minn.

 ### Cheese 'N' Limas In Onion Shells

6 med. or lge. white onions
1 ½ c. cooked lima beans
¼ c. catsup
¼ tsp. ground sage
Dash of pepper
¼ lb. sharp process American cheese, shredded
¼ c. hot water
6 slices bacon, cooked and crumbled

Peel onions; cook in boiling, salted water for 15 to 20 minutes or until partially tender. Drain and cool. Slice off ends and remove centers. Place onions in 10 x 6 x 1½-inch baking dish. Chop onion centers; place around whole onions. Combine lima beans, catsup, sage, pepper and half of cheese; fill onions with mixture. Pour hot water around onions. Bake at 375 degrees for 25 minutes or until tender. Sprinkle remaining cheese and bacon over top. Bake 5 minutes longer or until cheese melts. Yield: 6 servings.

Mary Post, Atlanta, Ga.

178

Island-Inspired Onions

    8 med. onions
    1 tbsp. butter
    1 15½-oz. can corned beef hash
    1 8½-oz. can sliced pineapple
    2 tbsp. brown sugar
    1 tsp. cornstarch
    ½ tsp. dry mustard
    1 8-oz. can tomato sauce

Cook onions in boiling salted water until tender, about 20 minutes. Drain and cool. Slice tops from each onion and lift out centers. Chop centers to make ½ cup; cook in butter until lightly browned. Add corned beef hash and stir until well mixed. Fill onions with mixture and arrange in baking dish. Drain pineapple slices, reserving syrup. Cut pineapple slices in half and place a half slice on top of each stuffed onion. Combine brown sugar, cornstarch and mustard in a small saucepan. Add pineapple syrup and tomato sauce; cook, stirring constantly, until thickened. Pour over onions. Bake in a 400-degree oven for 20 to 25 minutes. Yield: 4-6 servings.

Photograph for this recipe on page 167.

 ### Onions With Sage Stuffing

    6 lge. onions
    4 c. dry bread cubes
    3 tbsp. melted fat
    ½ tsp. chopped parsley
    1 tsp. sage
    1 tbsp. chopped celery
    4 to 6 tbsp. stock or water
    ½ tsp. salt

Boil onions for 10 minutes or until almost tender. Drain and hollow out, leaving a ¾-inch shell. Chop pulp and combine with remaining ingredients; stuff into onions. Bake at 325 degrees for 30 minutes in pot with roast. Yield: 6 servings.

Mrs. Ruth Williams, Mt. Sterling, Ky.

 ### Supper Dish

    12 sm. onions
    1 can cream of mushroom soup
    1 c. grated cheese

(Continued on next page)

Boil onions in salted water until tender; drain. Place onions in casserole. Stir mushroom soup; pour over onions. Sprinkle cheese over top. Bake at 350 degrees for 15 to 20 minutes or until browned. Yield: 4 servings.

Mrs. Chelsea A. Merritt, Home Economics Teacher, Tollesboro, Ky.

 ### Spiced Glazed Parsnips

> 6 medium-sized fresh parsnips
> Boiling water to cover
> 2 tbsp. butter or margarine
> ¼ c. light brown sugar
> ⅛ tsp. salt
> ¼ tsp. ground cloves
> 3 tbsp. fresh orange juice

Wash parsnips and cook them in their skins in boiling water to cover, 30 minutes until they are tender. Lift out of water and cool until they can be handled. Remove skins and cut parsnips in half lengthwise. Set aside. Melt butter or margarine in a skillet. Blend in sugar, salt, cloves and orange juice. Heat. Add parsnips and cook slowly until they are hot and glazed. Serve as a vegetable. Yield: 6 servings.

Photograph for this recipe below.

Baked Parsnips

1 lb. parsnips
4 tbsp. butter
¼ c. hot water

Scrape or pare parsnips; cut in lengthwise slices, removing hard core if necessary. Place parsnips in baking dish. Add butter and hot water. Cover and bake at 375 degrees for 30 to 40 minutes or until tender. Uncover during last few minutes of baking. Yield: 4-6 servings.

Mrs. Jeanette Bogne, Clara City, Minn.

 ## Candied Parsnips

6 med. parsnips
⅔ c. brown sugar
1 tsp. salt
⅓ c. butter or margarine
1 tbsp. lemon juice

Boil parsnips for 20 minutes or until almost tender; drain and slice. Arrange parsnips in layers in greased casserole, sprinkling each layer with brown sugar, salt and lemon juice; dot with butter. Bake at 375 degrees for 25 to 30 minutes. Yield: 6 servings.

Mrs. Effie G. Hoyle, Newport News, Va.

 ## Parsnip Balls

8 parsnips
½ c. flour
4 tbsp. butter
2 c. plus 2 tbsp. milk
½ tsp. salt
¼ tsp. pepper
2 c. fine dry bread crumbs
3 eggs, beaten

Boil parsnips in salted water until soft. Cool; remove outer coating and core. Mash parsnips. Blend flour with melted butter; gradually add 2 cups milk, salt and pepper. Cook until very thick, stirring constantly; mix with parsnips. Refrigerate overnight. Shape into 1-inch balls; roll in crumbs. Dip in eggs mixed with 2 tablespoons milk; roll again in crumbs. Fry in deep fat until golden brown.

Kathryn Davis, Home Economics Teacher, Pinckneyville, Ill.

Panfried Parsnips

1 stick butter or margarine
1 lb. fresh young parsnips, peeled and sliced ¼-in. thick

Melt butter in preheated 300 degree 12-inch skillet. Place parsnips in butter. Cover and cook for 10 minutes. Turn parsnips; cover and cook until browned. Turn parsnips; cook, uncovered, until tender. Yield: 6 servings.

Mrs. Bud Gaulke, Riddle, Ore., Favorite Recipes Food Fair

Parsnips In Orange Sauce

12 sm. parsnips, cooked
½ c. orange juice
2 tbsp. brown sugar
2 tbsp. light syrup
½ tsp. salt
⅛ tsp. paprika
2 tbsp. butter
Grated orange peel

Place parsnips in shallow 8 x 12-inch casserole. Combine orange juice, sugar, syrup, salt and paprika; pour over parsnips. Dot with butter; sprinkle with orange peel. Bake at 400 degrees for 20 minutes. Yield: 6 servings.

Mrs. Bette Eckre Johnson, Raymond, Minn.

Rosemary Parsnip Casserole

12 parsnips
6 tbsp. butter
¼ tsp. fresh or dried rosemary
2 tbsp. flour
¼ grated Parmesan cheese
2 c. half and half
½ c. salted cracker crumbs

Peel parsnips; cook in boiling, salted water for 30 minutes or until tender. Drain and cut in half lengthwise. Arrange half of parsnips in greased 2-quart baking dish. Dot with 1 tablespoon butter; sprinkle with half of rosemary, flour and cheese. Drizzle with half of cream. Repeat. Melt remaining butter; toss with cracker crumbs. Sprinkle over top of casserole. Bake at 400 degrees for 20 minutes. Yield: 6 servings.

Marcia E. Nordquist, Home Economics Teacher, Castle Rock, Wash.

Peas and Peppers

Barley And Peas Casserole

2 c. pearl barley
1 pkg. frozen peas
3 tbsp. margarine
1 med. onion, diced
1 c. chicken broth or soup
Salt

Cook barley and peas as directed on packages. In a large skillet, melt margarine and lightly brown onion. Add barley, peas and broth; season to taste. Heat about 5 minutes and serve. Yield: 6-8 servings.

Gwen Morgenstern, Home Economics Teacher, Hamden, Ohio

 ## Hopping John

8 oz. black-eyed peas
½ lb. ham bone
1 sm. onion, chopped
1 tsp. salt
¼ tsp. pepper
1 c. instant rice
1 1-lb. can tomatoes (opt.)

Cover peas with boiling water; add ham bone, onion, salt and pepper. Cook for 1 hour and 15 minutes. Place rice on top; add water to cover rice. Bring to boiling point; cover and remove from heat. Let stand until rice is tender; add tomatoes. Yield: 6 servings.

Mrs. Malta O. Ledford, Jupiter, Fla., Favorite Recipes Food Fair

 ## Texas Caviar

2 No. 2 cans black-eyed peas, drained
⅓ c. peanut oil
⅓ c. wine vinegar
1 clove of garlic
¼ c. finely chopped onion
½ tsp. salt
Cracked pepper

Place peas in bowl with remaining ingredients; store in refrigerator for 24 hours. Remove garlic; store for 2 days to 2 weeks before eating. Yield: 6-8 servings.

Mrs. Rachel Pearce, Home Economics Teacher, Fort Worth, Tex.

Cowboy Black-Eyed Peas

1 No. 303 can black-eyed peas
1 med. sweet onion, sliced
½ tsp. Worcestershire sauce
2 tbsp. butter

Drain half the liquid from peas; add remaining ingredients. Heat thoroughly; serve hot. Yield: 5 servings.

Colleen Stevenson, Neroosa, Wis.

 ## Bologna Cups With Peas

6 ⅛-inch slices Bologna
2 tbsp. butter
2 c. seasoned cooked peas
2 c. cooked rice
1 peeled tomato

Spread bologna with butter; place in heated broiler. As slices heat, bologna will take the shape of cups. Fill with hot peas; arrange around mound of rice. Cut tomato into wedges and place between cups. Garnish with sliced, hard-cooked egg, if desired. Yield: 6 servings.

Maybelle Ferrell, Dunnelton, Fla.

 ## Browned Rice With Peas

1 c. uncooked regular rice
2 ½ c. boiling water
½ c. butter
¼ c. minced onion
1 4-oz. can sliced mushrooms, drained
1 10-oz. pkg. frozen peas, thawed
1 8-oz. can water chestnuts, diced
3 tbsp. soy sauce

Saute rice in skillet, stirring often until lightly browned. Turn into a 1½-quart casserole; add water and stir with fork to separate rice grains. Cover and bake in preheated 350-degree oven for 30 minutes or until rice is tender. Melt butter in skillet over low heat. Add onion and mushrooms; saute until onion is transparent. Remove from heat; add peas, water chestnuts and soy sauce. Add rice and blend gently; return to casserole. Bake, uncovered, for an additional 15 minutes. Yield: 8 servings.

Mrs. Theodore J. Fronczak, Officers' Wives, Club, Jusmag, Philippines

Casserole Of Peas

    1 No. 2 can peas
    2 hard-cooked eggs, chopped
    ¼ tsp. salt
    Pepper
    1 tbsp. flour
    1 tbsp. butter
    1 c. buttered cracker crumbs
    ½ c. cheese, grated

Drain peas, reserving juice. Place peas in a buttered casserole. Add eggs and seasonings. Pour liquid from peas into a saucepan; heat. Thicken with flour; add butter and pour over peas. Brown buttered crumbs slightly. Mix crumbs with cheese and pour over peas. Bake for 30 minutes at 350 degrees. Yield: 6 servings.

Mrs. Beulah Meyers, Home Economics Teacher, Defiance, Ohio

 Cheese Loaf With Peas

    1 c. milk
    1 tsp. salt
    1 tbsp. butter
    1 tbsp. mustard
    ½ c. sugar
    3 egg yolks, beaten
    ½ c. vinegar
    1 sm. can pimento, chopped
    1 lb. grated cheese
    1 c. saltine cracker crumbs
    1 No. 303 can or 1 pkg. frozen peas, cooked

Blend milk, salt, butter, mustard, sugar, egg yolks and vinegar; cook until thickened, stirring constantly. Combine pimento, cheese and cracker crumbs with cooked mixture; pour into buttered 8-inch ring mold. Bake at 350 degrees for 30 minutes. Cool for 5 minutes; invert onto plate. Fill center with hot, seasoned peas. Yield: 8 servings.

Mrs. Hester R. Harding, Home Economics Teacher, Mt. Olivet, Ky.

Herbed Peas

½ c. sliced green onions
2 tbsp. butter
2 10-oz. pkg. frozen field peas
½ tsp. sugar
½ tsp. salt
⅛ tsp. pepper
¼ tsp. basil
1 tbsp. parsley flakes
¼ c. water

Saute onions in butter until soft; add frozen peas. When peas come to a boil, stir in remaining ingredients. Simmer, covered, for 10 minutes. Yield: 4-6 servings.

Sister Mary Albertus, Home Economics Teacher, Tyler, Tex.

 ## Almondine Peas And Onions

1 c. diagonally-cut celery
½ c. slivered blanched almonds
½ c. melted butter
1 sm. can whole onions
1 10-oz. pkg. frozen English peas, cooked
Salt and pepper to taste

Cook celery in boiling salted water until tender but crisp; drain. Lightly brown almonds in butter; add onions, peas and celery. Season with salt and pepper. Serve hot. Yield: 8-10 servings.

Mrs. Marie M. Hubbard, Providence, R. I.

 ## Citrus-Honey Peas

1 tbsp. grated orange and lemon rind
2 tbsp. butter
Juice of 1 orange
Juice of 1 lemon
¼ c. honey
1 No. 303 can early garden peas, drained
¼ c. chopped pimento

Saute rind in butter for 2 to 3 minutes; stir in juices and honey. Cook rapidly for several minutes or until thickened. Add peas and pimento; heat. Yield: 4 servings.

Mrs. Marie Hayes, Home Economics Teacher, St. Paul Park, Minn.

Creole English Peas

    1 sm. onion, chopped
    1 med. green sweet pepper, diced
    1 1-lb. can tomatoes
    1 tbsp. butter
    Red pepper and salt to taste
    1 c. cheese, grated
    1 1-lb. can small English peas, drained

Cook onion, green pepper and tomatoes until thick. Add butter, red pepper and salt. Cook until very little juice is left. Blend half the cheese into mixture. Add peas; mix and pour into casserole. Spread top with remaining cheese. Bake at 350 degrees for 20 minutes. Yield: 4-6 servings.

Mrs. Rowena McCarty, Beaumont, Miss.

 ## Deviled English Peas

    1 1-lb. can English peas, drained
    4 hard-cooked eggs, sliced
    ½ c. chopped pimento
    1 c. grated cheese
    1 can cream of mushroom soup
    1 No. 2 can French-fried onion rings

Arrange a layer of peas, egg slices, pimento and cheese in casserole; spread half the soup over top. Repeat layers. Bake at 350 degrees for 15 minutes. Cover with onion rings; return to oven until thoroughly heated. Yield: 6-8 servings.

Mrs. John L. Rummell, Raymond, Wash.

 ## Frozen Peas Continental

    1 bunch green onions
    Butter or margarine
    1 tsp. flour
    ⅓ c. light cream
    Salt and pepper
    1 pkg. frozen green peas
    2 tbsp. water
    1 tsp. sugar

Cut onions into 1-inch lengths; saute in 1 teaspoon butter for 3 to 4 minutes, stirring constantly. Blend in flour and cream; cook until thickened, stirring constantly. Add dash of salt and pepper. Cook peas with 1 tablespoon butter, water, ½ teaspoon salt and sugar. Simmer, covered, for 3 minutes; combine with onion mixture. Bake at 300 degrees for 12 minutes. Yield: 4 servings.

Mrs. Retha George, Home Economics Teacher, Biloxi, Miss.

English Pea Casserole

    2 c. English peas
1 can cream of mushroom soup
4 hard-cooked eggs, sliced
1 c. grated cheese
1 sm. green pepper, chopped
1 c. cracker crumbs
2 c. milk
2 tbsp. flour
2 tbsp. butter
1 tsp. lemon juice
1 tsp. grated lemon rind
1 tsp. Worcestershire sauce
Salt and pepper to taste

Make layers of peas, soup, eggs, cheese, pepper and cracker crumbs until all are used. Make a sauce of milk, flour and butter. Add remaining ingredients; pour over layers. Bake at 350 degrees for 30 minutes. Yield: 8-10 servings.

Mrs. Cliff Winstead, Union, Miss.

 ### English Peas A La Orange

    2 pkg. frozen peas, cooked
3 tbsp. orange juice
1 orange, sectioned

Partially drain peas; add orange juice. Heat for 3 minutes. Place in serving dish; top with orange sections. Serve immediately. Yield: 9 servings.

Jean Ray, Home Economics Teacher, Savannah, Ga.

 ### Green Peas

    1 lb. green peas
½ tsp. lemon juice
Pinch of sugar (opt.)
Butter or hot cream

Hull and wash green peas. Drop peas in ⅛ inch boiling water or stock. Add lemon juice and sugar. Simmer, covered, 10 to 15 minutes or until peas are tender; drain. Season with melted butter.

Mrs. J. P. Williamson, Chattanooga, Tenn.

Frozen Green Peas In Sour Cream

1 c. sliced, fresh or canned mushrooms
2 tbsp. butter or margarine
1 10-oz. pkg. frozen green peas, partially thawed
3 green onions, halved lengthwise and cut into 2½-in. lengths
2 tbsp. water
¾ tsp. salt
Dash of pepper
½ c. sour cream
1 tbsp. flour
Paprika (opt.)

Brown mushrooms lightly in butter; add peas, onions, water, salt and pepper. Cook, covered, for 5 minutes or until peas are tender. Blend sour cream and flour; stir into peas. Heat thoroughly; sprinkle with paprika. Yield: 4 servings.

Mrs. Lucille Reid Marker, Robertsdale, Ala., Favorite Recipes Food Fair

Green Pea Casserole

2 pkg. frozen green peas
1 can cream of chicken soup
1 can onion rings or 1 pkg. frozen onion rings

Boil peas for 4 minutes; put in greased casserole with cream of chicken soup. Spoon 4 tablespoons soup over peas. Put onion rings over top. Bake for 20 minutes in 350-degree oven. Yield: 4-6 servings.

Mrs. Nathan N. Withington, Officers' Wives' Club, Reese AFB, Lubbock, Tex.

Green Peas, French-Style

5 or 6 outer lettuce leaves
3 lb. fresh or frozen peas
12 sm. onions
2 sprigs parsley
½ c. butter, softened
2 ½ tsp. sugar
2 tsp. salt

Lay lettuce leaves in heavy saucepan with tight-fitting lid. Gently mix peas with onions, parsley, butter, sugar and salt. Put mixture onto bed of lettuce. If fresh peas are used, sprinkle with 3 tablespoons water; add none if frozen peas are used. Cover and cook over low heat for 15 minutes or until peas are tender but moist. Remove from heat. Lettuce may be shredded and gently mixed with peas or discarded. Yield: 6 servings.

Lorraine R. Fiedler, Carleton, Mich.

Green Peas In Casserole

2 c. frozen or canned green peas
¼ c. onion, chopped fine
2 tbsp. butter or bacon fat
1 lb. ground beef
1 ½ tsp. salt
1 tsp. Worcestershire sauce
1 c. tomatoes
3 tbsp. buttered bread crumbs

If frozen peas are used, cook in ½ cup boiling salted water. Drain peas. Put 1 cup peas in buttered baking dish. In frying pan, cook onion in butter until tender, but not brown. Add meat; stir and cook until meat loses color. Add seasonings and tomatoes; let simmer 5 to 10 minutes, stirring to keep from sticking. Pour half the meat sauce over peas; add remaining peas. Top with sauce and buttered bread crumbs. Bake in 350-degree oven for 15 to 20 minutes. Baby lima or butter beans may be substituted for peas. Yield: 6 servings.

Effie W. Brock, Kokomo, Ind.

 ## Green Peas With Rice

½ c. rice
2 c. shelled green peas
1 sm. onion, chopped
3 tbsp. butter
½ c. chopped mushrooms
1 tbsp. Parmesan cheese
Buttered bread crumbs

Boil rice in 2 quarts salted water; drain. Rinse rice with hot water. Cook peas in a small amount of water for 10 to 15 minutes. Fry onion in butter; add mushrooms. Fry for 10 minutes. Combine all ingredients except cheese and crumbs. Sprinkle top with cheese and buttered bread crumbs before baking. Bake in casserole at 350 degrees for 30 minutes. Yield: 6-8 servings.

Sister M. Roberta, Home Economics Teacher, Richmond Dale, Ohio

 ## Peas And Ham Curry

1 1-lb. 1-oz. can sweet peas, drained
¼ lb. cooked cubed ham
2 tbsp. butter
½ tsp. curry powder
¼ tsp. monosodium glutamate
2 tbsp. flour
¼ tsp. salt
1 c. milk

(Continued on next page)

Combine peas and ham in 1½-quart casserole. Blend butter, curry powder, monosodium glutamate, flour, salt and milk. Cook until thickened, stirring constantly; remove from heat. Fold into peas and ham. Bake, covered, at 325 degrees for 30 minutes. Yield: 4 servings.

Patricia A. Glass, Home Economics Teacher, Dill City, Okla.

 ### Pea Souffle

    1 No. 2 can English peas
½ *onion, sliced*
    1 c. cream
    3 tbsp. flour
    3 eggs, separated

Simmer peas with onion for 30 minutes; remove onion. Drain peas; mash. Add cream, flour and egg yolks; fold in stiffly beaten egg whites. Place in greased mold. Bake at 250 degrees until knife inserted comes out clean. Yield: 6 servings.

Mrs. Rush Valentine, Starkville, Miss.

 ### Peas Pagoda

    1 No. 303 can early garden peas, drained
½ *c. pea stock*
    1 ½ tsp. seasoned chicken stock
¼ *tsp. ginger*
½ *tsp. sugar*
    1 tbsp. salad oil
    1 5-oz. can water chestnuts, drained and sliced
    1 2 to 3-oz. can sliced mushrooms, drained
    1 ½ tsp. cornstarch
    1 tbsp. soy sauce

Combine all ingredients except cornstarch and soy sauce; heat, covered, until hot. Blend cornstarch with soy sauce; stir gently into mixture until thickened. Serve hot. Yield: 4-5 servings.

Phyllis L. Barton, Alexandria, Va.

 ### Peas And Rice Provencal

    2 c. cooked rice
    Butter to taste
    Salt to taste

(Continued on next page)

Just plain baked beans are excellent, but these beans have been lifted to heavenly heights with the addition of one ingredient—tart and tasty cranberry juice. The first recipe is for the times you want to start from scratch—the second is for those days when you're short on time. Either way, the result is delicious and different.

CRANBERRY BAKED BEANS

1½ c. dried pea, kidney, lima or marrow beans
1½ tsp. salt
2 c. cranberry juice cocktail
2 c. water
⅓ c. chopped onion
2 tbsp. molasses
1 tsp. dry mustard
⅛ tsp. ginger
¼ c. catsup
2 tbsp. (firmly packed) dark brown sugar
¼ lb. salt pork, sliced

Place beans, salt, cranberry juice and water in saucepan; bring quickly to a boil. Remove from heat; set aside for 1 hour. Cover and bring to a boil again. Reduce heat and simmer until beans are tender, adding more water if necessary. Drain beans; reserve liquid. Combine beans and all remaining ingredients except salt pork. Pour half of bean mixture into a bean pot or 2-quart casserole. Top with half of salt pork. Repeat bean and pork layers. Add 1½ cups reserved bean liquid. Bake, covered, at 250 degrees for 6 to 8 hours. Uncover during last hour of baking. Add more of the reserved liquid if necessary to keep beans from drying. Yield: 6-8 servings.

QUICKIE CRANBERRY BAKED BEANS

1 1-lb., 12-oz. can baked beans with pork
1 7-oz. can whole berry cranberry sauce

Combine beans and cranberry sauce; mix well. Pour into 1½-quart casserole. Cover and bake at 350 degrees for 30 minutes or until heated. Yield: 4 servings.

See photograph on reverse page.

1 17-oz. can English peas, drained
¼ c. chopped onion
½ c. sliced green olives
4 tbsp. cooking oil
Pimento strips

Gently combine hot rice with butter, salt and hot peas. Saute onion and olives in oil until tender; add to peas and rice. Garnish with pimento strips. Yield: 6 servings.

Doris Williamson Law, Home Economics Teacher, Pensacola, Fla.

 Penny-Wise Casserole

½ lb. bacon
1 11-oz. can condensed cheddar cheese soup
½ c. milk
2 tsp. instant minced onion
1 ½ tsp. parsley flakes
1 7-oz. pkg. elbow macaroni, cooked and drained
1 17-oz. can sweet peas
⅓ c. grated Parmesan cheese

Fry bacon until crisp; drain and dice. Combine soup, milk, onion and parsley flakes in 2-quart casserole dish. Stir in bacon, macaroni, peas and Parmesan cheese; sprinkle with additional Parmesan cheese. Bake at 350 degrees for 35 minutes. Yield: 6-8 servings.

Mrs. Marcia Murdock, Logan, Utah

 Pineapple-Lemon Peas

1 pkg. frozen green peas, cooked
½ tsp. salt
¼ c. water
2 tbsp. butter
¾ c. drained pineapple chunks
½ tsp. grated lemon rind
1 tsp. lemon juice

Cook peas in salted water until tender; add butter to liquid in pan. Increase temperature; when bubbly, add pineapple, lemon rind and juice. Heat for a few minutes, stirring constantly. Yield: 4 servings.

Mrs. Lucille Bradbury, San Angelo, Tex.

Jiffy Gourmet Peas

1 can sm. young peas
⅓ c. split, toasted almonds
1 can cream of mushroom soup
1 tbsp. milk
1 c. fine bread crumbs
Melted butter

Combine peas, almonds and mushroom soup. Add milk; mix well. Top with bread crumbs which have been tossed in melted butter. Bake 20 minutes at 350 degrees or until crumbs are golden brown. Yield: 6 servings.

Mrs. R. V. Coffel, Officers' Wives' Club, NAS, Bermuda

 ### Peas Chambourd

1 17-oz. can peas with onions, drained
½ c. catsup
½ tsp. salt
Dash of pepper
⅓ c. grated Parmesan cheese

Combine peas and onions with catsup, salt and pepper in greased casserole. Sprinkle with cheese. Bake at 350 degrees for 20 minutes. Yield: 4 servings.

Mrs. Karen Williams, Home Economics Teacher, Perham, Minn.

Peas Continental

1 c. canned sliced mushrooms, drained
¼ c. minced onion
2 tbsp. butter or margarine
¼ tsp. salt
Speck of pepper
¼ tsp. nutmeg
⅛ tsp. dried marjoram
2 c. cooked or canned peas

Saute mushrooms and onion in butter until onion is transparent; add salt, pepper, nutmeg and marjoram. Combine with hot peas; serve. Yield: 4 servings.

Alberta Ball Bickerdike, Home Economics Teacher, Milton, Ill.

 ### Pea Timbales

1 ½ c. pea puree
2 tbsp. melted butter

(Continued on next page)

3 eggs, well beaten
Salt and pepper

Blend all ingredients well; pour into greased molds. Set molds in pan of hot water. Bake at 250 to 325 degrees until set. May be served with white sauce. Yield: 6-8 servings.

Katherine Potter, Frontenac, Kan., Favorite Recipes Food Fair

Souper Special Vegetables

1 10½-oz. can condensed cream of mushroom soup
⅓ c. water or milk
1 c. shredded cheddar or process cheese
1 tbsp. chopped parsley
Generous dash of crushed tarragon
Cooked peas

In saucepan, stir soup until smooth; gradually blend in water, cheese, parsley and tarragon. Heat until cheese is melted. Stir now and then. Serve over cooked peas.

Photograph for this recipe below.

Split Pea Casserole

1 ½ c. green split peas
3 tbsp. onion, chopped
Salt and pepper
2 ½ tbsp. butter
4 tbsp. flour
1 c. milk
1 No. 2 can tomatoes
1 ½ c. cooked rice
Buttered bread crumbs

Soak peas overnight in water; add onion and cook until tender, but not mushy. Add ¾ teaspoon salt toward end of cooking time. Drain and boil liquid down to ½ cup. In a saucepan, melt butter; stir in flour. Add split pea liquid and milk, stirring constantly. Cook until thickened. Season with salt and pepper to taste. Drain tomatoes and sprinkle with salt. Place peas, hot sauce, tomatoes and cooked rice in alternate layers in a buttered baking dish. Cover with crumbs. Bake at 375 degrees for 25 to 30 minutes. Serve with bacon, if desired. Yield: 6-8 servings.

Mrs. Marjorie P. Kibelbek, Brownsville, Pa.

 ### Steam-Fried Peas

2 slices bacon, diced (opt.)
1 sm. onion, chopped (opt.)
2 tbsp. butter
2 c. peas
2 tbsp. water

Saute bacon and onion in butter; add remaining ingredients. Simmer, covered, for about 20 minutes or until tender. Yield: 4 servings.

Mrs. Hazel R. Johnson, Basin, Wyo.

 ### Vegetable Casserole

1 c. thick white sauce
1 c. sharp cheese, grated
1 can tomato soup
1 sm. can pimento, drained and chopped
1 lge. can small English peas, drained
1 onion, finely chopped
1 green pepper, finely chopped
½ c. almonds

(Continued on next page)

Combine white sauce, cheese and soup. Mix all vegetables together. Alternate layers of sauce and vegetables in a baking dish. Top with almonds. Bake at 350 degrees for 30 minutes. Yield: 15 servings.

Mrs. Alton D. Lewis, Home Economics Teacher, Lexington, Tenn.

 ## Venetian Rice And Peas

4 slices bacon
1 sm. onion, minced
3 tbsp. butter
1 10-oz. pkg. frozen peas
¾ c. uncooked rice
2 c. chicken broth
1 tsp. salt
Dash of pepper
¼ c. Parmesan cheese

Saute bacon in heavy skillet. Remove bacon and grease. Saute onion in butter; add frozen peas. Cook 5 minutes; stir frequently. Add rice; cook until well coated with butter. Pour in chicken broth, salt and pepper. Cover and simmer. Stir occasionally for 20 minutes or until liquid is absorbed. Toss with crumbled bacon and Parmesan cheese. Yield: 6-8 servings.

Mrs. Tom W. Barron, Metairie, La.

 ## Creole Pepper Casserole

8 lge. sweet peppers
¾ c. water
1 ½ tbsp. butter
1 ½ tbsp. flour
1 c. milk
Salt to taste
1 can mushroom soup
1 ½ c. cheese, grated
1 c. bread or cracker crumbs

Coarsely grind peppers. Cook in water until tender; drain well. Make a cream sauce of butter, flour, milk and salt; mix with mushroom soup and peppers. Put mixture in buttered casserole; add cheese and bread crumbs. Bake for 30 minutes at 300 degrees. Yield: 6-8 servings.

Grace Evelyn Miller, Elkton, Ky.

Banana Peppers Crespo

1 ¼ c. flour
½ tsp. salt
¼ tsp. baking powder
½ tsp. chili powder
1 c. milk
12 med. banana peppers

Combine flour, salt, baking powder and chili powder; add milk and stir to form a batter. Wash peppers and remove core, veins and seeds; cut into halves. Coat peppers evenly with batter on both sides; fry until golden brown. Drain on absorbent paper; serve warm. Yield: 6 servings.

Mrs. Ann H. Hutchings, Midvale, Utah

French-Fried Pepper Rings

Green peppers, cut in rings
Milk
Seasoned flour

Dip pepper rings in milk then in seasoned flour. Fry in deep hot fat until brown. Drain; sprinkle with salt.

Mrs. Lee Trammell, Nashville, Tenn.

Fried Ortega Peppers

Cheddar cheese, cut into 1½x½-in. pieces
1 No. 2½ can Ortega peppers, drained
1 egg, beaten
Cornmeal
Fat

Insert a piece of cheese into each pepper. Dip peppers into egg; roll in cornmeal. Fry in a small amount of fat; drain. Yield: 10 servings.

Mrs. Margaret Hollingsworth, Home Economics Teacher, Tuscaloosa, Ala.

Fried Peppers With Eggs

6 green peppers, sliced
1 onion, sliced
¼ c. olive oil
4 eggs, beaten

(Continued on next page)

Brown green peppers and onion in hot olive oil; add eggs and cook until done. Yield: 4 servings.

Mrs. Louise O. Smith, West Harwich, Mass.

Green Pepper Casserole

4 or 5 green peppers, chopped
1 tbsp. butter
2 tbsp. flour
1 c. milk
¾ c. grated cheese
½ c. cracker crumbs

Cook green peppers in a small amount of water until tender. Melt butter in saucepan; blend in flour. Gradually add milk. Cook and stir until thickened. Add cheese and stir until melted. Stir in peppers; pour into baking dish. Cover with cracker crumbs. Bake at 350 degrees until bubbly and browned. Yield: 5-6 servings.

Mrs. Martha Young, Franklin, Ky., Favorite Recipes Food Fair

 ## Green Pepper Stew

1 onion, chopped
4 tbsp. shortening
2 c. water
2 green peppers, chopped
2 tomatoes, chopped
1 tsp. salt
½ tsp. (scant) pepper
4 potatoes, diced
2 tbsp. flour

Brown onion in shortening. Add water, peppers, tomatoes, salt and pepper; cook for 20 minutes. Add potatoes and cook until potatoes are soft, but not mushy. Mix flour with a small amount of water; add enough to vegetables to thicken. Yield: 4 servings.

Mrs. Alfred Berger, Garwood, Tex.

Pepper Casserole

  7 lge. green peppers
  1/4 lb. margarine
  2 c. bread crumbs
  1/2 lb. sharp cheese
  3 eggs, beaten
  2 c. evaporated milk
  1 tsp. salt
  1/4 tsp. black pepper

Cook green peppers until tender. Place a layer of green pepper strips in a buttered casserole; dot with margarine. Cover with a layer of bread crumbs and cheese. Repeat layers until all green pepper has been used. Combine eggs, milk, salt and pepper. Pour over green pepper. Cook at 325 degrees until eggs and milk set, about 40 minutes. Yield: 10 servings.

Mrs. Doran Ingram, Home Economics Teacher, Scottsboro, Ala.

 ### Stewed Peppers

  3 slices bacon, diced
  6 green peppers, cut into 1/4-in. strips
  1/3 c. water
  1/2 bottle chili sauce
  2 tbsp. catsup
  1/4 tsp. salt
  1/4 tsp. monosodium glutamate
  Dash of pepper

Fry bacon until crisp in 1-quart pan; pour off most of grease. Add peppers to bacon; add water. Cover and simmer gently for 15 minutes. Add chili sauce, catsup, salt, monosodium glutamate and pepper. Simmer 5 minutes longer. Yield: 4 servings.

Marian Hahalyak, Williamsville, N. Y.

 ### Cheese-Stuffed Peppers

  6 med. green peppers
  6 bacon strips
  1/3 c. onion, chopped
  3 c. cooked rice
  3 c. cheddar cheese, shredded
  2 tbsp. pimento, chopped
  1/2 tsp. salt
  1/2 c. bread crumbs
Bacon curls
  1 can green beans or 1 pkg. frozen beans, cooked and seasoned

(Continued on next page)

Cut off tops of green peppers; remove seed and membrane. Cook 5 minutes in boiling salted water; drain. Cut bacon in small pieces; saute with onion until crisp and brown. Drain on absorbent toweling. In a mixing bowl, combine bacon, onion, rice, cheese, pimento and salt; toss to blend. Spoon into green pepper cups. packing lightly. Place peppers in baking dish. Bake about 30 to 40 minutes at 375 degrees. Garnish with bread crumbs over top and bacon curls, if desired. Place green beans around peppers to serve. Yield: 6 servings.

Mrs. Lola S. Pevehouse, Home Economics Teacher, Amarillo, Tex.

 Barbecue-Stuffed Peppers

>   4 *lge. green peppers*
>   1 *lb. ground meat*
>   ⅔ *c. instant nonfat dry milk*
>   2 *tbsp. catsup*
>   2 *tsp. salt*
>   ⅛ *tsp. pepper*
>   1 *egg*
>   1 *slice day-old bread, cubed*
>   ¼ *c. finely cut onion*
>   3 *tsp. Worcestershire sauce*
>   1 *8-oz. can tomato sauce*
>   1 *tbsp. vinegar*
>   ¼ *tsp. dry mustard*
>   ½ *tsp. chili powder*
>   2 *tbsp. brown sugar*

Remove stems and seed from peppers. Combine meat, milk, catsup, 1½ teaspoons salt, pepper, egg, bread, onion and 2 teaspoons Worcestershire sauce. Mix well. Combine remaining ingredients for a sauce. Place peppers in baking dish; place 1 tablespoon sauce in each. Fill with meat mixture. Spoon 1 tablespoon sauce over peppers. Cover and bake at 350 degrees for 55 to 60 minutes. Heat remaining sauce; serve with peppers. Yield: 4 servings.

Velma Young, Tacoma, Wash.

 Corn-Stuffed Green Peppers

>   4 *to 6 med. green peppers*
>   1 *½ c. canned or fresh corn*
>   1 *c. diced raw tomatoes*
>   4 *tbsp. finely chopped celery*
>   1 *tbsp. finely chopped onion*
>   2 *tbsp. melted butter*
>   2 *eggs., slightly beaten*
>   1 *¼ tsp. salt*
>   ⅛ *tsp. pepper*
>   ½ *c. soft bread crumbs*
>   1 *tsp. sugar (opt.)*

(Continued on next page)

Wash peppers; remove tops and seeds. Parboil in salted water for 3 to 5 minutes; drain. Combine remaining ingredients; add sugar if canned corn is used. Stuff peppers; replace tops. Place in greased casserole with small amount water. Bake, covered, at 325 to 350 degrees for 50 to 60 minutes. Yield: 4 servings.

Bertha Keller Benthien, Batavia, Ohio

 ### Curry-Stuffed Green Peppers

¼ lb. ground beef
½ c. rice
½ c. whole kernel corn or ½ c. English peas
2 tsp. curry
Salt and pepper
1 sm. onion, chopped
4 lge. green peppers, cored
Stuffed green olives

Cook meat; add all ingredients except green peppers and olives. Stuff peppers; top with olives. Place in shallow pan; add water. Bake at 350 degrees for 45 minutes.

Jacque Floyd, Lakeland, Fla.

 ### German-Style Peppers

2 hard rolls or slices of bread
6 med. green peppers
1 ½ lb. ground beef
1 med. onion, chopped
2 eggs
Salt and pepper to taste
2 or 3 drops Worcestershire sauce
1 tbsp. parsley flakes
Water
1 tbsp. lard
Flour
1 bouillon cube

Soften rolls in water. Cut off tops of peppers; remove seed. Combine beef, onion, eggs, salt, pepper, bread, Worcestershire sauce, parsley flakes and 2 cups water. Mix well. Stuff peppers with mixture; replace tops of peppers. Fry peppers in hot lard for 5 minutes; add water. Cover; cook for 45 minutes or until peppers are done. Remove peppers to warm oven. Thicken cooking liquid with a smooth paste of flour and water; stir in bouillon cube. Season to taste. Bring to a boil; pour over peppers. Yield: 3-6 servings.

Mrs. Hannelore McKinney, Burns, Ore.

Green Peppers Stuffed With Maine Sardines

  4 green peppers
  3 tbsp. chopped celery
  ¼ c. chopped onion
  3 tbsp. melted butter
  2 4-oz. cans Maine sardines, drained
  1 c. cooked rice
  1 tsp. chopped parsley
  ⅛ tsp. curry powder
  ¼ tsp. salt
  Dash of pepper
  ¼ c. dry bread crumbs
  1 tbsp. grated Parmesan cheese
  1 can tomato sauce

Cut thin slice from stem end of peppers; remove seed. Parboil peppers in salted water for 5 minutes. Saute celery and onion in 2 tablespoons melted butter until barely tender. Break sardines into small pieces and add to vegetables with rice, parsley, curry powder, salt and pepper. Mix well. Stuff peppers with mixture. Combine remaining melted butter, bread crumbs and cheese; sprinkle over stuffing. Place peppers in baking dish; pour tomato sauce around them. Bake in preheated 350-degree oven for 30 minutes. Yield: 4 servings.

Photograph for this recipe on front cover.

 ## Quick No-Bake Stuffed Peppers

  4 lge. green peppers
  1 lb. ground beef
  1 8-oz. can tomato sauce
  ⅔ c. grated cheddar cheese
  Salt and pepper to taste
  ¼ tsp. garlic salt
  Herb meat seasoning (opt.)
  1 c. cooked instant rice

Remove stems, seeds and membrane from peppers. Boil peppers for 15 minutes or until fork tender. Cook meat until done in medium frying pan; drain off grease. Stir in tomato sauce, cheese, seasonings and rice; simmer and stir until cheese has melted and mixture is hot. Spoon into hot cooked peppers. Yield: 4 servings.

   Mrs. Rose Ann Murphy, Home Economics Teacher, Trenton, N. J.

 ## Stuffed Green Pepper Boats

  3 to 4 lge. green peppers, halved lengthwise
  2 to 2¼ c. cooked rice
  ¾ lb. American cheese, cubed
  1 10½-oz. can cream of tomato soup

(Continued on next page)

Remove seeds from peppers; parboil for 5 minutes. Drain. Combine rice, cheese and soup; fill peppers with mixture. Place each pepper in cups of aluminum foil; set in baking pan. Bake at 350 degrees for 30 minutes. Yield: 6-8 servings.

Mrs. Lee Sandager, Forest Lake, Minn., Favorite Recipes Food Fair

 ## Ham And Macaroni-Stuffed Peppers

    3 lge. green peppers
    1 ½ c. elbow macaroni
    1 tbsp. butter or margarine
    1 tbsp. flour
    1 c. milk
    ½ tsp. Tabasco sauce
    ½ tsp. salt
    1 c. diced cooked ham
    3 tbsp. grated cheese

Wash peppers; cut in half. Remove seeds. Boil peppers in boiling salted water for 10 minutes or until just tender. Cook macaroni according to package directions; drain. Melt butter in saucepan; add flour and stir to make a paste. Stir in milk, Tabasco and salt; cook until slightly thickened, stirring constantly. Pour over cooked drained macaroni; add ham. Stir in 2 tablespoons grated cheese. Fill peppers; sprinkle with remaining grated cheese. Bake at 375 degrees for 30 minutes on greased baking sheet. Yield: 3 servings.

Photograph for this recipe on page 183.

 ## Green Peppers Stuffed With Carrots

    2 onions, chopped
    ⅔ c. plus 2 tbsp. olive oil
    1 lb. carrots, grated
    Salt
    Sugar
    ½ tsp. parsley
    6 to 8 green peppers
    1 c. water
    4 tomatoes, peeled

Fry onions in 2/3 cup olive oil; add carrots to onions with ½ teaspoon salt and 1 teaspoon sugar. Cover; simmer. When carrots are almost done, add parsley; stir occasionally. Stuff peppers loosely with carrot mixture. Place in large pan; add water. Bake at 350 degrees until water is absorbed; cool in pan. Cut tomatoes into small pieces; cook in remaining olive oil. Mixture will be like paste; add sugar and salt to taste. Pour over cooled peppers; serve cool. Yield: 6-8 servings.

Mrs. Wanda Meador, Irwin, Idaho

Potatoes

Au Gratin Potatoes

2 tbsp. margarine
2 tbsp. flour
1 tsp. salt
1 c. milk
1 c. grated cheese
2 c. cooked cubed potatoes

Melt margarine; blend in flour, salt and milk gradually. Cook until thickened, stirring constantly. Add cheese; remove from heat. Place potatoes in greased baking dish; cover with sauce. Bake at 400 degrees for 30 to 40 minutes. Yield: 4-6 servings.

Orlena Wagner, Home Economics Teacher, Hampton, Tenn.

 ## Baked Potato Surprise

Medium baking potatoes
Butter
Salt and pepper
Spanish onions, sliced

Peel potatoes; cut into ½-inch slices. Place each potato on foil; butter, salt and pepper each one. Place onion slices between potato slices; seal in foil. Bake at 375 degrees for 30 minutes. Invert potatoes; bake for 15 minutes longer. Open foil; bake for 15 minutes longer. Cheese or bacon may be substituted for onion. A longer baking time at a lower temperature is suggested for cheese.

Mrs. Charles Goodwyn, Sherman, Tex.

 ## Baked Potatoes With Chef's Sauce

5 or 6 baking potatoes
½ c. sour cream
¼ c. soft margarine
1 c. shredded sharp process American cheese
2 tbsp. chopped green onion

Scrub potatoes; dry. For crunchy skins, bake ungreased; for soft skins, rub with shortening. Place on pan. Bake at 425 degrees for 50 to 60 minutes or until done. Roll gently to make insides mealy; cut across tops. Press ends to fluff. Combine remaining ingredients; spoon over potatoes. Yield: 5-6 servings.

Mrs. Ina P. Vance, Home Economics Teacher, Jefferson, Pa.

Baked Potatoes In Rock Salt

Rock salt
4 potatoes

Place rock salt 1 inch deep in 3-pound coffee can. Place potatoes in salt without touching can or each other. Pour rock salt around potatoes. Place metal cover on can; place on bed of white coals. Place hot coals on top of can. Bake for 25 minutes or until fork tender. Yield: 4 servings.

Mrs. John H. Rogers, West Allis, Wis.

 ## Idaho Baked Potatoes

4 Idaho potatoes, 2½-in. thick
2 egg whites
¼ cup salt

Scrub potatoes until clean. Coat potatoes with egg whites; roll in salt until lightly coated. Prick a few holes with fork. Bake at 350 degrees for 1 hour and 30 minutes or until soft. Make a crisscross cut on each potato; squeeze until gash pops open. Garnish with dried parsley or paprika. Serve with sour cream and chives, shredded cheese, crisp bits of bacon or fresh ground pepper. Yield: 4 servings.

Ann Moore, Home Economics Teacher, Bliss, Idaho

 ## Baked Potato

8 baking potatoes
½ c. hot milk
¾ tsp. salt
¼ tsp. pepper
1 tsp. grated onion
4 tbsp. melted butter
Grated cheese

Scrub potatoes thoroughly and dry; rub with fat. Arrange on baking sheet; bake at 450 degrees for 45 to 50 minutes or until done. Cut a slice from top of each potato; scoop potato into bowl. Add milk and beat until fluffy; season with salt, pepper and onion. Add part of the butter; pile lightly into potato shells. Brush with remaining melted butter; sprinkle with grated cheese. Broil until cheese melts. Yield: 8 servings.

Mary Ella Ingram, Wagram, N. C., Favorite Recipes Food Fair

Baked Stuffed Potatoes

> 6 baking potatoes, scrubbed
> ¼ c. warm milk
> Salt and pepper
> 4 tbsp. butter
> ¾ c. shredded American cheese (opt.)
> Paprika

Bake potatoes at 375 degrees for 1 hour; halve lengthwise. Scoop out insides; reserve shells. Blend pulp with milk, salt, pepper and butter; stuff shells. Top each with cheese. Lightly brown under broiler or bake for 15 to 20 minutes longer; sprinkle with paprika. Serve. Yield: 6 servings.

Mrs. Ada Sue Diamond, Bennington, Vt.

 Potatoes Stuffed With Peanut Butter

> 3 lge. potatoes
> ¼ tsp. salt
> ¼ tsp. pepper
> 2 tbsp. butter
> 2 tbsp. peanut butter
> Grated cheese or crisp fried bacon (opt.)

Rub potato skins with softened fat; bake until done. Halve lengthwise; scoop out the inside of potatoes, being careful not to break skins. Mash the potatoes with seasoning, butter and peanut butter until fluffy. Use an electric beater about 2 minutes for fluffier potatoes. Fill shells. Sprinkle with cheese or bacon. Bake at 350 degrees until brown and hot. Yield: 6 servings.

Mrs. Variel Garner, Home Economics Teacher, Moody, Tex.

 Souffled Potatoes

> 6 lge. baking potatoes, washed
> Butter or margarine
> 1 c. sour cream
> 1 egg, beaten
> 1 tsp. salt
> ⅛ tsp. pepper
> 9 slices bacon, cooked and crumbled

Rub potato skins with butter. Bake at 400 degrees for 45 minutes or until tender. Cut off tops. Scoop out potato. Mash potatoes with sour cream, ¼ cup butter, egg, salt and pepper; stir in bacon. Stuff potato shells. Bake at 400 degrees for 45 to 60 minutes or until heated through. Potatoes may be frozen before the final baking period. Yield: 6 servings.

Novice D. Littleton, Home Economics Teacher, San Angelo, Tex.

Seashore Stuffed Potatoes

> 1 10-oz. can frozen cream of shrimp soup
> ¼ c. milk
> 1 tbsp. grated onion
> Dash of pepper
> ½ c. shredded sharp cheese
> 4 med. potatoes, baked
> 1 7-oz. can crab meat, cleaned and flaked
> Paprika

Combine soup, milk, onion and pepper; heat slowly, stirring frequently. Add cheese; stir until melted. Halve potatoes lengthwise; scoop out insides. Blend with soup mixture slowly; beat until fluffy. Fold in crab meat; spoon into potato shells. Bake on cookie sheet at 450 degrees for 15 minutes. Sprinkle with paprika; serve. Yield: 4 servings.

Eva Jane Schwartz, Gettysburg, Pa.

 ### Barbecued Potatoes

> 6 lge. baking potatoes
> Butter
> Salt

Peel and slice potatoes into ¼-inch slices. Melt ½ cup butter in skillet or cake pan. Coat potato slices with butter on both sides; place directly on charcoal grill. Brown on one side; turn and brown on other side. Serve hot and crisp directly from grill. Spread with butter; sprinkle with salt. Yield: 8 servings.

Mrs. Evling Rohm, Decorah, Iowa

 ### Boiled Mature Potatoes

> 6 med. potatoes
> ½ tsp. salt
> 2 to 3 tbsp. melted butter
> 3 to 4 tbsp. chopped parsley

Wash and pare potatoes; quarter or leave whole. Cook, covered, for 20 to 40 minutes in 4 cups boiling salted water. When tender, drain well; roll potatoes in butter-parsley mixture. Add additional seasoning, if necessary. Chives may be substituted for parsley. To mash potatoes, boil as directed; drain and place in mixing bowl. Break potatoes up with hand potato masher, fork or electric mixer until there are no lumps and texture is uniform. Add butter and seasoning to taste.

Mrs. R. L. Fagan, Montgomery, Ala.

Cheese-Potato Casserole

1 sm. onion, chopped
½ stick melted margarine or butter
4 tbsp. flour
2 tsp. salt
½ tsp. dry mustard
½ tsp. paprika
¼ tsp. pepper
2 c. milk
6 to 8 med.-sized potatoes, peeled and diced small
2 8-oz. pkg. American process cheese

Saute onion in butter or margarine until tender. Remove from heat. Stir in seasonings and slowly add milk. Cook, stirring constantly, over low to medium heat until it thickens and boils one minute. Cut cheese into small pieces and stir with potatoes into sauce. Put into buttered 8-cup baking dish or casserole. Bake at 350 degrees about 45 minutes.

Mrs. John Chafee, Wife of Governor of Rhode Island, Providence

 ### Cheese-Potato Strips

5 med. potatoes
⅔ c. milk
½ tsp. Tabasco
1 ½ tsp. salt
1 tbsp. butter
¼ lb. process American cheese, coarsely grated or thinly sliced
Paprika

Peel potatoes and cut into strips as for French-fried potatoes. Turn into greased shallow baking dish. Combine milk, Tabasco and salt; pour over potatoes. Dot with butter. Cover and bake at 425 degrees 40 minutes or until potatoes are tender. Top with cheese and bake, uncovered, 5 minutes longer. Sprinkle with paprika. Yield: 6 servings.

Photograph for this recipe on page 205.

 ### Country-Style Potatoes And Mushrooms

½ lb. mushrooms, chopped
½ c. chopped onion
3 tbsp. butter or margarine
1 tsp. salt
Dash of pepper
4 c. cooked mashed potatoes
1 tbsp. chopped parsley

(Continued on next page)

Saute mushrooms and onion in butter or margarine for 8 minutes or until tender; salt and pepper. Fold into seasoned mashed potatoes; sprinkle with parsley. Yield: 6 servings.

Diane M. Brown, Home Economics Teacher, Grayville, Ill.

 ### Curried Potato Casserole

½ c. chopped onion
¼ c. butter
2 tsp. curry powder
5 tbsp. flour
2 tbsp. tomato paste
Freshly ground black pepper to taste
2 ½ c. chicken bouillon
5 c. diced boiled potatoes

Saute onion in butter for 5 minutes. Add curry, flour, tomato paste and pepper. Mix well. Add bouillon gradually; cook until thickened, stirring constantly. Add potatoes and pour into casserole. Bake at 375 degrees for 30 minutes. Yield: 6 servings.

Mrs. Curtiss E. Knighton, Pres. Officers' Wives' Club, Frankfurt, Germany

 ### Dakota Potatoes

4 slices bacon
4 c. pared sliced potatoes
1 onion, diced
2 c. cooked or canned tomatoes
2 tsp. salt
¼ tsp. pepper
½ tsp. mustard
1 tsp. sugar
¼ tsp. celery salt

Fry bacon crisp; drain on absorbent paper. Saute potatoes and onion in drippings for 10 minutes. Add remaining ingredients; simmer for 20 minutes or until potatoes are tender and tomato juice is slightly thickened. Garnish with crumbled bacon. Yield: 4-6 servings.

Phyllis Ann Lankalis, Lexington, Mass.

211

Duchess Potatoes

 3 c. hot mashed potatoes
 Butter
 6 tbsp. milk
 1 ½ tsp. salt
 ⅛ tsp. pepper
 3 eggs, separated

Blend potatoes with 3 tablespoons butter, milk, salt, pepper and egg yolks. Fold in stiffly beaten egg whites. Place mixture in pastry bag and tube; form rosettes on a greased baking sheet or shape border around meat or fish. Brush with butter. Bake at 425 degrees for 5 minutes or until brown. Yield: 6-8 servings.

   Mrs. Charlene Strickland, Home Economics Teacher, Danielsville, Ga.

 ## Raw Potato Dumplings

 2 c. cooked riced potatoes
 2 c. uncooked grated potatoes
 2 eggs, beaten
 1 sm. onion, minced
 Chopped parsley to taste
 ¾ c. flour
 1 tbsp. baking powder
 1 tbsp. salt
 ¼ c. butter
 ½ c. toasted bread crumbs

Blend potatoes, eggs, onion and parsley. Stir in flour sifted with baking powder and salt; add more flour if needed. Drop by tablespoonfuls into boiling salted water. Cook, covered, for 10 to 12 minutes; lift from water. Place in serving dish; top with butter and bread crumbs. Yield: 6-8 servings.

   Mrs. James Massa, Winner, S. D.

 ## French-Fried Potatoes

 2 ¼ lb. potatoes
 Solid all-vegetable shortening for deep frying
 Salt

Pare potatoes and cut into sticks about ¼-inch thick. As they are cut, place potatoes in cold water. When ready to fry potatoes, heat shortening to 365 degrees. Drain and dry potatoes thoroughly. Fry about ¼ at a time for 10 to 15 minutes, or until potatoes are golden brown. Drain on paper towels. Sprinkle with salt. Keep in warm oven until all potatoes are fried. Yield: 6 servings.

Whole Browned Potatoes

2 ¼ lb. sm. new potatoes
Boiling salted water
Solid all-vegetable shortening for deep frying
Salt

Pare potatoes and add to boiling salted water. Cook until just tender; drain. Fry potatoes in shortening at 365 degrees for 5 to 10 minutes or until golden brown. Drain on paper towels. Sprinkle with salt. Yield: 6 servings.

 ## Saratoga Chips

2 ¼ lb. potatoes
Solid all-vegetable shortening for deep frying
Salt

Pare potatoes and cut into very thin slices. As potatoes are sliced, place in cold water. When ready to fry potatoes, heat shortening to 365 degrees. Drain and thoroughly dry potatoes. Fry about ¼ at a time in shortening for 5 to 8 minutes, or until golden. Drain on paper towels. Sprinkle with salt. Keep in warm oven until all potatoes are fried. Yield: 6 servings.

Photographs for these recipes below.

213

Fresh Fried Potatoes

¼ c. butter or margarine
4 c. thinly sliced potatoes
¾ tsp. salt
Pepper to taste

Melt butter in heavy skillet; arrange a layer of sliced potatoes over bottom of skillet. Add one-third of remaining potatoes; sprinkle with salt and pepper. Add two more layers of potatoes and seasoning. Cover tightly and cook over medium heat until steam escapes. Reduce heat and cook for 25 to 30 minutes. Remove from heat for 1 minute; invert serving plate over pan and flip. Serve. Yield: 4 servings.

Cornelia M. Merwin, Hummelstown, Pa.

 ### German Hot Potatoes

6 med. potatoes
½ med. cabbage, shredded
½ c. vinegar
½ med. onion, chopped
Salt and pepper to taste

Boil potatoes in jackets until done. Simmer shredded cabbage until done; add water as needed. Add peeled, sliced potatoes, vinegar, onion and seasonings to cabbage; simmer. Serve. Yield: 6 servings.

Mrs. Dorothy Schulz, Home Economics Teacher, McLaughlin, S. D.

 ### Hashed Brown Potatoes

4 peeled cooked potatoes, chilled
¾ tsp. salt
⅛ tsp. pepper
1 tbsp. finely chopped onion
2 tbsp. margarine
2 tbsp. bacon fat

Grate potatoes with medium grater; sprinkle with salt, pepper and onion. Heat margarine and fat over medium heat; add potatoes. Saute for 5 to 10 minutes or until golden on underside, without stirring. Turn; brown other side. Yield: 3-4 servings.

Mrs. Katherine Long, West Hyattsville, Md.

Hot German Potato Salad

½ lb. bacon, cooked and crumbled
½ c. chopped celery
½ c. sliced onion
¼ c. bacon drippings
3 tbsp. sugar
1 tbsp. flour
1 ½ tsp. salt
½ tsp. celery seed
¼ tsp. pepper
½ c. water
⅓ c. vinegar
5 med. potatoes, cooked and cubed

Cook bacon until crisp; drain and crumble. Saute celery and onion in bacon drippings until tender. Combine sugar, flour and seasonings; stir into drippings. Add water and vinegar, stirring until smooth. Bring to a boil; add potatoes and bacon. Mix thoroughly. Yield: 6 servings.

Mrs. Mel Kuethe, Home Economics Teacher, Edwardsville, Ill.

 ## Idaho Patio Potatoes

6 med. potatoes
1 c. cottage cheese
1 c. sour cream
2 tbsp. chopped green onions
2 tbsp. butter
¼ c. Parmesan cheese

Cook potatoes in jackets; cool and mash. Salt and pepper to taste; add sour cream, cottage cheese and chopped green onions. Turn into lightly buttered casserole. Dot with butter and sprinkle with Parmesan cheese. Bake at 350 degrees for 25 minutes or until thoroughly heated. Mixture may be placed in potato shells, dotted with butter, sprinkled with Parmesan cheese and thoroughly heated.

Mrs. Don Samuelson, Wife of Governor of Idaho, Boise

 ## Luncheon Potato Puff

3 c. hot mashed potatoes
4 tbsp. butter or oleo, melted
1 c. bread crumbs
⅓ c. mayonnaise
1 tsp. salt
½ tsp. basil

(Continued on next page)

1 tbsp. grated lemon peel
1 ½ tbsp. lemon juice
½ c. milk
3 eggs, separated
¼ c. grated cheddar cheese

Combine melted butter with crumbs; spread in shallow 9-inch casserole. Combine mayonnaise, salt, basil, lemon peel and juice, milk and beaten egg yolks. Add to mashed potatoes; beat until smooth and fluffy. Beat egg whites stiff; fold into potato mixture. Pour into casserole. Sprinkle cheese over top. Bake in 350-degree oven for 30 minutes. Turn oven to 375 degrees and bake 10 minutes or until browned. Yield: 6 servings.

Mrs. J. G. Bauer, Officers' Wives' Club, Davisville, R. I.

Lyonnaise Potatoes

6 med. new potatoes
4 tbsp. butter
2 tbsp. cooking oil
½ c. finely sliced onions
Seasoning to taste

Drop new potatoes into boiling water to cover. Cook, covered, until tender, from 20 to 30 minutes. Remove skins; while still hot, slice thinly. Saute slices in 2 tablespoons butter and cooking oil till evenly browned. Saute onions in remaining butter; mix onions and potatoes gently. Season with salt, pepper and parsley.

Mrs. Clifford Bolden, Millbrook, Ala., Favorite Recipes Food Fair

Springtime Potatoes

1 ½ lb. small new potatoes
1 ½ tbsp. chopped green onions
⅓ c. chopped cucumber
2 tbsp. sliced raidshes
1 tsp. salt
Dash of pepper
½ c. sour cream
2 tbsp. chopped green pepper

Scrape potatoes; cook for 10 to 15 minutes in boiling water. Drain. Combine remaining ingredients; heat but do not boil. Pour mixture over hot potatoes. Yield: 4 servings.

Mrs. Harold C. Doty, Candor, N. Y.

New Potatoes With Cornflakes

6 med. potatoes, cooked and peeled
½ c. melted butter
1 c. finely crushed cornflakes
1 tsp. salt
¼ tsp. pepper

Dip potatoes in butter, then in cornflakes. Place in shallow baking dish; sprinkle with salt and pepper. Bake in preheated 250-degree oven for 20 minutes or until browned. Yield: 6 servings.

Charlotte Critchfield, Home Economics Teacher, Clay, Va.

 ### New Potatoes In Sour Cream

2 lb. new potatoes
1 ½ tsp. salt
2 tbsp. butter or margarine
½ c. sour cream
Dash of pepper

Wash and scrape potatoes. Place in saucepan with ½ inch boiling water and salt. Cover; cook for 15 minutes or until potatoes are tender. Drain. Add butter or margarine; heat until melted. Add sour cream and pepper. Heat only until hot. Yield: 4-6 servings.

Hazel Culbertson, Freeport, Tex.

 ### Patrician Potatoes

3 c. cream-style cottage cheese
4 c. cooked mashed potatoes
¾ c. sour cream
1 ½ tbsp. finely grated onion
2 ½ tsp. salt
⅛ tsp. white pepper
Melted butter
½ c. toasted almonds

Sieve cottage cheese; blend with warm mashed potatoes. Add sour cream, onion, salt and pepper; spoon into shallow, buttered 2-quart casserole. Brush surface with butter. Bake at 350 degrees for 30 minutes. Lightly brown under broiler; sprinkle with almonds. Yield: 8 servings.

Esther F. Intermill, Home Economics Teacher, Chassell, Mich.

Party Potatoes

8 to 10 med. potatoes, cooked
1 8-oz. pkg. cream cheese
1 c. sour cream
1 tsp. garlic salt
Butter
Paprika

Beat potatoes with electric mixer until smooth; add cream cheese and sour cream. If mixture is too stiff, add milk. Place in 2-quart casserole. Season with garlic salt; dot with butter. Sprinkle with paprika. Bake at 350 degrees for 30 minutes. Yield: 12 servings.

Mrs. Shirlee Johnson, Home Economics Teacher, Mt. Zion, Ill.

 ### Potatoes Chantilly

6 med. potatoes, cooked
½ c. butter
½ tsp. salt
¼ tsp. pepper
Scalded milk
½ to ¾ cup whipping cream, whipped
⅓ c. grated cheese

Mash potatoes through ricer and return to pan; add butter, salt and pepper. Gradually stir in scalded milk to obtain desired consistency. Beat until fluffy. Spread into buttered baking dish. Top with whipped cream and sprinkle with grated cheese. Bake in 400-degree oven until cheese is melted and topping is golden brown and bubbling. Yield: 6 servings.

Mrs. Francis Sheridan, Officers' Wives' Club, Abilene, Tex.

 ### Potatoes With Mushrooms And Cheese

4 to 5 med. Irish potatoes, peeled and thinly sliced
¼ tsp. salt
¼ tsp. pepper
1 clove of garlic, thinly sliced
¼ lb. butter
1 ½ lb. mushrooms
1 c. grated Swiss or cheddar cheese
Small bunch parsley, chopped
1 sm. onion, finely chopped
1 pt. heavy cream

Season potatoes with salt and pepper. Rub baking dish with garlic, then butter. Alternate layers of potatoes and mushrooms in baking dish, sprinkling each

(Continued on next page)

layer with cheese, parsley and onion. Repeat layers until all is used, ending with potatoes and reserving some cheese. Pour cream over potatoes; sprinkle remaining cheese over cream. Dot with butter. Bake at 375 degrees for 45 minutes or until potatoes are done. Yield: 6-8 servings.

Pat Baldwin, Home Economics Teacher, Woodville, Miss.

 ### Potatoes O'Brien

> 5 or 6 med. potatoes
> 1 ½ c. milk
> 2 tbsp. butter
> 1 c. diced cheese
> 1 sm. onion, finely diced
> ½ med. green pepper, diced
> 1 sm. jar pimento, diced
> ½ tsp. salt
> Cracker crumbs

Cook potatoes in jackets; peel and dice. Combine milk and butter; cook until slightly thickened. Add all remaining ingredients except potatoes and crumbs. Pour sauce over cooled potatoes; pour into baking dish. Cover with fine cracker crumbs. Bake at 375 degrees for 40 minutes. Yield: 5-6 servings.

Mrs. Virginia Golden, Big Stone Gap, Va.

 ### Potatoes-Onions Au Gratin

> 9 c. cooked, diced potatoes
> 2 lb. small white onions
> ½ c. each butter and flour
> 3 c. milk
> 3 c. light cream
> 1 c. chicken broth
> 1 lb. sharp cheddar cheese, coarsely grated
> 1 c. grated Parmesan cheese
> ½ tsp. pepper
> 1 ¾ tsp. salt
> 1 tsp. seasoned salt
> 1 clove garlic, crushed

Cook potatoes; cool. Peel and dice into ½-inch cubes. Peel onions; cook in boiling salted water only until just tender. Drain. Melt butter in large skillet; blend in flour. Add milk, cream and chicken broth; cook until thickened, stirring constantly. Add cheese, cooking gently until melted; add seasonings and garlic to taste. Mix sauce with cooked potatoes and onions; pour into 9 x 13 x 2-inch casserole or baking dish. Bake at 350 degrees for 45 minutes or until bubbly and lightly patched with brown. Yield: 10 servings.

Mrs. C. E. Koeninger, Pres. Officers' Wives' Club, Columbus, Ohio

 ## Potato Filling Casserole

14 med. potatoes
⅔ c. milk
2 eggs
1 lge. onion, minced
4 tbsp. butter
3 slices fresh bread, cut in ½-in. cubes
1 c. celery, diced finely
1 tbsp. fresh parsley
1 tsp. salt
¼ tsp. pepper
¼ tsp. marjoram

Peel and boil potatoes. Mash potatoes adding milk and eggs; beat well. Saute onion in butter until soft, not brown. Add to potatoes with remaining ingredients. Place in 3-quart casserole; dot with butter. Bake, uncovered, at 350 degrees for 45 minutes or until top is slightly puffed and browned. Yield: 12 servings.

Mrs. Tom Sherman, Birmingham, Ala.

 ## Potato-Ham Scallop Supreme

2 qt. pared potatoes, thinly sliced
¼ c. minced onion
¼ c. chopped green pepper
1 to 1½ lb. chopped ham
1 can cream of mushroom or celery soup
1 c. milk
Salt and pepper
1 can asparagus, drained

Layer potatoes, onion, green pepper and ham in 2-quart casserole; season. Combine soup and milk; season to taste. Pour over casserole. Bake, covered,

(Continued on next page)

at 350 degrees for 45 minutes. Uncover; bake for 20 to 30 minutes longer or until potatoes are tender. Top with asparagus; return to oven for 5 to 8 minutes. Serve. Yield: 8-10 servings.

Sister St. Anne-du-Sauveur, Van Buren, Maine, Favorite Recipes Food Fair

 ## Potato Souffle

>   6 med. potatoes, cooked
>   1/4 c. butter or margarine
>   2 eggs, separated
>   1 c. hot milk
>   3 drops Tabasco sauce
>   1 tsp. salt
>   1/2 tsp. dry mustard
>   1/4 tsp. monosodium glutamate
>   1/8 tsp. white pepper
>   1/2 c. grated cheddar cheese

Drain potatoes; whip or rice thoroughly. Beat in remaining ingredients except egg whites and cheese. Add cheese; beat until cheese melts. Fold in stiffly-beaten egg whites; turn mixture into greased 1½-quart casserole. Bake at 325 degrees for 50 minutes or until a knife inserted comes out clean. Yield: 6-8 servings.

Mrs. Marion Oster, Concord, Cal.

 ## Potato Stuffing

>   1/2 c. chopped onion
>   1/2 c. chopped celery
>   1/2 c. butter
>   1 loaf bread, crumbled
>   3 1/2 c. milk
>   2 tsp. salt
>   1/2 tsp. pepper
>   3 eggs, beaten
>   4 lb. potatoes, cooked and mashed
>   1 tbsp. parsley flakes

Saute onion and celery in ¼ cup butter until tender. Soak bread in milk. Blend salt, pepper, eggs and 1 tablespoon butter with hot potatoes. Combine all ingredients in large casserole; dot with remaining butter. Bake at 325 degrees for 1 hour or until brown and puffy. Leftovers may be sliced and fried. Yield: 8-10 servings.

Mrs. Elizabeth Yocom, Home Economics Teacher, Pottstown, Pa.

Potato Pancakes

    3 c. finely grated raw potatoes
    1 c. sifted flour
    2 tsp. salt
    2 tsp. baking powder
    ⅛ tsp. white pepper
    2 eggs
    1 c. milk
    4 tbsp. melted margarine
    2 tbsp. grated onion

Grate potatoes just before using to prevent discoloration. Combine all ingredients in large mixer bowl; beat on number three speed until blended. Drop by spoonfuls into hot fat; spread out with spoon. Brown; drain on paper towel. Yield: 10 servings.

Mrs. Robert Gould, Home Economics Teacher, Maryville, Tenn.

 ## Scalloped Potatoes

    2 tbsp. butter
    2 tbsp. flour
    ¾ tsp. salt
    1 ¾ c. milk
    5 c. sliced potatoes

Melt butter in saucepan; stir in flour and salt. Add milk slowly, stirring constantly, until sauce boils and thickens. Add potatoes; heat, stirring occasionally, until sauce boils. Pour into a greased casserole. Cover and bake at 350 degrees for 30 minutes or until potatoes are tender. Serve hot. Yield: 5 servings.

Mrs. Leslie Nuckolls, Richlands, Va.

 ## Stewed Potatoes

    1 sm. onion, chopped
    ¼ c. butter or margarine
    4 med. potatoes, pared and diced
    1 tsp. salt
    ½ c. water

Saute onion in butter until transparent. Add potatoes, salt and water. Simmer, covered, until done. Yield: 6 servings.

Mrs. Lucille King, Home Economics Teacher, Nazareth, Tex.

Rutabagas and Spinach

Baked Pumpkin Casserole

  1 1-lb. 13-oz. can pumpkin
  2 tbsp. sugar
  2 tbsp. butter or margarine, melted
  ¼ tsp. mace
  ½ tsp. salt
    Dash of pepper
  2 eggs, slightly beaten
  ½ c. coarsley chopped pecans
  ½ c. (firmly packed) light brown sugar
  ¼ c. maple syrup
  ½ c. pecan halves

Combine pumpkin, sugar, butter, mace, salt, pepper, eggs and chopped pecans in greased 1-quart casserole. Heat brown sugar and syrup until sugar is dissolved; bring to a boil. Cool slightly. Arrange pecan halves around edge of casserole; cover with glaze. Bake in preheated 350-degree oven for 40 minutes. Yield: 6-8 servings.

Mrs. Kenneth J. Leyden, Officers' Wives' Club, Oahu, Hawaii

 ## Fried Pumpkin Blooms

  12 to 16 fresh pumpkin blooms
  1 or 2 eggs, well beaten
  Fine cracker crumbs
  Salt and pepper to taste

Blooms must be cut in early morning before closing. Divide in half; wash and place in salt water until ready to use. Remove from water and dip in eggs; roll in crumbs. Place in well-greased skillet. Cook at low temperature until a golden brown. Serve while hot. Yield: 4 servings.

Kay Mathias, Home Economics Teacher, Nokomis, Ill.

 ## Steamed Pumpkin With Corn

  1 sm. pumpkin
  Salt and pepper to taste
  Monosodium glutamate
  Butter
  6 slices bacon
  2 tbsp. chopped onion
  1 16-oz. pkg. cream cheese
  1 can whole kernel corn
  2 tbsp. Worcestershire sauce

(Continued on next page)

Boil or steam pumpkin; drain and mash. Add salt, pepper, monosodium gluta-mate and butter as for mashed potatoes. Fry bacon until crisp; chop fine. Fry onion in bacon fat. Add cream cheese; fry until melted. Add pumpkin, bacon, corn and Worcestershire sauce; mix well. Pat mixture into baking dish. Cover and keep hot until ready to serve. Canned pumpkin may be used. Yield: 8 servings.

Mrs. M. Jean Henk, Canonsburg, Pa.

Cooked Radishes

Radishes
Seasoning to taste

Drop radishes into salted boiling water to cover. Simmer, uncovered, about 6 to 8 minutes or until tender. Drain; correct seasonings.

Mrs. K. J. Ashcraft, Montgomery, Ala., Favorite Recipes Food Fair

Creamed Radishes

4 pkg. fresh radishes
2 tbsp. flour
1 c. milk
1/8 tsp. curry powder
1 tbsp. margarine

Pare and cut off ends of radishes. Cover radishes halfway with cold water in saucepan. Cover and cook for 10 minutes. Remove from heat; add flour and milk. Stir; add curry powder, blending well. Cook until sauce is smooth. Add margarine; serve. Yield: 4 servings.

Janet L. Glen, Home Economics Teacher, Brick Town, N. J.

Buttered Rutabagas

1 1/2 to 2 lb. rutabagas
1 1/2 tsp. Worcestershire sauce
1/4 tsp. onion powder
1/4 c. sugar
1 tsp. salt
3 to 4 drops Tabasco sauce
Butter to taste

(Continued on next page)

Peel rutabagas; cut into small pieces in saucepan. Add Worcestershire sauce, onion powder, sugar, salt and Tabasco sauce. Cover with water; bring to a boil. Cook until tender. Add butter and mash with a fork.

Mrs. Anne Sutphen Welch, Knoxville, Tenn.

 ### Mashed Rutabaga

> 1 lge. rutabaga
> 1 tsp. salt
> Pepper to taste
> 2 tbsp. butter
> ¼ c. heavy cream

Peel rutabaga; cut into slices or cubes. Cook in boiling, salted water for 15 to 20 minutes or until tender. Drain thoroughly. Mash rutabaga until fine with potato masher; add pepper and additional salt if needed. Add butter and cream. Heat and serve. Yield: 6 servings.

Mrs. Audra Reich, Home Economics Teacher, Webster, S. D.

 ### Finnish Rutabaga Pudding

> 3 c. or 2 lb. mashed rutabaga
> Boiling water
> 1 tsp. salt
> 2 tbsp. milk
> 2 tbsp. butter or margarine
> ½ tsp. sugar
> ⅛ tsp. ground nutmeg
> ⅛ tsp. ground black pepper
> 2 tbsp. butter or margarine, melted

Wash, peel and cut rutabagas in quarters. Place in saucepan with 1 inch boiling water and salt. Bring to boiling point and cook, uncovered, 5 minutes. Cover

(Continued on next page)

and continue cooking 20 minutes or until rutabagas are soft. Mash and put through a sieve. Add 2 tablespoons butter or margarine, milk, sugar, nutmeg and ground black pepper. Mix well. Turn into a buttered 9-inch pie plate. Make indentations over the top with the tip of a tablespoon. Pour melted butter or margarine over the surface. Bake at 375 degrees for 40 to 45 minutes or until top is lightly flecked with brown.

Photograph for this recipe on page 223.

 ### Rutabaga Casserole

>1 med. rutabaga
>2 tbsp. butter
>2 tbsp. coarse ground white flour or white toast crumbs
>½ c. milk
>1 egg
>White pepper to taste
>1 tbsp. brown sugar or syrup
>Salt to taste
>Nutmeg to taste

Peel, rinse and slice rutabaga. Cook until soft; mash. Mix in butter and 1 tablespoon flour; gradually add the milk and other ingredients except nutmeg. Pour into well-greased mold or casserole; sprinkle remaining flour and nutmeg on top. Bake at 350 degrees for 30 minutes. Yield: 6-8 servings.

Sharon Ailie, Goodhue, Minn.

 ### Rutabagas

>4 med. rutabagas
>½ tsp. salt
>Melted butter
>Lemon juice
>Chopped parsley

Pare and dice rutabagas; drop into boiling water. Cook, uncovered, until tender, about 25 to 35 minutes. Drain well; sprinkle with salt. Combine remaining ingredients; serve with rutabagas. Rutabagas may also be French-fried or baked as for potatoes.

Mrs. J. G. McDavid, Madison, Wis.

 ### Sauteed Rutabaga

>2 slices bacon
>1 lge. rutabaga, thinly sliced

(Continued on next page)

Cut bacon crosswise into small pieces; fry until crisp. Remove bacon. Cover and cook rutabaga in bacon grease over medium high heat for 20 minutes or until tender, turning occasionally. Add bacon; heat and serve. Yield: 3-4 servings.

Mrs. Marguerite Stetson, Home Economics Teacher, Salem, Ore.

 ## Boiled Oyster Plants (Salsify)

1 tbsp. flour
2 tsp. lemon juice
½ tsp. salt
2 c. peeled oyster plant

Dissolve flour, lemon juice and salt in 3 cups boiling water. Peel oyster plant; dice. Drop into boiling water; cook for 7 to 10 minutes or till tender. Chive or parsley butter may be served with oyster plant.

Mrs. Kenny Lehto, Burbank, Cal.

 ## Sweet Rutabaga

2 tbsp. brown sugar
1 No. 2 can rutabaga
1 tbsp. corn syrup
2 tbsp. butter
Marshmallows

Combine brown sugar and rutabaga in a casserole; pour corn syrup over mixture. Dot with butter; cover with marshmallows. Cover and bake at 350 degrees for 20 to 30 minutes. Yield: 5-6 servings.

Fran Mollet, Conde, S. D.

Salsify Casserole

12 oysters plants or 1 pt. canned oysters plants, sliced
6 plain crackers, crumbled
½ tsp. salt
½ tsp. pepper
1 tbsp. margarine
1 ½ c. milk

Place in alternate layers in a casserole, oyster plants and crackers until all have been used. Mix remaining ingredients; pour over mixture. Bake at 350 degrees about 30 minutes. Yield: 4 servings.

Louise Hunt, Kevil, Ky.

 ## Baked Spinach

1 pkg. frozen spinach
1 c. boiling water
2 tbsp. fat
2 tbsp. flour
1 ¼ c. milk
½ c. plus 2 tbsp. grated American cheese
1 tsp. salt
Dash of pepper
1 c. buttered bread crumbs

Drop spinach into briskly boiling water; bring to a boil and cook for 4 to 6 minutes or until tender, separating leaves with fork. Drain and chop. Melt fat in saucepan; add flour and stir until smooth. Add milk gradually; cook until thickened, stirring constantly. Add spinach, ½ cup cheese and seasonings; blend well. Turn into greased shallow baking dish. Cover with mixture of buttered crumbs and remaining cheese. Bake at 350 degrees for 30 minutes. Yield: 4 servings.

Elizabeth Curry, Home Economics Teacher, Marianna, Fla.

 ## Chinese Spinach

2 lb. fresh spinach or 2 10-oz. pkg. spinach
2 cloves of garlic
2 tbsp. peanut or corn oil
1 ½ tsp. salt
1 to 1½ tsp. sugar
¼ tsp. monosodium glutamate (opt.)

(Continued on next page)

Wash and drain the spinach, removing any wilted leaves. Crush the garlic. Heat the oil with the garlic in fry pan over high flame. Add spinach and stir until oil is thoroughly mixed with spinach. Discard garlic. Add remaining ingredients and stir again. Cover and cook for 2 minutes. Place in serving dish. Garnish with bits of crisp bacon, ham or hard-cooked eggs. Yield: 4-6 servings.

Mrs. Janice Ritchie, Home Economics Teacher, Reedsville, Ohio

 Fresh Spinach Piquant

> 6 *slices bacon*
> ½ *c. onion rings*
> 2 *lb. fresh spinach*
> ½ *tsp. oregano leaves*
> 1 *tbsp. cider vinegar*
> ⅛ *tsp. pepper*
> 1 ½ *tsp. salt*

Fry bacon; remove from skillet. Drain off all but 2 tablespoons bacon fat; discard excess fat. Add onion rings to fat and saute until transparent. Remove from fat; set aside. Wash spinach; add to fat. Add oregano; cover and cook for 8 to 10 minutes or until spinach is tender. Add vinegar, pepper, salt, onion rings and crumbled bacon. Toss lightly; garnish with additional fresh onion rings. Yield: 4-5 servings.

Photograph for this recipe below.

Florentine Spinach

4 tbsp. butter
4 tbsp. flour
1 ¾ c. milk
1 tsp. salt
3 med. eggs, slightly beaten
3 c. chopped spinach
¼ c. buttered crumbs

Melt butter in saucepan; blend in flour. Gradually add milk and salt; cook and stir until thickened. Mix beaten eggs, white sauce and spinach lightly; pour into buttered casserole. Cover and bake at 350 degrees for 45 minutes. Sprinkle on buttered crumbs. Bake, uncovered, 15 minutes longer. Yield: 6 servings.

Caroline E. Duffy, Home Economics Teacher, Turlock, Cal.

 ## Fried Spinach

1 c. finely chopped fresh wilted spinach or 1 c. chopped
     canned spinach
¾ to 1 c. saltine cracker crumbs
¼ tsp. salt
1 egg, well beaten
4 tbsp. shortening

Wilt spinach; cool. Add spinach, crackers crumbs and salt to eggs; mix. Melt shortening in skillet; add spinach mixture. Fry slowly, chopping and turning frequently, until nicely browned. Yield: 4 servings.

Mrs. Vera Grimm, Home Economics Teacher, Holgate, Ohio

 ## Spinach Patties

3 tbsp. salad oil
2 c. chopped spinach, cooked
1 egg, slightly beaten
3 tbsp. grated Romano cheese
Salt to taste
¼ tsp. garlic powder

Place salad oil in skillet. Combine all other ingredients thoroughly. When oil is hot, drop mixture by tablespoonfuls into skillet; cook until firm. Yield: 4 servings.

Mrs. Vincent A. Ciccone, New Hartford, N. Y., Favorite Recipes Food Fair

Spinach Balls

  2 c. cooked spinach
  2 tbsp. butter (opt.)
  ½ to 1 tsp. salt
  ¼ tsp. pepper
  2 eggs
  Bread crumbs
  2 tbsp. grated onion
  2 tbsp. grated cheese
  ¼ tsp. oregano
  ⅛ tsp. allspice
  ¼ c. water

Combine spinach, butter, salt, pepper, 1 egg, 1 cup bread crumbs, onion, cheese and spices. Let stand for 10 minutes; shape into balls. Blend remaining egg and water. Roll spinach balls in bread crumbs, egg mixture and again in crumbs. Fry in deep fat at 375 degrees until brown or at 350 degrees in deep butter. Drain on absorbent paper, Yield: 6 servings.

Violet Kueker, Waterloo, Ill.

 ## Stir-Fry Spinach

  4 slices bacon
  3 qt. spinach
  2 tbsp. tarragon vinegar
  Salt and pepper to taste

Cook bacon until crisp in heavy skillet; drain bacon, reserving 2 tablespoons fat. Chop or crumble bacon. Wash and trim large stems on spinach; add to hot fat in skillet. Stir and toss spinach over moderately high heat for 3 minutes or until barely tender and bright green. Sprinkle with tarragon vinegar; season with salt and pepper. Garnish with bacon; serve immediately. Yield: 8 servings.

Mrs. Frances Schneider, Home Economics Teacher, Menomonie, Wis.

 ## Hot Bacon-Spinach Dressing

  3 to 6 slices of bacon
  5 tbsp. sugar
  ½ tsp. salt
  1 tbsp. flour
  1 egg, slightly beaten
  3 tbsp. vinegar
  3 tbsp. water
  Cooked spinach

(Continued on next page)

Dice bacon; fry until done. Drain off most of fat. Mix sugar with salt and flour; blend in egg. Add vinegar; mix well. Add water; mix. Add spinach to bacon over low or medium heat; add dressing. Cook until dressing begins to thicken. Serve hot. Yield: 4-6 servings.

Jane E. Spangler, Shippensburg, Pa.

 Green Rice Casserole

> *4 beaten eggs*
> *1 tbsp. grated onion*
> *2 tsp. salt*
> *1 lb. grated sharp cheese*
> *1 c. milk*
> *4 c. cooked rice*
> *1 pkg. frozen chopped spinach*
> *½ tsp. marjoram*
> *½ tsp. thyme*
> *½ tsp. rosemary*
> *1 tbsp. Worcestershire sauce*
> *¼ c. melted butter*

Cook spinach 5 minutes; drain. Mix all ingredients. Put in casserole. Pour melted butter on top. Bake 30 minutes at 350 degrees. Yield: 8 servings.

Mrs. Fred R. Peck, Officers' Wives' Club, Wheeler AFB, Hawaii

 Spinach-Cheese Bake

> *1 10-oz. pkg. frozen spinach, cooked and drained*
> *2 tbsp. finely chopped onion*
> *2 beaten eggs*
> *½ c. milk*
> *½ c. shredded, sharp process American cheese*
> *1 3-oz. can sliced mushrooms, drained*
> *¼ tsp. salt*
> *Dash of pepper*
> *½ c. buttered soft bread crumbs*

Combine all ingredients except crumbs. Turn into 9 x 5-inch loaf pan. Top with crumbs. Bake at 350 degrees for 20 minutes or until knife inserted in center comes out clean. Yield: 4 servings.

Mrs. James E. Petitmermet, Officers' Wives' Club, Waverly AFS, Iowa

Spinach Loaf

    1 No. 2 can spinach, drained and chopped
    ½ c. finely chopped onion
    ½ c. finely chopped green pepper
    ¼ tsp. pepper
    1 tsp. salt
    ¼ c. finely chopped pimento
    1 ½ c. fine cracker crumbs
    1 egg, slightly beaten
    3 tbsp. melted butter or bacon drippings

Combine all ingredients thoroughly; place in well greased 1-pound coffee can or covered baking dish. Steam, covered, for 1 hour and 30 minutes. Yield: 8-10 servings.

Margaret Jones, Mobile, Ala.

 Texas Spinach Loaf

    2 eggs, separated
    2 c. ground or finely chopped spinach
    ½ tsp. salt
    ½ tsp. pepper
    ½ tsp. nutmeg
    1 c. bread crumbs
    1 onion, finely chopped
    1 green pepper, finely chopped
    ½ clove of garlic, chopped (opt.)

Beat egg whites until stiff. Beat egg yolks. Combine all ingredients, folding in egg whites last. Place in buttered casserole. Bake at 350 degrees for 1 hour. Yield: 6 servings.

Mrs. Fritz Michalke, Schulenburg, Tex.

 Spinach

    ½ c. white sauce
    2 c. cooked spinach, drained
    1 ½ c. cooked macaroni
    2 hard-cooked eggs, chopped
    2 tbsp. grated Italian style cheese

Mix white sauce with cooked spinach. In a buttered baking dish, make alternate layers of spinach, macaroni and chopped eggs. Sprinkle top layer with grated cheese. Heat 20 minutes at 350 degrees. Yield: 6 servings.

Mrs. A. F. Hickey, Camas, Wash.

Savory Spinach Squares

2/3 c. milk
1/4 c. melted butter
1/2 c. minced onion
2 tbsp. dry parsley flakes
1 tsp. Worcestershire sauce
1 1/2 to 2 tsp. salt
1/2 tsp. thyme
1/2 tsp. nutmeg
4 eggs, beaten
2 10-oz. pkg. frozen chopped spinach, cooked and drained
2 c. cooked rice
2 c. shredded process American cheese

Combine milk, butter, onion, parsley flakes, Worcestershire sauce, salt, thyme and nutmeg; mix well. Add to eggs. Combine remaining ingredients; add egg mixture and mix well. Pour into a greased shallow 2-quart baking dish. Bake in a preheated 350 degree oven for 40 to 45 minutes. Cut into squares for serving. Yield: 8 servings.

Sister Roserita, Home Economics Teacher, Newark, Ohio

Sesame Spinach

2 pkg. frozen leaf spinach
1/4 c. soy sauce
2 tbsp. cider vinegar
1/4 tsp. sugar
1 med. onion, cut into rings
2 tbsp. toasted sesame seed

Cook spinach according to package directions; do not overcook. Combine soy sauce, vinegar and sugar. Drain spinach and add onion rings; add soy sauce mixture and toss. Chill for 1 hour, tossing frequently. Serve in portions as a salad; garnish with toasted sesame seed just before serving. To toast sesame seed, gently heat a 2 or 3-ounce box sesame seed in small skillet. Stir frequently until each seed is toasted, but not burned. Press seed using the bottom of a water tumbler to extract oil and enhance flavor. Yield: 6-8 servings.

Mrs. Jean Prebeck, Lexington, Ill.

Spinach With Cream Cheese Dressing

1 12-oz. pkg. frozen spinach
1 3-oz. pkg. cream cheese
2 tsp. chopped chives or 1/2 tsp. grated onion (opt.)
Salt and pepper

(Continued on next page)

Cook spinach according to package directions; cook until all liquid has evaporated. Add cream cheese to hot spinach with chives or onion; season to taste. Serve. Yield: 4 servings.

Echo P. Schepman, North Bend, Ore.

 ## Spinach Delight

> 1 pkg. frozen spinach or 1 lb. fresh spinach
> 1 tbsp. butter
> 1 tbsp. flour
> ½ c. sour cream
> ½ tsp. minced onion
> ¼ tsp. monosodium glutamate
> ½ tsp. salt
> ¼ tsp. pepper

Cook spinach until tender. Melt butter; blend in flour. Add sour cream; cook, stirring constantly, until thickened. Add spinach, onion and seasonings. Heat over low heat. Yield: 4 servings.

Mrs. Muriel F. Richards, Home Economics Teacher, Battle Creek, Neb.

 ## Spinach Fondue

> 2 pkg. frozen spinach
> 5 tbsp. butter
> ½ c. chopped onion
> 1 tbsp. flour
> 2 eggs
> 2 c. milk
> 1 c. soft bread crumbs
> ½ c. grated Old English cheese

Cook spinach as directed on package; drain. Melt butter in a saucepan; add onion. Cook until transparent; do not brown. Add flour; stir. Combine and beat eggs and milk; add to flour mixture. Stir. Fold bread crumbs and cheese into cooked spinach. Combine spinach with hot mixture. Place in buttered casserole. Bake at 350 degrees for 30 minutes. Serve with mushroom-cheese sauce.

SAUCE:

> 1 can cream of mushroom soup
> 3 hard-cooked eggs, chopped
> ½ c. grated Old English cheese

Combine all ingredients. Heat in top of double boiler. Yield: 6 servings.

Gertrude Quinby Brubaker, Portage, Pa.

Spinach Divine

    1 can cream of mushroom soup
½ stick butter
    Grated onion to taste
    4 pkg. frozen choped spinach, cooked and drained
½ pkg. cheddar cheese, grated
    4 strips bacon, diced

Combine soup, butter and onion in double boiler; cook until smooth. Grease casserole with bacon fat. Combine spinach and sauce; place in casserole. Sprinkle with cheese and bacon. Bake at 350 degrees for 40 to 50 minutes. Yield: 8 servings.

Mrs. Doris Burr, Hayward, Cal.

Spinach-Macaroni Bake

    2 lge. onions, chopped
    3 cloves of garlic, minced
    3 tbsp. olive oil
    2 1½-oz. pkg. spaghetti sauce mix
    2 3 or 4-oz. cans mushrooms
    2 8-oz. cans tomato sauce
    2 8-oz. cans tomato paste
    2 c. water
    1 lb. elbow macaroni, cooked
    4 eggs, well beaten
    3 pkg. frozen chopped spinach, thawed and drained
    2 c. cottage cheese
½ c. grated Parmesan cheese

Lightly brown onions and garlic in oil; combine with spaghetti sauce mix, mushrooms, tomato sauce, tomato paste and water in large saucepan. Combine drained macaroni with 2 eggs; mix well. Combine remaining eggs with spinach, cottage cheese and Parmesan cheese. Alternate layers of one-third of sauce, one-half of macaroni and one-half of spinach mixture in 9 x 13 x 2-inch baking pan. Repeat layers using same amounts. Cover with remaining sauce. Cover with foil. Bake at 350 degrees for 45 minutes; uncover and bake for 5 minutes longer. Yield: 12 servings.

Mrs. Robert V. Smith, Officers' Wives' Club, Key West, Fla.

Spinach Madeline

    2 pkg. frozen chopped spinach
    4 tbsp. butter
    2 tbsp. flour
    2 tbsp. chopped onion

(Continued on next page)

½ c. evaporated milk
½ tsp. black pepper
 Red pepper to taste
¾ tsp. celery salt
¾ tsp. garlic salt
½ tsp. salt
1 tsp. Worcestershire
1 6-oz. roll Jalapeno pepper cheese, cut into small pieces
 Buttered bread crumbs

Cook spinach; drain and reserve ½ cup liquid. Melt butter; add flour and stir until well blended and smooth but not brown. Add onion; cook until soft. Add milk and spinach liquid slowly, stirring constantly. Cook until smooth and thick; add seasonings, Worcestershire sauce and cheese. Combine cream sauce with spinach. Place in casserole; top with buttered crumbs. Bake at 350 degrees for 25 minutes.

Mrs. Ethel Robbins, Jennings, La., Favorite Recipes Food Fair

 ## Spinach And Oyster Casserole

2 doz. large oysters or 1 pt. small oysters
2 qt. spinach
2 tbsp. chopped onion
1 sm. clove of garlic
½ c. butter or margarine
2 eggs, slightly beaten
2 tbsp. cream
¼ tsp. pepper
1 tsp. salt
 Bread crumbs

Scald one-half of the oyster liquid; chop the remaining one-half. Cook spinach for 3 minutes; drain well and chop fine. Saute onion, garlic and chopped oysters in butter; add to spinach. Stir in eggs and cream; season. Place scalded oysters in a well greased 2½-quart casserole; pour oyster mixture over them. Top with bread crumbs. Bake at 325 degrees for 1 hour. Yield: 8 servings.

Hazel Edberg, Home Economics Teacher, Modesto, Cal.

 ## Spinach Pie

2 lb. spinach
½ lb. feta cheese, crumbled
½ lb. cottage cheese
½ c. chopped parsley or mint leaves may be added, if desired
 Salt and white pepper
6 eggs, separated

(Continued on next page)

½ lb. pastry sheets
¾ lb. butter, melted

Clean and chop spinach; place in large mixing bowl. Add feta, cottage cheese and seasonings. Add egg yolks and mix thoroughly. Beat egg whites until stiff and fold into spinach mixture. Grease 9 x 13-inch pan and place 6 pastry sheets into pan, brushing each with melted butter. Spread spinach mixture evenly; cover with 6 individually buttered pastry sheets. Bake at 350 degrees for approximately 1 hour or until golden brown. Cut in squares and serve hot or cold. Yield: 6 servings.

Mary Germany, Detroit, Mich.

 ## Spinach Ring

> 3 c. cooked spinach
> ½ c. coarse crumbs
> 1 tsp. onion juice
> 1 tbsp. chopped celery
> ¼ tsp. salt
> ¼ tsp. pepper
> 2 tbsp. butter or margarine
> 3 eggs, beaten

Mix all ingredients; pour into a buttered ring mold. Set in pan of hot water. Bake at 300 degrees for 30 minutes. Unmold onto large platter; fill center with a white vegetable such as creamed cauliflower or mashed potatoes. Make a border of buttered carrots. Yield: 6 servings.

Martha June Graber, New Paris, Ind.

 ## Spinach Souffle

> 4 tbsp. butter
> 1 tbsp. minced onion
> 1 tbsp. minced green pepper
> 1 tbsp. minced celery
> 3 tbsp. flour
> ½ tsp. salt
> ⅛ tsp. pepper
> 1 c. milk
> 4 eggs, separated
> 2 c. cooked spinach, drained

Melt butter; add onion, green pepper and celery. Cook until soft but not brown. Blend in flour, salt and pepper; add milk. Cook, stirring, until thickened. Beat egg yolks until thick and lemon colored; stir slowly into white sauce.

(Continued on next page)

Add spinach. Beat egg whites until stiff; fold in. Turn into buttered 1-quart casserole; set in pan of hot water. Bake at 350 degrees for 50 minutes or until dry on top. Yield: 6 servings.

Toni Guast, Factoryville, Pa.

 ### Spinach Timbales

    1 pkg. frozen chopped spinach
    2 tbsp. butter or margarine
    2 tsp. lemon juice
    Milk
    2 eggs
    2 tbsp. flour
    1 tsp. salt
    ⅛ tsp. pepper

Place spinach in saucepan; do not add water. Turn heat on low and break with a fork. After thawing, continue to cook and stir for 5 minutes. Drain well and reserve water. Add butter and lemon juice to spinach. Add enough milk to water to make 2/3 cup liquid; pour into mixing bowl. Add eggs, flour and seasonings; beat until well blended. Add spinach. Pour spinach mixture into greased custard cups. Place cups in a pan of hot water. Bake at 350 degrees for 45 minutes or until firm; test as for custard. Loosen timbales with a spatula and turn onto platter. Serve with hollandaise or cheese sauce. Yield: 4-5 servings.

Margaret Marie Godfrey, Macclenny, Fla.

 ### Sweet And Sour Spinach

    3 tbsp. sugar
    1 ½ tbsp. cornstarch
    ½ tsp. salt
    1 egg, beaten
    ½ c. milk
    3 tbsp. vinegar
    1 tbsp. butter
    1 No. 2½ can spinach
    4 strips bacon, fried and chopped
    2 hard-cooked eggs

Combine sugar, cornstarch and salt with egg and milk. Cook in double boiler until thickened; add vinegar and butter. Combine spinach, bacon and boiled dressing. Bake at 350 degrees for 20 minutes. Garnish with hard-cooked eggs. Yield: 6 servings.

Frances H. Judy, Home Economics Teacher, Richwood, W. Va.

Squash and Sweet Potatoes

Crunchy Baked Acorn Squash

Acorn squash
Butter
Brown sugar
Crushed pecans
Coconut

Wash squash and cut in halves. Boil in salted water until tender; drain and place in baking dish. Add 1 teaspoon butter and 1 tablespoon brown sugar to each half. Sprinkle with pecans and coconut. Bake at 350 degrees until sugar bubbles.

Helene Arnold, Home Economics Teacher, Frankfort, Ky.

 ## Acorn Squash With Applesauce

2 acorn squash, washed and halved
Melted butter
Brown sugar (opt.)
Cinnamon (opt.)
2 to 2½ c. applesauce

Remove squash seed. Bake, cut-side down, at 350 degrees for 35 minutes. Turn; bake for 25 minutes longer. Brush insides with butter; sprinkle with brown sugar and cinnamon. Heat applesauce; spoon into squash. May be garnished with cherries, jelly or preserves. Yield: 4 servings.

Mrs. Billye Tingle, Carthage, Miss., Favorite Recipes Food Fair

 ## Acorn Squash Stuffed With Ham And Apple

3 med. acorn squash
½ tsp. salt
1 c. diced tart apples
2 c. diced cooked ham
1 tsp. dry mustard
¼ tsp. pepper

Wash and cut squash in halves, lengthwise; remove seed. Sprinkle inside with salt; place cut-side down in pan. Pour in ¼-inch boiling water. Bake in preheated 425 degree oven for 30 minutes or until almost tender. Turn squash halves cut-side up. Combine remaining ingredients; spoon into squash cavities. Reduce heat to 375 degrees and bake for 20 minutes or until apples are tender. Serve hot. Yield: 6 servings.

Mrs. Eddith M. Davis, El Paso, Tex.

Acorn Squash Stuffed With Pork

3 *acorn squash, halved and seeded*
1 *lb. pork sausage, cooked and drained*
⅔ *c. milk*
1 *tsp. salt*
¼ *tsp. pepper*
1 *tsp. dry mustard*
½ *c. pickle relish*
¾ *c. uncooked oats*

Place squash cut-side down in baking pan; pour a small amount of water in pan. Bake in preheated 425 degree oven for 30 minutes. Remove from oven; turn squash cut-side up. Combine sausage with remaining ingredients; spoon into squash centers. Add a small amount of water to pan; return to oven. Reduce temperature to 350 degrees; bake for 30 minutes or until tender.

Vesta L. Glessner, Home Economics Teacher, Shanksville, Pa.

 Stuffed Acorn Squash Au Gratin

1 *acorn squash*
1 *tsp. chopped onion*
1 *tsp. finely chopped green pepper*
2 *tbsp. butter*
½ *c. grated cheese*
1 *c. soft bread crumbs*
Salt and pepper

Bake squash at 400 degrees for 35 minutes or until tender. Cut lengthwise into halves; discard seed and scoop out center, leaving shells ¼-inch thick. Mash pulp; add remaining ingredients. Pile into squash shells. Bake at 350 degrees until browned on top. Yield: 2 servings.

Mrs. Nancy H. Davis, Washington, Ohio

 Texas Acorns

1 *acorn squash*
2 *tbsp. oleo*
4 *tbsp. brown sugar*

Cut squash in half, lengthwise. Remove seeds and turn cut side down in ½ inch water in a shallow pan. Bake at 350 to 375 degrees until squash is tender when mashed with fingers; remove from oven. Drain any remaining water from pan. Turn squash cut side up. Melt oleo and brown sugar; spoon mixture over cut edges of squash and pour in cavity. Return to oven; cook until mixture is bubbly. Yield: 2 servings.

Mrs. L. L. Withrow, Ft. Worth, Tex.

Baked Squash

4 or 5 fresh squash, cut up or 1 can
1 sm. onion, cut up
Salt to taste
1 egg, beaten
2 tbsp. butter
¼ c. grated cheese
1 c. cracker crumbs

Cook squash and onion in small amount of salted water; drain and mash. Add egg, butter, cheese and ½ cup cracker crumbs; mix well. Place in buttered baking dish; top with remaining crumbs. Bake at 350 degrees for 25 minutes. For variation, shape mixture into balls and roll in cracker crumbs. Fry in deep fat. Yield: 6 servings.

Myrtle F. Campbell, Rockmart, Ga.

 ### Baked Squash Dressing

6 med. yellow squash
3 c. bread crumbs
1 c. grated cheese
1 med. onion, coarsely grated
1 tsp. salt
⅛ tsp. pepper
2 tbsp. butter
2 eggs, beaten
Cracker crumbs

Cook squash in a small amount of boiling water; drain, saving water. Mash squash. Soak bread crumbs in enough squash water to soften. Blend all ingredients except cracker crumbs; place in a buttered casserole. Cover with cracker crumbs. Bake at 350 degrees for 1 hour. Grated cheese may be sprinkled on top. Yield: 6-8 servings.

Jane Carr, Covington, Tenn.

 ### Baked Banana Squash

½ banana squash
½ c. butter
¾ c. brown sugar

Wash squash; remove seed. Place in long baking pan or roaster. Parboil until tender; drain. Sprinkle with butter and sugar. Bake at 425 degrees until brown. Yield: 6 servings.

Sylvia B. Prater, Richmond Dale, Ohio

Bleu Cheese-Squash Casserole

4 med. yellow squash
1 tsp. salt
1 egg, beaten
⅓ wedge bleu cheese
1 tbsp. butter
Black pepper to taste
Cracker crumbs

Cook squash in salted water until tender. Drain and mash thoroughly. Mix in all remaining ingredients except crumbs. Pour into baking dish and top with crumbs. Bake for 30 minutes in a 375-degree oven. Yield: 4 servings.

Marjorie Bullard Turner, Jackson, Miss.

 ### Butternut Squash Casserole

3 c. ground butternut squash
1 c. sugar
¼ c. butter
1 c. milk
½ c. flaked coconut
Dash of salt

Combine all ingredients; pour into a 9-inch casserole. Bake at 325 degrees for 45 minutes. Yield: 8 servings.

Mrs. David L. Sayers, Danville, Va.

 ### Butternut Squash With Topping

4 c. cooked mashed squash
3 c. sugar
2 eggs, beaten
1 tsp. vanilla flavoring
1 sm. can crushed pineapple
1 sm. jar maraschino cherries, chopped
2 tbsp. cornstarch
Food coloring
½ c. finely chopped nuts

Combine squash, 2 cups sugar, eggs and flavoring in casserole. Bake at 350 degrees for 40 minutes. Blend remaining ingredients; cook until thickened, stirring constantly. Serve over squash. Yield: 6-8 servings.

Mrs. Regina Duncan, Home Economics Teacher, Blue Ridge, Ga.

Dorothy's Squash Casserole

3 med. butternut squash
Cracker crumbs
1/2 c. grated cheese
1/4 c. minced onion
Salt and pepper
Butter
1/4 c. cream or milk
Paprika

Slice squash and arrange slices in layers in buttered casserole. On each layer sprinkle cracker crumbs, cheese, onion, salt and pepper. Dot with butter. Add cream. Top casserole with crumbs, cheese, butter, and sprinkle with paprika. Cook, covered, at 375 degrees for about 20 minutes; remove top and brown about 10 minutes. Yellow crook-neck squash may be used if desired. Yield: 4-6 servings.

Mrs. Dorothy A. Foster, Mathews, Va.

 ## Honey-Glazed Squash

1 med. butternut squash
1/4 c. honey
2 tbsp. butter
1 tbsp. lemon juice
1 tbsp. water
1/8 to 1/4 tsp. mace

Pare squash and cut in pieces. Steam until nearly tender. Combine remaining ingredients; bring to a boil. Pour sauce over squash in baking pan. Bake at 350 degrees until squash is tender and well glazed, basting occasionally. Yield: 4-5 servings.

Elma M. Senn, Yakima, Wash.

 ## Spiced Butternut Squash

1 lge. butternut squash
3 tbsp. butter or margarine
1/4 c. brown sugar
Ground nutmeg

Peel and seed squash; cut into 1-inch cubes. Cook until tender in salted water. Arrange squash in buttered casserole. Dot with butter; sprinkle with brown sugar and nutmeg. Bake at 350 degrees for 20 minutes or until browned. Yield: 4 servings.

Mrs. Virginia Smith, Evansville, Ind.

Mashed Butternut Squash

        2 lb. butternut squash
        3 tbsp. butter
        3 tbsp. brown sugar
        3 tbsp. orange juice
        ½ tsp. grated lemon peel
        ¾ tsp. salt

Wash whole unpeeled squash; place in saucepan with boiling water. Cover and cook for 45 minutes or until tender. Remove from water; split lengthwise. Scoop out seed; discard. Scoop out squash; mash. Blend in remaining ingredients. Serve hot. Yield: 6 servings.

Mrs. Marijo W. Rawlings, Home Economics Teacher, Ackerly, Tex.

 ### Chili Squash

        6 sm. squash, peeled and quartered
        1 c. grated sharp cheese
        ½ can Ortega chili
        1 c. bread crumbs

Cook squash until tender; drain. Add cheese and chili. Pour into casserole; top with bread crumbs. Bake at 350 degrees for 30 minutes. Yield: 6 servings.

Mrs. Ralph E. Lund, Ft. Sumner, N. M.

 ### French-Fried Squash

        1 med. white squash
        Salt and pepper
        Cornmeal

Peel squash; slice thinly. Crisp in water for 30 minutes; drain. Dip each slice in seasoned cornmeal. Fry in deep fat to a golden brown; drain. Yield: 3 servings.

Mrs. Ruth Brown, Fenton, La.

French-Fried Summer Squash

    3 eggs, beaten
    ½ c. milk
    1 tsp. salt
    4 med. summer squash, thinly sliced
    2 c. cornmeal
    Oil

Combine eggs, milk and salt to make a batter. Dip squash in batter; roll in cornmeal. Fry in deep fat until done. Yield: 6 servings.

Mrs. Frances W. Banner, Home Economics Teacher, Castlewood, Va.

 ### Squash Fritters

    ½ c. flour
    ½ tsp. baking powder
    2 c. cold cooked mashed squash
    2 c. milk
    2 eggs
    1 tsp. salt

Sift flour and baking powder; combine with all remaining ingredients. Fry cakes on griddle until done. Yield: 4 servings.

Mrs. Janice Sawyer, St. Johnsbury, Vt.

 ### Wagon Wheels

    1 firm long yellow or green squash, thinly sliced
    ¼ c. cornmeal
    ½ tsp. salt
    Few dashes of pepper
    2 tbsp. cooking oil

Dip squash into mixture of cornmeal, salt and pepper. Saute squash in hot oil until a delicate brown, turning once. Add more oil if necessary. Yield: 4-6 servings.

Irene G. Carlson, Home Economics Teacher, Mt. View, Alaska

 ### Squash Puppies

    3 med. yellow squash, thinly sliced
    3 eggs, beaten

(Continued on next page)

1 c. self-rising cornmeal
1 c. vegetable oil
Salt to taste

Dip squash into eggs; roll in cornmeal. Drop squash into preheated oil; fry until golden brown. Remove from heat; add salt. Yield: 4 servings.

Mrs. Charles D. Ward, Thomasville, N. C.

 Homewood Farm Squash Pie

    2 lb. small yellow squash
    ½ tsp. salt
    Dash of white pepper
    2 tbsp. butter
    1 sm. onion, grated
    1 c. heavy cream
    1 c. Spanish peanuts
    8 slices crisp cooked bacon, crumbled
    ¼ c. dry bread crumbs

Cook squash in small amount salted boiling water until tender and all water has disappeared. Mash squash; add salt, pepper, butter, onion and cream. Mix well; spoon into a greased 9-inch shallow baking dish. Bake in preheated 350 degree oven for 50 minutes. Sprinkle top with peanuts, bacon and bread crumbs. Yield: 6 servings.

Dixie T. Giannini, Princeton, Ky.

 Baked Hubbard Squash

    Hubbard squash
    Butter
    Brown sugar

Cut squash into pieces; remove seeds and strings. Place pieces in dripping pan in a 350-degree oven for 1 hour. Cover generously with butter and sprinkle with brown sugar. Cook for 1 hour longer, basting frequently. Add butter if necessary. Cooked squash may be scalloped with drained crushed pineapple, dotted with butter and covered with bread crumbs if desired. Bake until top is browned.

Mrs. Agnes Thomas, Townley, Ala.

Honey-Spice Squash

1 qt. diced cooked hubbard squash
½ c. honey
¼ c. melted butter
1 tsp. salt
½ tsp. pepper
½ tsp. ginger

Drain squash; mash. Mix squash with honey, butter, salt and pepper. Place in buttered casserole; sprinkle with ginger. Bake at 325 degrees for 20 minutes. Serve. Yield: 6 servings.

Mrs. Doris Daby, Sacred Heart, Minn.

 ### Jo's Squash

7 to 9 med. yellow squash
1 sm. onion
Salt and pepper to taste
1 c. bread crumbs

Boil squash and onion in water with salt and pepper until tender. Drain and mash. Place squash mixture into casserole dish; mix in 1 cup white sauce. Sprinkle with buttered bread crumbs. Bake at 350 degrees for 30 minutes. Bread crumbs may be made by placing slices of bread in blender.

WHITE SAUCE:

2 tbsp. butter
2 tbsp. flour
2 c. milk

Melt butter in 1-quart saucepan. Add flour; stir until all flour is dissolved. Pour milk into flour mixture; stir until smooth and thick. Yield: 6 servings.

Mrs. Lillian King Wier, Home Economics Teacher, Odem, Tex.

 ### Squash Chili Verde

2 tbsp. butter
6 to 8 sm. yellow squash, sliced
1 med. onion, sliced
1 to 3 hot green chili peppers
Salt and pepper to taste
4 slices American cheese

Melt butter in electric skillet. Cook squash and onion in butter at 200 degrees for 30 minutes or until tender and slightly browned. Keep tightly covered except to stir four times. Add peppers and seasonings; heat for 15 minutes. Pour into casserole; cover surface with cheese. Bake at 350 degrees until melted or brown. Yield: 8 servings.

Mrs. Jerry Whish, Evergreen, Ala.

Squash Custard

2 eggs
1 c. milk
3 tbsp. bacon drippings or butter, melted
Salt and pepper to taste
2 c. cooked yellow squash
1 c. bread crumbs

Beat eggs; add milk, bacon drippings, salt and pepper. Combine with squash in buttered casserole. Top with bread crumbs. Bake at 350 degrees for 30 minutes or until browned. Yield: 4 servings.

Mrs. Lillian Barber, Haines City, Fla., Favorite Recipes Food Fair

Squash Pie

2 lb. med.-sized squash, peeled
¼ c. finely chopped onions
3 well-beaten eggs
1 tsp. salt
¾ c. sugar
½ tsp. white pepper
¼ c. melted butter
30 saltine crackers, finely crushed

Cut squash into medium slices; add onions. Cook in enough water to cover, until well done. Stir constantly. Press through a coarse sieve; pour into mixing bowl. Add remaining ingredients; mix well. Pour into 9-inch casserole bowl. Sprinkle crackers over top until covered. Bake at 350 degrees for 45 minutes.

Mrs. John Connally, wife of Governor of Texas, Austin

Squash Souffle

1 lb. squash
1 lge. onion, chopped
Salt and pepper to taste
1 c. grated sharp cheese
¼ c. butter
2 eggs, separated
½ c. milk
8 or 10 crackers, finely crumbled

Cook squash and onion until tender; drain. Mash until fine; add salt, pepper, cheese, butter, egg yolks, milk and crackers. Fold in stiffly beaten egg whites. Pour into buttered casserole; bake at 350 degrees until brown and firm. Serve hot. Yield: 10 servings.

Mary Davis, Section, Ala.

Squash And Pineapple En Casserole

3 c. cooked squash
3 tbsp. butter
½ c. brown sugar
¼ c. pineapple juice
5 slices pineapple
10 marshmallows
English walnuts

Select well-ripened squash. Cut in halves; remove seeds. Cook in oven until tender; remove shell. Mash with potato masher or press through ricer. Add butter, part of sugar and pineapple juice; beat until light and smooth. Cover with layer of wedge-shaped pineapple pieces and marshmallows; cut in halves. Fill dish with squash; lay pineapple slices on top. Sprinkle with brown sugar. Place whole marshmallows in holes of pineapple slices. Put English walnut kernels on each marshmallow. Bake in 350-degree oven until marshmallows brown and melt slightly.

Fannie Kerns, St. Joseph, Mo.

 ## Squash Piquant

1 pkg. frozen or fresh squash
1 tbsp. butter
½ tsp. salt
¼ tsp. pepper
¼ tsp. sugar
¼ c. chopped onion
1 tbsp. chopped green pepper (opt.)
1 slice cooked bacon, chopped
¾ c. crushed cracker crumbs
1 egg, beaten

Cook squash in small amount of water; add butter. Mash squash. Mix all remaining ingredients with drippings from bacon; add to squash. Place in baking dish. Bake, uncovered, at 350 degrees for 30 to 40 minutes. Serve hot. Yield: 8 servings.

Flora Fry, Home Economics Teacher, Coleman, Tex.

 ## Squash Ring

1 ½ qt. yellow squash, cut into ½-in. pieces
1 med. onion, diced
½ med. green pepper, diced
1 clove of garlic, diced
1 tsp. salt

(Continued on next page)

2 tbsp. sugar
¼ c. butter
1 tbsp. Worcestershire sauce
½ tsp. pepper
½ tsp. Tabasco sauce
1 c. bread crumbs
3 eggs, well beaten
½ c. milk

Cook squash, onion, green pepper and garlic in water until tender; drain well. Add remaining ingredients; mix well. Fill a greased 1½-quart ring mold. Bake over water at 350 degrees for 40 minutes. Keep warm until ready to serve; unmold and fill center of ring with buttered green lima beans or English peas. Garnish around ring with tiny whole pickled beets. Yield: 12 servings.

Mrs. Roy Wesley, Arlington, Va.

 ### Squash Timbale

3 eggs, beaten
2 c. mashed cooked squash, drained
1 c. cream of mushroom soup
½ c. cracker or bread crumbs
1 tbsp. minced onion
Salt and pepper to taste
½ c. grated cheese

Combine all ingredients except cheese; pour into greased casserole. Sprinkle with cheese. Place dish in shallow pan of water. Bake at 350 degrees for 40 minutes. Yield: 8-10 servings.

Mrs. Reed Wilson, Lawndale, N. C.

 ### Baked Squash And Cheese

2 lb. yellow crookneck squash
2 tsp. salt
¼ lb. cream cheese
2 tbsp. minced parsley
½ c. melted butter

Select small, uniform squash. Pare lightly and cut into halves lengthwise. Arrange in deep skillet and almost cover with water. Add the salt. Cover; bring to a boil. Cook over medium heat for 10 minutes. Drain well. Have the cream cheese at room temperature and blend in the parsley. Spread on the cut halves of the squash and put the halves together. Arrange in a buttered baking dish; pour the butter over them. Bake in a 375-degree oven for 20 minutes or until browned. Cut into halves crosswise. Yield: 6-8 servings.

Mrs. Lane B. Kennedy, Home Economics Teacher, Savannah, Ga.

Smothered Squash

3 to 4 tbsp. margarine
1 pkg. frozen crookneck squash
1 med. onion, sliced
½ tsp. salt
¼ tsp. sugar (opt.)
Paprika (opt.)

Melt margarine in heavy pan; add all remaining ingredients except paprika. Stir until mixture begins to sizzle. Simmer, covered, until squash and onion can be mashed. Uncover; allow excess liquid to evaporate. Pour into serving dish; sprinkle with paprika. Yield: 3-4 servings.

Lois G. Salter, Zwolle, La.

 ## Squash

4 or 5 yellow crookneck squash
1 med. onion, chopped
2 tbsp. bacon drippings or butter
Salt and pepper to taste

Wash and scrape squash; cut into ¼ to ½-inch thick rounds. Bring to boil in small amount salted water; cook for 4 to 5 minutes or until almost tender. Saute onion in bacon drippings. Drain squash; add to onion. Season with salt and pepper. Heat until tender but not mushy. Yield: 4 servings.

Mrs. Patricia Goza, Home Economics Teacher, Denison, Tex.

 ## Squash-Herb Casserole

2 lb. yellow crookneck squash
4 tbsp. butter
½ c. cheddar cheese, grated
1 onion, finely chopped
Dash of oregano
Dash of thyme
Dash of garlic powder
3 eggs, separated
Bread crumbs
Paprika

Cook squash in salted water until tender. Drain; press through a colander. Combine squash, butter, cheese, onion and herbs. Add beaten egg yolks. Beat egg whites until stiff; fold into mixture. Pour into casserole; sprinkle with bread crumbs and paprika. Bake at 325 degrees for 30 minutes. Yield: 8 servings.

Mrs. J. E. Franks, Columbus, Miss.

Squash Stuffed With Ground Beef

8 to 10 med. yellow crookneck squash
½ lb. mixed ground meat
⅓ c. uncooked rice
1 med. onion, chopped
Salt and pepper
1 tbsp. diced green pepper (opt.)
1 sm. can tomatoes
1 can tomato paste
½ c. water

Cut neck off squash; scoop out inside with apple corer. Whittle neck so it can be inserted back in squash. Mix ground meat, rice, onion, salt, pepper and bell pepper; stuff squash. There will be meat and rice mixture left over. Put necks into squash; secure with toothpicks. Shape most of the remaining meat and rice mixture into small balls. Arrange squash in casserole; place meat balls around squash. Combine tomatoes, tomato paste, water and remaining meat mixture; pour over squash and meat balls. Cover; cook over medium heat for 30 minutes. Continue simmering for 1 hour, lifting the lid occasionally; add water as needed.

Mrs. C. L. Morgan, Dothan, Ala.

 ## Stuffed Squash

4 med. yellow crookneck squash
3 slices bacon
¼ c. chopped onions
½ c. grated cheddar cheese

Clean and peel squash; peeling may be left on if not bruised or discolored. Boil for 15 minutes in a medium saucepan. Remove and cut in half lengthwise. Scoop out seeds and pulp; set aside. Place hollowed out squash in lightly greased, flat casserole dish. Cut bacon into small bits and saute with onions in skillet. Add seeds and pulp from squash, mixing well. Fill hollowed out squash with mixture. Sprinkle with grated cheese. Place in a 350-degree oven for 15 minutes or until cheese melts. Yield: 4 servings.

Nancy J. Ross, Home Economics Teacher, Del Rio, Tex.

 ## Yellow Crookneck Squash

2 qt. sliced tender crookneck squash
Water
2 tbsp. butter
1 tsp. salt
⅛ tsp. pepper

(Continued on next page)

½ c. evaporated milk
2 tbsp. sugar

Do not peel squash; place in container, adding just enough water to cook. Cook until tender; drain well. Add butter, salt and pepper; mash well. Heat milk with sugar until sugar is well dissolved. Add milk mixture to squash; mix well. Serve hot. Yield: 6-8 servings.

Mrs. Ila Vaughan, Tahlequah, Okla.

Yellow Squash Casserole

2 lb. yellow crookneck squash
1 lge. onion
2 tbsp. butter
1 can frozen shrimp soup
1 can water chestnuts, sliced
Salt to taste
Bread crumbs

Chop squash and onions. Saute in butter over low heat until tender. Add frozen shrimp, soup and water chestnuts. Add salt to taste and pour into greased casserole. Cover with bread crumbs and dot with additional butter. Bake in a 350-degree oven for 30 minutes. Yield: 6-8 servings.

Mrs. John T. Brown, Pine Bluff, Ark., Favorite Recipes Food Fair

Baked Zucchini In Sour Cream

6 zucchini
⅔ c. sour cream
1 c. grated cheddar cheese
1 tbsp. butter
½ tsp. salt
3 tbsp. fresh bread crumbs
2 tbsp. grated cheese

Cut squash into ½-inch slices; simmer in water for 10 minutes. Place in 8-inch casserole. Combine sour cream, cheddar cheese, butter and salt; heat until blended. Pour sauce over squash. Combine bread crumbs and remaining cheese; sprinkle over casserole. Bake at 375 degrees for 10 minutes. Let stand for 5 minutes before serving. Yield: 6 servings.

Mrs. Charles Higgins, Honolulu, Hawaii

Baked Zucchini Parmesan

    4 to 5 sm. zucchini squash, thinly sliced
    2 tbsp. butter
    ½ tsp. salt
    Dash of pepper
    1 c. stewed tomatoes
    2 tbsp. grated Parmesan cheese

Combine zucchini, butter, seasonings and tomatoes in casserole. Bake at 350 degrees for 20 minutes or until zucchini is tender. Sprinkle with cheese; bake for 10 minutes longer. Serve. Yield: 4 servings.

Frances Fischer, Home Economics Teacher, Burlington, Wash.

 ### Baked Zucchini Squash

    3 or 4 zucchini, chopped
    ¼ c. salad oil
    1 tsp. salt
    Dash of pepper
    Garlic salt to taste
    1 sm. can evaporated milk
    1 egg
    1 slice bread, broken
    1 c. grated cheese

Combine squash, oil, salt, pepper and garlic salt with a small amount of water in saucepan. Cook for 10 minutes. Combine milk and egg; beat until blended. Pour over bread crumbs; let stand until bread is soaked. Place a layer of one-half the squash mixture in a 9 or 10-inch casserole; add a layer of cheese. Pour one-half the milk-egg mixture over the casserole. Repeat layers, using all remaining ingredients. Bake at 350 degrees for 45 minutes. Yield: 5-6 servings.

Mrs. Coral Hawkins, Tehachapi, Cal.

 ### Fried Zucchini

    1 med. zucchini squash
    ½ tsp. salt
    2 eggs, beaten
    Cracker crumbs

Peel squash; slice crosswise into ⅛ to ¼-inch slices. Dip in salted eggs; coat with cracker crumbs. Fry in ½-inch deep shortening until golden brown. Drain on absorbent paper. Yield: 6-8 servings.

Mrs. Eleanor Roberts, Home Economics Teacher, Thompsonville, Ill.

Panned Zucchini With Dill

  1 sprig fresh dill
  ½ sm. onion, chopped
  2 tbsp. bacon fat
  1 qt. sliced zucchini
  ½ tsp. salt
  Pepper to taste

Cook dill and onion in hot fat until almost browned; add squash, salt and pepper. Cover and simmer for 10 minutes or until just tender. Add ¼ cup of water if needed. Yield: 4 servings.

Polly J. Hanst, Accident, Md.

 ## Zucchini Pancakes

  1 lge. zucchini, grated
  1 egg
  2 tbsp. flour
  ½ tsp. baking powder
  1 tbsp. sugar
  ½ tsp. salt

Combine all ingredients; mix well. Fry as for pancakes in a small amount of oil or margarine. Yield: 2 servings.

Ruth Marier, North Highlands, Cal.

 ## Zucchini Patties

  5 med. zucchini
  3 eggs
  1 tbsp. grated Parmesan cheese
  1 clove of garlic, minced or mashed
  2 tbsp. flour
  ½ c. finely chopped parsley
  1 tsp. salt
  1 tsp. pepper
  ½ c. olive oil or salad oil

Remove both ends of zucchini, but do not peel. Coarsely shred zucchini; press out water. Mix in remaining ingredients. Heat small amount of oil in skillet. Drop heaping tablespoons of mixture into fat; fry until brown. Serve immediately. Yield: 6 servings.

Mrs. Judy McIntyre, Columbus, Ga.

Skillet Squash Au Gratin

¼ c. butter or margarine
4 c. thinly sliced zucchini or other squash
1 med. onion, sliced
1 tsp. salt
Dash of pepper
¼ c. water or 2 peeled sliced tomatoes
½ c. grated American cheese
Soy sauce (opt.)

Melt butter in skillet. Add squash, onion, salt, pepper and water or tomatoes. Cook, covered, for 10 to 15 minutes or until squash is tender. Sprinkle with cheese and soy sauce. Yield: 4-6 servings.

Mrs. Paralee Coleman, Home Economics Teacher, Wellington, Tex.

 ### Sour Cream Zucchini

6 med. zucchini
½ tsp. salt or to taste
1 tbsp. diced onion
¼ tsp. brown sugar
Dash of Worcestershire sauce
¼ c. sour cream

Wash zucchini; do not pare. Cut off ends; slice about ⅛-inch thick. Cook in very small amount of water with all ingredients except sour cream until just tender. Zucchini slices should not lose their shape; do not overcook. Drain off water; add sour cream. Toss; do not break. Serve immediately. Yield: 6 servings.

Mrs. Irma Whitehead, Modesto, Cal.

 ### Stuffed Zucchini With Tomato Sauce

6 med. zucchini, cooked
1 lb. hamburger
1 c. uncooked rice
1 med. onion, chopped
½ tsp. salt
¼ tsp. pepper
1 qt. tomatoes
2 mint leaves

Scoop centers out of zucchini. Mix all remaining ingredients except tomatoes and mint leaves; stuff zucchini. Stand upright in heavy skillet; pour tomatoes

(Continued on next page)

over top. Add mint leaves. Cook slowly for 1 hour or until tender. Yield: 6 servings.

Mrs. Catherine Mordan, Home Economics Teacher, Millville, Pa.

 ## Zucchini Stuffed With Tuna Fish

> 8 med. zucchini
> Olive oil
> 1 6½ to 7-oz. can tuna, drained and flaked
> 2 tbsp. grated Parmesan or Romano cheese
> ⅓ c. sweet fresh cucumber pickles, chopped
> 1 tsp. salt
> ⅛ tsp. pepper
> ½ c. Italian-style bread crumbs
> 1 c. creamed cottage cheese
> 1 egg, slightly beaten

Wash zucchini and pat dry. Use sharp paring knife to cut slice from one side of each squash. Scoop out centers, reserving ¼-inch thick shells. Chop scooped-out pulp; saute in 2 tablespoons oil until tender and lightly browned. Cool. Combine with tuna, Parmesan cheese, pickles, salt, pepper and bread crumbs. Sprinkle shells with additional salt, if desired; stuff with tuna mixture. Combine cottage cheese and egg in electric blender or electric mixer; spread over tuna stuffing. Brush zucchini with oil. Place in lightly oiled 13 x 9 x 2-inch baking pan. Bake in 375-degree oven 35 to 40 minutes or until fork tender.

Photograph for this recipe below.

Sausage-Zucchini Boats

    4 med. zucchini
    ¼ lb. bulk pork sausage
    ¼ c. chopped onion
    4 c. fine cracker crumbs
    1 slightly beaten egg
    ½ c. grated Parmesan cheese
    ½ tsp. monosodium glutamate
    ¼ tsp. salt
    ¼ tsp. thyme
       Dash of garlic salt
       Dash of pepper

Cook whole zucchini in boiling water until barely tender, 7 to 10 minutes. Cut in half lengthwise; scoop squash from shells and mash. Cook sausage with onion; drain off excess fat. Stir in mashed zucchini. Reserving 2 tablespoons Parmesan cheese, add remaining ingredients. Mix well; spoon into zucchini shells. Place shells in a shallow baking dish; sprinkle with reserved Parmesan cheese and dash of paprika. Bake in 350-degree oven for 25 to 30 minutes. Yield 4 servings.

Mrs. Janell McClellan, St. Paul, Minn.

 ### Sweet And Sour Zucchini

    1 pkg. dehydrated onions
    ⅛ c. wine vinegar
    ¾ c. sugar
    1 tsp. salt
    ½ tsp. pepper
    ⅓ c. salad oil
    ⅔ c. cider vinegar
    ½ c. chopped green pepper
    ½ c. sliced celery
    5 zucchini, sliced paper thin

Soak onions in wine vinegar. Add sugar, salt, pepper, oil and cider vinegar. Pour over vegetables; mix well. Marinate for 6 hours or overnight. Drain and serve. Yield: 12 servings.

Leulla Blankenship, Biggs, Cal.

 ### Zucchini Casserole

    2 ½ c. cooked zucchini
    1 c. chopped onion
    1 chopped green pepper

(Continued on next page)

3 tbsp. butter
     1 c. cooked rice
     6 eggs, slightly beaten
     Salt and pepper
     2 c. buttered bread crumbs
     ½ c. mild cheese, grated

Cook zucchini; do not drain. Fry onion and green peppers in butter. Add to zucchini and rice. Add eggs, salt and pepper to taste. Cover with bread crumbs and cheese. Bake at 350 degrees for 30 minutes or until eggs are cooked. Yield: 6 servings.

                                        Eva Foremaster, Caliente, Nev.

   Zucchini-Chili Casserole

     3 lb. tender zucchini, thinly sliced
     1 med. onion, chopped
     1 can tomato sauce
     1 tbsp. bacon fat
     ½ tsp. salt
     3 to 4 chili tepines, crushed
     1 tsp. chili powder
     1 c. grated cheese
     ¼ c. cracker crumbs

Combine zucchini, onion, tomato sauce and fat in saucepan. Bring to a boil; simmer for 20 minutes or until tender. Remove from heat; add seasonings. Alternate layers of squash mixture and cheese in 2-quart casserole; sprinkle with cracker crumbs. Bake at 350 degrees for 30 minutes. Yield: 6-8 servings.

          Evelyn Gaines Johnson, Home Economics Teacher, Tucson, Ariz.

   Zucchini Custard

     1 lb. zucchini
     4 eggs, lightly beaten
     1 c. shredded cheddar cheese
     1 ½ c. milk, scalded
     1 tbsp. butter
     1 tsp. salt
     ¼ tsp. paprika
     1 tsp. chopped green onion

Cook zucchini in boiling salted water until tender; drain and chop. Combine eggs, cheese, milk, butter, seasonings and onion; add zucchini. Pour into greased casserole; place casserole in pan of water. Bake at 325 degrees for 50 to 55 minutes. Yield: 6 servings.

          Geneva Wheeler, Lincoln, Neb., Favorite Recipes Food Fair

Zucchini And Olive Casserole

1 ½ lb. zucchini
2 eggs, well beaten
1 tsp. salt
½ c. milk
2 tbsp. grated onion
1 c. dry bread crumbs
1 c. grated American cheese
½ c. diced ripe olives

Simmer zucchini until tender; drain. Combine all remaining ingredients; add to zucchini. Pour into buttered casserole. Bake at 350 degrees for 35 minutes. Yield: 6 servings.

Mrs. Polly M. Page, Yerington, Nev.

 ## Zucchini Pancake

4 or 5 med. zucchini
5 tbsp. salad oil
1 med. onion, chopped
1 green pepper, chopped (opt.)
1 tbsp. dry parsley flakes
1 8-oz. can tomato sauce
1 tsp. each basil and oregano
5 eggs
½ c. milk
Salt and pepper to taste
¾ c. grated cheddar cheese
Paprika

Slice zucchini thin. Place salad oil in heavy 10-inch ovenproof skillet. Add zucchini, onion, green pepper and parsley flakes. Cook until zucchini is lightly browned and wilted. Add tomato sauce, basil and oregano. Simmer over low heat until mixture is moist, but not soupy. Beat eggs; add milk, salt and pepper. Pour over hot zucchini mixture. Cover and cook over low heat until eggs begin to set. Sprinkle with grated cheese and paprika. Slip under broiler until cheese is melted and lightly browned. Cut in wedges and serve. Yield: 6-8 servings.

Mrs. Betty G. Alexander, Home Economics Teacher, Norwalk, Cal.

 ## Banana-Pecan Yams

6 med. yams, mashed and cooked
1 can chopped pecans
¼ c. mashed bananas

(Continued on next page)

¾ c. (firmly packed) brown sugar
¼ tsp. salt
1 tsp. cinnamon
1 tsp. lemon juice
¼ c. melted butter or margarine

Combine all ingredients; mix until well blended. Turn into a casserole. Bake at 350 degrees for 20 minutes or until lightly browned. Top with whipped cream.

Mrs. Ernest Seawright, Vernon, Tex.

 Brandied Sweet Potatoes

2 tbsp. cornstarch
½ tsp. nutmeg
2 tsp. salt
½ c. sugar
1 c. water
1 tbsp. lemon juice
⅓ c. brandy
6 lge. sweet potatoes, cooked
Miniature marshmallows

Combine cornstarch, nutmeg, salt and sugar in 1-quart saucepan; gradually stir in water. Cook until clear, stirring constantly. Stir in lemon juice and brandy. Peel potatoes; cut crosswise into ¼ to ½-inch thick slices. Place in buttered shallow casserole; cover with sauce. Cover and bake in preheated 375 degree oven for 30 minutes or until glazed, basting occasionally. Sprinkle with marshmallows; broil until golden brown. Yield: 8 servings.

Jeanne C. Conner, Home Economics Teacher, Greenwood, Del.

 Candied Sweet Potatoes

4 med. sweet potatoes
Salt
2 tbsp. butter or margarine
½ c. light brown sugar
¼ c. water

Boil sweet potatoes in salted water to cover until nearly tender; peel and cut in halves lengthwise. Place butter, sugar and water in skillet and cook until syrupy; add sweet potato halves. Cook slowly, turning until brown on both sides. Potatoes may be baked with syrup for 30 minutes at 375 degrees. Yield: 4 servings.

Estelle Greene, Yreka, Cal.

Candied Sweet Potatoes With Honey

4 lge. sweet potatoes, cooked and halved
¼ c. melted butter
¾ c. honey
¾ c. orange juice
¼ tsp. salt
1 tbsp. cornstarch

Place potatoes in greased 8 x 8 x 2-inch pan. Blend butter, honey, orange juice, salt and cornstarch; cook until slightly thickened, stirring constantly. Pour over potatoes. Bake at 450 degrees for 10 minutes. Yield: 6-8 servings.

Jeanne Yoxall, Home Economics Teacher, Stafford, Kan.

 ## Orange-Glazed Sweet Potatoes

½ c. brown sugar
½ c. sugar
½ c. orange juice
1 tbsp. cornstarch
4 tbsp. butter
2 c. sliced cooked sweet potatoes

Cook sugars, juice and cornstarch until thickened, stirring constantly; add butter. Pour over potatoes in casserole. Bake, covered, at 350 degrees for 30 minutes. Yield: 4 servings.

Sandra J. Jacobson, Home Economics Teacher, Mahnomen, Minn.

 ## Coconut-Broiled Louisiana Yams

8 med. yams, cooked, peeled and halved
1 ½ c. shredded coconut
¼ c. butter or margarine
½ c. (firmly packed) brown sugar
¼ c. heavy cream
¼ c. maraschino cherries

Arrange yams in lightly greased shallow 2-quart casserole; sprinkle with 1 cup coconut. Combine butter, brown sugar and cream; pour over yams. Top with remaining coconut and cherries. Broil 4 to 5 inches from source of heat for 4 minutes or until coconut is lightly browned. If desired, two 1-pound cans drained and halved yams may be used. Yield: 8 servings.

Mrs. Joan Howlett, Jackson, Miss.

Pineapple-Glazed Yams

> 4 lge. sweet potatoes, cooked
> ⅓ c. (firmly packed) brown sugar
> 1 tsp. salt
> ¼ c. butter
> ½ c. unsweetened pineapple juice

Cool potatoes. Cut crosswise into 2-inch pieces. Spread half of sugar in greased shallow casserole; add potatoes. Sprinkle with salt; dot with butter. Add remaining sugar; pour on pineapple juice. Bake in preheated 375 degree oven for 15 minutes, basting occasionally. Turn potatoes; bake 15 minutes longer. Yield: 6 servings.

Carolyn Shidaker, South Bend, Ind.

 ## French-Fried Sweet Potato Chips

> 2 to 3 sweet potatoes, peeled
> Fat
> Confectioners' sugar (opt.)

Cut potatoes in 1-inch strips or very thin slices; cover with cold, salted water. Soak for 30 minutes; drain and dry. Fry in hot deep fat. Sprinkle with sugar.

Mrs. Florence D. Sorrell, Home Economics Teacher, Benson, N. C.

 ## Sweet Potato-Bread Crumb Balls

> 1 can sweet potatoes, well drained
> 1 tsp. brown sugar
> Melted butter
> Salt and pepper
> Bread crumbs

Mash sweet potatoes; add sugar, 3 teaspoons butter and seasonings. Chill; form into balls. Roll in bread crumbs. Fry in butter. Yield: 6 servings.

Marjorie Scott, Bethany, Ill.

 ## Cajun-Fried Yams

> 2 lb. boiled yams or 2 cans yams, drained
> ¼ c. cooking oil
> ¼ c. brown sugar
> ¼ tsp. salt
> 2 dashes of cinnamon

(Continued on next page)

Peel and slice yams ¼-inch thick. Brown in oil on both sides over medium heat. Remove to warmed platter; sprinkle with sugar, salt and cinnamon.

Mrs. Mildred H. Harris, Schofield Barracks, Hawaii

 ## Sweet Potato Croquettes

5 med. sweet potatoes, cooked
2 tbsp. sugar
2 tbsp. butter
1 tsp. lemon juice
6 marshmallows
2 egg whites, slightly beaten
2 c. crushed cornflakes

Peel potatoes; mash. Add sugar, butter and lemon juice. Shape potatoes around marshmallows; chill for 1 hour. Dip into egg whites; roll in cornflakes. Fry in deep fat at 375 degrees until golden brown. Drain; serve at once. Yield: 6 servings.

Grace Womack Buford, Home Economics Teacher, Plainview, Ark.

 ## Island-Style Ham And Sweet Potatoes

1 No. 2 can pineapple chunks
6 med. sweet potatoes, cooked
6 to 8 tbsp. butter
Salt and pepper to taste
Pinch of nutmeg
Milk
2 c. coarsely chopped ham
½ green pepper, diced
1 tbsp. cornstarch
2 tbsp. brown sugar
2 tbsp. vinegar

Drain pineapple, reserving ¾ cup juice. Mash potatoes; add 4 to 6 tablespoons butter, salt, pepper, nutmeg and milk. Whip until fluffy. Saute ham in remaining butter, stirring until golden; add green pepper and pineapple chunks. Cook for 2 to 3 minutes. Blend cornstarch with pineapple juice, brown sugar and vinegar; stir until clear and thickened. Pour into casserole; drop mashed sweet potatoes on top. Bake at 350 degrees for 45 minutes or until brown and bubbling. Yield: 4-6 servings.

Mrs. Edwin Hoysradt, Jr., Island Falls, Maine

Sweet Potato Puffs

1 c. flour
1 ½ tsp. baking powder
½ tsp. salt
¼ tsp. cloves
¼ tsp. ground cinnamon or nutmeg
2 eggs
2 c. cold mashed sweet potatoes

Sift dry ingredients together. Beat eggs and potatoes together and add dry ingredients. Roll out ½-inch thick; cut in circles, squares or strips. Fry in 360 to 370-degree deep fat as doughnuts for 2 to 3 minutes. Roll or sprinkle with sugar as soon as they are drained but still warm, if desired.

Mrs. Jean Johnson, Memphis, Tenn.

 ## Louisiana Yam And Apple Scallop

6 med. yams, cooked, peeled and sliced
4 tart apples, cored and sliced
¼ c. soft butter or margarine
½ tsp. grated orange peel
¼ tsp. allspice
½ c. apple juice

Arrange yams and apple in greased, shallow 2-quart casserole. Mix butter and orange peel; dot yams and apples with mixture. Stir allspice into apple juice; pour over yams and apples. Cover and bake at 350 degrees for 30 minutes. Uncover and bake 15 minutes longer, basting occasionally. Yield: 6 servings.

Photograph for this recipe on page 241.

 ## Scalloped Sweet Potatoes And Apples

4 sweet potatoes, cooked and sliced
3 med. tart apples, pared and sliced
½ c. butter or margarine
½ c. sugar
Salt
¼ c. hot water

Alternate layers of potatoes and apples in ½-quart shallow casserole; dot each potato layer with butter or margarine. Sprinkle each apple layer with sugar and salt; add water. Bake, covered, at 375 degrees for 25 minutes. Uncover; bake 20 minutes longer or until liquid has evaporated and top is brown. Yield: 8-10 servings.

Anita Colter, Genoa, Neb.

Raisin-Filled Sweet Potatoes

1 egg
4 c. mashed sweet potatoes
1 tsp. salt
⅛ tsp. cinnamon
⅛ tsp. ginger
¼ c. melted butter
1 c. orange juice
¼ c. sugar
1 tbsp. cornstarch
1 tbsp. finely sliced orange peel
1 c. seedless raisins

Beat egg slightly; add potatoes and seasonings. Blend well; add butter. Shape into nests on greased baking sheet. Bake at 450 degrees for 20 minutes or until edges are slightly browned. Blend orange juice with sugar and cornstarch. Cook over low heat, stirring, until mixture thickens. Add orange peel and raisins. Cook for 2 minutes. Fill centers of potato nests. Yield: 6-8 servings.

Mrs. Helen R. Geren, Home Economics Teacher, Comstock Park, Mich.

 ### Scalloped Sweet Potatoes And Pineapple

2 c. cooked sweet potatoes, thinly sliced
1 c. pineapple chunks or crushed pineapple, drained
½ c. brown sugar
4 tbsp. melted butter
1 tsp. salt
6 slices pineapple
¾ c. pineapple juice

Layer potatoes and pineapple chunks in buttered baking dish. Sprinkle with sugar. Dot with butter; sprinkle with salt. Repeat layers. Top with pineapple slices; cover with pineapple juice. Bake, covered, at 350 degrees for 30 minutes. Uncover; bake until top is brown. Yield: 6 servings.

Mrs. Carolyn Saxe, Home Economics Teacher, Moultrie, Ga.

 ### Skillet Sweet Potatoes

2 tbsp. butter or margarine
½ c. orange marmalade
¼ c. water
1 tbsp. lemon juice
1 lge. can sweet potatoes
6 stewed prunes, cut

(Continued on next page)

269

Heat butter, marmalade, water and lemon juice in frying pan. Add potatoes and prunes. Cook slowly for 15 minutes, basting once or twice. Yield: 4 servings.

Mrs. James V. DeCoster, Pres. Officers' Wives' Club, Scott AFB, Ill.

Sweet Potatoes Denise

> 1 ½ c. whole cranberry sauce
> 3 tbsp. dry sherry
> ½ c. water
> ¼ c. brown sugar
> ¼ tsp. nutmeg
> 2 tbsp. butter
> 6 sweet potatoes, cooked, peeled and sliced
> ¼ c. chopped pecans
> ¼ c. raisins

Combine cranberry sauce, sherry, water, brown sugar and nutmeg in saucepan. Bring to boil; cook over low heat 5 minutes. Stir in butter until melted. Arrange sweet potatoes, pecans and raisins in casserole; pour sauce over. Bake in 350-degree oven for 25 minutes. Yield: 6-8 servings.

Mrs. Linda Riccio, Tuscaloosa, Ala.

Sweet Potatoes With Marshmallows

> 6 to 8 med. sweet potatoes, cooked and mashed
> 2 tbsp. butter or margarine
> ½ c. hot milk or half and half
> ½ tsp. salt
> 1 tsp. nutmeg or cinnamon
> ¼ tsp. paprika
> ¼ c. concentrated orange juice
> ½ c. dark brown sugar
> Few grains of allspice
> 1 to 1½ c. chopped English or black walnuts
> ½ lb. marshmallows

Combine all ingredients except walnuts and marshmallows; beat until light and fluffy. Fold in nuts; pour into greased 4-quart casserole. Cover with marshmallows. Bake at 350 degrees until mixture is hot and marshmallows are brown. Yield: 8-10 servings.

Mrs. Mary Kaye Hancock, Home Economics Teacher, Sesser, Ill.

Tomatoes
and Turnips

Baked Tomato Rarebit

  3 c. fresh bread cubes
  1 ½ c. grated cheese
  2 eggs
  ½ tsp. mustard
  1 ½ tsp. salt
  1 lge. can tomatoes

Arrange layers of bread cubes and cheese in greased casserole. Beat eggs; pour over bread and cheese. Add seasonings; pour tomatoes over all. Let stand 10 minutes. Bake at 350 degrees for about 30 minutes. Serve with crisp bacon. Yield: 4 servings.

Mrs. Allan Watson, Lincoln, Neb.

 ### Breaded Tomatoes

  2 tbsp. melted butter
  2 tbsp. flour
  Dash of salt
  1 c. milk
  1 pt. tomatoes
  2 tbsp. sugar
  2 slices bread, broken into lge. pieces

Blend half the butter, flour and salt; slowly add milk. Simmer until thickened, stirring constantly. Heat tomatoes, remaining butter and sugar; add to hot sauce. Stir in bread; remove from heat. Serve. Yield: 4 servings.

Jane Choate, Home Economics Teacher, Welch, Okla.

 ### Broiled Tomato Napoli

  4 lge. tomatoes
  1 c. fresh bread crumbs
  ¼ c. melted butter
  2 tbsp. grated Parmesan cheese
  ½ tsp. Italian herb seasoning

Wash tomatoes; remove stems. Slice; place in large broiler pan. Blend bread crumbs, butter, cheese and seasoning; spoon mixture over tomatoes. Broil 10 inches from unit for 4 to 5 minutes or until tomatoes are hot and crumbs are browned. Serve at once. Yield: 4 servings.

Mrs. Barbara Hammerberg, Home Economics Teacher, Hortonville, Wis.

Broiled Tomatoes

> 5 tomatoes
> Dash of salt and pepper
> 1 tbsp. butter, melted

Remove stem ends from tomatoes and cut in half. Place in greased shallow baking dish. Add salt, pepper and butter. Place under direct heat in broiler, far enough from heat to allow tomatoes to cook before browning. Broil for 10 to 20 minutes. Serve on crisp buttered toast, garnished with parsley. Yield: 5 servings.

Mrs. Pruda Caudill Prather, Carter, Ky.

 ## Curried Tomatoes

> 1 tbsp. chopped onion
> 2 tbsp. butter
> 6 tomatoes, peeled and sliced or 2 to 3 c. stewed tomatoes
> ½ c. canned milk or cream
> 1 tbsp. flour
> 1 tsp. curry powder
> Pinch of salt

Saute onion in butter until transparent; add tomatoes. Simmer. Blend remaining ingredients; pour over tomatoes. Cook until thickened, stirring constantly. May be served over hot buttered toast. Yield: 4 servings.

Mrs. Beth Beck, Kaysville, Utah

 ## Curried Tomatoes And Onions

> 1 c. diced onions
> 2 tbsp. butter
> 4 tbsp. flour
> 2 c. cooked tomatoes
> 1 tsp. salt
> ¼ tsp. curry powder

Brown onions in butter; sprinkle flour over cooked onions, stirring lightly. Add tomatoes and salt; cook until thickened, stirring constantly. Add curry powder. May be served on rice. Yield: 4 servings.

Reva Wilson, Home Economics Teacher, Drummond, Mont.

Danish Tomatoes

Fresh tomatoes
Sugar
Salt
Buttered croutons
Crumbled bleu cheese

Cut tops off tomatoes; spread out flowerlike. Sprinkle with sugar and salt; place in pan. Bake at 375 degrees for 10 minutes. Add croutons and cheese. Bake until cheese bubbles.

Rosemary Martine, Erie, Pa., Favorite Recipes Food Fair

 ## Creole-Fried Tomatoes

1 clove of garlic, minced
1 tbsp. chopped parsley
½ tsp. salt
Dash of pepper
1 onion, minced
1 tbsp. vegetable oil
2 lge. red or green tomatoes, thickly sliced
1 c. cornmeal

Combine garlic, parsley, salt, pepper and onion with oil. Spread mixture on tomato slices; sprinkle with cornmeal. Brown in lightly-oiled skillet. Yield: 4 servings.

Doris Y. Burnette, Fort Defiance, Va.

 ## French-Fried Tomatoes

1 egg
2 c. milk
1 ½ c. flour
½ tsp. baking powder
⅛ tsp. salt
1 tbsp. sugar
Tomatoes, sliced ¼-in. thick

Combine all ingredients except tomatoes. Dip tomato slices in additional milk and flour; dip into batter. Fry in 350-degree fat until brown.

Helen Larson, Home Economics Teacher, Crosby, Minn.

Fried Ripe Tomatoes

    6 med. tomatoes, thickly sliced
    ⅓ c. plus 2 tbsp. flour
    1 tsp. salt
    1 tsp. sugar
    ¼ c. plus 2 tbsp. butter or margarine
    1 ¼ c. milk
    ¼ tsp. sweet basil

Dip tomatoes in 1/3 cup flour blended with salt and sugar. Brown quickly in ¼ cup butter; remove to serving dish. Add remaining butter to drippings; blend in remaining flour and milk. Cook until thickened, stirring constantly. Pour over tomatoes; sprinkle with basil. Serve. Yield: 6 servings.

Mrs. Doris Gustafson, Brethren, Mich.

 ## Tomato Croquettes

    ½ c. flour
    ½ tsp. baking powder
    ¼ tsp. salt
    Few grains of pepper
    1 tsp. melted butter
    1 egg, beaten
    ¼ c. milk
    1 16-oz. can whole tomatoes, drained

Make a batter of all ingredients except tomatoes. Dip tomatoes into batter; brown in hot fat. Drain; serve hot.

Annie Laurie Clark, Westminster, Md.

 ## Fried Green Tomatoes

    4 or 5 med. green tomatoes
    ⅓ c. flour
    ¾ tsp. salt
    Few grains of pepper (opt.)
    ¼ c. shortening

Wash tomatoes; remove stem ends. Cut crosswise into ½-inch slices. Blend flour, salt and pepper; dip tomato slices into mixture. Brown quickly on one side in shortening; turn. Reduce heat; cook until soft in center. Remove to hot platter; serve hot. Yield: 4-5 servings.

Mrs. Patricia D. Chappell, Griffin, Ga.

Tomato Pie

½ pkg. pie crust mix
6 lge. tomatoes, cut in ½ inch thick slices
Salt and pepper to taste
½ c. cornmeal
4 tbsp. butter or margarine
1 tsp. sugar
½ c. grated cheese
1 tbsp. melted butter

Prepare pie dough as directed on package for 1 crust. Season tomatoes with salt and pepper. Coat with cornmeal; fry in butter. Turn with spatula to brown both sides. Sprinkle each slice with sugar. Line a pie pan with pastry dough. Place layer of tomatoes on bottom; sprinkle with grated cheese. Repeat. Top with cheese; sprinkle with melted butter. Bake at 425 degrees for 10 minutes. Lower heat; bake 15 minutes more.

Mrs. Richard Humphreys, Boise, Idaho

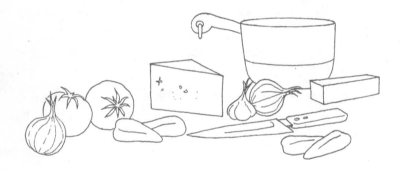

 ## Heartburn Special

1 No. 2½ can tomatoes
1 can green chili peppers, seeded and chopped
1 lge. onion, diced
3 cloves of garlic, chopped
¼ c. butter or margarine
Grated cheese

Combine tomatoes, peppers, onion and garlic; simmer until slightly thickened. Pour into greased casserole; top with butter and cheese. Bake at 350 degrees until bubbly. Leave seeds in peppers to make casserole hotter. Yield: 4 servings.

Mrs. Nel L. Estill, Home Economics Teacher, Maxwell, Cal.

Herbed Tomato Slices

4 lge. ripe tomatoes, peeled
½ c. cooking oil
¼ c. vinegar
¼ c. chopped parsley
¼ c. sliced green onions
1 tsp. salt
¼ tsp. pepper
½ tsp. dried thyme or marjoram

Slice tomatoes into thick slices; place in flat dish. Combine all remaining ingredients in a glass jar. Shake well; pour over tomatoes. Cover and chill for several hours or overnight. At serving time, transfer tomato slices to a platter; sprinkle with additional chopped parsley. Yield: 8 servings.

Mrs. Audrey Miles, Chicago, Ill.

Scalloped Tomatoes

1 tbsp. butter or margarine
2 tsp. minced onion
¼ c. diced green pepper
¼ tsp. Tabasco sauce
3 c. quartered peeled fresh tomatoes
1 tsp. sugar
1 tsp. salt
1 tbsp. flour
½ c. buttered bread crumbs

Melt butter in saucepan. Add onion and green pepper; cook until tender, but not brown. Stir in Tabasco. Add tomatoes, sugar salt and flour. Bring to a boil; reduce heat and simmer for 10 minutes. Tomatoes may be served immediately or turned into a 1-quart casserole. Sprinkle edge with buttered bread crumbs. Place under broiler until crumbs are lightly browned. Yield: 4 servings.

Photograph for this recipe on page 271.

Sour Cream-Scalloped Tomatoes

1 No. 2½ can tomatoes, drained
1 c. chopped onion
½ c. cheese cracker crumbs
1 ½ tsp. sugar
½ tsp. monosodium glutamate
½ tsp. salt
¾ c. sour cream
3 slices bread, cubed and toasted
1 tbsp. melted margarine

(Continued on next page)

Break tomatoes into pieces with a spoon. Layer in greased 1½-quart casserole with ½ cup onion, cracker crumbs, sugar, monosodium glutamate and salt. Cover with remaining onion; top with sour cream. Sprinkle bread crumbs over cream; brush with margarine. Bake at 325 degrees for 20 minutes or until thoroughly hot. Yield: 6 servings.

Judith G. Collins, Albany, N. Y.

 ## Spanish Rice

> 4 strips bacon
> ½ c. thinly-sliced onion
> 2 ½ c. peeled cubed tomatoes
> ¼ green pepper, cut into strips
> 2 tsp. salt
> 1 tsp. paprika
> 1 clove of garlic, minced
> Dash of pepper
> 2 ½ c. cooked rice

Fry bacon crisp; remove from pan. Add onion, tomatoes, green pepper, salt, paprika, garlic and pepper to drippings; cook until vegetables are transparent. Fold in rice and crumbled bacon; place in casserole. Bake at 350 degrees for 10 minutes or until heated through. Serve hot. Yield: 4-5 servings.

Ollie Lee Arter, Home Economics Teacher, Kiowa, Okla.

 ## Baked Dill-Stuffed Tomatoes

> 6 med. tomatoes
> Salt and pepper
> 1 ½ c. coarse dry bread crumbs
> 1 tbsp. finely chopped onion
> 1 tbsp. chopped parsley or chives
> ½ tsp. dillseed
> ¼ c. butter, melted

Slice stem end from tomatoes; remove pulp. Sprinkle insides with salt and pepper; invert to drain. Combine remaining ingredients with tomato pulp; stuff tomatoes. Place in shallow baking dish. Bake at 350 degrees for 15 to 20 minutes. Yield: 6 servings.

Mrs. Doris G. Kruger, Bumsville, Minn.

Bean-Stuffed Tomatoes

1 green pepper, chopped
1 can pork and beans
Seasoning to taste
6 tomatoes
6 strips bacon

Combine pepper and beans; season. Scoop out insides of tomatoes; fill tomatoes with bean mixture. Top with bacon. Bake at 350 degrees for 1 hour. Yield: 6 servings.

Mrs. Joanne Bloom, Home Economics Teacher, Atlanta, Ill.

 ## Baked Stuffed Tomatoes Dothan

6 med. ripe tomatoes
½ c. smooth or crunchy peanut butter
¾ c. soft bread crumbs
1 tsp. salt
⅛ tsp. freshly ground pepper
½ tsp. oregano
2 tbsp. finely chopped onion
¼ c. finely diced celery

Remove stem ends from tomatoes; cut a thin slice from top. With a spoon remove tomato pulp and chop. Mix with peanut butter and remaining ingredients. Fill tomato shells; place in a greased flat baking dish. Bake in 400 degree oven for 25 to 30 minutes. Yield: 6 servings.

Mrs. Lucy Givens, Seattle, Wash.

 ## Baked Tomato Cups

¾ c. bread crumbs
2 tbsp. butter
6 med. tomatoes
½ tsp. salt
Pepper
1 c. whole kernel corn
¾ c. mushrooms
1 c. tomato pulp

Saute bread crumbs in butter. Cut thin slices from stem ends of tomatoes; remove pulp. Combine salt, pepper, corn, mushrooms, tomato pulp and ½ cup buttered crumbs; fill tomatoes with mixture. Sprinkle with remaining crumbs; place in baking dish. Bake at 350 degrees for 30 minutes. Yield: 6 servings.

Mrs. Ella Jo Adams, Kaneohe, Hawaii

Baked Tomatoes With Meat Stuffing

    12 med. tomatoes
    Salt
    1 lb. ground meat
    ½ lb. bulk sausage
    1 lge. onion, diced
    ½ clove of garlic, minced
    ¼ tsp. pepper
    1 c. dry bread crumbs
    3 strips bacon, quartered

Slice stem ends from tomatoes; remove pulp leaving ½-inch shells. Sprinkle insides with salt; invert to drain. Brown ground meat and sausage with onion, garlic, 1 teaspoon salt and pepper. Add tomato pulp; simmer for 20 minutes. Soak bread crumbs in small amount of water; fold into meat mixture. Fill tomato shells; lay a piece of bacon on each tomato. Place tomatoes in shallow baking dish. Bake at 375 degrees for about 25 to 30 minutes. Yield: 12 servings.

Mrs. Ellen Gimon, Home Economics Teacher, Groves, Tex.

 ### Baked Tomatoes With Rice

    6 tomatoes
    Salt
    ½ c. diced celery
    ¼ c. diced green pepper
    2 tbsp. chopped onion
    2 tbsp. butter
    ⅔ c. instant rice
    ¾ c. water
    Dash of pepper

Remove seed and pulp from tomatoes; salt insides. Bake in shallow baking dish at 375 degrees for 15 minutes. Saute celery, green pepper and onion in butter for 3 minutes; add rice, water, ½ teaspoon salt and pepper. Bring to boil; cover. Let stand for 10 minutes; add tomato pulp. Fill baked tomatoes with mixture; bake for 5 minutes longer. Yield: 6 servings.

Janet Chamness, Mascoutah, Ill., Favorite Recipes Food Fair

 ### Cheese-Stuffed Tomatoes

    6 slices bacon, chopped
    1 med. onion, chopped
    1 med. green pepper, chopped
    1 c. grated cheese

(Continued on next page)

2 tsp. dry mustard
1 tsp. parsley
4 med. tomatoes
¼ c. bread or cracker crumbs
Butter

Saute bacon, onion and pepper until golden brown; remove from heat. Stir cheese, mustard and parsley into sauteed vegetables until blended. Scoop out centers of tomatoes; fill tomatoes with cheese mixture. Sprinkle with crumbs; dot with butter. Place in greased casserole. Bake at 350 degrees for about 20 minutes or until crumbs are brown and tomato skins are crinkly. Yield: 4 servings.

Mrs. Jeanette Cason, Home Economics Teacher, Webster, Tex.

 ## Tomato-Cheese Casserole

4 med. tomatoes, cut into ½ in. slices
1 c. process cheddar cheese, grated
⅓ c. onions, thinly sliced
½ tsp. salt
⅛ tsp. pepper
1 c. potato chips, crushed

Arrange half the tomato slices in bottom of 1½-quart casserole. Arrange half the cheese and onion slices in layers over tomatoes; sprinkle with half the salt and pepper. Repeat; top with crushed potato chips. Bake at 350 degrees for 30 minutes or until cheese is melted and bubbly. Yield: 4 servings.

Mrs. Gay E. Robb, Providence, R. I.

 ## Tomato Pudding

1 10-oz. can tomato puree
¾ c. brown sugar
¼ tsp. salt
⅛ tsp. basil
⅛ tsp. oregano
1 c. fresh white bread, cut into 1-in. cubes
⅓ c. melted butter

Combine puree, sugar, salt and spices; simmer for 3 to 5 minutes. Place bread cubes in buttered casserole; add puree. Pour melted butter over puree and bread cubes. Bake, covered, at 350 degrees for 40 to 50 minutes. Yield: 4 servings.

Mrs. Howard Green, Birmingham, Mich.

Tomato Pot Pie

1 lge. can tomatoes
2 c. water
1 ½ tbsp. plus ½ tsp. salt
1 tsp. pepper
3 c. flour
2 ½ tbsp. shortening
2 tsp. baking powder
2 med. potatoes, sliced
2 tsp. butter

Combine tomatoes, water, 1½ tablespoons salt and pepper; bring to a boil. Mix flour, shortening, baking powder and remaining salt. Add enough water to make dough. Roll out on bread board; cut into medium squares. Add to boiling mixture; make layers of pastry and sliced potatoes until all are used. Add butter. Boil for 30 minutes or until potatoes are done. Yield: 6-8 servings.

Marion Magnani, Freeport, Ill.

 ## Cooked Turnips

1 lb. sliced young turnips
Seasoning to taste
Butter
Lemon juice and vinegar

Wash, pare and slice turnips; place in steamer. Steam for 20 to 30 minutes; drain. Season; serve with butter, lemon juice and vinegar. If turnips are old, parblanch sliced or whole turnips for 3 to 5 minutes. Drop into rapidly boiling water to cover; add ½ teaspoon each salt and sugar. Cook, uncovered, for about 20 minutes if sliced, 25 minutes if whole. Season; serve with butter, lemon juice and vinegar.

Mrs. Marion Walker, Gladstone, Ore.

 ## Scalloped Turnips

5 or 6 med. turnips
1 egg
½ c. cream
Cheese

Boil turnips in salted water until tender. Drain; slice or cut into chunks. Place in baking dish. Beat egg and cream together; pour over turnips. Grate or cut cheese into thin strips; sprinkle over turnips. Bake at 350 degrees until cheese melts. Yield: 6 servings.

Olive DeFord, Gassville, Ark.

Dog Patch Turnips

1 lb. turnips
4 tbsp. butter, melted
4 tbsp. flour
1 tbsp. minced onion
⅓ c. cream
Salt and pepper to taste
3 eggs, separated

Wash, pare and slice turnips. Cook for 30 minutes or until soft. Drain and mash, reserving 1/3 cup liquid. Blend butter and flour. Gradually add onion, reserved water and cream. Add mashed turnips and seasonings. Add to well-beaten egg yolks. Fold in stiffly beaten egg whites. Pour into buttered baking dish. Cover and bake at 350 degrees until thoroughly heated. Yield: 6 servings.

Frances Moore, Kingfisher, Okla.

 ### Stuffed Turnips

8 med. turnips, peeled
½ lb. ground beef
2 tbsp. catsup
1 c. bread crumbs
1 tsp. finely chopped onion
Salt and pepper to taste
Butter

Cook turnips in salted water until tender but firm; drain. Cool; scoop out centers, reserving 2 tablespoons for stuffing. Mix meat, catsup, ½ cup bread crumbs, onion, reserved mashed turnip pulp, salt and pepper. Fill turnip cups. Cover with remaining bread crumbs; dot with butter. Bake at 350 degrees for 35 to 40 minutes. Yield: 8 servings.

Mrs. Ted Scott, Twin Falls, Idaho

 ### Turnip Cups

6 sm. white turnips, pared
1 tbsp. lemon juice
3 med. beets, diced and cooked
4 tsp. butter

Cook turnips in water with lemon juice until tender. Scoop out centers of turnips. Mix drained beets with butter; stuff into turnips. Serve garnished with parsley. Yield: 6 servings.

Mrs. Bert Johnson, Home Economics Teacher, Bruce, Miss.

Turnip Casserole

> 2 c. mashed cooked yellow or white turnips
> 4 tbsp. butter or margarine, melted
> 1 tbsp. sugar
> 1 tsp. salt
> Dash of pepper
> 1 c. soft bread crumbs
> 2 eggs, beaten

Combine turnips, 3 tablespoons butter, sugar, salt, pepper, ¾ cup bread crumbs and eggs. Mix well. Turn into a buttered 1-quart casserole. Mix remaining bread crumbs with melted butter; sprinkle over top. Bake in preheated 350-degree oven for 30 minutes or until brown. Two pounds turnips equal 2 cups mashed turnips. Yield: 6 servings.

Mrs. Jewell Tidwell, Burns, Tenn., Favorite Recipes Food Fair

 ### Turnip Greens

> 2 lb. bacon or cottage ham
> 2 to 3 lb. greens

Add meat to enough water to cover; simmer for about 2 hours. Wash greens carefully, cutting out bruised areas and tough stems. Drop greens into simmering water with meat. Cook until just tender, 35 to 40 minutes.

Mrs. Jack Ashcraft, Warner Robbins, Ga.

 ### Turnip Greens With Cornmeal Dumplings

> Turnip greens
> ½ c. sifted flour
> 1 tsp. baking powder
> ½ tsp. garlic salt
> ½ c. yellow cornmeal
> ⅛ tsp. pepper
> 1 egg
> ¼ c. milk
> 1 tbsp. melted butter

Cook turnips until done, using plenty of liquid; remove turnips. Sift dry ingredients into mixing bowl; add egg, milk and butter. Stir until batter is well mixed. Drop dumplings by teaspoonfuls into simmering broth. Cover tightly and simmer for 15 minutes. Do not lift cover while dumplings cook. Chicken broth may be used instead of turnip broth. Yield: 4 servings.

Mrs. Thelma L. Fowler, Home Economics Teacher, Conce, Tenn.

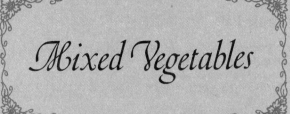

Mixed Vegetables

Broccoli Pie

4 c. peeled broccoli, cut in large pieces
1 pkg. frozen lima beans
1 c. cooked carrot slices
3 hard-boiled eggs
3 c. milk
2 tbsp. minced onion
3 tbsp. mayonnaise
1 tsp. prepared mustard
Crushed cornflakes
Butter

Cook all vegetables in salted water until tender, but not completely done. Combine milk, onion, mayonnaise and prepared mustard. Arrange vegetables and eggs in layers, beginning with broccoli, using sauce to separate layers. Cover with sauce; sprinkle with crushed cornflakes. Dot with butter. Bake at 325 degrees for 25 minutes. Yield: 8-10 servings.

Venna Von Almen, La Mirada, Cal.

 ### Brussels Sprouts And Carrots In Mushroom Sauce

2 pkg. frozen Brussels sprouts
4 lge. carrots, sliced
½ c. boiling water
1 tsp. salt
1 can cream of mushroom soup
½ c. grated cheese

Simmer Brussels sprouts and carrots in boiling salted water until tender; add soup. Heat; add cheese. Stir slightly; serve immediately. Yield: 6 servings.

Mrs. Dorotha Danel, Home Economics Teacher, Coyle, Okla.

 ### Brussels Sprouts With Turnips

2 oz. salt pork
1 ½ c. water
4 c. peeled sliced turnips
¾ tsp. salt
3 tbsp. sugar
1 pkg. frozen Brussels sprouts
1 tbsp. butter or margarine
½ tsp. sugar
¼ tsp. dry mustard
½ tsp. horseradish

(Continued on next page)

Boil salt pork in water for 20 minutes; add turnips. Boil over medium heat for 20 to 30 minutes or until turnips are tender. Season with salt and sugar. Prepare Brussels sprouts according to package directions. Season with butter, sugar, mustard and horseradish. Place turnips in a bowl; place sprouts in a mound in center of turnips. Yield: 6-8 servings.

Doris S. Viears, Wise, Va.

 ### Carrot-Corn Casserole

1 ½ c. white sauce, cooled
3 eggs, beaten
1 c. grated cheese
1 c. grated carrots
1 ½ c. cream-style corn

Pour small amount of sauce into eggs; pour eggs into remaining sauce. Add cheese, carrots and corn. Place in well-greased dish; bake about 40 minutes in 300-degree oven.

Mrs. Rowan Burdette, Greer, S. C.

 ### Cauliflower And Onion Fromage

1 med. cauliflower
2 tsp. salt
½ stick margarine
¼ c. flour
⅛ tsp. pepper
1 ¼ c. milk
¼ lb. grated sharp cheese
1 tsp. Worcestershire sauce
1 No. 2 can sm. canned onions or 2 c. sm. onions, boiled
   tender

Break cauliflower into pieces; soak in cold water 1 hour before cooking. Cover with water and 1 teaspoon salt; boil until slightly tender, about 10 minutes. Drain. Place layer of cauliflower in 1½-quart casserole; then layer of onions. Melt margarine; add flour and blend well. Add remaining salt and pepper; slowly add milk, stirring constantly. Stir in cheese and Worcestershire sauce; pour over layers of onion and cauliflower. Bake 30 to 40 minutes in 350-degree oven.

Sue Jones, Flora, Miss., Favorite Recipes Food Fair

Chevron Casserole With Celery Seed Crust

  ¼ c. chopped onion
  3 tbsp. fat
  4 tbsp. flour
  1 tsp. salt
  ⅛ tsp. pepper
  2 c. meat stock, gravy or vegetable liquid
  1 c. cooked diced meat
  ½ c. diced cooked carrots
  ¾ c. diced cooked celery
  1 c. diced cooked potatoes
  1 c. cooked green beans

Fry onion in fat until brown. Add flour and seasonings. Add liquid; cook until smooth and thick. Add meat and vegetables; turn into baking dish.

CELERY SEED CRUST:
  1 ½ c. flour
  2 ½ tsp. baking powder
  ½ tsp. salt
  ½ tsp. celery seed
  ¾ tbsp. shortening
  ½ c. milk

Sift flour, baking powder and salt. Add celery seed. Cut in shortening. Add milk. Roll to fit top of casserole; place over filling. Slash center. Bake at 400 degrees until crust is brown. Yield: 6 servings.

Ann Havemann, Muscatine, Iowa

 ### Cole Cannon

  4 lge. carrots, peeled and chopped
  1 sm. parsnip, chopped (opt.)
  1 sm. cabbage, chopped
  ¼ med. turnip, chopped
  15 lge. potatoes, halved
  1 med. onion, halved
  Salt and pepper to taste
  1 pt. cream
  ¼ lb. butter

Cook carrots and parsnip for 10 minutes; add cabbage and turnip. Cook until nearly done; add potatoes and onion. Cook until done; drain. Mash fine; add salt and pepper. Heat cream; add with butter to vegetables. Mix well. Yield: 8 servings.

Mrs. Jennie Stewart, Dallas, Tex.

Colorful, healthful, and delightfully tasty, Brussels sprouts are appearing on more and more American tables as their popularity continues to rise. A complete meal guaranteed to please, Bubble and Squeak combines Brussels sprouts with old-fashioned corned beef, other vegetables and a tangy sauce.

BUBBLE AND SQUEAK

1 5-lb. corned beef brisket
1 med. onion, halved
1 clove of garlic
6 whole cloves
8 peppercorns
2 bay leaves
1 c. celery, cut into 2-in. pieces
6 med. potatoes, peeled
6 whole white onions
4 10-oz. pkg. frozen California Brussels sprouts
1 1-lb. can whole baby carrots
2 tbsp. snipped parsley

Place corned beef in large pot and cover with cold water. Add halved onion, seasonings and celery. Bring to a boil. Reduce heat; cover and simmer for 3 to 4 hours until tender. Skim excess fat off liquid and remove corned beef. Cook potatoes and whole onions in corned beef liquid, covered, until nearly tender; add Brussels sprouts. Cover and cook 15 minutes longer. Add carrots and heat through. Serve beef and vegetables on hot platters. Garnish potatoes with parsley.

ENGLISH MUSTARD SAUCE:

1 tbsp. cornstarch
2 tsp. sugar
1 tsp. dry mustard
$\frac{1}{2}$ tsp. salt
1 c. water
1 tbsp. butter
$\frac{1}{4}$ c. vinegar
1 tsp. horseradish
2 egg yolks, beaten

Mix cornstarch, sugar, mustard and salt in top of double boiler; add water. Cover and stir over direct low heat until mixture thickens and boils for 1 minute. Remove from heat; mix in butter, vinegar, horseradish, then egg yolks. Cook over boiling water until sauce thickens slightly. Serve with Bubble and Squeak. Two pounds fresh California Brussels sprouts may be substituted for frozen Brussels sprouts.

See photograph on reverse side.

Confetti Corncake

> 2 pkg. frozen mixed vegetables
> 2 tbsp. butter
> Salt and pepper to taste
> 1 pkg. corn muffin mix

Cook vegetables as directed on package; drain. Add butter and seasonings. Place in a buttered baking dish. Make corn muffins as directed on package; spoon over vegetables. Bake at 425 degrees for 25 minutes or until brown. Let stand for 3 minutes; invert onto serving plate.

CREAMY CHEESE SAUCE:
> 2 tbsp. butter
> 2 tbsp. flour
> ½ tsp. dry mustard
> ½ tsp. salt
> Dash of pepper
> 1 ½ c. milk
> 1 ½ c. diced Velveeta cheese

Melt butter in top of double boiler. Remove from heat; blend in flour, mustard, salt and pepper. Slowly stir in milk; cook until mixture thickens. Add cheese; continue cooking until it melts. Serve over wedges of corn cake. Yield: 4-6 servings.

Marjorie A. Wetzler, Peru, Ill.

 ### Egg-Vegetable Cutlets

> 3 or 4 eggs, beaten
> 3 c. mixed vegetables
> 2 to 3 c. oats
> 1 tbsp. chopped onion
> 1 tsp. salt
> Dash of pepper
> 2 tbsp. fat

Combine all ingredients except fat; mix well. Drop by spoonfuls into hot fat. Brown on both sides. Yield: 6 servings.

Betty Harrington, Beachwood, N. J.

Corn And Tomato Scallop

2 c. tomatoes
¼ tsp. paprika
3 tbsp. chopped celery
½ c. bread crumbs
1 egg, beaten
2 c. corn
3 tbsp. chopped onion
2 tbsp. chopped green pepper
5 tbsp. melted butter
2 tbsp. sugar
1 tsp. salt
Crushed Ritz crackers or Ritz cheese crackers

Combine all ingredients except cracker crumbs; pour into buttered baking dish. Top with crackers. Bake at 350 degrees for 30 minutes.

Mrs. Pauline S. Slate, Home Economics Teacher, Emporia, Va.

 ### French Peas Or Peas Etuvee

2 slices bacon, cut in strips
Lettuce, shredded
1 No. 303 can sm. peas, drained
1 No. 303 can thin onions, drained
Flour
Butter, softened
Salt and pepper to taste

Render bacon in saucepan, but do not brown. Add lettuce; saute until it becomes dry. Add liquid drained from vegetables to lettuce mixture; cook until liquid is reduced to half its original volume. Add peas and onions and bring to a boil. Mix flour with softened butter; blend into peas, stirring until it comes to a boil. Season to taste. Yield: 6 servings.

Mrs. Hulett C. Smith, Wife of Governor of West Virginia, Charleston

 ### Green Broccoli Ring And Beets

2 pkg. frozen broccoli, chopped
2 tbsp. butter
3 tbsp. flour
1 can evaporated milk
½ tsp. salt
3 eggs, beaten

(Continued on next page)

¾ c. mayonnaise
1 sm. can beets
1 tbsp. vinegar

Cook broccoli as directed on box; drain and mash. Melt butter; stir in flour. Add milk gradually, stirring constantly; cook and stir until thickened. Add salt. Stir in eggs gradually; add mayonnaise and broccoli. Place in an oiled ring mold; set in pan of hot water. Bake at 350 degrees for 45 minutes. Unmold and fill center with beets that have been heated with vinegar. Yield: 8 servings.

Jimmie Garvin Harris, Aiken, S. C.

 ## Green Vegetable Casserole

1 pkg. frozen lima beans, cooked
1 pkg. frozen English peas, cooked
1 can green beans, cooked
2 green peppers, cut into strips
½ pt. heavy cream, whipped
½ c. mayonnaise
1 sm. can Parmesan cheese

Drain cooked vegetables. Layer in large casserole with green peppers. Blend whipped cream and mayonnaise; pour over vegetables. Sprinkle with cheese. Bake at 350 degrees for 45 minutes or until light brown. Yield: 8 servings.

Mrs. Lehman Jones, Home Economics Teacher, Spade, Tex.

 ## Harvard Beets With Greens

1 tbsp. sugar
2 tsp. cornstarch
¼ c. vinegar
¼ c. water or beet juice
1 tbsp. butter
Dash of salt
1 c. cooked diced beets
2 c. wilted spinach or other greens

Combine sugar and cornstarch; add remaining ingredients except beets and greens. Cook over low heat until thickened, stirring constantly. Add beets; heat. Serve over hot wilted greens. Yield: 4 servings.

Isabelle Staley, Home Economics Teacher, Huron, S. D.

Indian Succotash

    1 12-oz. can whole kernel corn, drained
    1 1-lb. can or 2 c. green lima beans, drained
    2 tbsp. oleo
    ½ c. light cream
    Salt and pepper to taste

Combine all ingredients; heat and serve.

Mrs. Opal Maloch, Emerson, Ark.

 ### Indian Summer Succotash

    1 qt. water
    1 qt. fresh butter beans
    1 slice bacon
    1 tbsp. butter
    3 potatoes, cut up
    1 sm. onion
    3 tomatoes, peeled
    2 stalks celery, chopped
    Salt and pepper to taste
    1 c. fresh corn

Bring water to boil. Add butter beans, bacon and butter; cook for 30 minutes. Add potatoes, onion, tomatoes, celery, salt and pepper. Cook slowly for 1 hour. Ten minutes before serving time, add corn. Yield: 6 servings.

Mrs. J. W. Bonniville, Suffolk, Va.

 ### Marinated Vegetable Bowl

    1 cucumber, sliced (opt.)
    1 No. 303 or No. 2 can French-style green beans, drained
    1 No. 303 or No. 2 can large English peas, drained
    1 onion, sliced
    3 to 5 stalks celery, chopped
    1 green pepper, cut into rings
    1 red sweet pepper or 1 sm. jar pimento
    2 can artichoke hearts (opt.)
    ½ c. corn oil
    1 c. vinegar
    ½ to 1 c. sugar
    1 tsp. salt

Blend all ingredients; refrigerate for at least 48 hours. Drain; serve. Yield: 25 servings.

Joanne Crow, Home Economics Teacher, Newnan, Ga.

Marinated Fresh Vegetable Kabobs

    8 sm. white onions, peeled
    8 cherry tomatoes
    1 sm. eggplant, cut into 3-in. cubes
    ½ lb. fresh mushrooms, washed and cleaned
    1 med. green pepper, cubed
    1 pkg. Italian French salad dressing mix

Place vegetables in bowl. Prepare Italian French dressing according to package directions; pour over vegetables. Marinate for 3 to 4 hours; string on skewers. Grill over hot coals for 12 to 20 minutes or until done. Yield: 8 servings.

Mrs. J. Dee Cates, Home Economics Teacher, Tempe, Ariz.

 ## Mary's Favorite Casserole

    2 tbsp. butter or margarine
    1 tsp. onion powder
    3 c. Corn Chex, crushed to 1⅓ c.
    2 cans cream of mushroom soup
    ½ c. milk
    ¼ tsp. salt
    ¼ tsp. onion juice
    Dash of Tobasco sauce
    2 c. fresh cooked peas or 1 10-oz. pkg. frozen peas
    1 2-oz. can mushrooms
    2 lb. tiny new potatoes, cooked and peeled

Melt butter and onion powder over low heat; stir in Corn Chex. Heat and stir until crumbs are coated. Combine soup, milk, salt, onion juice and Tabasco sauce, mixing well. Rinse frozen peas in warm water and drain. Add mushrooms, peas and potatoes to soup; mix well. Pour mixture into a buttered 2-quart baking dish. Top with additional crumbs. Bake at 325 degrees for 45 minutes or until bubbly. Yield: 4 servings.

Mrs. Debra Ray, Falls Church, Va.

 ## Mexican Casserole

    ½ c. chopped onion
    2 cloves of garlic, pressed
    ½ lb. lean pork, ground
    2 lb. ground beef or hamburger
    2 tbsp. shortening
    ½ tsp. salt
    ½ tsp. pepper

(Continued on next page)

½ tsp. monosodium glutamate
½ tsp. Tabasco sauce
1 4-oz. can pimento, sliced
1 No. 2 can tomatoes
1 4-oz. bottle ripe olives
1 No. 2 can green peas, drained
1 ½ c. cooked elbow macaroni
1 8-oz. can mushroom stems and pieces
½ lb. cheese, diced

Brown onion, garlic and meats in hot shortening, stirring to crumble meat. Drain off excess fat. Add all remaining ingredients except cheese. Pour into two 1-quart casseroles. Bake at 350 degrees for 1 hour. Top with cheese during last 10 minutes of baking time. Yield: 20 servings.

Blanche Minks, Liberty, Miss., Favorite Recipes Food Fair

 ## Mixed Vegetable Casserole

½ stick margarine
4 tbsp. flour
½ tsp. dry mustard
½ tsp. salt
⅛ tsp. pepper
½ tsp. Worcestershire sauce
2 c. milk
1 pkg. frozen peas, cooked and drained
1 pkg. frozen green beans, cooked and drained
16 small onions, cooked or canned
1 c. buttered bread crumbs
¼ c. grated cheddar cheese

Melt margarine over low heat. Blend in flour and seasonings. Remove from heat; slowly stir in milk. Mix vegetables in sauce. Turn into buttered 8-cup casserole. Sprinkle buttered bread crumbs in a ring around top; fill center with grated cheddar cheese. Bake 30 minutes at 350 degrees. Yield: 6-8 servings.

Mrs. Richard B. Goebel, Officers' Wives' Club, Madison, Wis.

 ## Mixed Vegetables With Orange Butter Sauce

2 tbsp. frozen orange juice concentrate, thawed
2 tbsp. butter
Beets, carrots, green beans, spinach

Stir orange juice concentrate into melted butter and heat just until warm. Serve over hot cooked vegetables. Yield: 3-4 servings.

Photograph for this recipe on page 285.

Mixed Vegetables Au Gratin

2 pkg. frozen mixed vegetables, cooked
1 2-oz. can sliced mushrooms, drained
½ c. finely chopped onion
½ stick butter
¼ c. flour
2 c. milk
1 c. shredded sharp American cheese
Salt and pepper to taste
2 tbsp. melted butter
½ c. dry bread crumbs

Combine drained vegetables with mushrooms. Saute onion in butter until transparent; add flour and milk. Cook until thickened, stirring constantly. Fold in cheese; melt. Season; pour into 1½-quart buttered baking dish. Blend butter and crumbs; sprinkle over vegetable mixture. Bake at 350 degrees for 25 minutes or until heated and lightly browned. Yield: 6-8 servings.

Mary Ellen Trowbridge, Home Economics Teacher, Spangle, Wash.

 ### Mixture Of Summer Vegetables

3 tbsp. olive oil
1 med. onion, chopped
1 med. green tomato
3 c. summer squash
1 cucumber
1 green pepper
3 ripe tomatoes, peeled
Salt and pepper to taste

Heat olive oil in heavy or electric skillet. Add onion; saute until golden. Cut green tomato, squash, cucumber and green pepper into bite-sized pieces; add to onion. Toss lightly to coat with oil. Cut ripe tomatoes into bite-sized pieces; add to other vegetables. Sprinkle with salt and pepper. Cook for 15 minutes or until tender. Yield: 4-6 servings.

Mrs. Ruby G. Jasper, Eliot, Maine

 ### Pinwheel Vegetable Casserole

8 sm. carrots, cooked
8 sm. onions, cooked
1 ½ c. green beans, cooked
1 c. peas, cooked
4 tbsp. butter or margarine
4 tbsp. flour

(Continued on next page)

>   2 c. milk
> ½ lb. cheese, shredded
> ½ tsp. salt
> ½ tsp. pepper

Place well-drained vegetables in a casserole. Melt butter; stir in flour. Add milk gradually; cook, stirring, until thickened. Add cheese; stir until melted. Season to taste; pour over vegetables. Cover with pinwheel biscuits; bake at 425 degrees for 20 minutes or until biscuits are light brown.

PINWHEEL BISCUITS:

>   2 c. flour
>   3 tsp. baking powder
> ½ tsp. salt
> ½ c. butter or margarine
> ¾ c. milk

Sift dry ingredients; cut in 4 tablespoons butter until the consistency of coarse cornmeal. Stir in milk; turn out onto floured board. Knead for 30 seconds; roll out to ¼ inch thickness. Spread with remaining melted butter; roll up like jelly roll. Cut off 1-inch slices; place on casserole. Yield: 6 servings.

Mrs. William L. Wright, Pres. Officers' Wives' Club, Fort Riley, Kan.

 Ratatouille

>   2 c. yellow summer squash, cut into ½-in. cubes
>   1 ½ tsp. salt
>   3 cloves of garlic, minced
> ⅓ c. salad oil
> ⅓ tsp. cumin or comino seed
>   2 c. peeled eggplant, cut into ½-inch cubes
> ½ tsp. oregano
>   3 med. onions, sliced
>   2 green peppers, cut in strips
> ½ tsp. marjoram
>   3 medium tomatoes, sliced
> ⅓ tsp. dill seed

Cover bottom of greased 2½-quart casserole with squash cubes. Sprinkle with one-third of the salt, garlic and oil. Add cumin. Make a second layer with eggplant. Sprinkle with one-half of remaining salt, garlic and oil. Add oregano. Make a third layer of onion slices and a fourth layer of green pepper. Sprinkle with remaining salt, garlic, oil and marjoram. Cover; bake at 350 degrees for 1 hour. Add a layer sliced tomatoes. Sprinkle with dill seed. Bake, uncovered, for 15 minutes longer. Yield: 6 servings.

Mrs. Emma Lou Leftwich, Home Economics Teacher, Mount Pleasant, Tex.

Rice Medley

2 med. onions, diced
2 med. green peppers, diced
Butter
2 c. cooked rice
¾ c. diced cooked carrots
1 sm. can pimento, diced
1 can cream-style golden corn
Salt and pepper to taste
1 tsp. cumin powder
1 c. milk or half and half

Saute onions and green peppers in butter. Mix all ingredients except milk; allow to stand several hours or overnight. Add milk. Mixture should have a custard-like consistency. Put in casserole. Bake 1 hour or until set at 325 degrees. Yield: 8-10 servings.

Mrs. Oscar J. Ogren, Washington, D. C.

 ### Rutabaga And Carrots

1 2-lb. rutabaga
2 med. carrots
1 tsp. sugar
¼ c. butter
Salt and pepper to taste

Pare and cube rutabaga and carrots; boil in small amount of water with sugar until tender. Drain; mash. Add butter, salt and pepper; serve hot. Yield: 6 servings.

Mrs. Allen S. Lawrence, Home Economics Teacher, Sinton, Tex.

 ### Rice With Mushroom Casserole

1 c. uncooked rice
½ c. chopped onion
1 c. chopped canned tomatoes
1 lb. sliced mushrooms
½ c. butter
3 c. chicken broth
½ c. Burgundy
Salt and pepper to taste
1 c. cooked frozen peas
¼ c. Parmesan cheese

In electric skillet, cook rice, chopped onion, tomatoes and mushrooms in butter for 10 minutes at 300 degrees. Add broth, wine and seasoning; mix well.

(Continued on next page)

Cover skillet; simmer for 40 minutes or until rice is tender and liquid has cooked down. Stir in peas; sprinkle on Parmesan cheese. Three chicken bouillon cubes in 3 cups water may be substituted for broth. Yield: 6 servings.

Mrs. Paul D. Werner, Hon. Pres. Officers' Wives' Club, Calumet AFS, Mich.

 ### Scalloped Broccoli 'N' Onions Imperial

> 1 10-oz. pkg. frozen broccoli, cooked and drained
> 1 1-lb. can sm. whole white onions, drained
> 1 10½-oz. can condensed cream of mushroom soup
> ⅓ c. milk
> ½ to 1 tsp. curry powder
> ¼ c. toasted slivered almonds

In 1½-quart shallow round casserole, arrange broccoli in spoke fashion. Place onions between broccoli. Stir soup until smooth; blend in milk and curry. Pour over vegetables. Top with almonds. Bake at 350 degrees for 30 minutes. Yield: 4 servings.

Photograph for this recipe below.

Savory Julienne Vegetables

  2 lge. yellow onions
  2 c. celery
  2 tbsp. soy sauce
  2 tbsp. salad oil
  2 tbsp. cold water

Cut onions into thin slices lengthwise; cut celery into thin diagonal slices. Combine all ingredients; cover and steam for 3 to 5 minutes, stirring once or twice. Do not overcook. Cooked julienne slices of meat may be added. Yield: 4 servings.

         Mrs. Minnie B. Russell, Jerome, Idaho

 ### Scalloped Corn And Okra

  2 lb. fresh or 1 can okra
  4 tbsp. butter or fat
  1 can corn
  Salt and pepper to taste
  2 tbsp. flour
  1 c. milk
  ¼ lb. sharp cheese
  1 c. fine dry bread crumbs

Drain okra; fry in 2 tablespoons fat for 10 minutes, stirring frequently. Layer okra and corn in greased baking dish; sprinkle each layer with salt and pepper. Combine remaining fat, flour and milk. Cook until thickened, stirring constantly. Add cheese; stir until melted. Pour over okra and corn; cover with crumbs. Bake at 350 degrees until brown. Yield: 4 servings.

    Mrs. Audrey Shaw, Home Economics Teacher, Springhill, La.

 ### Southern Succotash

  1 lge. onion
  2 green peppers
  1 No. 2 can tomatoes
  1 No. 2 can cream-style corn
  ½ lb. bacon, fried crisp

Saute onion and green peppers; add tomatoes and corn. Heat. Top with crisp bacon; serve. Yield: 6 servings.

        Mrs. Ross Finley, Farmington, N. M.

Six-Layer Dinner

    6 potatoes, sliced
    1 ½ lb. ground steak
    3 to 4 onions, sliced
    3 to 4 green peppers, sliced
    3 to 4 carrots, sliced
    1 qt. cooked tomatoes
    1 tbsp. salt
    1 tsp. sugar
    ½ tsp. pepper

Layer potatoes, steak, onions, green peppers and carrots in buttered casserole. Cover with tomatoes; season with salt, sugar and pepper. Bake, covered, at 325 degrees for 2 hours and 30 minutes. Yield: 10-12 servings.

Mrs. Delia McClurg, Merino, Colo., Favorite Recipes Food Fair

Smorgasbord Casserole

    1 15-oz. can cut green beans, drained
    1 15-oz. can cut asparagus spears, drained
    1 c. chopped cooked ham
    2 tbsp. butter, melted
    ¼ c. flour
    2 c. milk
    ¾ tsp. salt
    ⅛ tsp. celery seed
    1 ½ tbsp. mustard
    2 hard-cooked eggs, finely chopped

Arrange beans, asparagus and ham in layers in greased 2-quart casserole. Blend butter and flour; stir in milk. Cook until thick and smooth; add salt, celery seed and mustard. Pour over vegetables and ham; top with eggs. Bake at 350 degrees for 25 minutes. Yield: 6 servings.

Mrs. Alva Moe, New York, N. Y.

Spanish Casserole Delight

    3 tbsp. butter
    2 lb. summer squash, diced
    2 cans green chili peppers or fresh green chili peppers, chopped
    2 cans whole kernel yellow corn

(Continued on next page)

4 med. onions, chopped
2 cloves of garlic, chopped
2 lb. Velveeta cheese

Melt butter in large pan. Add all ingredients except cheese. Cover and simmer until squash is tender. Add cheese; heat until melted. Pour into casserole; keep hot until ready to serve.

Mrs. JoAnn Westbrook, Dyess AFB, Tex.

 ### Spinach And Corn Parmesan

1 tbsp. dried onion
1 can cream-style corn
1 10-oz. pkg. frozen spinach, thawed and drained
1 tsp. vinegar
½ tsp. salt
¼ tsp. pepper
¼ c. fine bread crumbs
2 tbsp. grated Parmesan cheese
2 tbsp. melted butter or margarine

Combine all ingredients except bread crumbs, cheese and butter. Place in lightly greased baking dish. Blend crumbs, cheese and melted butter; sprinkle over vegetables. Bake at 400 degrees for 20 minutes.

Mrs. James Borland, Indianapolis, Ind.

 ### Sweet And Sour Carrots And Onions

8 sm. carrots, cooked
4 to 8 sm. onions, cooked
2 tbsp. butter or margarine
2 tbsp. flour
¼ tsp. salt
2 tbsp. sugar
2 tbsp. vinegar
¼ tsp. paprika

Drain carrots and onions; add water to carrot stock to measure 1 cup. Melt butter; add flour, salt, sugar, vinegar, paprika and carrot stock. Cook until thickened, stirring constantly. Add vegetables; let stand over low heat for 15 to 20 minutes, stirring occasionally. Yield: 4 servings.

Mrs. Nancy Hoffman, McComb, Ohio

Stewed Okra, Corn And Tomatoes

2 c. sliced okra
1 sm. onion, chopped
2 tbsp. bacon drippings
2 c. cooked or canned tomatoes
1 sm. can whole kernel corn
½ tsp. salt
Pepper

Lightly brown okra and onion in fat; add tomatoes, corn, salt and pepper. Cook over moderate heat for 20 minutes or until thickened. Stir occasionally. Yield: 6-8 servings.

Mrs. Gail Patton, Home Economics Teacher, Memphis, Tenn.

 ### Tart And Festive Vegetable Casserole

1 potato, diced
1 eggplant, diced
1 zucchini, diced
1 Bermuda onion, diced
2 green peppers, diced
2 sm. carrots, diced
½ c. green peas
2 tsp. parsley
Olive oil
3 tsp. salt
2 tsp. Tabasco
1 tsp. pepper
4 lge. tomatoes, sliced
½ c. raw rice
2 tbsp. white wine vinegar
½ c. water
1 ¾ c. shredded sharp cheese

Combine diced vegetables; add peas, parsley, 1/3 cup oil and seasonings. Oil flat 9 x 13-inch pan; cover with slices of 2 large tomatoes. Cover with one-half of vegetable mixture; add rice and rest of vegetable mixture. Add remaining slices of tomatoes. Pour ½ cup olive oil, vinegar and water over; cover with foil. Bake at 350 degrees 1 hour and 30 minutes to 2 hours. Just before serving, uncover; sprinkle with cheese. Put under broiler until browned. Yield: 6-8 servings.

Mrs. Lynn Cooke, Tampa, Fla.

Three Vegetable Casserole

    1 box frozen English peas
    1 box frozen lima beans
    1 can French beans
    4 hard-boiled eggs, cut fine
    1 c. mayonnaise
    1 med. onion
    Worcestershire sauce and Tabasco sauce to taste
    1 tsp. mustard
    4 strips of bacon, cooked

Cook peas and lima beans separately. Drain. Drain French beans. Combine remaining ingredients for sauce. Put peas on bottom of 1½-quart casserole; then add half of sauce. Add lima beans and balance of sauce; add French beans. Put strips of bacon on top. Bake about 20 minutes at 350 degrees. Yield: 6-8 servings.

Mrs. Leroy O. Blondeau, Officers' Wives' Club, Kure Beach, N. C.

 ### Tiskatash

    1 pkg. frozen English peas
    1 No. 303 can whole kernel corn
    ½ tsp. sugar
    ⅛ tsp. pepper
    Pinch of salt
    ½ c. cream or milk
    2 slices bacon, fried

Cook peas; drain and reserve liquid. Drain corn; mix corn liquid with the liquid from the peas. Add sugar, pepper and salt; simmer until liquid is reduced to ½ cup. Add peas, corn and cream. Heat and serve. Garnish with crumbled bacon. Yield: 4-6 servings.

Mrs. Walter Reichert, Jourdanton, Tex.

 ### Upside-Down Vegetable Bread

    2 8-oz. pkg. frozen mixed vegetables with onion sauce
    1 8½-oz. pkg. corn muffin mix
    ½ tsp. caraway seed

Cook vegetables as directed on package. Pour into greased 8-inch square baking dish. Prepare corn muffin mix as directed on package; stir in caraway seed. Spoon over vegetables. Bake in 400-degree oven for 20 minutes or until top is golden brown. Cut in squares. Yield: 6 servings.

Mrs. Calvin G. Gardner, Officers' Wives' Club, Norfolk, Va.

Thyme Enough Casserole

1 ½ c. carrots, sliced crosswise
1 ½ c. cut green beans
1 ½ c. celery, cut into ½-in. slices
⅔ c. water
¾ tsp. salt
Dash of pepper
½ tsp. powdered thyme
1 tbsp. finely chopped celery leaves
1 tbsp. finely chopped onion
¼ c. butter or margarine
1 can cream of mushroom soup
3 c. shredded bite-sized rice biscuits

Cook carrots, green beans and celery in water with salt, pepper and ¼ teaspoon thyme. Cover and cook for 15 minutes or just until tender. Save liquid. Place vegetables in buttered baking dish. Cook celery leaves and onion in 2 tablespoons margarine until onion is clear. Add soup and ½ cup reserved liquid; mix well. Pour mixture over vegetables. Add rice biscuits to 2 tablespoons margarine and ¼ teaspoon thyme. Coat and stir over low heat for 5 minutes. Top casserole with slightly crumbled rice biscuits. Bake in preheated 350 degree oven for 30 minutes or until bubbly and browned. Yield: 8 servings.

Mrs. Davis Nolte, Columbia, Ill.

 ### Vegetable-Cheese Loaf

1 c. cooked peas
1 c. cooked carrots
1 c. cooked string beans
2 c. cooked mashed potatoes
3 to 5 tbsp. butter
1 onion, minced
3 tbsp. flour
2 c. milk or vegetable broth
2 to 3 tsp. salt
½ tsp. pepper
½ tsp. celery salt
1 c. grated cheese
2 eggs, slightly beaten (opt.)
½ c. bread crumbs

Layer cooked vegetables in greased baking dish. Melt butter; add onion and flour. Brown; gradually add milk and seasonings. Cook until thickened, stirring constantly. Add cheese; stir until melted. Remove from heat; cool slightly. Stir in eggs. Pour over vegetables; sprinkle with crumbs. Bake at 350 degrees for 45 minutes. Yield: 8 servings.

Mrs. Ethel D. Finley, Home Economics Teacher, Silver Spring, Md.

Vegetable Casserole

1 pkg. frozen baby lima beans
1 pkg. frozen French-cut green beans
1 pkg. frozen peas and carrots
½ c. salad dressing
1 sm. onion, chopped
3 hard-boiled eggs, chopped
1 tsp. prepared mustard
1 tsp. Worcestershire sauce
4 tbsp. Wesson oil
Dash of Tabasco sauce

Cook vegetables according to directions on box; combine in casserole. Combine remaining ingredients and pour over vegetables. Heat in 350-degree oven until warmed through. Casserole may be made earlier in day and heated before serving. Yield: 10-12 servings.

Mrs. Robert J. Ray, Officers' Wives' Club, K. I. Sawyer, AFB, Mich.

 ### Vegetable Chow Mein

¼ c. butter
3 c. coarsley shreeded cabbage
1 c. sliced celery
1 c. thinly sliced carrots
1 green pepper, cut into thin strips
½ c. chopped onion
1 tsp. salt
Dash of pepper
1 6-oz. can evaporated milk

Melt butter in large skillet; add vegetables, salt and pepper. Cover and cook over medium heat just until vegetables are tender. Add milk; heat thoroughly, stirring once or twice. Serve over chow mein noodles or cooked rice. Yield: 6 servings.

Mrs. Maurie Metteauer, Broaddus, Tex.

 ### Vegetable Curry

1 ½ c. diced carrots
1 ½ c. diced potatoes
½ tsp. salt
1 can peas
1 sm. onion, chopped
2 tbsp. butter
2 tbsp. flour

(Continued on next page)

½ tsp. curry powder
Pepper
1 c. milk

Cook potatoes and carrots until tender; add salt and peas. Cook onion in butter until yellow; add flour, curry powder and pepper. Stir until thoroughly mixed; add milk. Bring to a boil; pour over hot vegetables. Serve at once. Yield: 8 servings.

Lucetta L. Metcalf, Winn, Mich., Favorite Recipes Food Fair

 ## Vegetable Deluxe

1 pkg. frozen baby lima beans
1 pkg. frozen whole-kernel corn
1 c. sour cream
1 sm. can deviled ham
3 tbsp. minced onion
1 tsp. salt
Bread crumbs or croutons

Prepare lima beans and corn by package instructions. Mix together, sour cream, deviled ham, onion and salt. Add to lima beans and corn in casserole. Sprinkle bread crumbs or croutons on top about ¼ inch thick. Bake 30 minutes at 350 degrees. Yield: 6-8 servings.

Mrs. Jack R. Russell, Officers' Wives' Club, Houma AFS, La.

 ## Vegetable Fondue

1 10½-oz. can cream of mushroom soup
1 c. grated process cheese
4 eggs, separated
1 10-oz. pkg. frozen mixed vegetables
Few drops Worcestershire sauce
¼ tsp. curry powder (opt.)
¼ tsp. salt
Dash of pepper
4 slices white bread, cubed

Heat soup; add cheese. Stir until melted. Beat egg yolks until thick and light; add slowly to soup mixture. Simmer for 1 to 2 minutes, stirring constantly. Place frozen vegetables in large bowl; add Worcestershire sauce, curry powder, salt, pepper and hot sauce. Stir; fold in bread cubes and stiffly beaten egg whites. Place in greased 8 x 8-inch pan. Bake at 350 degrees for 40 minutes. Yield: 10 servings.

Mrs. Patricia L. Wensel, Home Economics Teacher, Kokomo, Ind.

Vegetable Fritters

1 ¾ c. flour
1 tsp. salt
Few grains of pepper
3 ½ tsp. baking powder
2 eggs, beaten
½ c. milk
½ c. chopped cooked carrots
¼ c. cooked peas
¼ c. cooked lima beans
1 tbsp. chopped parsley
2 tbsp. melted fat

Sift dry ingredients. Combine eggs and milk; add to flour mixture and beat
thoroughly. Add carrots, peas, lima beans, parsley and fat; mix well. Drop
from tablespoon into deep hot fat at 375 degrees; fry until a delicate brown.
Serve hot with cheese sauce. Yield: 6 servings.

Patricia M. Chaffee, New London, N. H.

 ### Vegetable Medley

2 boxes frozen broccoli
1 box frozen artichoke hearts
3 c. med. white sauce
¾ c. grated cheddar cheese
½ c. mayonnaise
1 tbsp. horseradish
Salt and pepper to taste
1 can bamboo shoots
1 4-oz. can sliced mushrooms

Cook broccoli and artichoke hearts according to directions. Make white sauce;
add cheese. Stir until melted; remove from heat. Add mayonnaise, horseradish,
salt and pepper. In 2½ to 3-quart semi-flat casserole alternate layers of all vegetables. Pour white sauce over; top with additional grated cheese. Bake in 350
to 375-degree oven for 30 to 45 minutes or until cheese melts and bubbles
come through on top. Yield: 8 servings.

Mrs. Clifton E. Johnson, Officers' Wives' Club, Athens, Greece

 ### Vegetable Pie

1 sm. onion, sliced
3 tbsp. butter
1 tbsp. flour
1 ½ tsp. salt

(Continued on next page)

⅛ tsp. pepper
2 c. mixed vegetables and liquid
1 egg, slightly beaten
1 c. mashed potatoes

Fry onion in butter until soft; blend in flour, salt and pepper. Add vegetables; simmer slowly, stirring constantly, until mixture thickens. Turn into greased baking pan. Combine egg and potatoes; beat until fluffy. Spread potatoes over vegetable mixture. Bake at 400 degrees until brown. Yield: 6 servings.

Mrs. Mary Witt, Home Economics Teacher, Buffalo, Wyo.

 ## Vegetables With Creole Sauce

1 med. onion, grated
1 tbsp. prepared mustard
1 tbsp. Worcestershire
Dash of Tabasco
4 boiled eggs, grated
1 can sm. peas
1 can lima beans
1 can French-style green beans
2 c. mayonnaise

Layer peas and beans in casserole. Combine remaining ingredients, except eggs, to make sauce. Add creole sauce; top with grated eggs. Heat in 400-degree oven until sauce bubbles. Yield: 12 servings.

Mrs. James E. Rylee, Pres. Officers' Wives' Club, Lakehurst, N. J.

 ## Vegetarian Stroganoff

1 No. 2½ can vega steaks, cut into sm. strips
½ c. chopped onion
1 c. sliced canned or fresh mushrooms
Oil
2 cans cream of mushroom soup
2 c. sour cream
2 c. boiled rice

Brown vega steaks, onion and mushrooms in small amount of oil. Add mushroom soup; simmer for 20 minutes. Just before serving, add sour cream; heat thoroughly. Serve over rice. Yield: 6-8 servings.

Martha Lang, Lynwood, Cal.

Vegetable Soups

Asparagus With Chicken Broth

½ c. chicken broth
2 tbsp. oil
1 tbsp. sherry
½ tsp. salt
2 tbsp. soy sauce
1 tbsp. cornstarch
1 tsp. water
16 stalks fresh asparagus, cooked

Blend broth, oil, sherry, salt, soy sauce, cornstarch and water; cook for 1 minute, stirring constantly. Add asparagus; simmer for 3 minutes and 30 seconds. Yield: 4 servings.

Doris C. Johnson, Arvada, Colo.

 ## Augobouido

2 full heads of garlic
2 tsp. salt
¼ tsp. thyme
¼ tsp. sage
1 bay leaf
Saffron, if desired
2 whole cloves
2 qt. rapidly boiling water
3 egg yolks
4 tbsp. olive oil

Remove outer skin from garlic and cut into six large parts. Add garlic, salt, thyme, sage, bay leaf, saffron and cloves to water. Boil slowly for 20 to 30 minutes. Stir egg yolks, adding olive oil slowly until mixture thickens. Just before serving, add a small amount of soup to egg yolk mixture. Strain remainder of soup and add to egg yolk mixture. Serve with French bread. Yield: 6-8 servings.

Mrs. M. V. Walch, Home Economics Teacher, Bensenville, Ill.

 ## Avocado Soup With Garlic

4 fully ripe California avocados
2 c. chicken broth
2 tsp. lime juice
½ tsp. salt
⅛ tsp. garlic powder
2 c. heavy cream

(Continued on next page)

Halve avocados lengthwise, twisting gently to separate halves. Whack a sharp knife directly into seeds and twist to lift out. Peel avocado halves, then puree in electric blender with broth, lime juice, salt and garlic powder. Stir in cream. Chill thoroughly. Garnish with lemon slices or with heavy cream, whipped with a dash of garlic powder.

Mrs. Jeanette Heywood, Biloxi, Miss.

 Barley Broth

> 2 lb. lamb neck or breast
> ½ c. pearl barley
> Salt
> 6 whole black peppers
> 2 qt. water
> ¾ c. each chopped onion and celery
> ¾ c. each diced turnip and carrot
> 1 carrot, grated
> 1 c. cooked peas
> 2 tbsp. minced parsley
> Pepper

Put lamb, barley, 1 teaspoonful salt and peppers in large heavy pan; add water. Simmer about 1 hour and 30 minutes. Cool; skim. Remove meat. Trim off fat and bones and dice meat. Put meat back in soup. Add onion, celery, turnip and carrot. Bring to a boil. Simmer for 30 minutes or until vegetables are tender. Just before serving, add grated carrot, peas, parsley, more salt if needed and pepper to taste. Yield: 4-6 servings.

Valorie S. Jensen, Home Economics Teacher, Elko, Nev.

 Bean Soup

> 2 c. dried white beans
> 2 to 3 ham hocks, ham bone or salt pork
> 1 pkg. dry onion soup mix
> ½ c. catsup
> 1 tsp. salt
> ½ tsp. savory (opt.)
> Few grains of cayenne pepper
> 3 stalks celery, chopped (opt.)

Wash and sort beans; cover with 8 cups boiling water. Simmer until plump; add ham hocks, soup mix, catsup and seasonings. Cook until beans are almost tender; add celery and 5 cups water. Simmer until celery is tender. Yield: 6-8 servings.

Mrs. Shirley Gulbranson, Flandreau, S. D.

 ## Green Bean-Buttermilk Soup

¾ lb. snapped green beans
1 qt. buttermilk
½ tsp. pepper
1 tbsp. flour

Cook beans in salted water until done. Add buttermilk; stir often. Bring back to a boil; add pepper. Make a paste of flour dissolved in small amount of milk; let boil up again. Remove from heat; set aside to cool. Soup tastes better after it is cold.
Personal Comment: This is an old German recipe.

Mrs. H. H. Kierum, San Antonio, Tex., Favorite Recipes Food Fair

 ## Green Beans In Umido

2 lb. pork shoulder or beef stew
2 tbsp. oil
1 lge. onion, finely chopped
1 tsp. salt
½ tsp. pepper
2 tbsp. parsley, chopped
1 ½ c. tomatoes
Water (if needed)
4 c. fresh beans or 2 pkg. frozen beans

Cut meat into pieces and brown in oil. When medium brown, add onion, salt, pepper and parsley; finish browning. Add tomatoes. Cook on low heat for about 1 hour. Add beans; cook until done. Yield: 8 servings.

Pauline DiSora, Home Economics Teacher, Midland, Pa.

Old Faithful Navy Bean Soup

2 c. dried navy beans
4 oz. salt pork, finely diced
½ c. chopped onion
1 carrot, thinly sliced
1 c. finely diced potato
Salt and pepper to taste

Pick over beans, discarding any that are discolored. Wash in cold water; drain. Cover with water and allow to soak overnight. Cook pork in heavy soup kettle over moderate heat until golden brown. Add onion; cook until transparent but not brown. Add drained beans and cold water; bring to a boil. Reduce heat; cover pan and simmer gently for 2 hours. Add vegetables and continue to cook 30 minutes longer, until tender. Season to taste and serve immediately. For a richer, more mellow flavor, add 1 cup whole or evaporated milk; bring to serving temperature and serve at once. Yield: 6 servings.

Mrs. E. E. Bradford, Stephenville, Tex.

 ## Pasta E Fagioli

¼ c. chopped celery
¼ c. chopped onion
1 tbsp. chopped parsley
1 tsp. oregano, crushed
1 sm. clove garlic, minced
1 tbsp. olive oil
1 10¾-oz. can condensed tomato soup
1 soup can water
1 1-lb. 4-oz. can white kidney beans, drained
½ c. cooked elbow macaroni
½ tsp. lemon juice

Cook celery, onion, parsley, oregano and garlic in oil until vegetables are tender. Add remaining ingredients. Heat; stir occasionally. Yield: 4-5 servings.

Mrs. Dale Chambless, Madison, Wis.

 ## Beet Borsch

6 lge. fresh or canned beets
Water
3 tbsp. lemon juice
¼ c. sugar
1 tsp. salt
2 egg yolks
1 c. sour cream

(Continued on next page)

Peel and grate or cut beets into shreds. Cook beets in 3 pints water in saucepan until tender. Add lemon juice, sugar and salt; simmer for 5 to 15 minutes longer. Beat egg yolks with 1 tablespoon cold water; gradually add hot beet mixture, stirring constantly. Chill thoroughly. Beat sour cream into mixture before serving. Yield: 6 servings.

Rebecca Fader, Home Economics Teacher, Shelbyville, Ind.

Delicious Beet Soup

2 c. sliced or 10 sm. cooked beets
2 c. water
2 tbsp. sugar
Salt and pepper to taste
Cinnamon to taste (opt.)
3 tbsp. vinegar
4 eggs
Sour cream

Combine beets, water, sugar, salt, pepper and cinnamon. Heat to boiling; simmer for 10 minutes. Add vinegar; heat just to boiling. Beat 1 egg in each serving dish. Pour a portion of hot beet liquid over beaten egg; mix throughly. Add remaining soup with beets and 1 tablespoon sour cream to each serving. Boiled potatoes may be added. To serve cold, chill soup before adding to eggs. Yield: 4 servings.

Mrs. Annie Jones, Catawba, N. C.

Russian Cabbage Soup

1 ½ lb. flank steak
2 ½ qt. water
1 tbsp. salt
Pepper to taste
1 No. 2 can tomatoes or 2½ c. chopped fresh tomatoes
1 lge. onion
1 bay leaf (opt.)
½ clove garlic, cut fine (opt.)
1 med. head cabbage
2 tbsp. sugar
1 tbsp. vinegar or lemon juice

Place meat and water in 5-quart soup kettle. Add salt, pepper, tomatoes, onion, bay leaf and garlic. Bring to boiling point; reduce heat and simmer 1 hour and 30 minutes. Shred cabbage coarsely and add. Add sugar, vinegar and a little more salt to taste. Simmer gently for another 1 hour and 30 minutes. Serve hot. Yield: 4-6 servings. If desired, top each portion with 1 heaping tablespoon of sour cream.

Sister Mary Benedict Beehler, Home Economics Teacher, Crookston, Minn.

Cabbage Soup

2 ½ lb. brisket, cut up
1 lge. cabbage, shredded
1 bottle catsup
Salt to taste
⅓ box brown sugar

Cook brisket in 2 quarts water for about 1 hour or until meat is done. Do not let water cook down. Add remaining ingredients; cook for 30 minutes longer.

Mrs. Donald Estroff, Vidalia, Ga.

 ## Sweet-Sour Cabbage Soup

2 lb. brisket
2 lb. cabbage, chopped
1 No. 2 can tomatoes
1 lge. onion
Salt
Sugar to taste
Lemon or citric acid to taste

Boil brisket for 1 hour and 30 minutes, skimming when necessary. Add remaining ingredients; simmer for 1 hour and 30 minutes. Raisins or prunes may be added, if desired. Yield: 8-10 servings.

Mrs. Saul Cohen, Gary, Ind.

 ## Sweet And Sour Sauerkraut Soup

3 lb. beef brisket, cut in serving pieces
2 c. vegetable juice
1 qt. sauerkraut
1 tsp. powdered allspice
½ tsp. salt
½ tsp. pepper
2 tbsp. brown sugar

Place meat in a large kettle; completely cover with cold water. Bring to boil; add remaining ingredients. Heat to boiling; lower heat and simmer for 3 to 4 hours or until meat is fork tender. Yield: 4-6 servings.

Mrs. Phillip Goldman, St. Augustine, Fla.

Cabbage-Carrot Chowder

    4 c. shredded cabbage
    2 c. sliced carrots
    3 c. diced potatoes
    1 tbsp. salt
    ½ tbsp. pepper
    ½ tsp. sugar
    2 c. water
    2 tbsp. butter
    4 c. milk

Cook all ingredients, except butter and milk, over low heat until well done. Add butter and milk. Serve hot with crackers. Yield: 8 servings.

Mrs. Homer E. Miller, Fredericksburg, Ohio, Favorite Recipes Food Fair

Cream of Carrot Soup

    2 tbsp. butter
    2 tbsp. flour
    6 c. milk
    2 c. carrots, chopped fine
    1 sm. onion, minced
    ½ bay leaf
    4 tbsp. chopped celery
    1 tsp. salt
    ¼ tsp. pepper

Melt butter; add flour and mix well. Add milk stirring constantly. Cook until smooth and thick. Cook carrots, onion, bay leaf, celery, salt and pepper in 3 cups boiling water until tender. Press through sieve; add to white sauce and bring to a boiling point. Serve with croutons or crackers.

Mrs. Joseph P. Gereighty, New Orleans, La.

Aletha's Cheese Soup

    2 c. mashed potatoes, thinned with milk
    2 onions, cooked with stock
    ¼ lb. grated cheese
    Seasoning to taste
    3 c. beef stock

Mix all ingredients in beef stock; simmer together for 30 minutes. Serve hot with wheat waffers. Yield: 4 servings.

Mrs. Aletha Andrews, Home Economics Teacher, Hillsdale, Mich.

Canadian Cheese Soup

½ c. finely chopped onion
¼ c. butter or margarine
½ c. flour
4 c. milk
4 c. chicken broth
½ c. finely chopped carrots
½ c. finely diced celery
⅛ tsp. salt
Dash of paprika
1 c. diced sharp cheddar cheese

Cook onion in butter till tender, but not brown. Blend in flour; add milk, broth, carrots, celery salt and paprika. Cook and stir over medium heat; add cheese and stir until cheese melts. Simmer for 15 minutes. Garnish with toasted bread topped with olive slices.

Mrs. Frances Allen, Atlanta, Ga.

 ## Grandmother's Roasting Ear Soup

2 c. canned corn, cream-style
½ c. water
1 ½ c. whole milk
½ stick butter or margarine
1 tsp. salt
Dash of black pepper

Combine all ingredients in large saucepan. Bring to boil. Serve hot with crackers and sliced tomatoes. If fresh corn is used, it should be prepared cream-style and simmered ten minutes in 1 cup water instead of the half-cup water before adding remaining ingredients.

Mrs. Ona Raney, Allen, Okla.

 ## Scalloped Corn Chowder

3 tbsp. butter or margarine
1 lge. onion, sliced
5 med. potatoes, diced
½ pt. or 1 pkg. frozen scallops
2 c. boiling water
1 c. cooked whole kernel corn
2 tsp. salt
Dash of pepper
Dash of paprika
1 qt. milk
Chopped parsley

(Continued on next page)

Melt butter in Dutch oven; add onion and cook until tender but not browned. Add potatoes, scallops and boiling water. Cover and simmer 8 to 10 minutes until potatoes are tender. Add corn, salt, pepper, paprika and milk; heat thoroughly. Sprinkle with parsley when served, if desired. Yield: 6-8 servings.

Mrs. C. J. Fowler, Jasper, Ala.

 ## Creamy Vegetable Soup

¼ c. chopped green pepper
½ c. chopped onion
2 tbsp. fat
½ lb. ground beef
1 to 2 c. tomato juice
½ c. diced potato
¼ c. diced carrots
1 tsp. salt
2 tbsp. butter
2 tbsp. flour
2 c. milk

Cook green pepper and onion in fat until tender; add beef and cook until browned. Drain off excess fat; add tomato juice, potato, carrots and salt. Cover and simmer for 20 minutes or until tender. Melt butter and blend in flour; add milk gradually. Cook, stirring, until thickened; blend into soup mixture.

Mrs. Donece Harvey, Home Economics Teacher, Olathe, Kan.

 ## Cream Of Cucumber Soup

4 cucumbers, pared and finely chopped
1 c. chopped celery
2 tbsp. chopped onion
1 tbsp. chopped green pepper
4 c. milk
4 tbsp. butter, melted
4 tbsp. flour
1 tsp. salt
Dash of pepper
1 c. cream or evaporated milk

Place cucumbers in double boiler; add celery, onion, green pepper and milk. Cook for 20 minutes or until cucumbers are tender. Combine butter, flour, salt and pepper; gradually add to cucumber mixture. Cook for 10 minutes, stirring until thickened. Press mixture through sieve. Add cream; heat. Garnish with parsley. Yield: 6 servings.

Anna Brown, Butler, N. J.

Cucumber Soup

 2 lb. cucumbers, chopped
 Salt and pepper
 ½ c. hot water
 1 med. onion, chopped
 1 clove of garlic (opt.)
 1 green pepper, chopped (opt.)
 1 tbsp. butter or margarine
 2 c. light cream
 2 tbsp. chopped parsley

Combine cucumbers, salt, pepper, water, onion, garlic and green pepper. Cook until well done. Remove from heat to cool. Place in blender; add butter and light cream. Serve hot or cold; garnish with chopped parsley. Yield: 6 servings.

Isabel Dalmas, Valdese, N. C., Favorite Recipes Food Fair

Doukhabor Borsch

 1 sm. head cabbage
 3 med. potatoes
 3 qt. salted water or beef stock
 2 lge. onions
 1 28-oz. can tomatoes
 1 bunch carrots
 1 tbsp. chopped dill
 ⅓ lb. butter
 ½ pt. sour cream

Peel potatoes and carrots; slice fine, leaving 1 potato halved. Boil or pressure cook with 3 quarts salted water. Slice onions fine; fry in butter to golden brown. Add finely shredded cabbage and fry, stirring frequently to avoid burning. Do not overcook cabbage. Add tomatoes and dill. Simmer for a few minutes. When carrots and potatoes are done, mash the halved potato, using sour cream and return to boiling pot; add contents of frying pan and allow to simmer very slowly for 30 to 45 minutes. Yield: 6-8 servings.

Mrs. Jennifer Lacey, Valdosta, Ga.

Gazpacho

 5 very ripe tomatoes, peeled, seeded and chopped
 1 cucumber, peeled and chopped
 1 green pepper, seeded and chopped
 1 onion, chopped
 1 tbsp. finely chopped parsley

(Continued on next page)

1 clove of garlic, crushed
1 ¼ c. tomato juice
3 tbsp. salad oil
2 tbsp. vinegar
¼ tsp. paprika
Salt and pepper

Combine tomatoes, cucumber, green pepper, onion, parsley and garlic in blender; cover and blend until smooth. Stir in tomato juice, oil, vinegar, paprika, salt and pepper; chill thoroughly. Serve in individual chilled soup bowls; place an ice cube in each bowl. Serve with buttered croutons, crackers or cheese bread. Yield: 6-8 servings.

Mrs. William B. Dabney, Decatur, Tex.

 ## General Lee's Vegetable Bouillon

4 c. tomatoes
2 c. water
1 stalk celery, chopped
2 carrots, chopped
2 sprigs parsley
¼ green pepper, chopped
1 bay leaf
2 tsp. onion juice
Salt and pepper to taste
1 wineglass sherry wine

Combine all ingredients except sherry; boil for 30 minutes. Strain. Add sherry. Serve piping hot.

Mrs. W. Ludwell Harrison, Huntington, W. Va.

 ## Hearty Noodle Soup

1 1½-lb. soup bone
1 qt. water
1 tbsp. salt
⅛ tsp. pepper
1 tbsp. celery leaves
¼ c. chopped onion
3 ½ c. cooked tomatoes
½ c. sliced carrots
3 oz. very fine noodles

Put soup bone, water, salt and pepper in large kettle. Cover and simmer for 1 hour and 30 minutes. Remove soup bone and strain broth. Cut meat from bone; add meat, celery leaves, onion, tomatoes and carrots to broth. Cover and simmer for 20 minutes. Add noodles. Cover and simmer for 10 minutes longer. Yield: 4-6 servings.

Mary Fryman, Brookville, Ohio

Herb Soup

    3 No. 2 cans tomatoes
    2 cans consomme
    ½ tsp. dried basil
    ½ c. chopped celery
    4 whole cloves
    ½ c. chopped onion
    1 tbsp. salt
    ⅛ tsp. white pepper
    1 tbsp. margarine
    1 tbsp. sugar

Combine all ingredients; simmer until onion is completely cooked. Mash vegetables with potato masher. Serve with croutons, sour cream or any other soup condiment. Six to eight fresh tomatoes may be substituted for canned tomatoes. Yield: 6-8 servings.

Mrs. Gertrude D. Lape, Little Rock, Ark.

 ### Kidney Bean-Tomato Chowder

    1 pt. kidney beans
    2 qt. water
    1 qt. tomatoes
    6 med. potatoes, diced
    ½ lb. macaroni
    1 lb. bacon, chopped
    Salt and pepper to taste

Soak kidney beans in water overnight. Bring water, beans and tomatoes to a boil. When beans are soft, add potatoes and macaroni; cook until tender. Fry bacon until crisp; add to bean mixture. Season to taste. Yield: 12 servings.

Mrs. Lloyd H. Drybred, Mountville, Pa.

 ### Lemon Soup

    1 2½ to 3-lb. chicken
    2 tsp. salt
    ½ tsp. pepper
    ¾ c. rice
    2 eggs, separated
    Juice of 2 large lemons

Wash and inspect chicken; cut into pieces, if desired. Place in a large pot and cover with boiling water; add salt and pepper. Cover and cook until tender. Make sure to have at least 2 quarts of water during cooking time. Remove chicken from stock. Add rice to stock and cook until done. Remove pot from heat and allow rice to settle to the bottom of pot. In bowl, beat egg whites

(Continued on next page)

until creamy. Add an egg yolk at a time, beating until creamy. Add lemon juice, a little at a time and continue to beat. Stir 2 cups of hot broth in egg mixture and beat. Pour egg mixture in with rice and stock. Stir and heat. Do not boil. Serve hot. Boned chicken may be added. Yield: 4 servings.

Barbara A. West, Home Economics Teacher, Portsmouth, Va.

    ## Lentil Soup

> 1 ½ c. dried lentils
> 2 tbsp. butter
> ¼ c. diced onion
> ¼ c. diced celery
> 5 ½ c. water
> 1 1-lb. can tomatoes
> 2 tsp. salt
> ¼ tsp. Tabasco
> 1 c. beef bouillon
> 4 frankfurters, sliced
> 1 c. diced potatoes

Wash lentils. Melt butter in deep saucepan; add onion and celery. Cook until onion is tender, but not brown. Add water, lentils, tomatoes, salt and Tabasco. Cover. Cook over low heat in an electric blender; return to saucepan. Add bouillon, frankfurters and potatoes. Cook 20 minutes longer. Yield: 6-8 servings.

Photograph for this recipe below.

Lentil Soup Supreme

    1 1-lb. pkg. lentils
    ¼ lb. bacon, cut fine
    2 lge. onions, sliced
    2 lge. carrots, sliced
    2 qt. water
    1 c. celery, sliced at angle
    2 ½ tsp. salt
    ½ tsp. white pepper
    ½ tsp. dried thyme
    4 bay leaves
    1 lge. potato, grated
    1 ham hock
    2 tbsp. lemon juice
    1 lemon, sliced

Wash lentils; cover with cold water and soak overnight. Drain. Saute bacon; add onions and saute until golden. Add remaining ingredients except lemon juice and lemon. Simmer, covered, for 3 hours. Remove ham bone and bay leaves. Add lemon juice. Serve hot with lemon slices floating on top. Yield: 9-10 servings.

Mrs. Glenda Ballinger, Home Economics Teacher, Chattanooga, Tenn.

 ### Luncheon Soup

    1 can green pea soup
    1 can cream of tomato soup
    2 cans evaporated milk
    1 can crab meat or 1 sm. pkg. frozen crab
    ¼ c. Sauterne or sherry wine
    Dash of salt

Combine all ingredients; heat gently. Serve sprinkled with a dash of paprika and parsley flakes. Yield: 6 servings.

Mrs. Russell Norman, Rice Lake, Wis.

 ### Pottage A La California

    1 lb. ground beef
    ¼ lb. sausage
    1 lb. lentils, soaked
    6 to 10 onions, chopped fine
    1 or 2 carrots, chopped
    1 c. celery, chopped
    1 green pepper
    3 c. tomato juice

(Continued on next page)

2 tsp. salt
⅓ tsp. red pepper
¼ tsp. black pepper

Fry meats. Add undrained to all other ingredients. Simmer or boil gently for 1 hour. Yield: 12-16 servings.

Janice Bell, Home Economics Teacher, Perris, Cal.

Minestrone Soup

1 meaty beef or veal soup bone
Cooking oil
9 to 10 c. water
Dash of Worcestershire sauce
Salt and pepper
Garlic salt to taste
2 med. potatoes, shredded
3 carrots, shredded
1 leek or onion, shredded
1 med. turnip, shredded
1 c. string beans, cut into strips
¼ lb. thin spaghetti
Butter
Grated Gruyere cheese

Brown soup bone in oil; cover with water. Add seasonings; cook until meat leaves the bone. Remove bone. Add vegetables; cook over low heat for 1 hour and 30 minutes. Add spaghetti; cook for 9 to 12 minutes. Place a dot of butter and a small amount of grated cheese in each soup bowl; pour in soup. If soup becomes too thick as it cooks, thin with a small amount of water. Yield: 8 servings.

Mrs. Donald S. Cramen, Little Creek Amphib Base, Va.
Favorite Recipes Food Fair

Nannie Soup

7 or 8 med. Irish potatoes
Butter to taste
Salt to taste
½ tsp. sugar
1 can garden peas
½ box spaghetti
1 can tomatoes

Cut potatoes into small cubes; cook until tender. Season with desired amount of butter and salt. Add sugar, peas and spaghetti broken into 2-inch lengths.

(Continued on next page)

Bring to boil; cook until spaghetti is tender. Add tomatoes. Do not boil after adding tomatoes.

Personal Comment: This recipe is my own creation. Named by my 20 grandchildren.

Mrs. James Jackson, Sr., Leary, Ga.

 Normandy Soup Pot

    6 *lge. potatoes pared and quartered*
    3 *med. leeks, cut into 2-in. slices*
    2 *med. carrots pared and quartered*
    4 *10-oz. pkg. frozen Brussels sprouts*
    3 *qt. boiling water*
 ½ *c. sliced celery and leaves*
      Few sprigs parsley
    2 *tbsp. butter or maragrine*
    2 *tbsp. salt*
    1 *tsp. monosodium glutamate*
 ¼ *tsp. pepper*

Add potatoes, leeks, carrots and Brussels sprouts to boiling water; cover and simmer for 30 minutes. Stir in celery, parsley, butter and seasonings; simmer for 1 hour longer. Yield: 10 servings.

Mrs. Nancy Jameson, Dallas, Tex.

 Okra Gumbo

   1 *med. ham hock*
   2 *slices bacon*
   3 *qt. water*
   1 *tsp. salt*
   1 *tsp. pepper*
   1 *stalk celery, chopped*
   1 *onion, chopped*
   3 *lb. okra, washed and finely cut*
 10 *lge. tomatoes, cut or 1 No. 2½ can tomatoes*
   1 *c. corn (opt.)*

Cook meat in water until done. Add remaining ingredients. Simmer until done. Yield: 8-10 servings.

Mrs. W. W. Hill, Ridgeville, S. C.

Old-Fashioned Vegetable Soup

2 to 3 soup bones with meat
2 tbsp. fat
8 c. water
⅓ c. barley
1 med. onion, chopped
1 c. sliced carrots
1 c. chopped celery and leaves
2 1-lb. cans tomatoes
1 c. whole kernel corn
1 c. green peas
3 sprigs parsley, finely cut
1 tbsp. salt
¼ tsp. rosemary
¼ tsp. marjoram
¼ tsp. thyme
½ bay leaf, crushed
3 peppercorns

Cut meat off bone into small chunks; brown in hot fat. Add water and bone; simmer, covered, for 1 hour and 30 minutes to 2 hours. Remove bone; skim fat from top. Add barley; simmer for 45 minutes. Add vegetables and seasonings. Tie bay leaf and peppercorns in cheesecloth bag. Cook for 25 to 35 minutes or until vegetables are tender. Remove cheesecloth bag before serving. Yield: 10-12 servings.

Mrs. Jan Erickson, Home Economics Teacher, White Bear Lake, Minn.

 ### Onion Soup

1 lge. beef soup bone
6 lge. onions
4 tbsp. butter
¼ tsp. thyme
2 peppercorns
1 tsp. salt
½ tsp. Worcestershire sauce
6 slices French bread
½ c. grated Parmesan cheese

Cook soup bone in water to cover until meat is very soft. Strain and add water to make six cups of broth. Peel onions and thinly slice. Heat butter in large heavy skillet; add onions and cook slowly over low heat until they are soft and golden, stirring occasionally so they will cook evenly. Add broth, thyme, peppercorns, salt and Worcestershire sauce; simmer for 20 minutes. Remove peppercorns. Toast French bread; spread with butter and sprinkle with cheese. Put under broiler for 3 to 4 minutes. Serve soup with slice of cheese-toasted bread on top of each bowl. Bouillon cubes and water may be used to make broth. Yield: 6 servings.

Mrs. Paul W. Morton, Freeport, Ohio

Creamy Onion Soup

    1 lge. onion, cubed
    2 tbsp. butter
    ½ c. mashed potatoes
    2 c. milk
    ½ c. heavy cream
    Parsley flakes

Saute onion slowly in butter until soft but not brown. Pour into blender. Add potatoes and 1 cup milk. Cover; blend for 3 seconds. Pour into saucepan; bring to boil. Lower heat and add remaining milk. Simmer for 3 minutes. Add ¼ cup cream; chill. Just before serving, fold in remaining cream. Top with parsley flakes. Yield: 4 servings.

Mrs. J. R. Wiser, Manchester, Tenn.

 ### French Onion Soup With Wine

    6 lge. yellow onions, thinly sliced
    2 tbsp. butter or margarine
    1 tbsp. olive oil
    6 c. beef stock or bouillon
    ⅓ c. white or red wine (opt.)
    Salt and pepper to taste

Saute onions in butter and oil until limp in heavy-bottomed 3 or 4-quart covered pan. Simmer slowly for 15 minutes; pour in beef stock and wine. Simmer for 30 minutes or place in ovenware in 300-degree oven for 1 hour. Taste and add salt and pepper as desired. Yield: 6 servings. Ladle soup into individual bowls; top each serving with a slice of buttered, dry-toasted French bread. Sprinkle each toast round with shredded cheese or Parmesan cheese.

Mrs. Marie Edmunds, Home Economics Teacher, Bonners Ferry, Idaho

 ### Black-Eyed Pea Soup

    ¾ c. black-eyed peas
    6 c. water
    ¾ tbsp. salt
    ⅛ tsp. black pepper
    ½ tsp. garlic salt
    2 slices bacon
    1 sm. onion, cut up

Combine first 7 ingredients in a 2-quart pot; cook until peas are tender. Lightly brown flour in bacon grease in a small saucepan; cool. Add flour to soup and cook 5 minutes longer. Add more water if needed.

Mrs. Joe F. Dornak, Louise, Tex.

Dilled Split Pea Soup

3 strips bacon
1 c. split peas, washed
3 c. water
1 tsp. salt
2 tbsp. bacon fat
¼ c. finely chopped onion
1 tall can evaporated milk
½ tsp. dill weed
Few grains of cayenne

Fry bacon until crisp; drain on absorbent paper. Combine peas, water and salt in medium saucepan; bring to a boil. Boil for 2 minutes; remove from heat and let stand for 1 hour. Do not change water. Add bacon fat and onion; cover. Return to heat; bring to boil. Boil slowly for 40 minutes or until peas are tender; add milk, dill weed and cayenne. Heat to serving temperature, but do not boil. Garnish with crumbled bacon.

Mrs. W. H. Williamson, Audubon, N. J.

 ### Split Pea Soup

2 c. split peas
12 c. water
1 ham bone with meat or ½ lb. lean salt pork
1 onion, chopped
2 carrots, sliced
3 to 4 stalks celery with tops, chopped
5 frankfurters, sliced
1 c. milk
2 c. beef bouillon
2 tbsp. butter
Pinch of paprika
Freshly ground pepper
Salt to taste

Soak peas for 12 hours; drain. Place in large pot with water and ham bone; simmer, covered, for 3 hours. Add onion, carrots and celery; simmer, covered, for 1 hour. Strain soup; chill. Remove fat; add frankfurters, milk, bouillon and butter. Stir until soup boils; season. Simmer gently for 20 minutes. Yield: 20-30 servings.

Mary Jane Bertrand, Home Economics Teacher, Blackfoot, Idaho

 ### Ground Peanut Soup

2 4 to 6-lb. chickens, cut up
2 med. onions, chopped

(Continued on next page)

Salt to taste
4 med. tomatoes
1 lb. groundnut paste or peanut butter
Pepper

Place chickens, onions and salt in large saucepan; brown to a golden color or until dry. Add just enough cold water to cover; add tomatoes. Bring to a boil. Lower heat and simmer for 15 minutes. Remove tomatoes; add pulp to the stock. Mix the groundnut paste into a smooth cream with hot stock from saucepan. Pour creamed groundnut paste into saucepan; add 6 pints water and pepper. Cook slowly until oil rises to the top of the soup. Remove chicken if it becomes tender before the oil rises to the top. Return to the pot when the soup is cooked. Yield: 6 servings.

Marilyn Meyer, Minneota, Minn., Favorite Recipes Food Fair

 ## Pine Bark Chowder

2 c. diced bacon
1 qt. diced onions
4 qt. diced potatoes
¼ c. salt
1 tbsp. pepper
4 tbsp. Worcestershire sauce
¾ c. butter
6 c. tomato soup
12 c. tomatoes
12 c. tomato juice
1 gal. water

Brown bacon in heavy skillet; pour off part of fat. Saute onions in remaining fat. Place bacon and onions in heavy soup kettle with remaining ingredients; cook until potatoes are done. Yield: 50 servings.

Maude Haskin, Gilboa, N. Y.

 ## Pennsylvania Dutch Potato Soup

2 c. diced potatoes
1 c. water
2 tbsp. onion (opt.)
2 tbsp. margarine or butter
2 tbsp. flour
2 c. milk
⅛ tsp. celery salt
Salt and pepper to taste
1 hard-cooked egg, chopped

(Continued on next page)

329

Boil potatoes in water for 15 minutes or until tender. Brown onion in margarine; blend in flour. Add ½ cup milk. Add flour mixture, seasonings and remaining milk to potatoes. Cook, stirring occasionally, until thick. Garnish with egg. Yield: 4 servings.

Mrs. Rose Ann Murphy, Home Economics Teacher, Trenton, N. J.

 Spatzle Soup

  2 c. flour
  ½ tsp. salt
  1 egg
  ½ to ⅔ c. water
  2 c. diced potatoes
  4 c. chicken broth

Measure flour; add salt and blend. Add egg to flour mixture; stir until well mixed. Gradually add water until a stiff but spongy dough is formed. Boil diced potatoes in a small quantity of water. When cooked, add to chicken broth. Bring broth and potatoes to a boil. Cut dough into broth in very small pieces as for small dumplings. After all dough is added, bring mixture to a full boil. Serve. Yield: 4-5 servings.

Ruth I. Schwartz, Home Economics Teacher, Galesburg, Ill.

 Vichyssoise

  4 leeks
  ¼ c. butter, melted
  1 ½ c. thinly sliced potatoes
  1 c. chicken stock
  1 c. milk
  1 c. half and half
  ½ tsp. salt
  ⅛ tsp. white pepper
  ⅛ tsp. paprika
  1 tbsp. finely chopped chives or parsley

Slice leeks thin, using only white and very light green portions. Cook leeks in melted butter, stirring constantly, until transparent but not brown. Add potato slices and chicken stock; cover and cook over moderate heat until potatoes are tender. Press through a food mill or puree in blender. Return to saucepan; add milk, half and half and seasonings, stirring rapidly to blend. Heat only to serving temperature; do not boil. Garnish with chives or parsley. Serve hot or chilled. Yield: 6 servings.

Esther C. Whited, San Francisco, Cal.

Green Pumpkin Soup

    4 c. shredded very green pumpkin
    2 tbsp. margarine
    4 tbsp. flour
    4 c. water
    1 bay leaf
    Salt and pepper to taste
    Onion powder to taste
    ½ c. evaporated milk
    ½ c. sour cream

Use pumpkin that has not shown any signs of turning yellow. Peel, remove seeds and shred with medium cheese grater; set aside. In a large pan, brown margarine and flour; add water slowly. Cook for a few minutes with bay leaf, salt, pepper and a light sprinkle of onion powder. Add shredded pumpkin and cook gently for 20 minutes. Remove from heat and add evaporated milk mixed with sour cream. Stir in and serve.

Cathy Koszegi, Home Economics Teacher, Stockbridge, Mich.

 ### Pumpkin Soup

    1 ½ lb. soup meat
    ¾ lb. pig tails
    4 qt. water
    2 lb. pumpkin
    1 clove of garlic
    2 green onions
    ½ med. onion
    1 sprig of thyme
    1 hot pepper
    Salt to taste

Place soup meat, pig tails and 4 quarts of hot water in a large kettle. Boil until the meat is cooked; add the remaining ingredients except salt. Cook until pumpkin is soft. Remove meat and force pumpkin through a strainer. Return meat; add salt to taste. Soup is thick in consistency. Serve. Yield: 16 servings.

Sandra Amstutz, Sycamore, Ohio

 ### Wholesome Pumpkin Soup

    2 c. cooked pumpkin, drained
    6 tsp. sugar
    3 tbsp. butter
    2 qt. milk

(Continued on next page)

¼ *tsp. salt*
⅛ *tsp. pepper (opt.)*

Saute pumpkin and sugar in butter over medium heat for 15 minutes. Add milk, salt and pepper. Bring to a boil. Serve with toast or crackers. Yield: 6 servings.

Mrs. Arley A. Sarver, Crowley, La.

 Rutabaga Soup

1 3-lb. meaty beef shank bone
2 tbsp. salt or to taste
4 qt. water
2 lb. rutabagas, cubed

Boil soup meat in salted water until tender; add rutabagas. Cook until meat comes apart and rutabagas can be mashed with fork. Add water if necessary. Yield: 6 servings.

Mrs. Edith L. Barker, Home Economics Teacher, Fairfax, S. C.

 Soup Macedoine

2 tbsp. butter
½ c. finely chopped onion
2 c. sm. potato cubes
1 c. thinly sliced carrots
1 c. sliced green beans, asparagus, diced cauliflower or turnip
1 c. boiling water
2 c. diced cooked ham
1 qt. milk
Salt and pepper to taste
Finely minced parsley

Melt butter in a heavy saucepan or kettle; add onion and cook until transparent, but not brown. Add potato, carrot, green beans and water. Bring to a boil, cover and cook until vegetables are tender, about 25 to 30 minutes. Add a little more water, if necessary. Mash vegetables, leaving some small pieces for texture; add ham and milk and heat to serving temperature. Serve at once with a topping of finely miced parsley. Yield: 6-8 servings.

Photograph for this recipe on page 309.

Spinach Borsch

1 lb. fresh spinach
Salt to taste
Citric acid to taste
2 eggs, beaten
Sour cream
Chives or green onions (opt.)

Wash and cut spinach into pieces. Place in a large kettle; fill three-fourths full with water. Bring to a boil and simmer for 45 minutes. Add salt and citric acid very slowly, during last 15 minutes of cooking; cool. Add eggs to spinach; stir to avoid curdling. Cool until ice cold. Serve topped with sour cream and minced chives or green onions. Yield: 10 servings.

Mrs. Peter Pikofsky, Milwaukee, Wis.

 ### Vegetable-Beef Soup

1 2 to 3-lb. round beef bone
1 tbsp. salt
2 qt. cold water
3 med. carrots, sliced
2 c. chopped cabbage
1 c. cooked tomato
2 pieces celery with leaves, sliced
½ c. minced onion
1 med. parsnip, diced
1 c. cubed potatoes
Parsley

Simmer beef bone in salted water; remove bone. Skim off fat; dice meat. Return to broth with vegetables; cook until tender. Add parsley; cook for 30 minutes longer. Yield: 5-8 servings.

Mrs. June Patchett, Home Economics Teacher, Metcalf, Ill.

 ### Vegetable Soup

1 c. cubed carrots
1 c. cubed potatoes
1 c. cubed rutabaga
1 c. cubed turnip
2 tbsp. barley
1 small onion
1 can mixed vegetables

(Continued on next page)

Heat fresh vegetables to boiling; boil 5 minutes. Add mixed vegetables; heat again. Seal in sterilized jars. Pressure cook 1 hour at 10 pounds pressure. Yield: 6 pints.

Mrs. Lena Oleheiser, Grand Rapids, Minn., Itasca County Fair

 ## Cream Of Watercress Soup

1 ¾-oz. dry cream of leek soup mix
⅛ tsp. nutmeg
4 13¾-oz. cans clear chicken broth
2 c. light cream
1 bunch watercress, without stems
Round butter crackers, heated

Place soup mix and nutmeg in large kettle; gradually stir in chicken broth. Bring to boil, stirring frequently. Reduce heat and simmer, covered for 10 minutes. Blend ½ cup cream and portion of watercress at high speed until smooth. Gradually add remaining watercress and ½ cup cream, blending well. Add watercress mixture and remaining 1 cup cream to hot soup; simmer 5 minutes longer. Serve with crackers.

Mrs. Wanda Kyles, Cleveland, N. C.

 ## Healthy Soup

1 bunch watercress
3 c. water
1 tsp. salt
1 med. potato, peeled and sliced
⅓ c. coffee cream
Dash of pepper

Wash watercress; separate stems and leaves. Chop stems. Boil water; add salt, stems and potato. Cook for 10 minutes or until tender. Add leaves and cook for 2 minutes or until vegetables are soft. Rub through coarse sieve; add cream. Season. Yield: 4 servings.

Ruth E. Briggs, Home Economics Teacher, Clinton, Ill.

 ## Cream Of Zucchini Soup

3 c. or 1 lb. sliced zucchini
½ c. water

(Continued on next page)

1 tbsp. fresh or instant minced onion
1 tsp. all-purpose seasoning
½ tsp. parsley flakes
3 tsp. chicken-seasoned stock base
2 tbsp. butter
2 tbsp. flour
⅛ tsp. white pepper
⅛ tsp. monosidium glutamate
¼ tsp. each ground celery seed, onion powder
1 c. milk
½ c. light cream
Sour cream
Paprika
Slivered almonds

Combine first 5 ingredients and 1 teaspoon stock base. Cook until zucchini is tender and ony a small amount of water is left. Mash through sieve. Melt butter in saucepan; add flour, remaining stock base and seasonings. Blend well. Add milk and cream; simmer, stirring until thickened. Stir in zucchini, mixing well. If soup is thicker than desired, add additional milk. Serve topped with a spoon of sour cream; garnish with paprika. Set the soup bowl in a larger dish with generous amount of slivered almonds and radish roses. Yield: 4 cups.

Mrs. M. F. Brown, Tioga, Tex.

Cream Of Sweet Potato Soup

3 sweet potatoes
2 c. chicken broth or bouillion
1 tsp. sugar
⅛ tsp. each nutmeg, cloves
1 ½ c. milk
Salt to taste

Peel and slice potatoes; add broth and bring to boil. Simmer, covered, until tender, about 20 minutes. Force through food mill or puree in blender. Reheat with remaining ingredients. Serve hot or chilled. Yield: 1 quart.

Mrs. Fern Harmon, Julian, N. C., Favorite Recipes Food Fair

Cream Of Tomato Soup

3 ½ c. fresh or canned tomatoes
¼ c. plus 2 tbsp. chopped onion
2 tbsp. fat
3 tbsp. flour
½ tsp. sugar
3 c. milk
1 tsp. salt

(Continued on next page)

Cook tomatoes and onion for about 10 to 20 minutes; press through a sieve. Melt fat; blend in flour and sugar. Gradually add cooled tomatoes; cook until thickened, stirring constantly. Add tomato mixture to milk, stirring constantly. Heat slowly to serving temperature; add salt. Serve at once. Yield: 6 servings.

Laurice Hamlet, Home Economics Teacher, Gretna, Va.

 ## Tomato Bouillon

> *Beef knuckle soup bone or beef shank bone*
> *2 tsp. salt*
> *¼ tsp. pepper*
> *1 tsp. monosodium glutamate*
> *1 No. 2 can tomatoes*

Cover bone in large pot with 1 gallon water; add seasonings. Bring to boil; simmer for 2 hours. Add tomatoes; simmer for 20 minutes longer. Strain; cool. Remove fat; heat to boiling to serve. May be garnished with thin lemon slices. To serve chilled, garnish with sprig of parsley. Keeps well under refrigeration for five to six days. Yield: 6-8 servings.

Mrs. Ruth Yelvington, Corsicana, Tex.

 ## Tomato Soup

> *½ bushel tomatoes*
> *7 onions*
> *14 strips celery*
> *14 strips parsley*
> *14 bay leaves*
> *21 cloves*
> *1 small garlic*
> *½ lb. butter or oleo*
> *¼ c. salt*
> *½ tsp. pepper*
> *1 ½ c. brown sugar*
> *2 c. flour*

Cook first 7 ingredients until mushy; sieve. Add butter, salt, pepper and brown sugar; cook for 10 minutes. Mix flour with water to a thin paste; thicken tomato mixture and boil a few minutes. Put into hot, sterilized jars; seal.

Helen C. Fossell, Kennedy, Minn., Kittson County Fair

Pickles and Relishes

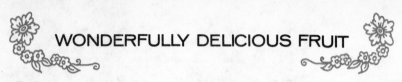

Fruit is one of the most wonderful products of nature. It has been the inspiration to painters, poets—and cooks. Fruit appeals to the eye, to the sense of smell—and its health-giving properties are great.

Although some fruit such as berries and melons are seasonal, fruit is available year 'round now. When fresh fruit is not suitable, buy it frozen, canned or dried.

Fruits in season are usually excellent buys. At this time, they are not only less expensive, but are of higher quality. Regardless of the season or price, buy fruits which are suitable to your needs.

Large, perfect fruit, for instance, will not be the best buy if you can use small fruits with blemishes that do not affect quality or flavor. In dishes where fruits are peeled and cut up, the small size that is not perfect would be the best bargain.

Store fresh firm fruit in a cool dry place or in the refrigerator. Do not wash it before storing since this increases the chance of spoilage. Unripe fruits should be allowed to ripen at room temperature, away from direct sunlight.

A guide for selecting the best fruit buys follows:

APPLES—Choose firm apples of good color. Immature apples are poor in color, flavor, and they shrivel after storage. Overripe apples are mealy. Brown-tinted area on the surface, called scald, is caused by gases given off by apples during storage. If slight, it affects the quality very little.

APRICOTS—Select uniformly colored fruit that is firm and plump. Ripe apricots are very perishable. Immature fruit is greenish-yellow, hard and slightly shriveled.

AVOCADOS—These vary from spherical to pear-shaped, from ½ pound to 3 pounds, green to almost black, thin smooth skin to thick rough skin. Shape and skin do not indicate quality. Look for bright, fresh-looking fruit just beginning to soften. Decay is indicated by dark sunken spots.

BANANAS—Best flavored ones are harvested green. Buy yellow-ripe fruit. Good eating quality is indicated by golden yellow or red color flecked with brown. Do not refrigerate.

BERRIES—Should have a bright, clean, fresh-looking, plump appearance. Overripe berries are dull in color, soft and lifeless.

CHERRIES—Select tart cherries for cooking, sweet ones for eating. Indications of good quality are bright fresh appearance, plumpness and good color. Avoid fruit with small brown circular spots of bruised fruit.

CRANBERRIES—Should have fresh, plump appearance, firmness and a luster. Avoid shriveled, dull, soft or moist berries.

FIGS—Choose fully ripe, soft figs. Color and size depend on the variety. Ripe figs sour and ferment quickly. Odor indicates souring.

GRAPEFRUIT—Should be firm and springy, not soft or flabby. Decay indicated by soft discolored area at button end.

GRAPES—To be served on the stem should be firm, highly-colored and adhere to the stem. Decay is indicated by mold, wet berries and stained containers.

LEMONS—Select heavy ones with smooth-textured skins. Avoid decay at stem end or soft, spongy fruit.

LIMES—Choose green, heavy-for-its-size fruit. Surface blemishes do not indicate poor fruit.

ORANGES—Firm, heavy fruit is best. Surface blemishes do not affect fruit. Avoid light, puffy fruit with badly creased skins.

PEACHES—Should be firm, fresh-appearing with whitish or yellowish color, and free from blemishes. Green color indicates they were picked too soon to allow ripening. Worminess is shown by small holes from which gum exudes. Decay, indicated by brown spots, spreads rapidly.

PEARS—Firm, not hard, free from blemish and clean are indications of properly ripe pears. Wilted or shriveled fruit has been picked too early and will never ripen or have good flavor.

PINEAPPLES—When ripe, has a dark orange-yellow color, fragrant odor, and the eyes are flat. Select fruit heavy for its size. Pineapple decays rapidly. Look for dark area at base or around eyes, sour odor, mold, moisture. Light colored area on side indicates sunburn; fruit will be dry, hard and pithy.

PLUMS AND PRUNES—Ripe fruit is plump and yields to slight pressure. Immature fruit is hard, shriveled, has poor color and flavor. Over-mature fruit is soft and leaky. Brownish color indicates sunburn and the flavor is likely to be poor.

RHUBARB—Choose fresh, firm, crisp, tender, thick stalks that are red or pink.

STRAWBERRIES—Choose bright, clean berries of solid red color and with caps attached. Small, misshapen berries have poor flavor and often have small hard green areas.

Guides for choosing melons are:

CANTALOUPES—Scar at stem should be slightly sunken and calloused. Pronounced yellowing indicates overripeness. Netting should be coarse, corky and greyish. Decay shows as soft sunken spots, mold or moisture at stem end.

HONEY DEW—Choose melon with light yellow rind that yields slightly to pressure. Dark sunken spots show decay. Flavor will be good, though, if spots have not penetrated rind. Greenish-white color and hardness show immaturity.

WATERMELONS—Should be firm, symmetrical, fresh, good color, a bloom on the surface, underside yellowish. Immature melons are hard, unripe in appearance. The underside is pale green or white. Overripe melons are dull, lifeless and feel spring to the touch. Decay occurs at the stem end and spreads rapidly. Fresh-cut stems are often painted with copper sulphate mixture to prevent decay.

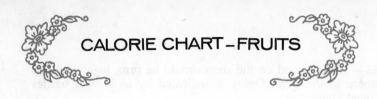

CALORIE CHART – FRUITS

Food	Amount	No. of Calories
FRUITS		
Apples, raw about 3 per lb.	1 apple	70
Apple juice, fresh or canned	1 c.	125
Applesauce		
Canned, unsweetened	1 c.	100
Canned, sweetened	1 c.	185
Apricots		
Canned, halves and heavy syrup	1 c.	200
Dried, cooked, unsweetened, with liquid	1 c.	240
Raw, about 12 per lb.	3 apricots	55
Avocados, raw		
California varieties, about 3 1/3 x 4¼ in.	½ avocado	185
Florida varieties, about 4 x 3 in.	½ avocado	160
Bananas, raw, about 3 per lb.	1 banana	85
Blackberries, raw	1 c.	80
Blueberries, raw	1 c.	85
Cantaloupe, about 1 2/3 lb.	½ melon	40
Cherries		
Raw, sour, sweet, hybrid	1 c.	65
Canned, red, sour, pitted	1 c.	120
Dates, fresh, dried, pitted	1 c.	505
Figs		
Dried, 2 x 1 in.	1 fig.	60
Raw, about 12 per lb.	3 figs	90
Fruit cocktail, canned	1 c.	175
Grapefruit		
Raw, medium, white	½ grapefruit	50
Raw, medium, pink or red	½ grapefruit	55
Canned, sections with syrup	½ c.	80
Grapefruit juice		
Fresh	1 c.	85
Canned, unsweetened	1 c.	95
Canned, sweetened	1 c.	120
Frozen, sweetened, water added	1 c.	95
Grapes, raw American type	1 c.	70
Grape juice, bottled	1 c.	165
Lemon juice, fresh or canned	1 c.	60

Food	Amount	No. of Calories
Lemonade concentrate, frozen, sweetened, water added	1 c.	75
Lime juice, fresh or canned	1 c.	65
Limeade concentrate, sweetened, water added	1 c.	75
Oranges, 3-in. diameter		
Naval, California	1 orange	70
Other varieties	1 orange	70
Orange juice, canned		
Frozen, sweetened, water added	1 c.	105
Peaches		
Canned, solids and syrup	1 c.	185
Raw, about 4 per lb.	1 peach	35
Raw, sliced	1 c.	65
Pears		
Canned, solids, syrup	1 c.	175
Raw, 3 x 2½-in, diameter	1 pear	100
Pineapple		
Canned, crushed with liquid	1 c.	205
Canned, sliced	1 slice; 2 tbsp. syrup	95
Raw, diced	1 c.	75
Pineapple juice, canned	1 c.	120
Plums, raw, 2 oz.	1 plum	30
Prunes		
Dried, uncooked	4 medium	70
Cooked, unsweetened	1 c.	295
Prune juice, canned	1 c.	170
Raisins, dried	1 c.	460
Raspberries, red		
Frozen, 10-oz. carton	1 carton	280
Raw	1 c.	70
Rhubarb, cooked, sugar added	1 c.	385
Strawberries		
Frozen, 10-oz. carton	1 carton	300
Raw	1 c.	55
Tangerines, raw, about 4 per lb.	1 tangerine	40
Tangerine juice, canned	1 c.	100
Watermelon, raw 4 x 8-in. wedge	1 wedge	120

Compiled from USDA Yearbook of Agriculture.

Cantaloupe Pickles

2 cantaloupes
1 ½ tsp. powdered alum
4 ½ c. sugar
2 c. vinegar
½ c. water
1 lemon, sliced thin
1 tbsp. pickling spices

Cut cantaloupes into 12 lengthwise pieces; remove seeds and peel. Place in enamel preserving kettle. Cover with cold water; add alum. Stir and cover; leave overnight. Drain fruit and rinse in cold water. Cover with cold water and heat to simmer. Cook about 20 minutes or until tender. Drain. Add to a syrup made of sugar, vinegar, water and lemon. Boil about 1 hour or until melon is transparent. Add spices during last 15 minutes. Pack in sterile jars; seal. Yield: 24 servings.

Donna Akeson, Chappell, Neb., Deuel County Fair

Pickled Peaches

20 to 24 small peaches
4 c. sugar
2 c. vinegar
4 pieces of stick cinnamon
1 tbsp. whole cloves

Choose ripe, but firm, cling peaches. Peel peaches without spoiling shape of fruit. Make a syrup of sugar, vinegar and spices tied loosely in a bag. Boil 5 minutes. Drop peaches into syrup and simmer for about 15 minutes or until tender. Pack into clean hot jars; strain syrup and pour over peaches in jars to within ½ inch of top. Seal according to manufacturer's directions. Yield: 4 pints.

Mrs. Callie Neal, McMinnville, Tenn., Warren County Fair

Quick Pickle Peaches

1 No. 2½ can peach halves
¾ c. brown sugar (packed)
½ c. vinegar
2 3-inch sticks of cinnamon
1 tsp. whole cloves
1 tsp. whole allspice

(Continued on next page)

Drain syrup from peaches; add brown sugar, vinegar and spices. Boil mixture for 5 minutes. Add peach halves and simmer 5 minutes longer. Let stand overnight in refrigerator. Yield: 7-8 servings.

Mrs. Myrtle Daniel, Lobelville, Tenn., Perry County Fair

Spiced Peaches

6 lb. small to medium cling peaches
White vinegar
4 c. sugar
2 ½ tsp. grated orange rind
6 1-inch sticks of cinnamon
Whole cloves

Scald 8 peaches at a time in boiling water for 1 minute; cool in ice water. Peel; place in solution of 2 quarts water and 2 tablespoons vinegar. Combine 1 cup water, 1½ cups vinegar, sugar, orange rind and cinnamon sticks in 3-quart saucepan. Cook over medium heat, stirring constantly, until sugar is dissolved. Bring to boil. Stick 2 cloves into each of one-third of the peaches; drop into syrup. Boil gently for 10 minutes or till just tender, turning them a few times. Drain peaches from syrup with wooden spoon; pack tightly into 3 hot quart jars. Add two sticks of cinnamon to each jar; fill jars with hot syrup. Seal jars. Yield: 3 quarts.
Personal Comment: This recipe also won ribbons at the following fairs: Kalamazoo County, Allegan County and St. Joseph County.

Mrs. Paul Grofvert, Kalamazoo, Mich., Michigan State Fair

Pear Pickle

1 gal. pears
6 c. sugar
2 c. water
4 c. vinegar
2 pieces gingerroot
2 sticks cinnamon
2 tbsp. whole allspice
1 tbsp. cloves

Select firm pears. Pare and cut in halves or quarters; remove core. Boil 20 to 30 minutes in clear water. Boil sugar, water, vinegar and spices tied in a bag for 10 minutes. Add pears; let stand overnight. Cook until pears are very tender. Pack pears into hot jars. Cook syrup until thick; pour over pears. Process 5 minutes in hot water bath; complete seal. Yield: 6-7 pints.

Mrs. Jesse Risener, Union Point, Ga., Green County Fair

Spiced Pickled Pears

3 c. light brown sugar
3 c. clear corn syrup
2 c. white vinegar
2 cinnamon sticks
2 tbsp. whole cloves
4 qt. pared small pears, with stems on or quartered pears

Cook sugar, corn syrup, vinegar and spices 20 minutes. Pour syrup in large, glass sterilized jar. Add pears and cook in boiling water bath until almost tender. Pour cooked syrup into enameled pan and cook until thick. Place cooked pears into hot pint jars, adding thick syrup alternately to within ½ inch of top. Remove air bubbles. Seal with hot sterilized lids and jar rings. Spices may be tied in cheesecloth so as not to darken the pears. Yield: 6 pints.
Personal Comment: This pickle recipe was first tried in 1963 and exhibited at Virginia State Fair, winning the Blue Ribbon in individual pickle class. It is also a 1963 winner of Blue Ribbon special award for best exhibit of pickles and relishes at Virginia State Fair.

Mrs. Tilden Lee, Appomattox, Va., Atlantic Rural Exposition

Prize-Winning Watermelon Pickles

5 lb. watermelon rinds
8 tsp. powdered alum
1 qt. cider vinegar
1 tbsp. whole cloves
2 cinnamon sticks
8 c. white sugar

Select firm watermelon rinds with large proportion of white rind. Cut off outer green skin and all pink from rind; cut into small triangular pieces. Place rind in large kettle; cover with water. Boil until rind is easily pierced with fork. Add alum. Remove from heat. Let stand overnight. Rinse under running water; drain. Return rind to kettle. Add vinegar, cloves and cinnamon sticks. Pour sugar over rind. Bring to boil, stirring constantly, until sugar is dissolved. Remove from heat. Let stand overnight. Bring to boil each day for 5 consecutive days. Pack rind in sterilized jars and fill with hot syrup; seal. Store 3 weeks before tasting. Yield: 6-7 pints.

Mrs. Richard de Malignon, Minneapolis, Minn., Minnesota State Fair

Watermelon Rind Pickles

9 lb. thick rind
1 bottle Lilly's lime

(Continued on next page)

½ *box cracked gingerroots*
4 ½ *lb. sugar*
2 *qt. vinegar*
2 *tbsp. whole allspice*
6 *drops oil of cloves*
6 *drops oil of cinnamon*

Cut rind into long 1½-inch wide strips. Remove green rind, leaving on about ¼ inch thick of red portion. Cut strips into cubes. Soak rind in dissolved lime and water to cover overnight. Remove rind from lime water; rinse in fresh water 3 times. Cover rind with fresh water; boil 1 hour with gingerroots tied in a piece of cloth. Drain for 1 hour. Make a syrup of sugar, vinegar, 2 cups water and spices; let come to a boil. Do not use ginger in syrup. Add rind to syrup; boil slowly for about 2 hours or until white spots show in rind. Pack into hot sterilized jars; fill with syrup and seal. Yield: 9 pints.

Mrs. Odie W. Underhill, Morganton, N. C., Burke County Fair

Pickled Beets

1 *gal. small beets*
3 ½ *c. cider vinegar*
½ *tsp. salt*
2 *c. sugar*
2 *tbsp. cinnamon*

Cook beets until tender. Dip into cool water; peel off skins. Combine remaining ingredients to make syrup; pour over beets. Bring to boil; pack into sterilized jars. Seal. Yield: 6 pints.

Mrs. Claude Brown, Vine Grove, Ky., Hardin County Fair

Sweet Pickled Beets

1 *gal. small whole beets*
3 *c. red vinegar*
3 *c. water*
3 *c. sugar*
1 *stick cinnamon*
1 *tbsp. allspice*

Boil beets until tender; peel. Set aside. Mix all other ingredients and boil 5 minutes. Add beets; simmer 15 minutes longer. Pack in sterile jars; cover with liquid. Seal according to directions. Yield: 10-12 pints.

Mrs. Don Wendel, Slaton, Tex., South Plains Fair

Dill Pickles

¾ c. sugar
½ c. salt
1 qt. vinegar
1 qt. water
3 tbsp. mixed pickling spices
Green or dry dill
Enough med. cucumbers, cut in quarters lengthwise, to fill
    7 pt. jars

Combine sugar, salt, vinegar and water. Put spices in a cheesecloth bag and add to vinegar mixture. Simmer 15 minutes. Place a head of dill in bottom of clean hot jars and pack with cucumber strips, standing them on end. Heat vinegar mixture to boiling and pour it boiling hot over cucumbers to within ¼ inch of the top of the jars. Adjust caps on jars and process for 15 minutes in a boiling water bath. Yield: 7 pints.

Mrs. Leo J. Schmidt, Grove City, Ohio, Ohio State Fair

Hot Dill Pickles

Cucumbers
Dill
Garlic
Hot peppers
13 c. water
3 c. vinegar
1 c. salt

Wash and wipe medium-sized cucumbers; sterilize jars. Pack cucumbers in ten 1-quart jars; add 2 small bunches of dill, 3 small garlic cloves and 3 small hot peppers to each jar. Pour hot water, vinegar and salt over cucumbers and seal tightly. Let stand several months to get best results.

Mrs. W. F. Pohley, Nevada City, Cal., Nevada County Fair

Kosher Dill Pickles

20 to 25 cucumbers, about 4 inches long
Alum
Garlic
Dill
Hot red pepper
Vinegar
Pickling salt
Water

Wash freshly picked cucumbers thoroughly; drop into cold water and leave for about 1 hour. Remove from water; wipe dry and pack into sterilized jars. To each quart jar, add ⅛ teaspoon powdered alum, 1 clove garlic, 2 heads dill and 1 small hot red pepper. Boil together 4 cups vinegar, 1 cup salt and 3 quarts water. Pour over cucumbers while hot and seal.

Mrs. Howard Claussen, Albert Lea, Minn., Freeborn County Fair

Sweet Dill Pickles

Cucumbers
Vinegar
Small piece of alum
Dill
¾ c. sugar

Place small or medium cucumbers in salted water overnight. Wash several times in clear water. Heat in water with vinegar and alum in kettle on stove; do not boil. Drain; pack in jars, adding dill as desired. Combine 1 cup vinegar, ¾ cup water and sugar; boil until syrupy. Pour hot syrup over cucumbers; seal. Yield: 1 quart.

Mrs. Joe F. Peitz, Hartington, Neb., Cedar County Fair

Icicle Pickles

2 gal. cucumbers
3 gal. boiling water
1 pt. salt
2 tbsp. alum
5 c. vinegar
2 ½ c. water
⅓ small box whole pickling spice
7 pt. sugar

Cut cucumbers lengthwise; pack in large earthen jar or any other large jar. Pour 1 gallon boiling water with salt over cucumbers. Cover with another gallon boiling water. Let stand 24 hours; drain. Pour remaining gallon boiling

(Continued on next page)

water with alum over cucumbers. Let stand 24 hours. Drain. Mix together vinegar, 2½ cups water, pickling spice and sugar; heat to boiling. Pour over cucumbers. Let stand 24 hours. Drain off liquid; heat to boiling and pour over cucumbers. Let stand 24 hours; drain off liquid. Pack cucumbers in hot sterilized jars. Heat liquid to boiling; pour over cucumbers. Seal jars. Yield: 12 pints pickles.

Beulah Bradshaw, Valdese, N.C., Burke County Fair

Lime Pickles

1 c. lime
1 gal. water
Cucumber slices
2 qt. vinegar
4 ½ lb. sugar
2 tsp. celery seed

Mix lime and 1 gallon cold water; pour over sliced cucumbers. Let stand overnight; drain. Wash well 3 times in water. Let stand 3 hours in cold water; drain. Mix together vinegar, sugar and celery seed; pour over cucumbers. Let stand overnight. Boil 35 minutes or until clear; pour into jars and seal. This recipe may be used for any amount of cucumbers by increasing liquid so there is enough to cover cucumber slices.

Mrs. Harvey Morrical, Assaria, Kan., Ottawa County Fair

My Blue Ribbon Sweet Pickles

2 gal. cucumbers, 1½ to 2 inches long
1 pt. salt, non-iodized
1 tbsp. powdered alum
5 c. vinegar, not less than 4% acidity
7 ½ c. white vinegar
4 tbsp. mixed pickling spices, most of pepper pods removed
1 tbsp. celery seeds

Wash and dry cucumbers; place in stone or glass jar. Boil 1 gallon water; stir in salt until well dissolved. Pour over cucumbers; cover with plastic or cloth and weight with plates. Let stand 1 week. Pour off brine; wash in cold water. Puncture each cucumber 2 or 3 times; cover with 1 gallon boiling water. Pour off water in 24 hours. Cover with alum in 1 gallon cold water; pour off water in 24 hours. Boil remaining ingredients; pour over cucumbers. Pour off every 24 hours and reheat; pour over cucumbers. Repeat for 3 days. Pack pickles in jars; turn upside down to drain. Boil vinegar solution; pour over pickles and seal. Yield: 7-8 pints.
Personal Comment: This recipe also won at Larue County Fair

Mrs. Morna Eastridge, Sonora, Ky., Hardin County Fair

Sweet Chip Pickles

1 gal. med. cucumbers
1 c. salt
2 tbsp. alum
2 tsp. ginger
1 qt. vinegar
3 lb. sugar
1 tsp. celery seed
Whole allspice
Whole cloves
2 sticks cinnamon

Wash and slice cucumbers; let stand 6 days in salt water. Use 1 cup salt to 1 gallon cold water. Stir a few times during 6 days. Drain; rinse well. Put on stove in enough cold water to cover; add alum. Cook 10 minutes; drain well. Add additional water and ginger. Cook 10 minutes; drain. Mix vinegar, 1 pint water and sugar; add spices. Cook until transparent in syrup. Can and seal in hot jars.
Personal Comment: This recipe has also won blue ribbons at Clay County Fair and Mid-American Fair.

Mrs. Horace Cowell, Wakefield, Kan., Central Kansas Free Fair

Aristocratic Slices

15 med. cucumbers
10 med. onions, chopped
½ c. salt to 1 gal. water
3 c. sugar
3 c. vinegar
3 tbsp. celery seed
3 tbsp. mustard seed

Slice cucumbers very thin. Mix slices and onions together; cover with salt water. Let stand 3 hours. Wash in clear water 3 times; drain well. Add sugar, vinegar, celery seed and mustard seed; cook in large container for 20 minutes. Place in hot jars; seal.

Mrs. Frieda B. Tupper, Clark, S. D., South Dakota State Fair

Bread And Butter Pickles

6 qt. thinly sliced med. cucumbers
12 med onions, thinly sliced
2 sweet red peppers, chopped
⅓ c. salt

(Continued on next page)

2 qt. vinegar
8 c. sugar
½ c. mustard seed
3 tbsp. turmeric
Pinch of powdered alum

Combine vegetables; arrange a 2-inch layer in enamel or earthenware container. Sprinkle with salt; repeat until vegetables and salt are used. Let stand 3 hours. Drain thoroughly; taste and, if too salty, rinse slightly. Add vinegar, sugar, mustard seed, turmeric and alum; mix well. Simmer 10 to 15 minutes or until cucumbers become a green color. Pack into hot sterilized jars; Seal. Yield: 4 quarts.

Mrs. Donald Ralph, Okemos, Mich., Michigan State Fair

Cinnamon Bread And Butter Pickles

3 tbsp. salt
8 c. cucumbers, sliced
3 c. onions, sliced
4 green peppers, chopped fine
2 c. vinegar
2 tsp. turmeric powder
2 tsp. celery seed
3 inches stick cinnamon
3 c. sugar

Sprinkle salt over vegetables; let stand 1 hour. Drain; add vinegar, spices and sugar. Bring to boiling point; hold to just simmering for 20 minutes. Pour into hot clean jars; seal. The secret of a crisp crunchy pickle is not to let it boil. Yield: 5 pints.

Mrs. Frank G. Brown, Center Harbor, N. H., Sandwich Fair

Crisp Pickle Slices

4 qt. thinly sliced cucumbers
6 onions, sliced thinly
⅓ c. salt
3 c. white vinegar
5 c. sugar
1 ½ tsp. turmeric
1 ½ tsp. celery seed
2 tbsp. mustard seed

Sprinkle vegetables with salt. Soak cucumbers and onions in cold water and ice cubes for 3 hours. Drain. Combine vinegar, sugar, turmeric, celery seed

(Continued on next page)

and mustard seed. Bring to a boil. Cook cucumbers and onions in boiling syrup until cooked through; can in hot jars and seal at once. Let stand for 24 hours. Yield: 8-10 pints.

Mrs. Gerald Yeoumans, St. Maries, Idaho, Benewah County Fair

French Mustard Pickles

    1 qt. 2-in. long green cucumbers
    1 qt. lge. green cucumbers
    1 pt. green tomatoes
    2 small hot red peppers
    2 stalks celery
    ½ head cabbage
    3 pt. fine white button onions
    2 heads cauliflower
    Salt
    1 lb. ground mustard
    1 tbsp. turmeric
    1 c. flour
    2 qt. vinegar
    ½ tsp. mixed spices
    2 c. brown sugar
    1 tsp. celery seed
    1 tsp. mustard seed
    1 tsp. curry powder

Leave small cucumbers whole; cut large cucumbers into cubes. Cut tomatoes, peppers, celery and cabbage into bits, size of a walnut; leave onions whole. Divide cauliflower into small flowerets. Soak vegetables in brine made from 1 cup salt to 1 gallon water. Scald them in brine after they have soaked for 24 hours. Drain well. Mix mustard, turmeric and flour with 1 cup vinegar, stirring mixture to a smooth paste. Add remaining vinegar and heat mixture, stirring constantly until it is thick. Add spices, brown sugar and remaining ingredients. Cook for 5 minutes; seal, boiling hot, in sterilized jars. Yield: 9 quarts.

Lillian E. Dagley, Alameda, Cal., Alameda County Fair

Garlic Pickles

    4 qt. sliced cucumbers
    6 med. white onions, sliced
    1 red pepper, chopped
    2 green peppers, chopped
    3 cloves of garlic
    ⅓ c. salt
    5 c. sugar

(Continued on next page)

1 ½ tsp. turmeric
1 ½ tsp. celery seed
2 tbsp. mustard seed
3 c. vinegar

Slice cucumbers thin. Add onions, peppers and whole garlic cloves; add salt. Cover with cracked ice and mix thoroughly. Let stand 3 hours; drain. Combine remaining ingredients and pour over cucumber mixture. Heat just to boiling. Seal in hot sterilized jars.

Mrs. LeRoy Jameson, Thedford, Neb., Thomas County Fair

Million-Dollar Pickles

4 qt. sliced cucumbers
8 to 10 small onions
2 small green peppers
2 small red peppers
½ c. salt
½ qt. cider vinegar
4 c. sugar
½ tsp. celery seed
1 tsp. turmeric powder
2 tbsp. white mustard seed
1 tsp. mixed pickling spices

Slice cucumbers, onions and peppers; place in a large crock. Sprinkle salt over them and cover with water. Soak in crock overnight. Drain. Combine vinegar, sugar, celery seed, turmeric powder, mustard seed and spices in a large kettle; bring to a boil. Add drained cucumbers and cook 20 minutes or until tender. Pack in hot sterilized jars. Yield: 6 pints.
Personal Comment: This recipe has been in my family for four generations. These pickles have won five blue ribbons and one grand award.

Marbena J. Fyke, Newburgh, N. Y., Orange County Fair

Old-Fashioned Pickle Slices

4 qt. thinly sliced unpared cucumbers
6 med. white onions, sliced
1 green pepper, cut in strips
1 sweet red pepper, cut in strips
3 cloves garlic, crushed
⅓ c. coarse salt
5 c. sugar
3 ½ c. white vinegar

(Continued on next page)

2 tbsp. mustard seed
1 ½ tsp. celery seed
1 ½ tsp. turmeric

Combine vegetables, garlic and salt. Cover with ice cubes and mix thoroughly. Let stand 3 hours. Drain well. Combine remaining ingredients; pour over vegetables. Bring just to boiling. Seal at once in hot sterilized jars. Chill before serving. Yield: 8 pints.
Personal Comment: This recipe also won a blue ribbon at Alameda County Fair.

Mrs. Maren K. Groves, Sebastopol, Cal., Contra Costa County Fair

Pickled Vegetables

2 c. carrots, peeled and cut up
Cauliflowerets
Small cucumbers
Small pearl onions, peeled
Celery, cut up
6 sweet red peppers, coarsley chopped
5 pt. white vinegar
6 pt. water

Place vegetables in crock; add enough brine to cover vegetables. Brine should be strong enough to float an egg. Weight vegetables down with a scalded heavy plate; place fruit jar of water over top. Let set for 1 week. Remove film that forms as fermentation takes place. Fermentation takes 2 to 3 weeks. Drain off brine. Boil vinegar and water. Place pickles in sterilized jar; pour hot vinegar and water mixture over pickles. Seal.
Personal Comment: This is my 4-time sweepstakes winner.

Mrs. James E. Fields, Los Olivos, Cal., Santa Maria Fair

Sandwich Pickles

1 qt. cucumbers, sliced
¼ c. non-iodized salt
2 qt. cold water
1 med. onion, cut in rings
1 tsp. mustard seed
½ tsp. celery seed
1 tbsp. mixed pickling spices
1 tsp. turmeric
½ c. white sugar
½ c. brown sugar
1 pt. cider vinegar

(Continued on next page)

Use large green cucumbers. Cut off ends; wash and slice. Dissolve salt in water; pour over cucumbers and onion rings. Let stand for 3 hours. Drain. Bring spices, sugars and vinegar to a boil; add drained cucumbers and onion rings. Heat to boiling point. Let boil for 1 to 2 minutes. Pack in sterilized jars while hot. Seal. Yield: 2 pints.

Mrs. Reed W. DePriest, Lobelville, Tenn., Perry County Fair

Seven-Minute Pickles

Cucumbers for 7 1-qt. jars
Onion
Mixed spices
Salt
6 c. vinegar
3 c. sugar
1 ½ c. water

Pack cucumbers tightly in jars. Put 2 slices of onion, 1 teaspoon spices and 1 teaspoon salt on top of each jar of pickles. Mix together vinegar, sugar and water; bring to a boil and pour over pickles. Cold pack 7 minutes after water starts to boil. Yield: 7 quarts.

Mrs. Jesse Crites, Petersburg, W. Va., Tri-County Fair

Sweet Dill Pickles

6 med. cucumbers
Ice water
Onions
Dill, fresh or dried
1 c. sugar
1 c. water
2 c. white vinegar
⅓ c. pickling salt

Soak whole cucumbers in ice water for 3 to 4 hours. Drain; slice crosswise or in strips. Place in sterilized jars along with few slices onion and a generous amount of dill. Combine sugar, water, vinegar and salt. Bring to a boil and pour over pickles; seal. Store in cool place until cucumbers look transparent. Yield: 3 parts.

Mrs. Cora Murphy, Waterloo, Ala., North Alabama State Fair

Sweet Mixed Pickles

1 c. salt
2 qt. unpeeled cucumber chunks
1 ½ qt. pickling onions
1 ½ qt. cauliflower pieces
1 med. red sweet pepper
1 qt. vinegar
1 tbsp. turmeric
1 tbsp. alum
5 c. white sugar
2 ¾ c. white vinegar
2 ¾ c. water
1 oz. mixed pickling spices
2 sticks cinnamon
1 tsp. whole cloves
1 tbsp. mustard seed

Make a mixture of 4 quarts water and salt; bring to a full boil. Pour over prepared vegetables; let stand 4 hours. Drain. Make a mixture of 2 quarts water, vinegar, turmeric and alum; pour over drained pickles. Bring to a boil; boil 5 minutes. Drain; run cold water over pickles until cool. Arrange in clean jars. Boil remaining ingredients together 20 minutes; pour over pickles and seal immediately. Spices in syrup should be·in a cheesecloth bag. Yield: 8 pints.

Ruth S. Hensen, Smithfield, Utah, Cache County Fair

Virginia Sweet Pickles

6 c. plus 1 tbsp. cider vinegar
1 lb. 9 oz. salt
Cucumbers
3 tbsp. powdered alum
9 c. sugar
⅓ c. pickling spice
1 tbsp. celery seed

Bring 1 gallon water to boil. Add 1 tablespoon vinegar and salt; cool. Place mixture in crock; add cucumbers and let set set for a few days to a week. Drain and cut in half or prick with fork. Combine 1 gallon water and 1 tablespoon alum; pour over cucumbers for 3 mornings. Drain and prepare fresh mixture each day. Combine remaining vinegar, 5 cups sugar, pickling spice and celery seed; bring to a boil. Pour over drained cucumbers; let set overnight. Drain vinegar mixture into pan; add 2 cups sugar and heat. Pour over cucumbers; let set overnight. Drain vinegar mixture into pan; add remaining sugar and heat. Place cucumbers in sterilized jars; pour vinegar mixture over cucumbers. Process in hot water bath for 10 minutes.
Personal Comment: This recipe has won first prize for the past 6 years.

Mrs. Styrk Myhre, Caledonia, Minn., Houston County Fair

Annie's Green Tomato Pickles

    5 lb. green tomatoes
    2 ½ lb. white onions
    ¼ c. plus 1 tbsp. salt
    1 pt. vinegar
    ½ c. sugar
    1 tbsp. celery seed
    1 tbsp. white mustard seed

Wash and slice tomatoes. Peel and slice onions. Place tomatoes and onions in crock in alternate layers; sprinkle each layer with salt. Cover with plate; weight down. Let stand overnight. Drain. Add 1 cup vinegar and 1 cup water. Heat to boiling; drain. Add remaining vinegar and 2 cups water, sugar, celery seed, and mustard seed. Boil slowly for 30 minutes, stirring occasionally. Pack in sterilized jars and seal.

Mrs. Annie Dussart, Trinidad, Colo., Las Animas County Fair

Garlic-Dilled Green Tomatoes

    3 qt. green cherry tomatoes, approximately
    12 cloves garlic
    6 sprays dill
    2 qt. white vinegar
    3 c. water
    ½ c. salt

Wash and pack tomatoes in jars. Add 2 cloves garlic and 1 spray dill to each pint. Boil vinegar, water and salt mixture about 5 minutes or until salt is dissolved. Pour over tomatoes; seal.

Mrs. Pat Carpender, Smithflat, Cal., Elhlorado County Fair

Green Tomato Pickle

    7 lb. green tomatoes, sliced
    2 gal. water
    3 c. lime
    3 pt. vinegar
    5 lb. sugar
    2 tbsp. pickling spice

Soak tomatoes in water mixed with lime for 24 hours; drain and wash well. Cover with water. Change water every hour for 4 hours; drain well. Heat vinegar, sugar and pickling spice; pour over tomatoes. Soak 24 hours or overnight. Cook for 1 hour. Put in clean jars and seal. Yield: 6 pints.

Mrs. Thomas E. Eaton, McMinnville, Tenn., Warren County Fair

Pear Tomato Pickles

7 c. green pear tomatoes
Salt
2 tbsp. mustard seed
1 tbsp. celery seed
2 c. vinegar
2 c. sugar
2 tbsp. turmeric

Cut pear tomatoes in half lengthwise; soak in ½ cup salt to 2 quarts water overnight. Drain. Add remaining ingredients; boil 10 minutes. Pack into sterilized jars and seal.

Mrs. Dan Smith, Hillsboro, Ore., Washington County Fair

Pickled Dill Okra

Okra
1 ¼ tsp. dill seeds
1 c. apple cider vinegar
1 c. water
1 tbsp. salt

Wash and cut off stems of small okra pods; place in pint jars. Sprinkle dill over top of okra. Cover with boiling vinegar, water and salt mixture. Place lids on jars and seal tightly. Place jars in deep container; cover with boiling water. Cover. Let stand overnight. Wait 3 weeks before eating.

Mrs. Luke Wood, Mountain Home, Ark., Baxter County Fair

Pickled Hot Pods

2 lb. tender fresh okra
5 pods hot red or green pepper
5 cloves garlic, peeled
1 qt. white vinegar
½ c. water
8 tbsp. salt
1 tbsp. celery seed or mustard seed (opt.)

Wash okra and pack in 5 hot sterilized pint jars together with 1 pepper pod and garlic clove per jar. Pack okra alternately with top end of pod toward bottom of jar. Bring remaining ingredients to boil. Pour over okra and seal. Let stand several weeks before serving and chill for crispness. Pimento may be used for garnish. Yield: 12 servings.

Mrs. George N. Phillips, Dallas, Tex., Texas State Fair

Pickled Okra

Okra
Red and green peppers (opt.)
Whole small carrots (opt.)
Alum
Garlic (opt.)
Dill seed, 1 tsp. per pt. or 1 head of green dill
1 qt. water
¼ c. salt
¼ c. vinegar

Wash and pack fresh tender okra in clean jars. Strips of red and green sweet peppers and carrots may be added for color. Add ¼ teaspoon alum per pint, garlic and dill. Heat other ingredients to boiling point and pour in filled jars; seal at once. Use zinc lids with rubber band. Yield: 6 pints.

Mrs. Lillie Lipps, Okeene, Okla., Fairview Fair

Barbecued Peppers In Sauce

¾ c. white vinegar
⅔ c. sugar
2 tbsp. salt
1 lge. can tomato juice
1 8-oz. can tomato sauce
1 bottle barbecue sauce (opt.)
1 crate red bell peppers

Mix first 6 ingredients together, adjusting to taste. Mixture is better slightly tart. Bring to boil; simmer. Barbecue red peppers over hot coals until completely cooked and skins are black. Peel off entire skin; quarter peppers and remove core. Bring sauce to rolling boil; add peppers to sauce. Cook until peppers have been heated through; place peppers in sterilized jars. Add sauce. Jar should not be packed. Allow enough sauce to give flavor. Seal jars; allow to cool. Yield: 14 pints.

Beverly A. Gabrielson, Los Angeles, Cal., Los Angeles County Fair

Hot Peppers

Hot peppers
1 qt. vinegar
1 c. salt
3 qt. water

Wash peppers; place in sterilized jars. Bring vinegar, salt and water to boiling point; pour over peppers in jars. Seal.

Mrs. J. A. Beauchamp, Detroit, Mich., Michigan State Fair

Pickled Jalapenos

12 jalapeno chilies
Cooking oil
1 small onion, sliced
1 carrot, sliced
1 tsp. salt
1 tsp. dry oregano
1 c. (about) boiled water
1 c. (about) white vinegar

In frying pan, place enough oil to coat bottom well; heat. Add chilies, 4 to 6 at a time, to hot oil. Turn in pan until all are barely blistered; remove to cool. Arrange chilies in sterilized pint jar; fit as snugly as possible, inserting a few slices of onion and carrot. Add salt and oregano. Fill jar with equal amounts of water and vinegar to within ½ inch of top. Cover jar with lid; place in pan. Add enough water to half cover jar; cover pan. Heat until jar is hot enough to seal. Do not leave over heat too long as chilies will cook and become soft.

Georgia Bejarano, Tulare, Cal., Tulare County Fair

Pickled Peppers

3 lge. red peppers
3 lge. green peppers
1 lge. onion
¾ c. sugar
1 ½ c. white vinegar
1 tbsp. mustard seed
1 tbsp. celery seed

Wash peppers; remove seeds and cut into strips. Slice onion into rings. Cover peppers and onion with boiling water; let stand 2 minutes. Drain; pack into hot pint jars. Boil sugar, vinegar and spices together 5 minutes; pour over peppers and onions. Seal. Yield: 2 pints.

Mrs. Maury C. Ballard, Warner Robins, Ga., Georgia State Fair

Pickled Peppers Olympia

1 qt. water
1 qt. vinegar
3 ½ c. sugar
5 tbsp. salt
2 bushels peppers

Boil water, vinegar, sugar and salt until mixture becomes syrup. Add peppers to syrup; boil until peppers become soft but still firm. Place in scalded jars; seal. Yield: 16 quarts.

Mrs. Olympia Dial, West Frankfort, Ill., DuQuoin State Fair

Pickled Sweet Banana Peppers

Mild banana peppers
11 pieces celery
11 heads dill
11 cloves garlic
5 ½ hot peppers (opt.)
4 ½ qt. water
1 ½ qt. cider vinegar
2 ½ c. plus 2 tbsp. sugar
¼ c. plus 2 tbsp. salt
1 ½ c. corn oil

Wash and cut each pepper in half lengthwise; remove seeds. Fill clean quart jars with peppers. Add to each jar 1 piece celery, 1 head dill, 1 clove garlic and ½ hot pepper. Bring remaining ingredients to a boil; pour over peppers. Seal. Personal Comment: This recipe also won ribbons at St. Louis County Fair

Mrs. Edward Martire, Nashwauk, Minn., Itasca County Fair

Beet And Cabbage Relish

1 qt. chopped cooked beets
1 qt. chopped cabbage
1 c. chopped onions
1 tbsp. salt
1 tbsp. prepared horseradish
1 ½ c. sugar
3 c. vinegar

Combine all ingredients; simmer about 10 minutes. Bring to boiling. Pack, boiling hot, into sterilized jars, leaving ⅛-inch head space. Adjust caps. Yield: 3 half-pints.

Mrs. Helmer Hultin, Ada, Minn., Norman County Fair

Cabbage And Pepper Relish

1 small cabbage
6 red peppers
6 green peppers
1 tsp. salt
2 c. sugar
1 qt. vinegar
1 tbsp. cinnamon
1 tsp. allspice
1 tbsp. white mustard seed
1 tsp. cloves

(Continued on next page)

Select a good firm head of cabbage and peppers. Cut cabbage in quarters, cutting out core. Cut peppers in half, removing all seed and pulp. Wash thoroughly. Put cabbage and peppers through a meat grinder. Sprinkle with salt; let stand 3 hours. Drain and wash in cold water. Mix sugar, vinegar and spices; boil for 5 minutes with cabbage and pepper. Quickly put it in hot jars and seal.

Mary Stewart, Fargo, N. D., Red River Valley State Fair

Cabbage Relish

        4 lb. fresh cabbage, ground
        9 lge. red bell peppers, ground
        9 lge. green bell peppers, ground
        8 lge. white Bermuda onions, ground
        4 med. carrots, ground
    ½ c. salt
        4 c. sugar
        2 ½ pt. apple cider vinegar
    ½ c. water
        2 tbsp. celery seed
        2 tbsp. mustard seed

Put ground vegetables in enamel kettle; add salt. Blend lightly. Cover and let stand for 6 hours. Put in cheese cloth bag; suspend and drain overnight. Put in large container; pour in remaining ingredients. Blend well; put in sterilized jars. Fill jars to within ½ inch of top. Add vinegar solution if necessary to cover top of relish. Cap jars; not necessary to seal. Will keep all winter in cool place or icebox. Yield: 6-8 pints.

Florence Austin, Dallas, Tex., Texas State Fair

Bordeaux Sauce

        2 qt. chopped green tomatoes
        4 qt. chopped cabbage
        6 lge. onions, chopped
        2 lb. sugar
        2 red peppers, chopped
        2 oz. celery seed
        2 oz. mustard seed
        4 tbsp. salt
        2 qt. vinegar
        1 tsp. turmeric

Mix all ingredients; cook slowly for 1 hour. Seal jars. Yield: 12 pints.

Mrs. Harry Hanson, Willard, Mont., Fallon County Fair

Green Tomato Relish

 1 qt. vinegar
 3 tbsp. flour
 3 tbsp. turmeric
 4 tbsp. salt
 1 tbsp. mustard
 2 tbsp. mixed pickling spice
 2 c. sugar
 4 or 5 chopped celery stems
 12 chopped red sweet peppers
 12 chopped green sweet peppers
 1 ½ qt. chopped onions
 2 ½ qt. chopped cabbage
 2 ½ qt. chopped green tomatoes

Mix a small amount of vinegar with flour and turmeric to make a paste. Place remaining vinegar in large kettle; bring to a boil. Stir in paste and let thicken like gravy. Tie spices in cloth bag. Add all remaining ingredients to vinegar mixture. Stir constantly until mixture boils; let boil 40 minutes. Place in hot pint jars and seal.

Personal Comment: This recipe has won prizes at fairs for 45 years.

Mrs. W. F. Cullum, Waverly, Tenn., Humphreys County Fair

Texas Chow-Chow

 1 gal. green tomatoes
 3 qt. cabbage
 4 green bell peppers
 2 red bell peppers
 1 or 2 hot long peppers
 2 c. chopped celery (opt.)
 8 med. onions
 2 tbsp. celery seed
 ¼ tsp. cinnamon
 ¼ tsp. allspice
 2 tbsp. salt
 3 c. sugar
 Vinegar

Grind tomatoes with coarse chopper. Put in bag or colander; drain overnight. Grind cabbage, peppers, celery and onions; add to celery seed, cinnamon, allspice, salt and sugar. Cover with white vinegar. Put over low flame and simmer. When mixture comes to boil, put in hot sterilized jars and seal.

Mrs. Cecil Berry, Crosbyton, Tex., Floyd County Fair

Vegetable Relish

½ bushel green tomatoes
2 c. salt
2 heads cabbage
12 green peppers
10 red peppers
12 onions
6 qt. vinegar
4 tbsp. celery seed
4 tbsp. mustard seed
1 tbsp. whole cloves
16 c. sugar

Grind tomatoes. Add salt. Put in bag; let drain overnight. Grind cabbage, peppers and onions. Mix in a large kettle with drained tomatoes. Add vinegar, celery seed, mustard seed, cloves and sugar. Cook until onions are tender, about 20 minutes. Seal in hot sterilized jars. Yield: 24 pints.

Mrs. Ella Henderson, Germantown, Md., Montgomery County Fair

Catsup

3 tsp. whole cloves
3 tsp. broken cinnamon stick
2 tsp. celery seed
½ tsp. cayenne pepper
2 c. white vinegar
16 lb. ripe tomatoes
1 med. onion, chopped
2 c. sugar
3 tbsp. salt
½ tsp. garlic salt

Measure spices in pan. Add vinegar; cover and bring to a boil. Remove pan from heat and let steep while preparing tomatoes. Wash and quarter tomatoes into kettle. Add onion; bring to a boil. Cook 15 minutes, stirring occasionally. Run cooked tomatoes through colander. Add sugar; bring to a boil and simmer until reduced about half. Strain vinegar-spice mixture into tomatoes, discarding spices. Add salt and garlic salt and simmer, stirring occasionally, until thick enough for catsup. Pour into hot sterilized jars and seal. Yield: 4-5 pints.

Mrs. Truman Smith, Mountain Home, Ark., Baxter County Fair

Baked Chili Sauce

1 lug tomatoes, peeled
6 to 7 bell peppers

(Continued on next page)

6 to 7 lge. onions
1 bunch celery
2 tsp. each cinnamon, allspice, cloves and nutmeg
1 pt. (or more) vinegar
4 c. sugar (about)

Grind and drain tomatoes. Place in large baking pan. Chop peppers, onions and celery fine. Add to tomatoes. Add spices. Add vinegar and sugar to taste. Bake until thickened at 250 degrees. Pour into sterilized jars and seal.

Ella K. Munson, Cardiff-by-the-Sea, Cal., San Diego County Fair

Chili Sauce

18 lge. ripe tomatoes
6 lge. onions, chopped
2 tsp. salt
½ tsp. each cloves and allspice
1 tsp. each cinnamon and nutmeg
1 ½ c. vinegar
4 c. sugar

Mix all ingredients; boil 3 hours. Bottle while hot; seal.

Leona Williams, Malad, Idaho, Oneida County Fair

Hot Chili Sauce

1 gal. ripe tomatoes
⅔ c. chopped white onions
1 ½ c. white sugar
1 tsp. nutmeg, grated
¾ tsp. Tabasco sauce
½ tsp. curry powder
2 c. vinegar
5 tsp. salt
2 tsp. ginger
1 tsp. cinnamon
1 tsp. dry mustard

Peel and core tomatoes before measuring. Put tomatoes and onions through food chopper, using fine blade. Add all other ingredients and boil for 2 hours or until thick, stirring frequently to prevent burning. When sauce is of desired consistency, pour into sterilized pint jars and seal at once. Yield: 3 pints.

Mrs. James S. Barnt, Gaylord, Mich., Otsego County Fair

Spicy Chili Sauce

1 gal. ripe tomatoes
½ c. chopped sweet red peppers
½ c. chopped white onions
1 c. brown sugar
1 pt. white vinegar
2 tbsp. salt
½ tsp. cayenne pepper
4 tbsp. pickling spices

Wash and scald tomatoes. Peel at once. Chop tomatoes into small pieces; mix with peppers and onions. Put in blender to finish pulverizing. Add sugar, vinegar, salt, cayenne and spices tied in a muslin bag. Cook until thick. Remove spice bag. Pour into hot, sterilized pint jars. Seal at once. Process jars in hot water bath 15 minutes. Place away from drafts to cool. If a blender is not available the tomatoes may be chopped and cooked to pieces.

Brenda Lee Peterman, Macon, Georgia State Fair

Chow Chow

8 c. green beans
8 c. shelled lima beans
1 bunch of carrots, pared and sliced
1 lge. head cauliflower
4 ears corn
2 lb. green tomatoes
5 green peppers
3 c. sugar
¼ c. salt
3 tbsp. celery seed
3 tbsp. mustard seed
2 tbsp. dry mustard
1 tbsp. turmeric powder
3 qt. vinegar
2 tbsp. Tabasco
2 lb. sm. white onions, peeled

Put whole green beans, shelled limas and carrot slices in a deep kettle. Break up cauliflower and cut corn from cob; add to vegetables. Add water to cover; bring to a boil. Reduce heat and cook 25 minutes; drain. While these vegetables are cooking, coarsely chop tomatoes and green peppers. Mix sugar, salt, celery seed, mustard seed, dry mustard and turmeric in deep kettle. Add vinegar. Cook over low heat, stirring constantly, until sugar is dissolved. Stir in Tabasco. Add drained cooked vegetables, chopped vegetables and onions. Cook 25 minutes. Spoon into sterilized jars; seal. Yield: 7 quarts.

Photograph for this recipe on page 337.

Carroll Fruit Chutney

4 mangos, peeled and chopped
6 apples, peeled and chopped
6 pears, peeled and chopped
6 white onions, peeled and chopped
2 No. 2 cans pineapple tidbits
2 tbsp. salt
3 tbsp. celery seed
6 chili peppers, chopped fine
1 qt. wine vinegar
4 cloves garlic, ground
1 lb. dates, coarsley chopped
1 lb. seeded raisins
2 lb. brown sugar
3 tbsp. mustard seed
3 tbsp. mixed pickling spice, tied in bag
½ lb. green ginger, ground
Juice and grated rind of 3 oranges
Juice and grated rind of 3 lemons

Blend all ingredients well. Cook over low heat, stirring often, for 1 hour or until thick and clear. Pour into pint jars; seal at once. Yield: 24 pints.

Frances Carroll, Dallas, Texas State Fair

 ## Hawaiian Chutney

4 c. crushed canned pineapple
2 c. chopped seedless golden raisins
½ c. (firmly packed) brown sugar
3 tbsp. white vinegar
1 tsp. salt
½ c. white sugar
¼ tsp. ground ginger
⅛ tsp. cayenne pepper
¾ tsp. ground allspice
¼ tsp. ground cloves
¼ tsp. cinnamon
Few drops Tabasco sauce
½ c. chopped almonds

Combine pineapple, raisins, brown sugar, vinegar and salt in large saucepan. In a small bowl combine white sugar, ginger, cayenne pepper, allspice, cloves, cinnamon and Tabasco sauce. Stir spice mixture into pineapple mixture; cook, stirring constantly, over low heat for 40 minutes or until mixture becomes clear. Remove from heat; add almonds. Pour into hot sterilized pint jars; seal at once. Yield: 3 pints.

Mrs. Mary Piechocki, Detroit, Michigan State Fair

Iowa Corn Relish

20 ears sweet corn
1 c. chopped green pepper
1 c. chopped sweet red pepper
1 ¼ c. chopped onion
1 c. chopped celery
2 c. sugar
1 ½ tbsp. mustard seeds or ¼ c. dry mustard
2 tbsp. salt
1 tsp. celery seeds
1 tsp. turmeric
1 qt. white vinegar

Boil corn for 5 minutes. Plunge into cold water. Cut kernels from cobs; measure 2½ quarts. Combine all ingredients; simmer 20 minutes. Pack into clean hot pint jars, leaving 1 inch head space. Make certain vinegar solution covers vegetables. Adjust lids. Process 5 minutes at 5 pounds pressure in canner or 15 minutes in boiling water bath. Yield: 6-7 pints.

Mrs. Edward Klopfenstein, Early, Iowa, Sac County Fair

Sweet Corn Relish

18 ears sweet corn
2 lge. green peppers
2 sweet red peppers
1 small cabbage
4 onions
1 c. chopped celery
1 qt. vinegar
2 c. brown sugar
2 tbsp. salt
3 tbsp. mustard

Cut corn from cobs. Seed peppers and chop with cabbage and onions. Mix vegetables together; add remaining ingredients. Cook, stirring occasionally, for 20 to 30 minutes or until tender. Pack in hot sterilized jars and seal. Yield: 5 pints.

Mrs. Wilbur Nye, Green Springs, Ohio, Seneca County Fair

Crisp Mustard Mix

6 med. chopped cucumbers
2 c. chopped onion
3 sweet peppers, chopped

(Continued on next page)

1 med. head cauliflower, cut up
1 qt. pickling onions
1 c. pickling salt
4 c. sugar
4 c. vinegar
¾ c. flour
¼ c. dry mustard
1 ½ tsp. turmeric
1 tbsp. celery salt

Layer vegetables and salt in large bowl; cover with cold water. Let stand over-night. Drain; rinse with cold water. Combine sugar and vinegar; heat to boiling. Mix remaining ingredients; add some vinegar mixture. Cool. Add spices to boiling mixture; stir well. Add drained vegetables; cook 10 to 15 minutes. Seal in hot sterilized jars. Yield: 6½ pints.

Dollie Campbell, Springfield, Ore., Lane County Fair

Hot Dog Relish

3 carrots, peeled
3 sweet red peppers, cored and seeded
2 qt. cucumbers, sliced
2 qt. green tomatoes, sliced
2 qt. onions
Sugar
Salt
1 ½ c. vinegar
½ tsp. cayenne pepper
2 tbsp. mixed pickling spices

Grind first 5 ingredients; add ½ cup sugar and mix well. Sprinkle with salt and let stand overnight. Drain; combine with vinegar, cayenne pepper, spices which have been tied loosely in cheesecloth and 1½ pounds sugar. Simmer for 45 minutes. Remove spice bag. Pour into clean, hot jars and seal. Yield: 6 pints.

Barbara R. Alexander, Greentop, Northeast Missouri Fair

Spiced Orange Wedges

4 oranges
2 c. sugar
½ c. vinegar

(Continued on next page)

12 whole cloves
3 pieces stick cinnamon

Put whole oranges in saucepan; add 1 quart water. Bring to a boil; boil 20 minutes. Drain and cut into eighths. Combine sugar, 1¼ cups water, vinegar, cloves and cinnamon; stir over low heat until sugar is dissolved. Bring to a boil; add pieces of orange and simmer about 20 minutes. Cool; cover and store in refrigerator. Serve as a relish. Yield: 5 cups.

Orange Cranberry Relish

2 oranges, quartered and seeded
4 c. fresh cranberries
2 c. sugar

Put orange quarters with peel and cranberries through food chopper. Add sugar to mixture. Chill in refrigerator several hours. Yield: 1 quart.

Photograph for these recipes below.

Pepper Jam

Red sweet peppers
2 tbsp. salt
6 c. sugar
4 c. vinegar

Wash and drain thick-walled peppers. Remove seeds and midribs; chop fine.
Mix 7 cups of peppers with salt. Let stand 3 to 4 hours. Add sugar and vinegar. Boil until thick. Pour, boiling hot, into hot jar. Seal at once.

Mrs. Anna Puckett, Lewistown, Mont., Midland Empire Fair

Pepper Hash

15 green sweet peppers
15 red sweet peppers
15 lge. white onions
1 ½ c. sugar
2 ½ tbsp. salt
1 pt. vinegar
¼ tsp. cayenne pepper

Chop peppers and onions fine or put them through food chopper. Cover with
boiling water; let stand 10 minutes. Drain. Add remaining ingredients; bring
to boil. Pack into sterilized jars and seal.

Mrs. Laura H. Holman, Benton, Ill., Franklin County Fair

Zucchini Relish

10 c. zucchini squash, peeled
4 c. onions
5 tbsp. salt
2 ¼ c. cider vinegar
6 c. sugar
1 tbsp. nutmeg
1 tbsp. turmeric
2 tbsp. cornstarch
2 tbsp. celery seed
½ tsp. pepper

Grind zucchini and onions; add salt. Let stand overnight. Drain and rinse
in cold water and drain again. Be sure all water is off or relish will be thin.
Add remaining ingredients; cook 30 minutes. Seal. Watch and stir often while
cooking. Red and green peppers may be added for coloring.

Mrs. Winston Weber, Odessa, Wash., Tri-County Fair

Jams, Jellies and Preserves

Apple Butter

1 peck apples, unpeeled
4 c. water
10 c. (about) sugar
2 tsp. ground cloves
2 tbsp. ground cinnamon
1 tsp. ground allspice

Wash, quarter and cook apples with water. Cover; let simmer slowly until tender. Rub through coarse sieve. Should be about 5 quarts pulp. Add half as much sugar as pulp; add spices. Simmer about 2 hours, stirring frequently as it will scorch easily. An asbestos mat placed under kettle will prevent scorching. When thickened, pour into hot sterilized jars; seal immediately. Apple Butter becomes stiffer when cool. Delicious served on hot buttered toast. Yield: 9-10 pints.

Mrs. Alfred Muth, Rocky Ford, Colo., Arkansas Valley Fair

Peach Butter

Fully ripe peaches
Sugar
Cinnamon (opt.)

Scald peels; pit peaches. Cook to pulp, using little water. Press through sieve or food mill. Measure pulp; add 1 cup sugar for every 2 cups peaches. Cook on low heat about 1 hour until thickened. Cool. Cinnamon may be added when half cooked. Stir often. Pour into sterilized jars; seal while hot.

Dorothy Graves, Crescent City, Cal., Del Norte County Fair

Peach Conserve

1 orange, quartered and sliced thin
7 c. chopped peeled peaches
5 c. sugar
½ tsp. ginger
¼ tsp. salt
⅔ c. sliced blanched almonds

Combine in kettle orange and peaches; boil 20 minutes. Stir in sugar, ginger and salt; boil until thick. Stir in almonds. Pour into sterilized jars and seal.

Mrs. Anna Olexa, Detroit, Mich., Michigan State Fair

Sand Plum Conserve

    8 *c. seeded sand plums, washed and cut up*
    4 *tbsp. lemon juice*
    1 ½ *tsp. grated lemon rind*
    1 *c. seedless raisins*
    6 *c. sugar*
    1 *c. black walnuts, chopped*

Combine all ingredients except nuts. Cook until thick. Blanch nuts 2 minutes; drain and cut or chop. Add to plum mixture when cooking is complete. Pour into sterilized jars; seal while hot. Yield: 5 pints.

Mrs. Oscar L. Hixson, Oklahoma City, Okla., Oklahoma State Fair

 ### Pineapple Honey

    Pineapple
  ⅛ *c. lemon juice*
  7 ½ *c. sugar*
    Butter
  ½ *bottle Certo or ½ pack other pectin*

Grind pineapple medium-fine, not to pulp. Measure 4 cups pineapple juice into a large saucepan. Add lemon juice and sugar. Add small amount of butter. Bring to a full rolling boil; boil hard 1 minute, stirring constantly. Remove from heat; immediately stir in Certo. Skim off foam with metal spoon. Stir or skim for 5 minutes to cool slightly to prevent floating fruit. Ladle into glasses. Cover with paraffin.

Mrs. Anna M. Snelbecker, Dover, Pa., York Interstate Fair

 ### Apricot Jam

  3 ½ *c. apricot nectar pulp*
  ⅓ *c. lemon juice*
  6 ½ *c. sugar*
  ½ *bottle Certo fruit pectin*

Bring all ingredients except pectin to a hard boil in large saucepan; boil 1 full minute, stirring to prevent sticking. Remove from heat; add Certo all at once. Stir for 5 minutes; put into hot sterilized glasses. Cover with ¼ inch of melted paraffin.
Personal Comment: This recipe also won ribbons at the following fairs: Bethlehem Fair, Harwinton Fair and Terryville County Fair.

Mrs. Mildred Knudsen, Torrington, Conn., Goshen Fair

California Blackberry Jam

1 ½ qt. fully ripe berries or fresh frozen blackberries
5 ½ c. sugar
2 tbsp. lemon juice
1 box Sure-Jel
¾ c. water

Completely crush berries. Mix sugar well with berries; add lemon juice. Mix Sure-Jel and water in a saucepan. Bring to boil; boil 1 minute, stirring constantly. Stir into fruit mixture. Continue stirring and cooking 2 minutes more. Cool for 5 minutes. Stir; skim by turns 5 minutes to prevent floating fruit. Ladle into glasses. Leave ½ inch space at top; cover at once with ⅛ inch melted paraffin or put jam in sealed jars. Yield: 20 servings.

Mrs. Laura Borders, Redwood City, Cal., San Mateo County Fair

 ### Pear Jam

6 lge. pears
2 green apples
1 orange
10 maraschino cherries
3 c. sugar

Wash fruit. Remove seeds and core but do not remove skins. Put through the medium grinder of food chopper. Add sugar. Bring to a boil, stirring constantly. Boil for 15 minutes. Pour in sterile jars and seal.

Patricia A. McCollum, Mahnomen, Minn., Mahnomen County Fair

 ### Strawberry Jam Delight

2 qt. (about) strawberries
¼ c. lemon juice
7 c. sugar
½ bottle pectin

Crush berries completely; measure 3¾ cups fruit and lemon juice in very large pan. Add sugar; mix well. Place over high heat; bring to a full rolling boil. Boil hard 1 minute; stir constantly. Remove from heat; stir in pectin. Skim off foam with metal spoon. Stir, skim and cool slightly. Ladle into ½-pint jars and seal.

Mrs. Donna McMahon, Glendora, Cal., Los Angeles County Fair

Buttered Strawberry Jam

4 c. (heaping) berries, not crushed
1 ½ tbsp. vinegar
4 c. sugar
½ tsp. butter

Put berries in kettle with vinegar; boil for 3 minutes, stirring gently with wooden spoon. Remove from heat; add sugar and butter. Boil for 10 minutes. Let stand for 24 hours. Yield: 2 pints.

Bonnie Kay Fjerstad, Fosston, Minn., East Polk County Fair

Apple Jelly

1 qt. apple juice
2 tbsp. strained lemon juice
3 c. sugar

Measure juices and sugar into kettle; place over high heat. Stir until sugar dissolves. Boil rapidly until last 2 drops of syrup poured from side of spoon, held high over kettle, join and slide off edge of spoon. This will happen when syrup has reached about 8 degrees above boiling point of water. Remove kettle from heat; skim off foam and pour jelly to within inch of top of glass. Yield: 3-4 jelly glasses.

Mrs. Charles McCloud, Kirksville, Mo., Adair Country Fair

Blackberry Jelly

6 qt. blackberries
1 box Sure-Jel
6 ½ c. sugar

Crush ripe berries; simmer, covered, 15 minutes. Place in jelly bag or 4 thicknesses dampened cheesecloth. Spread over colander; rest over bowl. Let juice drip through bag to measure 4½ cups juice in a 6 to 8-quart saucepan. If lacking juice, add a little water. Mix Sure-Jel with juice in saucepan over high heat; quickly bring mixture to a hard boil. Stir with wooden spoon. Stir in sugar; bring to a full rolling boil. Boil hard 1 minute, stirring constantly. Remove from heat; skim off foam with metal spoon. Pour at once into jars. Leave ⅛ inch space at top; seal.
*This recipe also won a blue ribbon in 1966 at Freeborn County Fair.

Mrs. Ray Cowell, New Richland, Minn., Minnesota State Fair

Red Currant Jelly

3 ½ qt. red currants
1 ½ c. water
1 box Sure-Jel
7 c. sugar

Crush fully ripe red currants; add water and simmer, covered, for 10 minutes. Place in jelly bag; squeeze out 6½ cups juice into 6 to 8-quart saucepan. Mix Sure-Jel with juice in saucepan over high heat; bring to hard rolling boil, stirring occasionally. Add sugar all at once; bring to rolling boil. Boil 1 minute. Remove from heat; skim off foam with metal spoon. Pour into jelly glasses. Leave ½ inch space at top. Cover with about ⅛ inch melted paraffin. Let cool; cover with lids and store. Yield: 12 glasses jelly.

Mrs. John Cafferty, Grand Rapids, Minn., Itasca County Fair

Dale's Concord Grape Jelly

3 lb. Concord grapes
½ c. water
7 c. sugar
½ bottle Certo

Stem fully ripe grapes; crush thoroughly. Add water; bring to a boil and simmer, covered, 10 minutes. Place in jelly cloth bag; squeeze out juice. Measure 4 cups juice into large saucepan. To measured juice in saucepan, add sugar; mix well. Place over high heat; bring to a boil, stirring constantly. Stir in Certo at once; bring to a full rolling boil. Boil hard 1 minute, stirring constantly. Remove from heat; skim off foam with metal spoon. Pour quickly into sterilized jelly jars or glasses. Seal immediately with self-sealing lids or ⅛ inch paraffin. Welch's grape juice may be substituted for fresh juice. Yield: 5 pounds.
*This recipe also won ribbons at the following fairs: Antelope Valley Fair and San Fernando Valley Fair.

Dale F. Zuber, Chino, Cal., Los Angeles County Fair

Mint Jelly

1 ½ c. fresh mint leaves, packed
3 ¼ c. water
Green food coloring
1 box powdered pectin
4 c. sugar

Pick and wash carefully fresh mint leaves. Heat to a boil with water; cover and allow to steep for at least 10 minutes. Strain through double cheesecloth;

(Continued on next page)

measure 3 cups mint infusion. Add a few drops green food coloring to tint. Add pectin; bring to a boil. Add sugar; bring to a hard rolling boil. Boil for 1 minute, stirring constantly. Remove from heat; skim off foam with metal spoon. Pour at once into hot sterilized jars, leaving ¼ inch space at top; seal immediately. Allow to cool in upright position. Yield: Six ½-pints.

James T. Trousdale, Louisville, Ky., Kentucky State Fair

 ### Strawberry Jelly

3 ½ c. strawberry juice or 2½ to 3 quarts berries
1 box powdered fruit pectin
5 c. sugar
A few drops red food color (opt.)

Wash, rinse, drain, cap and crush berries. Pour crushed berries in damp cotton flannel bag or on a square of the flannel tied over mouth of a deep bowl. For clearest of jelly, let juice drip through the cloth; if clearness is unimportant, help juice along by squeezing bag. Measure sugar. Put juice and pectin in kettle. Set kettle over high heat; stir to dissolve pectin. When mixture reaches a fast boil, add sugar; keep stirring. When mixture returns to fast boil, boil exactly one full minute. Remove kettle from heat; quickly skim off foam and pour jelly to within ½-inch of top of glasses. Unless to be refrigerated for use in a short time, glasses of jelly are sealed with paraffin. This may be done immediately or the lids may be put on the glasses until jelly cools. Glasses should be on level surface. Use hot, but not smoking paraffin, and use only enough to make a thin layer which touches the glass all the way around.

Photograph for this recipe below.

Fig Preserves

1 c. soda
6 qt. figs with stems
5 lb. sugar

Sprinkle soda over figs; cover with 6 quarts of boiling water. Soak 15 minutes; drain. Rinse figs in cold water. Mix sugar and 4 quarts water. Boil 10 minutes; skim. Add well-drained figs. Cook rapidly until figs are clear and tender and syrup is consistency of honey. Let stand overnight. Pack in pint jars; process 25 minutes at simmering temperature. Yield: 2-3 pints.

Mrs. Richard Eldridge, New Iberia, La., Sugarcane Festival and Fair

Strawberry Preserves Deluxe

1 ½ quarts stemmed, firm, red-ripe strawberries
5 c. sugar
⅓ c. lemon juice

Combine strawberries and sugar; let stand 3 to 4 hours. Bring slowly to boiling, stirring occasionally until sugar dissolves. Add lemon juice. Cook rapidly until berries are clear and syrup thick, about 10 to 12 minutes. Pour into a shallow pan. Let stand, uncovered, 12 to 24 hours in a cool place. Shake pan occasionally to distribute berries through syrup. Pack into hot Ball jars, leaving ¼-inch head space. Adjust caps. Process half-pints and pints 20 minutes at 180 to 185 degrees in hot-water bath. Berries with hollow cores should not be used. Yield: about 4 half-pints.

Photograph for this recipe on page 371.

Watermelon Rind Preserves Piquant

6 c. watermelon rind
1 lemon
2 c. sugar
½ c. pectin
Few drops red food coloring

Clean rind by removing red meat and green part of rind. Cut rind and lemon into small pieces. Mix fruit and sugar; let set overnight. Cook mixture for about 1 hour until thickened Remove mixture from heat; add ½ cup pectin and enough food color to give an attractive color. Seal preserves in jars.

Laura Wheeler, Hart, Tex., Olton Stock Show

INDEX

ACKNOWLEDGMENTS

We wish to express our appreciation for the use of photographs supplied us by the following: Cover—Maine Sardine Council (recipe on page 203) and Frontispiece—Louisiana Yam Commission.

Color photographs were supplied by the following: Brussels Sprouts Marketing Program; Carnation Instant Products Division; Artichoke Advisory Board; Ocean Spray Cranberries, Inc.; and United Fresh Fruit and Vegetable Association.

Title page and half page photographs were supplied by the following: McIlhenny Company (Tabasco); Filbert Hazelnut Institute; Idaho Bean Commission; Grandma's West Indies Molasses; Brussels Sprouts Marketing Program; Florida Citrus Commission; California Raisin Advisory Board; The R. T. French Company; South African Rock Lobster Service Corporation; United Fresh Fruit and Vegetable Association; Planter's Peanuts; American Spice Trade Association; National Meat Canners Association; Campbell Soup Company; Crisco; Louisiana Yam Commission; Pickle Packers International, Inc.; and Ball Brothers Company.